RELIGION, MARRIAGE, AND FAMILY

Series Editors

Don S. Browning
John Witte Jr.

Don Browning

THE EQUAL-REGARD FAMILY AND ITS FRIENDLY CRITICS

Don Browning and the Practical Theological Ethics of the Family

Edited by

John Witte, Jr.,
M. Christian Green, &
Amy Wheeler

William B. Eerdmans Publishing Company
Grand Rapids, Michigan / Cambridge, U.K.

Wm. B. Eerdmans Publishing Co.
2140 Oak Industrial Drive N.E., Grand Rapids, Michigan 49505 /
P.O. Box 163, Cambridge CB3 9PU U.K.

Printed in the United States of America

12 11 10 09 08 07 7 6 5 4 3 2 1

Library of Congress Cataloging-in-Publication Data

The equal-regard family and its friendly critics:
Don Browning and practical theological ethics of the family /
edited by John Witte, Jr., M. Christian Green & Amy Wheeler.
p. cm. — (Religion, marriage, and family)
Includes bibliographical references and index.
ISBN 978-0-8028-4569-6 (pbk.: alk. paper)
1. Family — Religious aspects — Christianity. 2. Browning, Don S.
I. Witte, John, 1959- II. Green, M. Christian (Martha Christian), 1968-
III. Wheeler, Amy.

BT707.7.E68 2007
241′.63 — dc22

2007019882

www.eerdmans.com

Contents

Editorial Preface

This volume is both a celebration and evaluation of the critical family theory developed by the distinguished University of Chicago scholar Don S. Browning. For the past two decades, Professor Browning has served as the dean of interdisciplinary family studies in North America. He has led a dozen major research projects that have brought hundreds of scholars around a common table and thousands of participants to public forums. He has published a dozen volumes of his own, catalyzed the publication of some six dozen volumes by others, and masterminded the production of a major PBS video on marriage. He has graced distinguished lecterns throughout North America, Western Europe, South Africa, South Korea, Malaysia, and Australia, addressing everything from kin altruism among the ancient Greeks to children's rights in the modern United Nations. He has brought all the main axial world religions into dialogue with his own tradition of Christianity, and brought many of the social sciences, humanities, and professions into interaction with his own disciplines of theology and ethics.

Professor Browning brings to the study of the family a distinctive methodology called "practical theological ethics." This is a method that combines his early work on pastoral or practical theology with his later work on theological ethics. Browning began his scholarly career as a leading scholar of pastoral care. His early research, begun already as a doctoral student in religion and personality at the University of Chicago in the early 1960s, gave rise to his volumes, *Atonement and Psychotherapy* (1966), *The Moral Context of Pastoral Care* (1976), and *Religious Ethics and Pastoral Care* (1983). He then moved gradually toward a wider dialogue among theology, ethics, and psychology in his volumes on *Generative Man* (1973, rev. ed. 1975), *Pluralism and Personality* (1980), and *Religious Thought and the Modern Psychologies* (1987). These first two phases merged into an effort to reconceptualize practical theology and, indeed, theology as a whole, in his signature volume, *A Fundamental Practical Theology* (1991).

In 1990, Browning began to widen the field of practical theology by drawing on other social sciences beyond psychology and by focusing his work on the concrete example of marriage and family life. Many of the contributors to this volume had the privilege to watch his work unfold as director of the decade-long Religion, Culture, and Family Project at the University of Chicago in the 1990s. Others thrived under his subsequent leadership of the five-year projects on "Sex, Marriage and Family & the Religions of the Book" and "The Child in Law, Religion, and Society" both at Emory University, and a dozen other smaller projects on related themes.

In the course of directing these projects, Browning has produced a stunning range of new interdisciplinary writings on marriage and family life. Particularly noteworthy are his co-authored volumes, *From Culture Wars to Common Ground* (1997, 2d ed. 2000) and *Reweaving the Social Tapestry* (2001), and his more recent monographs on *Marriage and Modernization* (2003), *Christian Ethics and the Moral Psychologies* (2006), and *Equality and the Family: A Fundamental Practical Theology of Children, Mothers, and Fathers in Modern Societies* (2007). All of these are pathbreaking volumes, both in their insights and in their methods, and they will remain anchor texts in family studies for many years to come. Also noteworthy are his four new co-edited anthologies on the enduring teachings on marriage and childhood in the urtexts of the world religions and on the shifting marital and family practices in modern American religions: *Sex, Marriage and Family and the World Religions* (2006), *American Religions and the Family* (2006), *Children and Childhood in American Religions* (2007), and *Children and Childhood in World Religions* (2007). He is now hard at work on a capstone monograph, *Christian Marriage and Modern Marriage Law*, which already has all the earmarks of another Browning classic in the making.

In this volume, we have asked scholars from several different disciplines who have worked with Browning to analyze his contributions to the study of marriage and family life, and to chart new pathways of potential scholarship in this vital interdisciplinary field. Gathered on the pages that follow are the reflections of several former students and fellow project leaders who together represent the fields of theology, ethics, pastoral care, evolutionary biology, law, demography, psychology, sociology, and history. Seven honorary forewords offer pithy assessments of Professor Browning's contributions to different guilds of family specialists. Ten chapters offer closer analysis of his development of specific themes.

The chapters cohere in part around one of the cardinal themes of Browning's work, namely, that marriage and family life must be guided and governed by an ethic of "equal regard." This is, in part, an internal family ethic that calls husband and wife to equal respect for the dignity and well being of the other, equal devotion to the procreation and nurture of their children, equal access to public and professional life, and equal sacrifice for the health, safety, welfare, and happiness of each other, of their children, and so far as possible of parents, grandparents, and other needy relatives. "Equal regard" is also, in part, an external family ethic that calls church, state, and society alike to give special protection and support to marriages and families. These domestic institutions are ancient, natural, and unique cradles of conscience, chrysalises of care, and cultivators of good citizens that cannot be eroded by condoning transient troth nor diluted by encouraging marital equivalents. This "equal regard" ethic, which Browning traces to some of the earliest Hebrew, classical, and Christian traditions of the West, is captured most poignantly today in Catholic sacramental and Protestant covenantal models of marriage and family life.

We have incurred a number of debts in the preparation of this volume — beyond the enormous debt of thanks that we owe to each of the contributors for sharing their time and talents with us. We express profound thanks to Dr. Craig Dykstra and his colleagues at the Lilly Endowment, Inc. for providing us with a generous grant to assemble this volume as well as two related volumes by Professor Browning. It was Craig Dykstra and his Lilly colleagues who had the foresight in 1990 to see that modern marriage and family life were in deep crisis, and needed the kind of deep interdisciplinary analysis on which Professor Browning had embarked. Their $4 million of support for Browning's Religion, Culture, and Family Project has permanently changed the field of interdisciplinary family study. It is a privilege to have a chance in this volume to illustrate and evaluate what Lilly's visionary philanthropy has wrought.

We wish to thank Kevin Jung, Sarah Schuurman, and Antonia Daymond, all from the University of Chicago Divinity School, for their research and editorial assistance in the preparation of this volume and the two related volumes by Professor Browning. We wish to thank Anita Mann of the Center for the Study of Law and Religion at Emory University for her skillful administration of this project, and Eliza Ellison for her editorial insights. And we wish to thank Jon Pott and his colleagues at Wm. B. Eerdmans Publishing Co. for taking on this volume and its companions, and seeing to their timely production.

Not least, we wish to thank Don Browning, our teacher, our colleague, and our friend, for his brilliant scholarship, inspired leadership, and sterling humanity. He has left a deep mark on each of our lives and has influenced a good deal of our work. We offer him this volume with deep appreciation, admiration, and affection.

John Witte, Jr.
M. Christian Green
Amy Wheeler

Honorary Forewords

Martin E. Marty

During a public program relating the concerns of the project "The Child in Law, Religion, and Society" to an academic public, President Jimmy Carter turned to the audience which included nineteen faculty members who were working on that project. He assumed that nineteen books would issue from their endeavor, but then asked, "but who of you are going to change the world?" Himself the author of nineteen books at the time he raised that question, Mr. Carter cannot have intended to devalue intellectual or literary endeavor. A response to his question could be: "but books themselves *can* change the world." Classics have done so, and works that combine intellectual effort with practical proposals and which show concern for the world of "doing" always stand the potential of being able to change the world through readers influenced by them.

Without pouring on praise of a sort that would embarrass Don Browning, I would say with confidence that the corpus of his work and his influence on colleagues and former students have already changed at least those zones of the world to which he reaches. And what a wide world that is, as evidenced by the essays in this *Festschrift!* When reading the manuscript I started to note all the terms, phrases, concepts, and revisions attributed to him by the authors and lost count, so plentiful are they — and so much more revealing and memorable are these when each is read in context as opposed to being given only a line or two of mention out of context in a Foreword.

Publishers, reviewers, and non-buyers of *Festschriften,* honorary works, know that, well-intentioned though these books be, many give evidence of the fact that contributors "cleaned out their desk drawers" or their computers' memories and unloaded them, no matter what the overall theme of the book of tribute may be. Anything but that is the case here. Having had the privilege of reading the chapters in a form which made them accessible to "Word-Search," I found that the name "Browning" showed up many scores, indeed, hundreds of times. This meant that the scrupulous editors and the conscientious contributors were disciplined to stick to the main theme(s), and thus produce a book destined to inform and challenge the scholars, practitioners, and interested laity who are concerned with marriage, sexuality, the family, "generativity," "practical theology," and so many more foci of Browning's work.

Their sticking to the point would have produced a banal and boring work were the point itself not engrossing. Which means: the Browning achievement is so detailed, so varied, so concerned with convergences and dialogue, with coherence and practical effect, that one could almost use the index of this work as a kind of access to a virtual encyclopedia on his subjects.

I like to make a distinction between persons who are "noted" or "famed" versus "celebrities." Browning is not a celebrity as were R. D. Laing and Thomas Szasz, Norman O. Brown, and so many others who arced above us mere decades ago, calling attention to themselves with extravagant, easily packaged, but soon largely forgotten claims and contentions. "Browning" is not a household word, but it belongs to a noted scholar who has drawn the attention of and then influenced two generations of serious reflectors on his themes. The chapters in this book themselves demonstrate how he has offered clues, hints, tantalizations, and pointings for other scholars.

While the scholars deal with Browningian themes, some of them cannot resist pointing also to personal aspects of his approach and method. As his close-up colleague at The University of Chicago for over three decades, I was privileged to learn from him on a week-daily basis and to enjoy the company of Don (and Carol!) on many a weekend evening. They as a couple and he as a scholar embody and exemplify so much of what his work propounds and proposes. Features of these show up in these essays. First, he is thoroughly grounded in the literature, from the works of Erik Erikson through Hans-Georg Gadamer and, it is not corny to say, all the way "back to the Bible and Aristotle" and ahead to futures rich in promise. Second, he is a "catholic" thinker in that he is ready to defend his approaches and findings while at the same time showing hospitality to and learning from scholars who differ vastly from him and who may represent other philosophies and diverse religions. Third, he was always known at "our" school, as I have seen him at work at Emory in two projects and in off-campus contexts of many sorts, as unfailingly curious and conscientious, eager to give credit to others whom his work inspires or nudges along.

Odds are good that this book will reach the desk of Jimmy Carter, who has shown interest in the projects of the Center for the Study of Law and Religion, "down the block," as it were, from The Carter Center at Emory University. So I am tempted to greet him with the words: "Here, Mr. President, stands a book with the potential of helping change the world insofar as it represents arguments with a scholar who has begun to change his many parts of the world." Readers, it's all yours!

David Popenoe

Don Browning is one of the true pioneers of the modern marriage movement. His interest in marriage as a scholarly pursuit and as a call to action on a national scale developed in the early 1990s, at a time when the Protestant establishment had drifted away from an outspoken support of marriage, instead choosing to accommodate the many "alternative" family forms and the exploding divorce culture that increasingly formed church congregations. Don argued that, given the high divorce and out-of-wedlock birth rates, the institution of marriage was weakening seriously, and this was proving to be an especially destructive problem for children. All of the good research up to the present day has found a strong correlation between the best child outcomes and, other things being equal, coming from a married-parent family. Marriage would weaken still further, he maintained, unless the church could find a way to continue its long-time support of the institution. Tolerance of the new family forms was important, but not at the expense of dropping the marriage support message altogether.

But there was a problem. In many circles, and especially among conservatives, the kind of marriage to be supported was the traditional marriage, with a bread-winning husband and economically dependent housewife. Yet in those domains where the women's movement had a major influence, such as among the mainline Protestant clergy together with many of their congregations, this form of marriage — a going back to the 1950s — was hardly something to be promoted. In dealing with this issue, Don came up with the clever and perfectly apt formulation of the "equal regard" marriage: marriage was not to be maintained as a one-sided bastion of dependency, but rather as a union of equal regard between husband and wife. This became a central theme of several of his books, caught on strongly in the national debate, and helped to bridge the gap between conservatives and liberals on the marriage issue.

In his work in the 1990s and early 2000s, Don and his colleagues plumbed the depths of theological understanding, with great success, to demonstrate the solid theological underpinnings for family life built around a strong marriage. What made his work especially innovative and highly regarded was his bringing to bear on the topic his broad understanding of the social sciences. Indeed, he is one of the world's intellectual leaders in bridging the gap between theology and the social sciences, generating what he calls a "practical theology." Few of us in the marriage movement even begin to have his breadth of scholarship, and we have learned much from his enlightening analysis, his wise counsel, and, of course, his friendship. We stand in awe of the reach of his mind, and the wisdom of his conclusions.

In every modern society today, the institution of marriage is weakening, and it seems that the more secular the society, the lower the rate of marriage. This suggests that, if a vital and sustainable marriage culture is ever to be redeveloped, religion will have to play a prominent role. One of the greatest legacies of Don's intellectual career is that he has shown us the way in this regard. Now it is up to the rest of us to be guided by his recommendations and insights, as well as by the warmth and kindliness with which he imparts them.

Barbara Dafoe Whitehead

Don S. Browning's contribution to the national conversation on the family is large, wide-ranging, unparalleled, and indispensable. As scholar, teacher, and public intellectual, he has enlarged the framework of the public debate; enriched its conceptual vocabulary; spanned the disciplines of social science, religion, history and public policy; and moved easily from the theoretical to the practical — all in pursuit of the goal of a cultural revitalization of marriage and the family.

Perhaps the first thing to say about Don's venture into this work is that he was willing to venture at all. Today, marriage and the family are respectable topics on the research and public policy agenda. That was not the case in the early 1990s, when Don launched his Religion, Culture, and Family Project. The bitter controversy over Daniel Patrick Moynihan's report on the black family in 1965 had cast a chill over research on the family. Few scholars — and especially those who, like Don, describe themselves as liberal — had any stomach for returning to the subject. Indeed, academic distaste for the topic became even stronger after the 1992 Republican Convention, when Marilyn Quayle and Pat Buchanan called for women to return to their traditional places in the home — a political blunder that helped put Bill Clinton in the White House.

However, by the late 1980s, rising rates of divorce, unwed teen pregnancy, father absence, and lone motherhood could no longer be ignored. A public debate over the "crisis of the family" began to take shape. It was cast largely in the evidence and argumentation of the social sciences. Don was almost alone in thinking that religion had anything to contribute to the discussion. Well-versed and practiced in the social sciences, he nevertheless saw them as insufficient to the larger challenge. For Don, the task of revitalizing the family was primarily a cultural work that must draw upon the institutions and resources of the civil society. Chief among these institutions was the church; chief among the cultural resources was the rich but neglected body of religious thought and tradition on marriage and the family.

At the same time, however, he took a critical approach to these traditions. His goal was not to cheerlead for the "traditional" family, but rather to mine the storehouse of religious thought for its insights and teachings on the goods of marriage and family life. From this critical stance, he and his colleagues were able to argue for a new family ethic of equal regard that would balance family unity and solidarity with mutual respect for, and commitment to, the individual flourishing of each family member.

Not all scholars are temperamentally or intellectually equipped to move back and forth between the theoretical and the practical, the abstract and the concrete. Yet as a practical theologian, Don has done so effortlessly and productively. He is as much engaged in formulating concrete public policy proposals as in articulating a public philosophy; as avid about marriage education as he is about marriage scholarship; as committed to fostering communication within marriage as he is to a global dialogue on marriage.

Let me not leave the impression that Don has worked in ivory tower seclusion. Through his leadership of the Religion, Culture, and Family Project, he has brought together a group of distinguished scholars, stimulated new research, and created a contemporary storehouse of thought and practice on marriage and the family that is unparalleled in its size, scope, and achievement. This body of work includes a raft of scholarly books; a PBS documentary on marriage; lecture series; journal articles; opinion pieces; policy recommendations; and a variety of marriage education materials for churches. Like his mind, Don's body is rarely at rest. He is an indefatigable traveler and tireless participant in the global conversation on family. He is the most generous of all teachers, creating opportunities for younger scholars to contribute to the work of reconstructing a public philosophy on the family and involving them in the task of formulating strategies to put that philosophy into practical use.

In looking over one of the early seminal works of the project, *From Culture Wars to Common Ground: Religion and the American Family Debate,* one cannot help but be struck by how many of its arguments and recommendations are now widely accepted by researchers and policymakers. Its public policy proposals — effective child support enforcement, elimination of the marriage penalty, support for marriage education initiatives — enjoy broad support. Likewise, the cultural work of marriage revitalization has caught on in the civil society. A grassroots marriage movement — involving individuals and organizations across the political and disciplinary spectrum — is now underway. Churches are beginning to awaken to their responsibilities to reach out to parents who need support and practical help in dealing with the stresses of work and the marketplace on their marriages and families.

No doubt Don would be the first to caution against any note of triumphalism in this litany of accomplishments. As he reminds us, the cultural work of renewal and reformation is complex and often difficult. But how lucky we are to have his guiding spirit and example to spur us on.

Herbert Anderson

I first read Don Browning in graduate school in the late 1960s. He was for me then a welcome antidote to the Barthian influence in pastoral theology. For the last twenty years, he has been a challenging but always honest tennis foe, a stimulating conversation partner, and a valued friend. More than anyone else I know, he embodies the capacity to "say the other side" with courage and confidence. For Browning, the first aim of "saying the other side" is critical consciousness, recognition of the assumptions that shape every theory and all practice. We had a mutual friend in Hyde Park who often described himself as a "radical centrist," a position that I believe Don Browning seeks to embody as well. I do not mean to suggest Don Browning is neutral. Far from it. His critical passions have led him to explore or even expose "the other side of everything," as the mystic Thomas Merton once observed.

When it was assumed that psychology and psychotherapy were ethically neutral, Don Browning wrote *Religious Thought and the Modern Psychologies* (1987, rev. 2004) insisting that psychological theories implicitly carried metaphors of ultimacy and principles of obligation. It is important, he said, to acknowledge that psychology, as well as religion, provides normative "concepts and technologies" for ordering the interior life. When pastoral care practice followed the clinical presumption of moral neutrality and focused almost exclusively on sustaining and support, Browning wrote *Religious Ethics and Pastoral Care* (1983), suggesting that every minister doing pastoral care is an ethical thinker. Browning's vision of the ethical dimension of care remains a necessary, though largely unfulfilled, perspective for pastoral care in an increasingly complex, pluralistic society.

When Don Browning took up the task of refurbishing practical theology, he was lifting up the other side of an ancient tradition. Along with David Tracy, Margaret Farley, and others, Browning moved practical theology beyond the clerical paradigm and beyond unreflected practice to a level of critical correlation between theory and praxis. Once critical consciousness is achieved, it is possible to clarify the issues and make choices regarding the norms and means of individual and social transformation. From my perspective as a pastoral theologian in the church, Browning's intellectual and organizing work in practical theology is his greatest achievement. Theological seminaries across the country are peopled with faculty trained by Don Browning in the short-lived program at the University of Chicago who are attentive to the way critical correlation of the tradition and the human sciences inform and are informed by ministerial practice.

When work on behalf of marriage and family life became the dominant focus for Don Browning, many old themes from his earlier work, such as mutuality/equal regard, social transformation, and critical consciousness, found a new place in his prolific writings. So did the practice of "saying the other side." The Religion, Culture, and Family Project was a monumental effort to "say the other side" on many matters pertaining to family living. That project also demonstrated Don Browning's organizational skills as well as his intellectual vision. As Don continues to take on new and even more challenging issues like family law, sustained by his courage and deep passions about the importance of family, I hope he will keep saying the other side, even to his own side.

Lisa Sowle Cahill

It was my privilege to be a part of Don Browning's Religion, Culture, and Family Project, funded by the Lilly Endowment. This ecumenical and interdisciplinary project offered the participants support to further their own related research and bring it to publication in a series of several books. We were encouraged to be both scholarly and practical, rigorous in our methods and arguments, but firmly grounded in the real-life issues confronting families, children, married people, and policymakers today. We engaged with the troubles besetting middle-class families in the socioeconomic and cultural "mainstream," but also learned from the lives, histories, and wisdom of those whose cultural voices have been marginalized, especially African Americans.

The most productive and unique aspect of this project was the fact that it provided a forum for contrasting and even oppositional points of view. Scholars who might have been natural adversaries were led by Don Browning's acute intellect and generous spirit to appreciate and even incorporate values and agendas quite different from their own. We project members were forced to face up to the numerous and ostensibly insuperable challenges and disruptions facing families in North America today — domestic violence, racism, sexism, poverty, and parental irresponsibility for the children brought into the world. We were also called, from within our various disciplines, to renegotiate the riches of Christian theology and church life in response to these problems.

I can well remember provocative and stimulating weekend conferences, arranged for venues that helped us cultivate a sense of social bonhomie, along with mutual respect and serious intellectual engagement. At times I experienced a certain frustration with some project advisory scholars who seemed to be advocating a pro-family stance that reinstated traditional nuclear family forms (against "hedonistic" self-fulfillment of adults) as well as with others whose radical critique of such forms led to a family based on liberal equality (against gender "oppression"). Yet the collegiality fostered by Don Browning eventually led most of us to recognize that these differing political agendas each stem from a valid concern, and that the occasional excesses of each can be ameliorated by respectful interaction. Those motivated primarily by a concern for children, and those equally motivated by a concern for women, were led to understand the merits of one another's positions by the exchanges the project fostered, leading to invaluable cross-fertilization and more nuanced, less ideological outcomes all around.

The "critical familism" proposed by Don Browning and colleagues in *From Culture Wars to Common Ground* is a good illustration of the ways in which our projects could productively converge. According to Browning, families and all their members are best served when they are committed and intact, active and supported in both public and private spheres, and most important, imbued with an ethos of love as "equal regard." Browning quite rightly, in my view, maintains that self-sacrifice is a necessary but secondary element in Christian love, essential to resolving the conflicts and failures that families confront, but not to be held up as the primary destiny of women or men, or of parents in general. Perhaps first devised in response to what Browning sees as the "male problematic" of loose ties to mates and children, and hence the need to shore up institutionally for men the obligations of marriage and fatherhood, the equal-regard family also reflects a growing consciousness of the gender injustices perpetrated by traditional "strong" family forms.

Also highly commendable and crucially important is Don Browning's developing analysis of the way economic conditions affect the health of cultures and families, and the status of women and children. In *Marriage and Modernization,* Browning lifts our sights beyond North America and offers innumerable on-target critiques of the negative impacts of globalization on families. He incisively shows why the "colonialism" of modernity disrupts cultures and traditions in ways that exacerbate asymmetries of power and lead to "gross injustices" for women and children. Advancing equal regard as a culturally pliable model for marriages and families, he also insists that it can and should guide public affairs, fair family and marriage policies, and the infrastructures of civil society and government that create or destroy local conditions of family flourishing.

Don Browning has the gift and the genius of a scholar who enables the work of others and raises the level of conversation in "the guild," as well as producing erudite monographs on the cutting edge of theory. As far as the latter is concerned, his recent work on praxis and Christian ethics in *Christian Ethics and Moral Psychologies* brilliantly breaks new ground in showing how to get past the impasse of "cultural difference" by understanding — and exercising — "practical reason" as a complex interaction of cultural context, action, moral reflection, and pursuit of objective goods to which humans organically respond.

The current work honoring his contributions displays Browning's own talent for moving creatively among a number of mutually informing base points to reach new levels of theological understanding as well as more responsible, equal-regarding practices in the church and in society. It is a fine and fitting tribute to his commitments, his style, and his impressive achievements.

Linda J. Waite

I want to highlight one important contribution that Professor Browning has made to both family life and social policy. I do this because, in my view, this is a seminal contribution that has not received the attention it deserves.

In 2002, Professor Browning published a book, *Reweaving the Social Tapestry: Toward a Public Philosophy and Policy for Families,* co-authored with Gloria G. Rodriquez. This book was commissioned for a national Assembly on American Families. In it, Browning and Rodriquez grapple with the most important challenges facing the family in the U.S. and most other similar societies. These include especially the well-being of children and the absolutely essential role of families in producing that well-being; the health of marriage as a social institution; the too-frequent absence of residential fathers in families; the unique difficulties faced by poor families; the need to balance paid employment and care for family members; and the challenges in achieving what Browning has elsewhere called "equal regard" between men and women in families.

All of these challenges are familiar. But Browning and Rodriquez bring a fresh perspective and the insights that come with it to them. They argue that we can only develop a consensus around these potential divisive issues by identifying and respecting the family philosophies and values of the various religious and cultural traditions that make up our society, and by building on the positive analogies between them. This approach gives Browning and Rodriquez the leverage to explicate concrete, clear, and principled guidelines for addressing the challenges facing us — a sort of "to do" list for policymakers, religious organizations, and families themselves. These suggestions should be disseminated, read, debated, and put into practice. I am particularly impressed with the idea of the sixty-hour work week for families with children. As always, when Don Browning attacks an issue, we see things in a new and clear light.

Carol Browning

Don and I have always been a team, parceling tasks out according to our various skills, which sometimes look traditional, sometimes not. For instance, he runs the sweeper; I'm in charge of the checkbook. But it was not until 1990 that we began to pull together in another kind of teamwork. It involved a long-term research project that lasted over a decade and absorbed our joint efforts in some way or another nearly every day. The waves and synergisms of that project go on even today.

We were at the Center of Theological Inquiry in Princeton, New Jersey, for eight months where we were enjoying a lovely townhouse in the woods, an office for Don at the Center, and the wonderful support from the staff of the Center. Don's main task was to finish *A Fundamental Practical Theology* (1991) and, along with that, prepare to write a proposal to the Lilly Endowment for a grant to support research on what he came to call the Religion, Culture, and Family Project.

Being a musician, I had been looking forward to some connection with the Westminster Choir College — organ lessons, etc. But because of back surgery very shortly before our arrival in Princeton, the strain of playing the organ was out, and all the other possibilities for occupying my time didn't work out for one reason or another. Don had brought along many books on family and marriage to read in preparation for the grant proposal to the Lilly Endowment. I found the titles and synopses of these books intriguing and, having nothing better to do, I started reading them. In fact, I became absorbed in them.

I had my own marriage and family to reflect upon, and our children were moving to the age where marriage was on the horizon for them. Don noticed my fascination with these books and seized the day. He put me to work. That is, he suggested that if I didn't mind doing so, it would be helpful if I took notes so that he could determine which books would be the best for him to give a careful reading. I readily agreed.

I also started reading two newspapers each day to ascertain what the media were saying about marriage, family, sex, children, mothers, fathers, and about fifty other categories relevant to the project. The number of topics we cover is still growing and so are the drawers upon drawers of articles that we have saved. I am still clipping. In the Princeton days, I read these newspaper articles along with my notes on books to Don in the car as we tooled around New Jersey. It is surprising that we never had an accident. Actually, he says it helps keep him awake while driving.

It was very enlightening to me to see him work out the plans for this project. He used his favorite advice that he also told his students when formulating their dissertation proposals and senior ministry papers. He would ask them, "What is the question?" He would go further and say, "Don't tell me the answer, at least not now. Let's first work on the question." It was quite a stimulating intellectual experience for me to do the same — to work on the question. The trouble is that one question leads to another. General questions lead to sub-questions. Practical questions cut across different fields; answers cannot be found within the borders of a single discipline. If you are not careful, you will work on the questions forever, and the direction they take you gets very complex.

After returning home from Princeton, I was unable to do the work as intensely because of my own responsibilities as a pianist and teacher of piano. But to this day, I check the papers for anything relevant to the project, even though it is officially closed. I think we are making progress. I am told that progress is made with a research question if it opens other good questions and stimulates other people to ask questions as well. The fine essays in this book written by these distinguished scholars suggest that Don's philosophy about the importance of questions may be paying off. I know that Don is delighted with the many good questions posed in these essays and the many excellent answers developed as well.

As I indicated above, the problem with asking questions is that the process never ends. I can see it now; we will be asking questions, reading, describing, analyzing, and posing tentative answers indefinitely into the future — two gray-haired people with articles and clippings on the kitchen table, pondering their meaning until the end of their days. I have always heard that marriage involves teamwork. However, no one ever told me that in some cases, marital teamwork is an endless research project. Maybe that would be a good title for a book — *Marriage as a Research Project.* Don't suggest this to Don, or I will have new articles to clip.

Introduction: The Equal-Regard Family in Context

Don S. Browning

I have been asked by the editors of this volume to provide an overview of my scholarly vocation. Since this volume, and its companion book titled *Equality and the Family* (2007), concentrate mainly on the bridge between my practical theological ethics and my research on marriage and family, some of what I say below may seem extraneous. But it should help explain how I became interested in making practical theological research a university enterprise — a discipline that could take its place in the interdisciplinary conversation of the modern university. Writing this essay leads me to talk about myself a bit more than feels comfortable, but my remarks may help explain why I chose to illustrate this approach to theology through research and writing on the family. It was probably a matter of accident that most of my work has unfolded in the university context. But that context made a difference. My thinking and writing, for good or ill, would doubtless have turned out much differently had circumstances put me within another institutional situation.

The following paragraphs will tell the story of how and why I traveled the road from a field called Religion and Psychological Studies, to practical theology or practical theological ethics, to trying to figure out what marriage and family should be in modern societies using the methods I had been developing over the years. To say it pointedly: the family research was an illustration — a case study — of the methods of practical theological ethics that I was beginning to envision. I could have used another problematic. As the reader will notice, the essays gathered in this volume concentrate on both the substance of my family research and the practical-theological methods that guided it. From time to time in the paragraphs below, I will identify how the authors in this volume have addressed various aspects of my theological trajectory.

The University Context

Except for two years that I taught at a denominational seminary in Oklahoma, my life as a teacher has been at a university-related divinity school with a large Ph.D. program and a smaller, but well-supported, program in Christian ministry. This university context was a favorable environment for pursuing the central question that has dominated my work, i.e., how does the Christian faith relate to, critique, and use the secular disciplines of the modern academy? It was difficult for me to do theology in a university context without being concerned with how it relates to other fields of knowledge.

This interest partially was induced by my primary field of study in my early days as a student and young professor. It was first called Religion and Personality and later named Religion and Psychological Studies. The rise of this field in several university divinity schools was due to the widespread cultural sense that religion and psychology (especially psychotherapeutic psychology) had overlapping, and sometimes competing, interests in human healing and transformation. Notice that both titles of the field contained the conjunction "and." This was probably done to emphasize that each discipline — religion *and* psychology — could be related to each other in a variety of ways but that neither should be reduced to the other. Hence, the field invited interdisciplinary thinking with all of its dangers, possible confusions, and potential creativity.

My Undergraduate Experience

But long before I thought about entering the field of Religion and Psychological Studies, I became interested in how theology relates to the disciplines of the modern academy. As an undergraduate, I was exposed to large doses of what I today call Christian humanism. In the church-related undergraduate school that I attended, I was exposed to a message that said the Christian faith contained two kinds of truth. It first witnessed to an ultimate truth about the ends of life and the nature of redemption, but it also secondarily had implications for more finite judgments about the common goods of this life and the optimal ordering of the major sectors of society such as business, medicine, education, government, law, and culture. I was first attracted to the category of culture in the form of imaginative literature; I came to the Divinity School of the University of Chicago to earn what was then called the Bachelor of Divinity Degree and then pursue a Ph.D. in the burgeoning new field of Religion and Literature. Very shortly, however, I became interested in the equally new and exciting field of Religion and Personality.

Little did I understand that as an undergraduate I was being challenged to develop a vocation — a *vocatio*. It was more of a Protestant vocation or calling than a classical Roman Catholic one. I was not being called to the specialized vocation of the monastery and the otherworldly disciplines of the love of God. I was being challenged to test the possibility of relating a Christian vision of the ends of life to wider areas of secular life — indeed, to aspects of the modern university disciplines. As an undergraduate, I was being challenged to investigate and test something of a monotheistic view of life, i.e., a view that said no matter what the diversity of finite values, cultures, and frames of meaning, some larger integrating moral and spiritual vision could be discovered and point to possible vantage points for seeing the whole. This vocation — the call to find wider frames of meaning for comprehending the grand diversity of values and disciplines — was more of an expectation and hope, but one toward which I believed real progress could be made.

Meanings of Christian Humanism

It took me several years to identify the vision received from my undergraduate studies as a kind of Christian humanism. It understood Christianity as interested in both ultimate ends and more proximate forms of human fulfillment such as health, beauty, knowledge, order, and even appropriate degrees of wealth. The question of Christian humanism is this: how do the grand themes of creation, fall, redemption, sanctification, and eternal life relate to, qualify, fulfill, transform, relativize, and finally even transcend the finite goods of health, education, art, and order? Christian humanism asks a *paradoxical question:*[1] how are finite goods affirmed, ordered, yet transcended and therefore relativized by visions and stories of

1. I gained this insight into the paradoxical nature of Christian humanism from Vigen Guroian, "G. K. Chesterton: Rallying the Really Human Things," *Intercollegiate Review* (Fall 2002): 26-34.

things infinite? There have been many great Christian humanists throughout history — Paul, Augustine, Aquinas, Melancthon, Erasmus, the philosophers and theologians of the Scottish Enlightenment, Tillich, and even the subtle blend of neoorthodoxy and American philosophical pragmatism that one finds in both Reinhold and Richard Niebuhr.

It is precisely the impulse of Christian humanism — this twofold interest in ultimate and proximate fulfillment and their dialectical relation — that has motivated my interdisciplinary interests. Furthermore, because of the biases of the University of Chicago, early in my work I came to believe that any integrating vision that found a place for both the Christian faith and humanism would need to risk confronting a variety of critical tests coming from experience, science, and philosophical analysis. Hence, my vocation was one shaped by both confession and philosophical critique. It was, I like to think, a "critical vocation" — one that I thought could fit in a modern university or liberal arts college.

Of course, there are a variety of Christian humanisms. There are those that are, in fact, reductionistic and use Christian themes as loose frameworks providing an ethos for otherwise thoroughly finite concerns to order proximate goods. Various forms of Christian existentialism and Christian Marxism exhibit this feature. And then there is the kind found in Edward Scribner Ames, the great philosopher of religion of American pragmatism.[2] Ames agreed with John Dewey in believing that religion was primarily a social process of bringing great ideals into actual social embodiment.[3] They both were far more interested in the social process than the symbols of transcendence that they sometimes invoked to encourage it.

Christian Humanism and the Multidimensionality of Life

Christian humanism understands the multidimensional character of human existence and how a properly developed Christian theology of creation, fall, and redemption both respects and transforms this multidimensionality. I will develop this claim at both the conceptual and autobiographical levels. In looking back over the years, my form of Christian humanism had affinity with the kind of theological thinking that incorporated the practical reason or *phronesis* of Aristotle and American

2. Edward Scribner Ames, *Religion* (New York: Henry Holt and Co., 1929) and *Psychology of Religious Experience* (New York: Houghton Mifflin Co., 1910).

3. John Dewey, *A Common Faith* (New Haven, CT: Yale University Press, 1934).

pragmatism into the grand theological themes of creation, human nature, justice, virtue, and moral obligation. Most recently, I have found the work of Paul Ricoeur,[4] Richard Bernstein,[5] and Hans-Georg Gadamer[6] (with a little help from nonreductionistic evolutionary theorists such as Mary Midgley)[7] as powerful resources for my brand of Christian humanism. They all are neo-Aristotelians in various ways, and Bernstein explicitly brings together American pragmatism with Gadamer's and Ricoeur's Aristotelian understanding of practical reason. Midgley updates and renders more flexible the psychobiological realism of Aristotle and makes it useable within a synthesis of pragmatism and hermeneutic philosophy advocated by Bernstein.

Why am I attracted by such a mélange of thinkers, and what problem am I trying to solve by turning to them? And how do they help me fulfill my *vocatio* of critically relating the Christian faith to the modern secular world, especially selected academic disciplines? I realize that since the writings of Karl Barth, there has been great skepticism in some theological quarters about developing friendly relationships with philosophy.[8] But when done well, as I think it was in the case of Aquinas,[9] Melanchthon,[10] and Erasmus,[11] philosophy was not arbitrarily imposed onto the Christian story. Instead, analogies were identified between the philosophy and the view of the human implicit in the Christian scrip-

4. Paul Ricoeur, *Oneself as Another* (Chicago, IL: University of Chicago Press, 1992).

5. Richard Bernstein, *Beyond Objectivism and Relativism* (Philadelphia: University of Pennsylvania Press, 1983).

6. Hans Georg-Gadamer, *Truth and Method* (New York: Crossroad, 1982).

7. Mary Midgley, *Beast and Man* (Ithaca, NY: Cornell University Press, 1978).

8. For his strongest statement of how theology is based on the self-revealing word of God totally independent of philosophical insights into human experience, morality, or reason, see Karl Barth, *Church Dogmatics* I (New York: Charles Scribner's Sons, 1936), 213-83.

9. I have been most informed by the Christian humanism in the marriage and family writings of Thomas Aquinas. See his *Summa Theologica* III, "Supplement," (New York: Benziger Brothers, 1948), QQ 1-99; see also his *Summa Contra Gentiles*, III, ii (London: Burns, Oates & Washbourne, 1928), chaps. 123-28.

10. Philip Melanchthon, *On Christian Doctrine* (New York: Oxford University Press, 1965). An explicit portrait of Melanchthon as a Christian humanist can be found in Clyde Manschreck's *Melanchthon: The Quiet Reformer* (Nashville, TN: Abingdon Press, 1958).

11. For a review of Erasmus as a Christian humanist, practical theologian, and rhetorician, see Manfred Hoffman, *Rhetoric and Theology: The Hermeneutics of Erasmus* (Toronto: University of Toronto Press, 1994).

tures. These analogies were amplified to become more generalizable descriptions of human being, feeling, thinking, and practical reason. These descriptions did not dictate the normative goals of Christianity but made it possible to relate the faith dialectically to the increasingly autonomous disciplines of psychology, economics, biology, philosophy, and law in the early and later modern academy. This has been the task of Christian humanism in the past and is, indeed, its mission today.

Christian Humanism as Antidote to Reductionism

Christian humanism sees human life as multidimensional. It is not reductionistic. It helps avoid psychological, biological, economic, legal, cultural, and even theological reductionism by giving attention to all the important dimensions of the human. There are strong forces in modern societies functioning to obscure the rich multidimensional character of human existence. Various modern disciplines fight for hegemony in interpreting the human. Economic, biological, psychological, sociological, and linguistic reductionisms compete for dominance in the contemporary intellectual and cultural scene.

Generativity and Equal Regard

Much of my own scholarship has been dedicated to critiquing examples of these reductionisms. Early in my research, I found that some psychoanalytic views claiming to explain all human action in strictly psychological terms actually lapsed into metaphysical and ethical speculations. In my *Generative Man: Society and the Good Man in Philip Rieff, Norman Brown, Erich Fromm, and Erik Erikson* (1973, 1975), I thought Rieff and Brown had crossed over these boundaries with tragic consequences but that, interestingly, Fromm and Erikson had done so fruitfully.[12] I mean by this that unwittingly the latter two psychoanalytic thinkers, in straying beyond the strict limits of scientific psychological statements, had nonetheless hit on creative syntheses of religious, moral, and psychological levels of thinking. This especially was true of Erikson and his concept of "genera-

12. Don Browning, *Generative Man: Society and the Good Man in Philip Rieff, Norman Brown, Erich Fromm, and Erik Erikson* (Philadelphia, PA: Westminster Press, 1973; reprinted as a Dell paperback, 1975).

tivity." Both Bonnie Miller-McLemore and Steven Tipton address in their essays my early work on these psychoanalytic ethicists and my interest in Erikson's view of the generative person.

In the intervening years since that volume was published, I have had the pleasure of learning that some psychologists who are Erikson scholars have come to agree with my analysis.[13] Erikson, along with the work of Louis Janssens and Paul Ricoeur, influenced my life-cyle theory of ethics, even my understanding of love as equal regard. Love as equal regard shifts in the balance between regard for the other, self-regard, and self-sacrifice as self and others (particularly our children) move through the stages of life. I consider love as equal regard as the core of Christian ethics and summarized in the principle of neighbor love ("You shall love your neighbor as yourself," Matthew 19:19). It means treating the other as an end — a child of God — and never as a means alone, but it also holds that you have a right to expect the other to treat you as an end as well. The ethic of equal regard is not just an ethic of mutual respect in a narrowly Kantian sense; it means willing and actively striving for the good (the flourishing) of the other, a good that may shift throughout the life cycle. It is not an ethic of reciprocity; love for the other is not conditioned by the response of the other Indeed, to continue community with the lovcd one, one must often sacrifice — go the extra mile — in order to restore a community of mutuality and equal regard.

My equal-regard ethic and its life-cycle context is addressed, and I must add challenged, in the chapters by Timothy Jackson and Miller-McLemore. And, as the reader will see, I attempt to defend myself in my response to my friendly critics in the concluding chapter. Indeed, as you will discover, there are some fireworks on the pages that follow — a bit of conflict and contention that, I believe, is also fruitful. It helps me clarify my thoughts and helps us all make progress.

Extending the Analysis

Later, in *Religious Thought and the Modern Psychologies* (1987, 2004), I extended the kind of analysis I ventured in *Generative Man* to other psychol-

13. Dan P. McAdams and Ed de St. Aubin, *Generativity and Adult Development* (Washington, DC: American Psychological Association, 1998). For my second look at the moral dimensions of Erikson, see "An Ethical Analysis of Erikson's Concept of Generativity," in *Generative Society*, ed. Dan McAdams and Edward de St. Aubin (Washington, DC: American Psychological Association Press, 2003).

ogies — Freud, Skinner, Rogers, Maslow, Jung, Kohut, and for a second time Erikson.[14] This study convinced me of the difficulty that any so-called secular discipline has, no matter how hard it tries, in remaining thoroughly reductionistic. I discovered in each of these psychologies implicit ethical theories and deep metaphors (mechanistic, harmonistic, dualistic, agonistic, or caring) that suggested entire worldviews and even narratives of a quasi-religious kind. I went so far as to call these personality and psychotherapeutic systems expressions of practical reason; they did contain elements of psychological description and explanation, but they also drifted time and again into moral prescriptions supported by implicit quasi-religious appeals to the way the world really is at its depths. I have been gratified to see that at least some academic psychologists have acknowledged the force of this argument and incorporated it into their own writings.[15] The kind of analysis that I did with the psychotherapeutic and personality psychologies in *Religious Thought and the Modern Psychologies* I did much later with the moral psychologies in *Christian Ethics and the Moral Psychologies* (2006), this time using the understanding of *phronesis* developed by Paul Ricoeur to examine the full range of the moral dimension implicit and explicit in these psychologies.

Sometimes the reductionisms of the modern disciplines are "soft" rather than "hard," more implicit than explicit or directly asserted. They do not attempt, in their public self-representations, to explain all aspects of human action, but they fail to specify the limits of their discipline. Hence, by default, their perspectives function as "soft reductionisms"; even though they do not claim exhaustive explanatory power, neither do they specify how their specialty fits in the context of other interpretive perspectives. To me, psychiatry constitutes one of the most intriguing examples of this kind of reductionistic maneuver. In the 1980s, I was fortunate to have convened a panel of scholars for the Park Ridge Center that

14. Don Browning, *Religious Thought and the Modern Psychologies* (Minneapolis, MN: Fortress Press, 1987, 2004).

15. For academic psychologists who have made use of the argument of *Religious Thought and the Modern Psychologies,* see the following: Stanton Jones, "A Constructive Relationship for Religion with the Science and Profession of Psychology; Perhaps the Boldest Model Yet," *American Psychologist* (March 1994): 184-99; Stanton Jones and Richard Butman, *Modern Psychotherapies* (Downers Grove, IL: InterVarsity Press, 1991); Daniel A. Helminiak, *Religion and the Human Sciences* (Albany, NY: State University of New York Press, 1998); P. J. Watson, "Changing the Religious Self and the Problem of Rationality," in *The Changing Self,* ed. T. M. Brinthaupt (Albany, NY: State University of New York Press, 1994).

addressed psychiatry in two volumes of essays.[16] These volumes, and some of my other psychological writings, led to an invitation in 1999 to address the Division of Religion of the American Psychiatric Association where I developed these observations even further. There was evidence, I argued, that modern psychiatry's unguarded soft reductionism actually was chasing some patients away from its services out of fear that the religious dimension of their lives would not be respected by psychiatric practitioners and their assistants.[17]

Various academic issues and challenges that I have faced have led me to risk a similar analysis of selected aspects of the field of economics, especially the rational-choice theories of my colleagues at the University of Chicago. I did this in connection with my investigations in the Religion, Culture, and Family Project partially because of the influence that economic theory has had on family theory in the social sciences.[18] Not unlike the field of psychology, neo-classical economics seems undergirded alternatively by deep metaphors of harmony or deep agonistic metaphors implying a metaphysics of conflict. In either case, as Donald McCloskey suggested in *If You're So Smart* (1990), a diffuse form of the Protestant work ethic permeates the moral sensibilities of this school of economics, showing how even soft reductionisms lapse into ethics and metaphysics.[19] With the encouragement of legal scholar John Witte, one of the editors of this volume, I have become emboldened to apply this kind of analysis to selected aspects of the field of marriage and family law.[20]

16. Don Browning, Thomas Jobe, and Ian Evison, eds., *Religious and Ethical Factors in Psychiatric Practice* (Chicago, IL: Nelson-Hall, 1990); Don Browning and Ian Evison, *Does Psychiatry Need a Public Philosophy?* (Chicago, IL: Nelson-Hall, 1991).

17. Don Browning, "Internists of the Mind or Physicians of the Soul: Does Psychiatry Need a Public Philosophy?" *Australian and New Zealand Journal of Psychiatry* (June 2003). This was my 1999 Oskar Pfister Award Lecture before the Division of Religion of the American Psychiatric Association.

18. Gary Becker, *Treatise on the Family* (Cambridge, MA: Harvard University Press, 1991); Richard Posner, *Sex and Reason* (Cambridge, MA: Harvard University Press, 1992). For my analysis of Becker and Posner, see "The Family Theory of the Chicago School of Economics," *The Annual: Society of Christian Ethics* (1995).

19. Donald McCloskey, *If You're So Smart* (Chicago, IL: University of Chicago Press, 1990).

20. Don Browning, "Critical Familism, Civil Society, and the Law," *Hofstra Law Review* 32:1 (Fall 2003): 313-30; Don Browning, "The Meaning of the Family in the Universal Declaration of Human Rights," in *The Family in the New Millennium,* vol. I, ed. A. Scott Loveless and Thomas Holman (Westport, CT: Praeger Perspectives, 2007), 38-53; Don Browning, "The United Nations Convention on the Rights of the Child: Should It Be Ratified and Why?" *Emory International Law Review* 20:1 (Spring 2006):

Theological Reductionism

But Christian humanism can be and, I think, should be just as skeptical of theological reductionisms. Theology itself can fail to grasp the multidimensional character of human existence. This kind of reductionism occurs when a theologian tries to account for everything from the angle of narrowly conceived theological themes. Such perspectives are unable to show how social, psychological, biological, and economic dimensions are not only qualified by theological views but also shape theological affirmations in turn. Most theologians who enter effectively into the modern critical conversation have succeeded in avoiding this kind of theological positivism. However, Barth, much of contemporary narrative theology, and the school of radical orthodoxy may be guilty of this form of reductionism.

On the other hand, many twentieth-century theologians were not theological reductionists; they did not reduce all meaning to God's action as though there were no stable structures of the world that God both created and then respected. Paul Tillich offered in his *Systematic Theology* III a multidimensional view that listed the inorganic, the organic, the psychic, and the spiritual as fundamental to human life.[21] More recently, William Schweiker, in an effort to develop a responsibility ethic for a new Christian humanism, lists three dimensions of basic human goods — premoral, social, and reflective goods. For both Tillich and Schweiker, social and individual ethical thinking entails making judgments about how, with regard to different issues and varying circumstances, these dimensions appropriately relate to each other.

The Centrality of the Practical

As the years rolled by, the influence of the hermeneutic philosophy of Hans-Georg Gadamer and Paul Ricoeur as well as my earlier studies in American pragmatism convinced me that interdisciplinary work proceeds best within a practical framework where the problem under consideration itself gives form to how the relevant disciplines relate in defining the issue, describing the forces that shape it, and searching for norms

157-84; Don Browning, "Linda McClain's *The Place of Families* and Contemporary Family Law: A Critique from Critical Familism," *Emory Journal of Law* (Spring 2007), in press.

21. Paul Tillich, *Systematic Theology* III (Chicago, IL: University of Chicago Press, 1963), 22-23.

that can address it. I became convinced that the integration of the disciplines was best seen as a practical, rather than a theoretical, enterprise. Theory was important, but now as a theory of the practical rather than a task in abstract *theoria* as such. Or to state the proposition more carefully, integration of the human sciences was best understood as a task of practical reason generously defined. This led to my work in practical theology and finally to various efforts to address contemporary issues in marriage and family as they relate to religion, society, and the law. This work unfolded during the 1990s as I simultaneously helped establish the International Academy of Practical Theology (1993) and launched, with the help of the Division of Religion of the Lilly Endowment and a host of excellent colleagues, the research of the Religion, Culture, and Family Project (1991-2003). The essays by Richard Osmer and Mary Van Leeuwen explicitly address this phase of my work.

The Five Dimensions of Practical Reason

The question began to arise, how then should one understand the nature of practical reason, practical wisdom, or *phronesis?* What is its structure? How does it proceed? And must it invariably have a religious or, at least, a faith dimension? My analysis of the implicit forms of practical thinking in the modern psychologies, law, and in other contexts gradually led me to believe that many allegedly neutral disciplines were actually exercises in practical reason. Furthermore, I became convinced that practical reason is thick; it is multidimensional within itself. Its multidimensionality is frequently obscured, if not repressed. But even when it is unmonitored and implicit, its structure can still be discovered, analyzed, and critiqued. Some forms of practical reason lurking in the horizons of particular disciplines may be quite faulty; other implicit forms of *phronesis* may be admirable even though hardly visible.

Nearly everywhere I looked, I seemed to find five levels or dimensions of practical reason. Many of these dimensions were assumed and not well thematized and brought to consciousness; yet they were operative nonetheless. Although my view of practical reason differs somewhat from that of Habermas, I agree with his argument that its dimensions can be derived from what he calls an empirical reconstructive process.[22] By

22. Jürgen Habermas, *Moral Consciousness and Communicative Action* (Cambridge, MA: The MIT Press, 1990), 98.

this, he means that a reflective analysis of actual concrete instances of practical reason will uncover the full scope of what they assume. I have concluded that when one does this, one will invariably find implicit in practical judgments deep metaphors about how the world is in its most final or ultimate context, e.g., whether warm or cold, dependable or unpredictable, affirming or indifferent. I call this the *visional* dimension of practical reason. Second, practical reason also contains some general principle about what is obligatory in human life, e.g., whether to follow tradition, to maximize the good for oneself (ethical egoism), to maximize the greatest good for the largest number (utilitarianism), to treat all persons as rational ends (Kant, Rawls) or as children of God (Judaism, Christianity), etc. I have called this the *obligational* dimension of practical reason. Most philosophers think that this dimension is all that practical reason is about and spend their time debating which of these principles is the most morally adequate. Third, practical reason is also about the ordering of goods, e.g., premoral goods such as pleasure, health, knowledge, wealth, or progeny. These goods reflect the desiring or aspirational aspects of life. Here, I agree with Aristotle, Aquinas, philosophical pragmatism, and Ricoeur that ethics is significantly about the actualization and ordering of this striving for the goods of life. I variously have called this the *tendency-need* or *premoral* dimension of practical reason. Erikson's concept of generativity and the concept of kin altruism found in Aristotle, Aquinas, Roman Catholic social teachings and scientifically amplified by evolutionary psychology illuminates some, but not all, of the premoral goods of life, especially as they apply to marriage and family. Stephen Pope reviews my use of evolutionary psychology to uncover and evaluate the importance of kin altruism to family formation and cohesion and M. Christian Green comments on the implication of this view and other considerations for my argument about the importance of fathers.

But there are two additional dimensions of practical reason that are often ignored. The fourth I have called the *environmental-social* or *contextual* level; it has to do with judgments or assumptions about which of our strivings for the good can be realized concretely in view of the constraints of natural and social forces that impinge upon the situation of our actions. In her chapter, Rebekah Miles deals with my analysis of what the social context of contemporary employment patterns means for family pressures today and the potentials, and limitations, of my proposal for a combined total of a 60-hour work week in paid employment for a husband and wife who are both in the workforce and who also have children.

Finally, the last of the five dimensions has to do with the most concrete level of actual practices; how does practical reason orchestrate these other four dimensions into a strategic set of actions, roles, rules, and social processes? Osmer and Van Leeuwen address this dimension of practical reason in their discussion of classroom teaching about marriage and family issues. I have called this the *practice* or *rule-role* level of practical thinking. In recent writings, I have started with this dimension first, shown the thickness of our practices, identified and analyzed the other four dimensions as they are embedded at the level of practice, and then gone backward and upward to a critical analysis and retrieval of the other levels in light of the classic practices of the Christian faith. I have developed and employed this multidimensional theory of practical reason in my writings since the early 1980s.[23] I gave them their most extensive elaboration in *A Fundamental Practical Theology* (1991)[24] but have used them as well in my writings on the family in the Religion, Culture, and Family Project.[25] Osmer explicitly addresses this work in his essay.

The modern university disciplines tend to specialize in one or more of these dimensions, but they seldom, if ever, avoid also making judgments about some if not all of the others. For example, the modern psychologies for the most part specialize at what I have called the premoral or tendency-need level. The difference between Freud, Jung, Rogers, Erikson, Kohut, and evolutionary psychology has to do with competing theories about our fundamental biosocial tendencies and needs and the various implications these theories have for the premoral goods that humans search for in life. But in spite of this specialization, these psychologies frequently spill over into the obligational and visional dimensions of practical reason, making them fair game for analysis from the perspective of systematic theology, moral theology, and philosophical ethics. Rational-choice economics also concentrates, not unlike the modern psychologies, on a rather narrow range of human desires or psychobiological

23. Use of the five dimensions probably first appeared in my *Religious Ethics and Pastoral Care* (Minneapolis, MN: Fortress Press, 1983). In this book, I used them to analyze and evaluate contemporary practices in pastoral care. Shortly thereafter, I used them to analyze the modern psychotherapeutic psychologies in *Religious Thought and the Modern Psychologies.*

24. Don Browning, *A Fundamental Practical Theology* (Minneapolis, MN: Fortress Press, 1991).

25. Don Browning, Bonnie Miller-McLemore, Pamela Couture, Bernie Lyon, and Robert Franklin, *From Culture Wars to Common Ground: Religion and the American Family Debate* (Louisville, KY: Westminster Press, 1997, 2000); Browning, *Marriage and Modernization: How Globalization Threatens Marriage and What to Do about It* (Grand Rapids, MI: Wm. B. Eerdmans, 2003).

inclinations that are thought to be both the fundamental goods of life as well as being largely commensurable. By commensurable, I mean that these goods are thought to be exchangeable with each other, such as the satisfactions of a new house might be exchangeable for a new car, the decision to have a child relinquished in hope of attaining a better television set, or a marriage forgone in order to have more individual discretionary income. But this form of economic theory also, as I have suggested above, often strays over its assigned boundaries to ethics and even metaphysics.

The field of family studies, which has been my preoccupation during the last fifteen years, exhibits the same multidimensional assumptions about the human. Secular family studies often explicitly reject the religious metaphors of covenant and sacrament and related ethics that have influenced family theory in the past. They present themselves as religiously and ethically neutral. I came to believe, however, that religious and ethical assumptions frequently appear in secular family studies, either in the form of old assumptions or new ones unwittingly substituted for more traditional ones. In the first edition of *From Culture Wars to Common Ground: Religion and the American Family Debate* (1997), my co-authors and I made no explicit reference to the five dimensions or the other theological methods spelled out in *A Fundamental Practical Theology.* But in the second edition (2000), we added a new appendix that demonstrated how we implicitly had used them to follow and critique the implicit normative arguments, both religious and secular, swirling around the contemporary debates over the family.

The Religion, Culture, and Family Project intentionally used the practical-theological method set forth in a *Fundamental Practical Theology.* The companion book to this present volume titled *Equality and the Family: A Fundamental Practical Theology of Children, Mothers, and Fathers in Modern Societies* (2007) traces in some detail the use of the practical theological methodology in that research project. This meant that we assumed, following Ricoeur and Gadamer, that there is a near identity between historical understanding *(verstehen)* and practical reason *(phronesis).* This meant that in order to think practically *(phronesis)* about the future of the family, we need to describe the present and understand *(verstehen)* how the past (both its classics on family and the distortions of them) affects the present. In an analogous way, to understand *(verstehen)* how we have been shaped, we need to bring to the past our descriptions of present problems and issues. Both John Wall and Garrett Paul address this aspect of the bridge between my practical theological ethics and the family project.

In *A Fundamental Practical Theology* and throughout the family project, I took this view of the relation of *phronesis* and *verstehen* and developed a view of theology called fundamental practical theology. It envisioned theology, when done well, as moving through four steps — from descriptive theology (describing questions), historical theology (retrieving the classics that have shaped who we are), systematic theology (critiquing and ordering the insight of the classics), and strategic practical theology (applying these insights to the issue in the original situation). The reader will notice that Richard Osmer both accepts these four steps but also modifies them. The arguments of *From Culture Wars to Common Ground,* my other family writings, and the Religion, Culture, and Family Project as a whole are designed to follow these four steps or movements.

Being a practical theologian with an eye cast toward contemporary practical issues, I was surprised how important the history of marriage and family became to the Religion, Culture, and Family Project. This is why we commissioned and used books on the Hebrew scriptures, the New Testament, and the interaction between law and religion such as John Witte's important *From Sacrament to Contract: Marriage, Religion, and Law in the Western Tradition* (1997).[26] The social sciences were used profusely throughout the project, and especially in *From Culture Wars to Common Ground,* my co-authored *Reweaving the Social Tapestry* (2002) (to which sociologist Linda Waite kindly refers in one of the forewords to this book), and *Marriage and Modernization* (2003). But I never moved from the so-called objectivity of the social sciences (for instance, the insights of sociology in two of our own national surveys or those of evolutionary psychology) to normative claims. Rather we used the social sciences to get "distance" (Ricoeur's concept of "distanciation") from the competing claims of history, especially on the question of the premoral goods of life, and to determine which of contending historical perspectives on marriage and family (for instance, Plato or Aristotle, or Christian Aristotelianism or Christian Platonism) had the stronger positions when it came to certain facts about human nature and social systems.

Conclusion

Because of the multidimensional character of practical thinking within a religious context, Christians who hold similar understandings of God,

26. John Witte, *From Sacrament to Contract* (Louisville, KY: Westminster John Knox, 1997).

Christ, the Holy Spirit, and the final consummation of life can nonetheless make very different decisions at other levels of practical thinking. Christians conflict with one another because they cannot follow their own arguments at these different levels and cannot trace the arguments of others. Hence, Christians often do not have clear ideas about where and how they disagree. They cannot come to agree because they cannot even carefully analyze where in the complex argumentation they actually disagree. Sadly, they continue to fight. I believe these five dimensions inform their disputes, but the contending parties do not understand how this happens, where in all of this thickness of practical thinking their differences lay, and how to gain control of their deliberations to find agreement and lasting community. These five dimensions continue to inform both the analysis and the constructive arguments in my more recent work on family issues in public policy, law, and the church.

I have told this bit of intellectual biography to illustrate what I mean by Christian humanism and how this rubric has informed my interdisciplinary vocation as a theological educator in the modern university. It is a vocation that I am gradually understanding more deeply. There is much more to say about both Christian humanism and my own approach to it. It has been my main goal, however, to describe a practically oriented Christian humanism as an example of how a theologically informed scholarly vocation can be defended in the modern university, both as a ground for various constructive research projects and as a framework for analysis and criticism of other disciplines. I have pursued this trajectory in the name of a larger vision no matter how partial and open ended — that of enhancing the possibility of a more integrated life.[27]

27. Parts of this introduction were first formulated for two conferences on scholarship as a Christian vocation sponsored by the Wabash Center during the summers of 2002 and 2003. I want to express my deep appreciation for the stimulus that these conferences provided me for thinking about my life and work in terms of the rubrics of *vocatio*.

1 Generativity, Self-Sacrifice, and the Ethics of Family Life

Bonnie J. Miller-McLemore

Like a good joke, a humorous Mother's Day card can sometimes speak volumes, capturing truths about love in families that evade empirical and theoretical research. This year my mom received a card that read, "Today you don't have to make dinner. You don't have to clean up. You don't have to vacuum or do laundry." Then on the inside it said: "Just pretend you're Dad. Happy Mother's Day!"

We laugh. But on some level we recognize a profound reality, at least for those who came of age prior to World War II and for many mothers who still carry the greater domestic load today. Women are well socialized to sacrifice themselves to make way for the welfare of others and sustain domestic tranquility. Christianity has done its fair share to keep this ideal in place. But many people have come to see this as unfair.

Scholars in ethics, theology, and feminist theory have supported this change. Despite divergent positions on the left and right, they agree about one claim: the need for greater gender equality in family relationships. In theology and ethics, Don Browning has made his own distinctive contribution. For four decades, from early publications on psychologist Erik Erikson to more recent work on marriage, he has championed generativity and equal regard, two concepts helpful in grounding mutuality in family life. Running like a thread through his work is ethical deliberation on self-fulfillment *(eros)*, self-sacrifice *(agape)*, and mutuality *(caritas)*, with sacrifice viewed increasingly as a means of reestablishing mutuality and not as an end itself.

Today's generation, however, faces a serious problem of family ethics that has gone largely unnoticed among scholars. Is there still a place for sacrifice? Embrace of mutuality has often meant less sacrifice, especially for women. But does it then mean more sacrifice for men? Few scholars raise this. Yet some men encounter it dramatically in their own lives when they go beyond just talking about equality and genuinely try to live it out. They discover what women have long known: families require unexpected costs on their part, especially when children are involved.

Instead the emphasis has fallen almost entirely on endorsing equal regard. If there is any worry at all, it has been concern, usually on the part of conservatives, about self-fulfillment. They worry that self-fulfillment as the new ethic contributes to high divorce rates. Accusations about self-centeredness, however, have not gotten us very far, especially when those already prone to hearing them are those who feel most guilty about failing children — women. Behind the attack on selfish individualism as a key factor in family decline hides an assumption, seldom overtly voiced, that someone needs to do a little sacrificing. But who? If people do not talk openly about this, isn't sacrifice likely to just fall back on the shoulders of women?

So is there a place for self-sacrifice? If so, what is it? What forms does it take? How is it related to mutuality? Who sacrifices under what circumstances? This chapter explores these questions by tracing one particular lifeline of this discussion through three instantiations — Erik Erikson's original insights on generativity, Browning's elaboration and turn to equal regard, and feminist theory in theology and ethics. In each case, I ask about the place of sacrifice in family life. In following a discussion on family ethics that informed Browning's own work and that he shaped, I agree with two important ideas he promoted. A psychological grasp of human needs is essential to any articulation of broader ethical imperatives and religious ideals. Modern psychology has operated as a formidable cultural force, defining fulfillment and the human good. I return to Erikson to ask how he, the father of the psychological concept of generativity, understood sacrifice before turning to Browning, feminist theology, and a reconsideration of sacrifice.

More central to my argument, however, I choose these sources because I suspect that each enriches a family ethics of mutuality but skirts the challenge of sacrifice in a different way — Erikson by omission, Browning by modification, and feminist theology by rejection. In short, discussions of generativity and equal regard have largely failed to locate sacrifice. More generally, contemporary Christian ethical theory of families lacks an adequate theory of sacrifice. This is particularly problematic when it comes to men's domestic involvement.

Generative Man

The second to last book Erikson published in his eighties, *The Life Cycle Completed,* brought his work to summation.[1] The book does not add anything remarkably new to his theory. It mostly reiterates his "eight ages of man" that captivated wide audiences and had a huge impact on mid-twentieth-century psychology. Most significantly, it added fresh appreciation for adult growth. Just as Sigmund Freud had discovered phases through which infants, toddlers, and young children move, so also do adults continue to develop until the end of their life. Adult development — psychological, moral, and religious — became the talk of the town, shaping who got attention in church circles, what studies got funded in the social sciences, and which books rose to the top of the best sellers list (e.g., Gail Sheehy's *Passages* and then *New Passages, Understanding Men's Passages, The Silent Passage,* and so forth).

This contribution sometimes gets lost in Erikson's initial claim to fame. He was best known for his idea of an identity crisis among youths, a crisis he himself experienced as he struggled with his Jewish and Christian background, his artistic proclivity in a scientific world, his work with children in a society centered on adults, and his European heritage as an immigrant to the United States. But each instance also represents for Erikson a crisis of generativity. His final book makes the importance of adulthood more evident by starting at the end of life and centering discussion around the "generational link" of adulthood. His first publication, *Childhood and Society,* actually anticipates this move. If it were not on children, he admits, its section on generativity "would of necessity be the central one."[2]

With the concept of generativity, Erikson had something especially unique. Or so argued Browning a few decades later in *Generative Man,* naming generativity the heart and soul — indeed, the "normative center" — of Erikson's theory.[3] For Browning, "generative man" offered a more ethically adequate image for modernity than the images of other prominent psychoanalytic psychologies at the time — Erich Fromm's productive man, Norman Brown's Dionysian man, and Philip Rieff's psychological man. Dedicated to the "maintenance and ecological strength of the

1. Erik H. Erikson, *The Life Cycle Completed: A Review* (New York: Norton, 1982).

2. Erik H. Erikson, *Childhood and Society,* 35th anniversary ed. (New York: Norton, 1963; original work published in 1950), 266.

3. Don S. Browning, *Generative Man: Psychoanalytic Perspectives* (New York: Delta, 1975), 24, 181.

human race," generative man promises a better solution to what Browning saw as the core problem of modernity — how to slow down the "runaway economic and technological expansion of Western society" without losing its benefits.[4] A decade or so later, even more convinced that psychology forms culture, Browning groups Erikson with William James and Heinz Kohut as proponents of a "culture of care," assuming in their psychologies a moral ethos that balances "self-love and self-transcending love for the other."[5] Psychologists in the United States and Japan resurrected the term recently, convinced that society faces crises that only investigation into social aspects of generativity might alleviate. Generativity has, Browning ultimately concludes in this context, all the necessary elements of a fully valid philosophical ethic.[6]

The word "generativity" plays on but pushes past Freud's definition of "genitality" as the crux of adult maturity, placing the climatic sexual act in its broader social context within the cycle of generations, as Erikson did each of Freud's sexual stages. It combines in one word another definition of health that Erikson liked to attribute to Freud — *"Leiben und arbeiten,"* or "to love and to work."[7] A generative person is, in a word, someone capable of the complicated balance of work and love.

How then does Erikson situate generativity in relationship to sacrifice? The first thing to notice is how much more he has to say about mutuality than self-sacrifice. He names the Golden Rule the "base line" of his theory and provides a whole new psychological framework for it that evolves out of his study of life cycle crises. He saw, he thought, a striking mutuality between adult and child at the crux of development. When a young infant smiles, an adult can hardly "help smiling back."[8] In responding to the child, the adult needs to feel recognized almost as much as the child needs recognition. "Mature man needs to be needed," and the ability to care for the next generation rests on this intricate link between adult

4. Browning, *Generative Man*, 7, 9.

5. Don S. Browning, *Pluralism and Personality: William James and Some Contemporary Cultures of Psychology* (Philadelphia: Fortress, 1980), 41, and *Religious Thoughts and the Modern Psychologies: A Critical Conversation in the Theology of Culture* (Philadelphia: Fortress, 1987), 6, 31.

6. Don Browning, "An Ethical Analysis of Erikson's Concept of Generativity," in *The Generative Society: Caring for Future Generations*, ed. Ed de St. Aubin, Dan P. McAdams, and Tae-Chang Kim (Washington, DC: American Psychological Association, 2004), 241-55.

7. Erik H. Erikson, *Identity, Youth, and Crisis* (New York: Norton, 1968), 136.

8. Erik H. Erikson, *Insight and Responsibility: Lectures on the Ethical Implications of Psychoanalytic Insight* (New York: Norton, 1964), 220, 231.

and child — what he sometimes called "cogwheeling" — of mutual need, response, feedback, guidance, and encouragement.[9] Mutuality denotes then "a relationship in which partners depend on each other for the development of their respective strengths." Put more simply, "it is best to do to another what will strengthen you even as it will strengthen" the other.[10]

The term "sacrifice" seldom appears at all in this pristine, almost beatific, vision of family harmony. This does not mean self-sacrifice has no place. But its place is definitely under-thematized and even untheorized. It is partly assumed in Erikson's initial definition of generativity as the inverse of self-absorption. Having children, he notes, does not automatically assure generativity, which requires a curbing of self-indulgence or giving up of the self. Those who do not succeed treat themselves "as if they were their own . . . one and only child."[11] His praise for care for children, in fact, comes partly from its very capacity to move one beyond such stagnating self-centeredness.

Brief mention of sacrifice also appears in the depiction of the prior stage of intimacy where the "capacity to commit oneself to concrete affiliation" with another adult "may call for significant sacrifices and compromises," an observation made only in his final rendition of the life cycle. Earlier he talks in more Freudian language about the capacity to "lose oneself" in the other, the "gradual expansion of ego-interests," and the "selflessness of joined devotion."[12] But in each case these sacrifice-like experiences occur on behalf of one adult for another and not on the part of adults for children. Care for the next generation may require giving up of one's desires, but this goes largely unmentioned. More often, generativity with children means receiving something back and sometimes it promises even greater self-affirmation.

Nor does Erikson notice the differing levels of self-diminishment required by different forms of generativity. Initially he says that synonyms of generativity — productivity and creativity — "cannot replace" care of children. A decade and a half later, perhaps as his own children became a distant reality, he amends this. Generativity means "man's love for his works and ideas as well as his children." In fact, an "adult man" needs the "necessary self-verification" that comes from "labor's challenge."[13]

9. Erikson, *Childhood and Society,* 266-67 and *Insight and Responsibility,* 152.

10. Erikson, *Insight and Responsibility,* 231, 233.

11. Erikson, *Childhood and Society,* 267 and *Insight and Responsibility,* 130.

12. Erikson, *The Life Cycle Completed,* 70; *Childhood and Society,* 267; and *Insight and Responsibility,* 128.

13. Erikson, *Childhood and Society,* 267; *Insight and Responsibility,* 131.

There are, however, significant differences in the level of self-forgetfulness that Erikson completely overlooks. Not all forms of generativity require to the same extent the "selfless" caring that Erikson identifies early on as the "instinctual power" behind generativity.[14] Creativity calls for a positive self-centeredness or self-focus, where one temporarily suspends consideration of the immediate needs of others, whereas procreativity calls for a postponement or suspension of one's needs in the service of another. This slight difference in semantics is a huge discrepancy in practice.

Part of Erikson's blindness results from inattention to the genderized context of generativity. Generative maturity involves mastery of two essential but all too often gender-stratified tasks — occupational or creative generativity and relational or procreative generativity. For the most part, Erikson and his followers simply accept a stark division of generative labor — what he even calls the "polarization of the two sexes":[15] men work, women love.

Behind Every Generative Man Stands Sacrificing Woman

The Life Cycle Completed first appeared in 1982. It was republished in 1998 four years after Erikson's death in an extended version with "New Chapters on the Ninth Stage of Development by Joan M. Erikson." Erik met Joan Serson, a Canadian dancer, at an experimental school for Americans in Vienna where they both taught. It was the beginning of a sixty-seven-year marriage and lifelong partnership.

Joan Erikson's preface is amazing, even the fact that it was written when she was ninety-three. Although one should not read too much between the lines, she leaves lots of leads that tempt one to follow. It begins with her version of the origin of the eight stages, specifically that of generativity. The original version of the theory, it turns out, completely omitted generativity.

Although her relationship with Erik was fairly conventional — he worked, she raised their three children — she uses first-person plural to describe the creation of the theory. "We received," she says, an invitation in the late 1940s to speak about children's growth at the Midcentury White House Conference on Children and Youth. "We went to work with

14. Erikson, *Insight and Responsibility*, 131.
15. Erikson, *Insight and Responsibility*, 129.

great enthusiasm." With Erik doing child analysis and Joan running the household, "we were sure we knew intimately about the early stages of development" and its adult parallels.[16]

It was, however, on a long drive between home and train station that Joan had her breakthrough. Erik was departing for a meeting and Joan planned to "hurry back" to the children. "We used the time to discuss the [life cycle] chart and its presentation." The chart sat on her lap as Erik drove when she "began to feel uneasy." "In a shocking moment of clarity I saw what was wrong": the stage where the Eriksons found themselves and their children was completely missing. She continues: "The seven chart stages jumped from 'Intimacy' (stage six) to 'Old Age' (stage seven). We surely needed another stage between the sixth and seventh, but time was short. Soon we included a new seventh stage entitled 'Generativity vs. Stagnation.' . . ."[17] They missed this, she speculates, because it is hard to recognize the stage in which one is situated. Its discovery, it seems, was very much hers, at least initially.

One of Joan's most cherished contributions was her weavings of the chart in multiple interconnected colors showing visibly how each stage lives on in the next and connects back to the first. The "life cycle chart becomes really meaningful," she argues in the preface, "only when you have observed it as a weaving or, even better, *have undertaken to weave it yourself.*"[18] She implies — and here I read with a feminist lens — that one only knows the cycle when one is involved intimately in stitching it together in the home, as most mothers are. Although men certainly weave, it is quintessentially something women do, making clothes for others, blankets for their warmth, pillows for their comfort, and rugs for them to walk on.

As a mother, Joan adds her own distinctive flavor to the theory. She inverts the order of each paired crisis, putting the challenging component first — mistrust vs. trust, shame and doubt vs. autonomy, and so forth. She clarifies that generativity is the most loosely defined and "longest stretch of time on the chart" because it includes starting a family and establishing oneself in work and community. Most tellingly, she uses the word "demanding" several times, perhaps because she knew well the steady demands of the domestic side of their generative partnership. This

16. Joan Erikson, "Preface," in *The Life Cycle Completed,* Extended Version with New Chapters on the Ninth Stage of Development (New York: Norton, 1998), 1-2.

17. Joan Erikson, "Preface," 3.

18. Joan Erikson, "Preface," 2 (emphasis added).

"demanding period" of life is "challenging, exciting at best" and "burdensome if rigid and demanding."[19]

In the 1950s when the life cycle theory emerged, generativity played out differently for men and women. Behind "generative man" stood "self-sacrificing woman," as hidden to us as the contributions of Joan herself have been hidden. Also hidden are the sacrifices or losses suffered by men whose work kept them away from intimate contact and care of children. But without an adequate theory of sacrifice neither loss can be acknowledged fully.

One should not promote a family ethic of generativity without a more serious accounting of gender and inequity in the distribution of the sacrifices of generativity.[20] Although Joan makes clear that it was children themselves — their own and those whom Erik had studied — who reoriented their thinking, later theorists were more than happy to interpret generativity apart from the demands and joy of their care. One of the more popular renditions, *Seasons of a Man's Life* by Jon Levinson, relies heavily on Erikson's theory but has little to say about children.[21] Browning himself says the idea of generativity was born "most especially" out of Erikson's experience as a "working therapist," not as a loving father.[22] I believe his theory emerged as much, if not more, from his experience as a parent.

Levinson's study captures a feature in male generativity during the mid- to late twentieth century: the focus is typically not self-sacrifice for the development of others. This is the woman's role. When listing factors that help resolve the crisis of generativity, such as success and satisfaction in one's job, another developmental psychologist (writing around the same time as Levinson) actually puts rearing children in parentheses.[23] Instead male development involves "Becoming One's Own Man," with

19. Joan Erikson, *The Life Cycle Completed: Extended Version*, 111-12.

20. I have raised this concern in several other places. See "Generativity and Gender: The Politics of Care," in *The Generative Society: Caring for Future Generations*, ed. Ed de St. Aubin, Dan P. McAdams, and Tae-Chang Kim (Washington, DC: American Psychological Association, 2003), 174-95. See also "Produce or Perish: A Feminist Critique of Generativity," *Union Seminary Quarterly Review* 43(1-4) (1989): 201-21 and *Also A Mother: Work and Family as Theological Dilemma* (Nashville, TN: Abingdon, 1994), chap. 2.

21. Daniel J. Levinson, with Charlotte N. Darrow, Edward B. Klein, Maria H. Levinson, and Braxton McKee, *Seasons of a Man's Life* (New York: Ballantine, 1978).

22. Browning, *Generative Man*, 24.

23. Douglas C. Kimmel, *Adulthood and Aging: An Interdisciplinary Developmental View* (New York: Wiley and Sons, 1974), 244-45.

women creating the "boundary space" within which his "Dream" develops and flourishes. That a husband might make similar sacrifices for his wife was (and still is) less socially acceptable. Analyzing gender dynamics around the same time, psychologist Jean Baker Miller says women base their self-image around the question, "Am I giving enough?" whereas men ask instead "Am I a doer?" Such self-giving becomes an "added luxury" after a man has paid his dues in productivity.[24]

The relegation of generativity to the second to last stage of the life cycle is part of the problem here. This position late in the life's stages tempts theorists to overlook generative challenges that arise long before mid-adulthood, especially for women. Young women regularly ask themselves about the timing of motherhood and the rhythms of paid employment, often long before marriage and children. They juggle, sometimes excruciatingly unsuccessfully, what Pamela Daniels describes as a "double generativity" with all its logistical and chronological nightmares.[25] Women fight an array of "can'ts" and "don'ts" that prevents them from allowing others to sacrifice for them.[26] The question of how to combine work and child rearing really comes down to an ethical quandary of grave consequence for family life: how to balance love of others and one's own desires, interests, talents, and a work of one's own. Simply put, how does one adjudicate self-sacrifice without complete self-loss?

Erikson's legacy on generativity and sacrifice is ambiguous. On the one hand, he makes a powerful ethnological and psychological case for mutuality as the source of human development. On the other hand, he restricts women's generativity to giving to others and makes greater allowance for alternative avenues of self-affirmation for men. Scholars in his wake progressively limited generativity to productivity outside the home and failed to attend to the gender disparities in who sacrifices what and how much for whom in families. Seldom did they consider sacrifice as part of generativity, whether inside or outside the home.

24. Jean Baker Miller, *Toward a New Psychology of Women* (Boston: Beacon, 1976), 49.

25. Pamela Daniels, "Dream vs. Drift in Women's Careers: The Question of Generativity," in *Psychology of Women: Selected Readings*, 2d ed., ed. Juanita H. Williams (New York: Norton, 1979, 1985), 435. See also Ruth Sidel, *On Her Own: Growing Up in the Shadow of the American Dream* (New York: Viking, 1990).

26. Nadya Aisenberg and Mona Harrington, *Women of Academe: Outsiders in the Sacred Grove* (Amherst: University of Massachusetts Press, 1988), 26; see also Carol Gilligan, *In a Different Voice: Psychological Theory and Women's Development* (Cambridge, MA: Harvard University Press, 1982).

Equal Regard: Dry Rhetoric for a Messy Reality

Survey research on models of love for a jointly authored book spearheaded by Browning, *From Culture Wars to Common Ground,* confirms the growing appeal of mutuality. Aided by George H. Gallup, the authors asked 1,019 randomly selected respondents which model of love — mutuality, self-sacrifice, or self-fulfillment — best correlates with good marriages and families. A majority rank mutuality ("giving your spouse and children the same respect, affection, and help as you expect from them") over self-sacrifice ("putting the needs and goals of your spouse and children ahead of your own"). Notably, when asked what they thought their own parents would say to the same question, respondents characterized them as more self-sacrificial, especially mothers. Only 9 percent thought mothers would select self-fulfillment (love "fulfills your personal needs and life goals"), whereas 28 percent believed fathers would.[27] In short, fewer people now accept, at least outright, the gender polarization of self-fulfillment and sacrifice that their parents presumed. Appreciation for mutuality has risen. The value of self-sacrifice has diminished.

In Browning's eyes, this is largely as it should be. His early work on generativity foreshadows a growing appreciation for self-love and a high appraisal of equal regard that comes to fruition in *From Culture Wars to Common Ground.* Shaped by humanistic and psychoanalytic psychologies, one of his contributions to ethical discussions of the family is his case for self-regard. Even early on he argues that *eros* is a "positive guide" in our efforts to love others. "We literally do not know how to assess the . . . needs of others unless we have some access to our own basic needs."[28] Humanistic psychologies establish the critical role of self-esteem in early development and counseling. But they fail to see the inevitable conflicts that would arise if everyone pursued an ethic of self-fulfillment. Browning favors psychoanalytic psychologists Erikson and Kohut precisely because they place self-love in generative relationship to care of others.

Both schools, however, suggest that the long Christian history of

27. Don S. Browning, Bonnie J. Miller-McLemore, Pamela D. Couture, K. Brynoff Lyon, and Robert M. Franklin, *From Culture Wars to Common Ground: Religion and the American Family Debate* (Louisville, KY: Westminster John Knox, 1997), 18-20. See also Don S. Browning, "Self-Sacrifice, Self-Fulfillment, and Mutuality: The Evolution of Marriage," *The Responsive Community* (Winter 1997-98): 58-62.

28. Don S. Browning, *Religious Ethics and Pastoral Care* (Philadelphia: Fortress, 1983), 73.

upholding selflessness has done more damage than good. Our problem is self-hate, not self-love. Kohut in particular dares to put a positive spin on narcissism itself, long defined as the nemesis of Christian love, by arguing that we are each born with healthy narcissistic needs for mirroring and idealization that we never outgrow. It is not a question of ridding ourselves of narcissistic desires. Rather maturity involves acquiring more constructive means of meeting them. There is actually such a thing as "mature narcissism" or healthy self-esteem that grounds empathy, humor, and the capacity to transcend the self.[29] Ultimately, these psychologies reinvigorate "older alternative traditions" in Christianity, Browning notes, that do not set self-love and self-sacrifice in such dire opposition.[30]

Here Browning enters a larger argument in twentieth-century theological ethics among those such as Anders Nygren, Gene Outka, Reinhold Niebuhr, Valerie Saiving, Judith Plaskow, and Susan Nelson, over whether *caritas*, often associated with mutuality, is more fundamental to the Christian message than unconditional sacrifice, often equated with love as *agape*.[31] Persuaded by psychology and aided by scriptures on neighbor love, he sides with those who argue for the former more Catholic view.

As he focuses more on families, Browning gradually changes his mind on the role of sacrifice. In the early 1980s he emphasizes "self-transcendence," a slightly gentler reading of self-sacrifice than self-denial.

29. See Heinz Kohut, *How Does Analysis Cure* (Chicago: University of Chicago Press, 1984); "Forms and Transformations of Narcissism," *Journal of the American Psychoanalytic Association* 14 (1965): 243-72; and "Introspective, Empathy, and the Semi-Circle of Mental Health," *International Journal of Psychoanalysis* 63 (1982): 395-407.

30. Don S. Browning, *Religious Thought and the Modern Psychologies: A Critical Conversation in the Theology of Culture* (Philadelphia: Fortress, 1987), 141.

31. See Reinhold Niebuhr, *The Nature and Destiny of Man* (New York: Charles Scribner's Sons, 1941); Anders Nygren, *Agape and Eros* (Philadelphia: Westminster, 1953); Gene Outka, *Agape: An Ethical Analysis* (New Haven: Yale University Press, 1972); Gene Outka, "Universal Love and Impartiality," in *The Love Commandments: Essays in Christian Ethics and Moral Philosophy,* ed. Edmund N. Santurri and William Werpehowski (Washington, DC: Georgetown University Press, 1992), 1-103 and *Agape: An Ethical Analysis* (New Haven: Yale University Press, 1972); Valerie Saiving (Goldstein), "The Human Situation: A Feminine View," *Journal of Religion* (April 1960): 100-112; Judith Plaskow, *Sex, Sin and Grace: Women's Experience and the Theologies of Reinhold Niebuhr and Paul Tillich* (Lanham, MD: University Press of America, 1980); and Susan Nelson Dunfee, *Beyond Servanthood: Christianity and the Liberation of Women* (Lanham, MD: University Press of America, 1989). See also David Tracy, "The Catholic Model of Caritas: Self-transcendence and Transformation," in *The Family in Crisis or in Transition,* ed. Andrew Greeley (New York: Seabury, 1979), 100-110.

One's own needs should be understood "not as an end in themselves," he says, "but as means toward a higher goal of self-transcendence in relating to others."[32] But by the late 1990s he repositions sacrifice itself. It now becomes the means to the higher goal of equal regard. In *From Culture Wars to Common Ground,* self-sacrifice is declared necessary *"to renew the true goal of love, which is mutuality."* Now it is sacrifice that is *"not an end in itself."* As he concludes in his prior work on the cultures of psychology, *"self-sacrifice is not the ideal of the Christian life."*[33]

Elevating self-love and equal regard means, in other words, downplaying self-sacrifice. Although Browning gives it a more central role than Erikson, he gives it little substance. Self-sacrifice has a temporary, fleeting quality; it is a transitional ethic on its way to somewhere else.[34] It is also derivative. *"Mutuality and equal-regard are the ideal, and sacrificial love is derived from them."* Niebuhr gives mutuality "secondary status," Browning charges.[35] But Browning essentially does the same to sacrifice.

In the end self-sacrifice results from human sinfulness, according to Browning. Because we live in a fallen world, not all our efforts to regard others highly will be rewarded. "There will always be unbalance, inequality, and injustice." Consequently, self-sacrifice is needed to "restore mutuality when it has broken down" or, as the Catholic ethicist who influenced Browning, Louis Janssens, says, "as long as we live in a world of conflict and sin."[36]

Is sacrifice only a consequence of the fall, however? This weekend I washed windows. As I leaned out the window to reach the outside pane, I glanced up at the gutter above me. There, chirping away, perched three tiny fluffy-feathered swallows. Then I saw what the racket was about. A larger swallow swept in, stuffed an insect in the open mouth of one baby bird and darted off. With thankless repetition, the parent bird returned again and again, nourishing each elated chick, until I grew tired of watching.

This glimpse of birdlife reminded me a bit of human parenting. The bird, as the parent, gives to others at a cost (or at least the bird could be

32. Browning, *Religious Ethics,* 68.

33. Browning et al., *From Culture Wars to Common Ground,* 282, emphasis in text and Browning, *Religious Thought and the Modern Psychologies,* 152.

34. On p. 119 in *Christian Ethics and the Moral Psychologies* (Grand Rapids: Eerdmans, 2006), Browning recognizes a similar criticism by Timothy Jackson in *The Priority of Love* (Princeton, NJ: Princeton University Press, 2003).

35. Browning, *Religious Thought and the Modern Psychologies,* 152, 149.

36. Browning, *Religious Thought and the Modern Psychologies,* 152; Janssens, "Norms and Priorities," 228.

doing something less taxing) not as a consequence of failed mutuality but because such giving is embedded, even instinctually, in nature. One father with whom I talked recently described his desire to give of himself as an almost "intuitive or primal consideration." Mothers have voiced a similar sentiment about the yielding of the body that happens in the physiology of pregnancy and nursing itself.[37] Neither the bird nor the human parent is thinking, at least not yet, about a future of mutual return.

In other words, the relationship between mutuality and self-sacrifice is more complicated than the one-up, one-down-manship that sees either as derivative. Sacrifice has a distinct place in creation, partly dictated by embodiment itself. It does not always arise in direct service to mutuality. Its relationship to mutuality is more fluid and less instrumental. Ethicists commonly identify forms of love, such as *eros* and *agape*, and debate their priority, but self-sacrifice itself needs greater nuance. It assumes a variety of forms, such as self-forgetfulness, self-suspension, self-extension, and self-giving.[38]

An ethic of equal regard is well and good at a rhetorical level. Questions arise when one moves closer to messy practice. Two other findings from the survey on models of love are noteworthy. When pushed beyond the question of what model of love is theoretically better and asked which model they actually use to resolve conflicts, the percentage of respondents choosing mutuality drops, while the choice of self-sacrifice rises by a full 10 percent and self-fulfillment rises by 5. In practice, mutuality is unwieldy, respondents seem to recognize. Real life often requires compromise.

Equally interesting, men rated sacrificial love higher than women. Whereas 44 percent of the male respondents say they value sacrifice, only 33 percent of the women do. Sixty-one percent of women rank mutuality higher, while only 48 percent of men do.[39] Men like self-sacrifice in theory, it seems, but women realize its import in practice. As a colleague remarked, "men like sacrifice when someone else is doing it."[40]

37. See, for example, Noelle Oxenhandler, *The Eros of Parenthood: Explorations in Light and Dark* (New York: St. Martin's, 2001) and Cristina Traina, *The Sensual Mother: Maternal Experience and the Boundaries of Sexual Ethics* (Chicago: University of Chicago Press, forthcoming).

38. For attention to this, see Gareth L. Hallett, *Christian Neighbor-Love: An Assessment of Six Rival Versions* (Washington, DC: Georgetown University Press, 1989), cited by Browning, *Christian Ethics*, 131.

39. Browning et al., *From Culture Wars to Common Ground*, 160.

40. Evon Flesberg, personal conversation. In general this essay benefited from conversation among colleagues at the Society for Pastoral Theology, June 2006.

Browning's concern about the male problematic or the "tendency for men to drift away from families" starts to get at this.[41] How does one entice men, evolutionally and biologically predisposed to plant seed and move on rather than care for offspring, to commit? Religious motifs, such as the Christian command that men imitate in the home Christ's sacrificial love of the church, augment natural proclivities to invest in one's own kin, Browning argues. But this simply does not go far enough. Instead of inspiring genuine sacrifice, Christianity has linked sacrifice with male headship and rule. Sacrifice requires giving up power. Shared responsibility for work and home means a kind of self-loss for which men have seldom been socialized by religion or otherwise.

Narrow focus on equal regard evades such messy negotiations. The dry, passionless flavor of the phrase "equal regard" itself contrasts sharply with the emotional and spiritual investment of other words for love, whether sacrifice, *eros,* or mutuality. Nonetheless Browning chose equal regard as his main motto for family ethics. Protestant ethicist Gene Outka also favors the term. But it is ultimately the tightly argued 1977 essay by Louis Janssens that convinces him.

Regard appeals to Browning as a universal, reversible principle. One respects every person "qua human existent," Outka and Janssens argue, regardless of traits, actions, personalities, and so forth.[42] Equal regard embodies the ideal of neighbor love as an impartial regard for all persons as children of God. In fact, this very impartiality pertains to both self and other. One should also impartially love oneself.

Impartially loving oneself or the other, however, seems a bit absurd, if not impossible, partly because "impartial" usually means neutral, objective, independent — qualities far removed from the entangled, complicated, painful, and pain-filled reality of love. There is really little that is impartial about it. Janssens writes at some distance from family life. Browning is closer to home. But because both attend primarily to the conceptual debate, neither one considers seriously enough the concrete materiality of families and the many requisite sacrifices. Instead of the hasty dismissal of sacrifice that has dominated the discussion in the past few decades, we now need to know how and when self-sacrifice is appropriate on the part of both men and women.

Finally, such discussion cannot avoid entanglement in the long his-

41. Browning et al., *From Culture Wars to Common Ground,* 106.

42. Outka, *Agape,* 9 and Louis Janssens, "Norms and Priorities in a Love Ethics," *Louvain Studies* 6 (Spring 1977): 219.

tory of vigorous debate over the place of sacrifice in Christian theology. A major oversight in theological ethics on the family concerns precisely the complex relationship between Christology, atonement, and theories of love. Only rudimentarily does Browning connect his reinterpretation of love with a reinterpretation of the cross. Niebuhr rests his case of self-sacrifice as the highest ideal on one particular reading of Jesus' death as sacrifice. So does Browning, even though he challenges Niebuhr. Neither Browning nor Janssens attempts to reinterpret the cross at all. Because Christ "loved us and gave himself up for us," they agree, so also should our love include self-sacrifice.[43] One wonders if Browning ever considers returning to his first book, *Atonement and Psychotherapy,* where he grapples with historical interpretations of the atonement that depart dramatically from the single-minded obsession in modern American Christianity with Christ's death as a sacrifice for our sins, shaped heavily along evangelical lines.[44]

Browning's ethics is removed from theological exploration in general. Except for his first book and an abiding interest in Niebuhr and Paul Ricoeur, he has shown greater enthusiasm in the course of his career for psychology, economics, and law than for systematic theology.[45] This contributes to a subtle disinterest in the cross and its impact on love in families. Greater attention to its meaning might turn what is usually an ethical discussion into a richer encounter with faith.

In the discussion of love in families more generally, serious reflection about self-sacrifice has quietly languished. Erikson seldom talked about sacrifice as essential to the creative and procreative work of mature adulthood. When others picked up on generativity as a useful construct, they often focused on the creativity of adult work and neglected family, children, and home. Browning has seldom drawn his 1960s reflection on Christian doctrines of atonement and sacrifice into direct conversation with his work on equal regard and families in the 1980s and 1990s. Meanwhile, throughout this time many secular theorists identified the morality of self-sacrifice as the bane of family life — an

43. Browning, *Religious Thought and the Modern Psychologies,* 152; Janssens, "Norms and Priorities," 228.

44. Don S. Browning, *Atonement and Psychotherapy* (Philadelphia: Westminster, 1966).

45. In *Generative Man,* he is most explicit about this. He says he will "bracket, for the time being, the fact that I am a listener to the Christian message" (16) and suspends direct theological exploration of the relationship between Erikson and the "great Christian image of man" (216).

"oppressive device which implements exploitation" as one scholar put it.[46] Generally theologians agree. Slowly, almost unnoticed, sacrifice has gone out of fashion.

Dumping Sacrifice

This eclipse of sacrifice coheres with feminist theology of our time. Unlike Browning, however, feminist theologians have spoken directly out of the throes of family struggles and have seen reinterpretation of the cross as absolutely central to any revised ethic of love. Valorie Saiving, for example, writes about women, love, and sin out of her own experience of self-loss as she single-handedly cares for an infant while pursuing her doctorate. Christine Gudorf considers self-sacrifice ludicrous praise for her adoption of two disabled children because she herself knows how deeply her own needs are entangled in this effort. Although they also relegate self-sacrifice to the back seat, they do so as women burdened by excessive expectations for self-sacrifice. This, they know, has not always been the case for men. Selfless love may be a Christian corrective for men but it is often detrimental to women. Then they, and many white feminist theologians since them, make a big mistake: they do not attempt to refashion self-sacrifice (for men) at all.

Many feminists have dumped sacrifice and for good reason. It has been a real "fishbone," to borrow from the title of a British volume on the challenge of Christianity for women.[47] The sheer number of women who have died from domestic violence, compelled to remain in dangerous contexts by Christian mandates to follow Christ, cannot help but make us sputter and choke.[48] That women should submit to their husbands unquestion-

46. Judith Farr Tormey, "Exploitation, Oppression, and Self-Sacrifice," in *Women and Philosophy: Toward a Theory of Liberation*, ed. Carol C. Gould and Marx W. Wartofsky (New York: Putnam, 1976), 206.

47. Daphne Hampson, ed., *Swallowing a Fishbone: Feminist Theologians Debate Christianity* (London: SPCK, 1996), xi. For further development of the ideas in this section, see Bonnie J. Miller-McLemore, "Salvaging Sacrifice: A Fishbone in the Throat of Feminist Theology," *Journal of Feminist Studies in Religion*, forthcoming 2007.

48. The basic premise runs like this: "Jesus suffers and so should I." See Mary D. Pellauer, Barbara Chester, and Jane A. Boyajiam, eds., *Sexual Assault and Abuse: A Handbook for Clergy and Religious Professionals* (San Francisco: Harper and Row, 1987); Joanne Carlson Brown and Carole R. Bohn, eds., *Christianity, Patriarchy, and Abuse: A Feminist Critique* (New York: Pilgrim, 1989); Carol J. Adams and Marie M. Fortune, eds., *Violence against Women and Children: A Christian Theological Handbook* (New York:

ingly has come under increasing suspicion. In addition, studies of abused children have found that a significantly higher number come from homes where Christian views of a punishing God and blood sacrifice are the staple.[49] Such findings have caused many to question Christianity's core belief in God's saving action as primarily one of substitutionary sacrifice.

This concern surfaced most powerfully throughout the 1980s largely as a result of classic publications by Beverly Wildung Harrison, Rita Nakashima Brock, Joanne Brown and Rebecca Parker, and Gudorf, all of whom connected the problem of sacrificial women with bad Christology. Sacrificial love is not the right religious ideal to hang over the heads of women already over-programmed to give and give, leaving them ashamed of the self-interest that accompanies their love. Nor is a Father God bent on sacrificing his son the appropriate image to promote from pulpit and communion table, condoning passivity before violence and perpetuating abuse. These are stark claims with which to reckon, even if one does not agree with them.

Gudorf shows how concrete practices of family life inform and are informed by the cross in a way Browning does not consider. The portrait of maternal love as heroic self-sacrifice results not just from a "radical misunderstanding of parenting" and "personal relationships in general," but also from a misunderstanding of Jesus. In Gudorf's words, "Jesus did not come to earth to give himself disinterestedly to save us. Jesus was motivated by a mutual love with 'Abba'" and "felt impelled not only to love others, but to bring others into the relationship he shared with 'Abba.'"[50]

Continuum, 1995); and Pamela Cooper-White, *The Cry of Tamar: Violence Against Women and the Church's Response* (Minneapolis, MN: Fortress, 1995). More women suffer from domestic violence annually than from "cancer, heart disease, and car accidents combined" (Lisa Isherwood, *Introducing Feminist Christologies* [London and New York: Sheffield Academic Press, 2002], 87).

49. Brandt F. Steele and Carl B. Pollock, "A Psychiatric Study of Parents Who Abuse Infants and Small Children," in *The Battered Child,* ed. R. Helfer and C. H. Kempe (Chicago: University of Chicago Press, 1968) and Kathryn Neufeld, "Child-Rearing, Religion, and Abusive Parents," *Religious Education* 74 (May-June 1979): 234-44 cited by Robert Wuthnow, *Growing up Religious: Christian and Jews and Their Journeys of Faith* (Boston: Beacon, 1999), 150. See also Philip Greven, *Spare the Child: The Religious Roots of Punishment and Psychological Impact of Physical Abuse* (New York: Alfred A. Knopf, 1991).

50. Christine E. Gudorf, "Parenting, Mutual Love, and Sacrifice," in *Women's Consciousness and Women's Conscience: A Reader in Feminist Ethics,* ed. Barbara Hilkert Andolsen, Christine E. Gudorf, and Mary D. Pellauer (San Francisco: Harper & Row, 1985), 176, 185-86. For other feminist theologians who have investigated the cross more

Although Jesus did urge sacrificial action, he did not pursue sacrifice as a good unto itself. He connected the demand for sacrifice — losing one's life, being last — with the promise of reward in the kingdom to come of which the present rewards of mutual love are already a partial taste.

Others go further than this. In a powerful essay, first published in 1981, "The Power of Anger in the Work of Love," Harrison rules out sacrifice completely, ultimately declaring, "Mark the point well: *We are not called to practice the virtue of sacrifice.*"[51] She reaches this conclusion in the context of a larger argument about the undervalued but powerful reality of women's history of bearing and nurturing life and the need for a fresh ethic of radically mutuality that appreciates this. Reappraisal of women's relational capacity to nurture others does not imply a return to sacrificial womanhood. "That we have turned sacrifice into a moral virtue has deeply confused the Christian moral tradition," Harrison believes. In contrast to Browning, however, she connects this directly to misconceptions about Christ. Christians have taken the crucifixion "out of its lived-world context in [Jesus'] total life and historical project and turn[ed] sacrifice into an abstract norm." Jesus did not seek death by crucifixion as an end in itself. He faced it because he refused "to abandon the radical activity of love," now redefined as "solidarity and reciprocity with the excluded ones in his community."[52]

Brock and Brown and Parker carry this idea to its logical extreme, positioning their argument at the heart of family life. Brock focuses on family "rather than race, gender, and class" because she believes it has had such a powerful influence on Christology.[53] However, where others

---

generally, see Mary M. Solberg, *Compelling Knowledge: A Feminist Proposal for an Epistemology of the Cross* (Albany: State University of New York Press, 1997); Darby Kathleen Ray, *Deceiving the Devil: Atonement, Abuse, and Ransom* (Cleveland: Pilgrim Press, 1998); Joanne Marie Terrell, *Power in the Blood: The Cross in the African American Experience* (Maryknoll, NY: Orbis, 1998); Cynthia S. W. Crysdale, *Embracing Travail: Retrieving the Cross Today* (New York: Continuum, 1999); Sharon G. Thornton, *Broken yet Beloved: A Pastoral Theology of the Cross* (St. Louis: Chalice, 2002); and Deanna A. Thompson, *Crossing the Divide: Luther, Feminism and the Cross* (Minneapolis: Fortress, 2004).

51. Beverly Wildung Harrison, "The Power of Anger in the Work of Love: Christian Ethics for Women and Other Strangers," in *Making the Connections: Essays in Feminist Social Ethics*, ed. Carol S. Robb (Boston: Beacon Press, 1985), 19, emphasis in the text (reprinted from *Union Seminary Quarterly Review* 36 [1981]: 41-57).

52. Harrison, "The Power of Anger," 18-19.

53. Rita Nakashima Brock, *Journeys by Heart: A Christology of Erotic Power* (New York: Crossroad, 1988), 3. See also her chapter, "And a Little Child will Lead Us: Christology and Child Abuse," in *Christianity, Patriarchy, and Abuse: A Feminist Critic*, ed. Joanne Carlson Brown and Carole R. Bohn (New York: Pilgrim, 1989), 42-61.

consider self-sacrifice from the perspective of adult life in relationship to partners, spouses, and children, Brock as well as Brown and Parker, regard it through the eyes of children with abusive parents. They accuse the traditional doctrine of sacrificial atonement of promoting what they christen as "cosmic child abuse" in which the "father allows, or even inflicts, the death of his only perfect son."[54] In Brock's reading, salvation comes not through sacrifice but through intimacy, the highest form of Christian love. Genuine love requires "self-awareness, self-affirmation, and concrete presence," not "egoless self-sacrifice."[55]

Black women theologians have different understandings of Christ and the cross.[56] Christ's suffering shows his love; the cross embodies the suffering of all marginalized and oppressed peoples at the hands of the dominant culture; so also then is human suffering, particularly that of black peoples, redemptive or already redeemed in Christ. Jesus is, as Jacquelyn Grant says, a "divine co-sufferer." But womanists still agree that common views of Christ's substitionary sacrifice have harmed women.[57] The Christian "hermeneutics of sacrifice," as ethicist JoAnne Marie Terrell remarks, has largely been an "ideological tool to impose the cross of slavery." Condoning injury or harm to someone for the sake of another "does *not* have divine sanction," she insists.[58] Williams goes one step further and concludes, "There is nothing of God in the blood of the cross."[59]

Of all the scholarship, Brown and Parker's essay, "For God So Loved the World," utters the most definitive manifesto. They run through the recognized doctrines of atonement — ransom, satisfaction, and moral influence — and declare all three bankrupt. They are all marred by their glorification of suffering, sacrifice, and death. Suffering

54. Brock, *Journeys by Heart*, 56.

55. Brock, *Journeys by Heart*, xii, 70.

56. See Jacquelyn Grant, *White Women's Christ and Black Women's Jesus* (Atlanta: Scholars Press, 1989); Kelly Brown Douglas, *The Black Christ* (Maryknoll, NY: Orbis, 1994).

57. See Jacquelyn Grant, "The Sin of Servanthood and the Deliverance of Discipleship," in *A Troubling in My Soul: Womanist Perspectives on Evil and Suffering*, ed. Emily Townes (Maryknoll, NY: Orbis, 1993), 199-218; Delores Williams, "Black Women's Surrogacy Experience and the Christian Notion of Redemption," in *After Patriarchy: Feminist Transformations of the World Religions* (Maryknoll, NY: Orbis, 1991), 1-14 and *Sisters in the Wilderness: The Challenge of Womanist God-Talk* (Maryknoll, NY: Orbis, 1993).

58. Terrell, *Power in the Blood*, 34, 124.

59. Terrell, *Power in the Blood*, 99 (citing Williams).

has no redeeming value. "We must do away with the atonement," they argue, "this idea of a blood sin upon the whole human race which can be washed away only by the blood of the lamb." The cross is purely a political event. Jesus died an "unnecessary, violent" death because he "challenged the unjust systems" of his time.[60]

Even if few people worry much over distorted understandings of Christian atonement, popular concern about the myth of the self-sacrificial mother has not abated. Interviews of 150 post–baby boom mothers among the middle and upper-middle class in a recent bestseller, *Perfect Madness: Motherhood in the Age of Anxiety,* reveal a population every bit as weighed down by motherhood as women forty years ago (dubbed the new momism or the mommy mystique), so "totally involved . . . they lose all sense of themselves and their boundaries."[61] Nor are guilt, anxiety, exhaustion, and anger over self-sacrifice limited to affluent white people. Out of grave concern for the welfare of her black sisters, author and biblical scholar Renita Weems makes an impassioned plea insisting that domestic abuse is not our Christian cross to bear. Trying to break the "inscrutable connection between suffering and redemption," she urges women to claim the value of their own lives.[62] Indeed, Terrell's own mother died at the hands of her lover and Weems forgives her mother for leaving home when her husband's abuse became unbearable. She made the "right choice."[63]

Salvaging Sacrifice

Several conclusions result from the work of this chapter, many of which suggest the need for research beyond it. The riskiest conclusion is that scholars in ethics and theology have given up on sacrifice too quickly. I say "risky" because sacrificial interpretations of love have done more

60. Joanne Carlson Brown and Rebecca Parker, "For God So Loved the World," in *Violence against Women and Children: A Christian Theological Handbook,* ed. Carol J. Adams and Marie M. Fortune (New York: Continuum, 1995), 55, 56 (reprinted from Joanne Carlson Brown and Carole R. Bohn, eds., *Christianity, Patriarchy, and Abuse: A Feminist Critic* [New York: Pilgrim, 1989], 1-30).

61. Judith Warner, *Perfect Madness: Motherhood in an Age of Anxiety* (New York: Riverhead, 2005). Quote comes from a review by Sylvia Karasu in *American Journal of Psychotherapy* 59(3) (2005): 283.

62. Renita J. Weems, "Sanctified and Suffering," *Essence* (December 2004): 162.

63. Terrell, *Power in the Blood,* 127; Weems, "Sanctified and Suffering," 164.

than their fair share of damage. One must carefully heed the critique of the last several decades. This means listening to those harmed, acknowledging the dangers and abuse of the doctrine of sacrifice, and avoiding oversimplification (i.e., either seeing sacrifice as the only way to interpret Jesus' death or ruling atonement out completely). Any project of reclamation comes only after consideration of economic and political inequities and warped emotional and spiritual reasons that lead women to sacrifice themselves inordinately and destructively. One must listen carefully for the distortions of glorification, subordination, and victimization.

Destructive sacrifice across classes and races, however, does not mean we should dump sacrifice altogether. Instead a better theory of sacrifice is more necessary now than ever before. The idea of "salvaging" is one way to proceed. *Webster's Dictionary* defines "salvage" as the "act of saving or rescuing property" in danger of destruction by a calamity, such as a wreck or fire. Self-sacrifice is a piece of intellectual and ritual capital that has long defined the church. But salvage implies a moderate path forward. The property has some value, despite all the damage, but the entire piece itself is not worth saving. Moreover, reentering the site of calamity involves some risk.

Any inclusion of self-sacrifice as part of family ethics must distinguish "life-giving" from "unhealthy, life-denying" forms, as pastoral theologian Brita Gill-Austern asserts.[64] Theological ethicist Barbara Andolsen, for example, specifies three occasions in which sacrifice is justifiable: when practiced by the privileged on behalf of the oppressed, when a party in greater need has a prima facie claim on others, and when occasions of sacrifice can be balanced out over the long run.[65] More explicit standards must be developed to assess sacrifice's legitimacy and to identify different kinds of sacrifice.

Ultimately, to discern the difference between exploitative and salvageable sacrifice, one must ask a series of complex questions raised by feminist and womanist theory pertaining to the motivation and aim of sacrifice and the nature of the person's selfhood. Is the sacrifice and surrender chosen and invited rather than forced or demanded? Is it motivated by fear or genuine love and faithfulness? Does the person remain a subject or is she turned into an object and a means to someone else's end?

64. Brita L. Gill-Austern, "Love Understood as Self-Sacrifice and Self-Denial: What Does It Do to Women?" in *Through the Eyes of Women: Insights for Pastoral Care*, ed. Jeanne Stevenson Moessner (Philadelphia: Westminster John Knox, 1996), 315.

65. Barbara Hilkert Andolsen, "Agape in Feminist Ethics," *Journal of Religious Ethics* 9(1) (1981): 80.

Does the sacrificial "loss" actually count as gain in some deeper way and enrich rather than destroy life?[66] Does sacrifice, in essence, lead to a more just and loving relationship?

As a basic rule, agency is key. Terrell makes this especially clear in her effort to determine exactly how black women find "power in the blood" of Christ. As she remarks, sacrifice is not genuine "unless it involves one's own agency."[67]

In this reassessment, gender stereotypes need to be challenged. When Erikson advocated generativity, a person (usually the man) who earned a living wage but spent long hours away from home was seen as selflessly serving his family. A woman who entered the workforce and left her children was seen as selfish. Today men who make domestic sacrifices — doing laundry, staying home, or moving for a wife's job — are still seen as odd; a "manly man" does not do domestic sacrifice. Such polarized views of self-sacrifice and selfishness serve neither men nor women well. Those who sacrifice in the domestic realm are often punished while those who sacrifice in the public realm receive rewards. At the same time, we have largely failed to account for the costs borne by those who give up caring for children to earn money.[68] Liberal feminism perpetuated a false and unfortunate dichotomy between the home as a site of sacrifice and the workplace as a site of self-fulfillment. This is not always the case, particularly for the working class where work does not guarantee personal satisfaction. Neither long work hours (formerly by men) nor endless domestic work and childcare (still largely women) constitute self-sacrifice or self-fulfillment de facto.

As this makes evident, there is a complex economy of sacrifice that is not always easy to adjudicate. Yet so often theological claims about love in families are oddly disconnected from serious questions about who works for how much money. We also know now in a way we did not a few de-

66. See Pamela Cooper-White, *The Cry of Tamar,* 93-95 for helpful consideration of these points. She also cites Sally B. Purvis, *The Power of the Cross: Foundations for a Christian Feminist Ethic of Community* (Nashville: Abingdon, 1993).

67. Terrell, *Power in the Blood,* 124.

68. Women's Studies professor Joan Williams confirms, for example, that even as women's wages catch up with men's in recent years motherhood itself continues to widen the gap: "mothers who work full time earn only sixty cents for every dollar earned by full-time fathers. Single mothers are most severely affected, earning the lowest percentage of men's average pay." Joan Williams, *Unbending Gender: Why Family and Work Conflict and What To Do About It* (Oxford: Oxford University Press, 2000), 2, citing Jane Waldfogel, "The Family Gap for Young Women in the U.S. and Britain," *Journal of Labor Economics* 16 (1998): 505.

cades ago that one cannot sustain domestic self-sacrifice without emotional health, institutional support, economic resources, and social capital. An economy that favors employers, privileges the white male worker, sees childcare as a private problem, and hires women at poor wages simply augments the strain of sacrifice for women and men alike.[69]

More work also needs to be done on what it takes to sustain sacrifice not just economically but politically and personally. Political philosopher Danielle Allen sheds fascinating light on the subject in her extraordinary work on the challenge of fostering social democracy. Like ethical theory, political theory has also lacked a "language to comprehend sacrifice, or the losses and disappointments" people endure for the sake of broader ideals of democracy.[70] Yet, Allen argues, sacrifice is an inevitable, inconspicuous, almost rudimentary part of democratic polity. To live with sacrifice requires habits of trust and rhetoric strong enough to assure reciprocal sacrifice or, in her words, the "constant redistribution of patterns of sacrifice."[71] Family democracy, like social democracy, also requires sacrifice and reassurance that people will share benefits and burdens.

In the end, the term "self-sacrifice" itself must be used with greater care not only practically but also theologically in worship and scholarship.[72] People need reminding that, contrary to popular understanding, the cross has never had a singular meaning but rather a whole host of conflicting interpretations, all of which have bearing on the practice of love in families. One of the "odd features of the Christian tradition," notes systematic theologian William Placher, is "that, while the notion *that* Christ saves lies at its heart, the church has never developed an official position on just *how* that salvation is accomplished."[73] Although the

69. See Gloria Albrecht, *Hitting Home: Feminist Ethics, Women's Work, and the Betrayal of "Family Values"* (New York: Continuum International Publishing, 2002).

70. Danielle S. Allen, *Taking to Strangers: Anxieties of Citizenship Since Brown v. Board of Education* (Chicago: University of Chicago Press, 2004), 35.

71. Allen, *Taking to Strangers,* 37.

72. When used in worship in particular, sacrifice "must be accompanied by a carefully structured catechesis and an illuminating hermeneutic," according to R. Kevin Seasoltz, "Another Look at Sacrifice," *Worship* 74(5) (Spring 2000): 411-12.

73. William C. Placher, ed., *Essentials of Christian Theology* (Louisville: Westminster John Knox, 2003), 188. He is partly summarizing the argument of Leanne Van Dyk in her essay in the book, "How Does Jesus Make a Difference?" 205-20. See also his essay, "The Cross of Jesus Christ as Solidarity, Reconciliation, and Redemption," in *Many Voices, One God: Being Faithful in a Pluralistic World: in Honor of Shirley Guthrie,* ed. Walter Brueggemann and George W. Stroup (Louisville: Westminster John Knox, 1998), 155-66 and Thornton, *Broken yet Beloved,* 70.

church has formal doctrines about Christ's nature and the trinity, we have no such doctrine about the cross.

The cross has many meanings, not just the one that has dominated Western Christianity of Christ's death as a vicarious sacrifice for our sins. The ransom theory, going back to patristic theology, understands Christ's death as paying a price owed to the devil that saves us from evil. Moral influence theory, suggested in the eleventh-century writings of Peter Abelard and linked with modern liberal theology, interprets Christ's death as an inspiring example of love that reconciles us to God. Contemporary liberation theory sees Christ's death as an unjust consequence of radical action on behalf of the oppressed and a sign of resistance to injustice that heralds the kingdom of God. Other contemporary theologians protest even the latter and portray the cross more bluntly as the evil use of violence by the powerful, literally an instrument of public execution and, as such, neither redemptive nor liberative.[74]

This complexity and multiplicity in the tradition must be more adequately represented in theological ethics of the family. Any attempt to consider love without locating it within this longer religious framework does not go far enough. Distinct from other principles, self-sacrifice requires religious grounding. For Christians this means addressing theological questions of Christ's life, death, and resurrection and ecclesial practices of worship. Examination of sacrifice also reveals how deeply Christian doctrine emerges out of and remains embedded within the dynamics of common life. The dynamics of family — who loves whom and in what way and, in particular, the sharp gender polarization between men and women — has had a powerful influence on doctrine and devotional life. To make changes in family life (e.g., share care of children) involves one most immediately in the thicket of Christian doctrine.

Self-sacrifice remains a delicate issue. No wonder Browning and others shied away from it in the last few decades. In the midst of what he called a "generation nourished by utopian images of free-flowing self-actualization," he introduces William James's idea of the strenuous life, with its distinctively self-sacrificial overtones. It is here that he acknowledges most clearly that most ethical action requires a dimension of self-sacrifice.[75] As we have seen, adult mutuality and generativity requires

74. For another statement of this position, see Regula Strobel, "New Ways of Speaking about the Cross: A New Basis for Christian Identity," in *Toward a New Heaven and a New Earth: Essays in Honor of Elisabeth Schüssler Fiorenza,* ed. Fernando Segovia (Maryknoll, NY: Orbis, 2003).

75. Browning, *Pluralism and Personality,* 28, 220.

more sacrifice than most contemporary theologians and developmental psychologists have understood. One cannot create without creating someone for whom or something for which one must care and assume responsibility. Those who have espoused mutuality have often done so in an adult-centric, chronological void, assuming equal adults and ignoring children, the aging, and those at different stages of non-equal dependency. Failure to include the routine realities of raising children has resulted in a lack of understanding of the inevitable restriction of one's own desires for the sake of one's children.[76]

Self-sacrifice still has weight and bearing in daily life. As several colleagues have pointed out, the word "sacrifice" technically means "to make sacred." Self-sacrificial love in families does have the potential to bless and sanctify, transforming care received in early childhood or in the present, as Erikson himself points out, into care given away.

76. See Bonnie J. Miller-McLemore, "Sloppy Mutuality: Love and Justice for Children and Adults," in *Mutuality Matters: Faith, Family, and Just Love,* ed. Edward Foley, Bonnie Miller-McLemore, Robert Schreiter, and Herbert Anderson (New York: Sheed & Ward, 2004), 121-35.

2 The Mutuality of Ethical Principles, Practical Virtues, and Social Institutions

Steven M. Tipton

The theological and ethical perspectives Don Browning brings to the study of human development and social institutions in the modern world come into sharp relief when compared with other critically interrelated views of these objects of inquiry and their evaluative implications. To pursue such comparison, this chapter concentrates on Browning's account of generativity as the cardinal virtue of adulthood in Erik Erikson's conception of the life cycle. I then compare this account with the institutionalized ethical stages in Lawrence Kohlberg's theory of moral development, Max Weber's classical analysis of institutional differentiation and modern moral contrariety, and a related recent account by the sociologist John Meyer.[1]

Erikson as Ethicist

In the chapter on "Generativity, Ethics and Hermeneutics: Revisiting Erik Erikson," in his *Christian Ethics and the Moral Psychologies,* Don Browning

1. See Lawrence Kohlberg, "Moral Development," in *International Encyclopedia of the Social Sciences,* ed. David L. Sills (New York: Macmillan, 1968), 483-94. Also Max Weber, "Religious Rejections of the World and Their Directions," in *From Max Weber: Essays in Sociology,* ed. H. H. Gerth and C. Wright Mills (New York: Oxford University Press, 1958), 323-59; and John W. Meyer, "Self and Life Course: Institutionalization and Its Effects," in *Institutional Structure: Constituting State, Society and the Individual,* ed. George M. Thomas, John W. Meyer, Francisco O. Ramirez, and John Boli (Newbury Park, CA: Sage Publications, 1987), 242-60.

mounts an insightful exploration and deft dissection of Erikson as ethicist. He sheds clear critical light deep into the body of his work, yet does so in elegant keeping with Erikson's own subtle, synthetic spirit.[2] In each of the eight stages of life, Erikson writes in "Life Cycle," we assume "a new drive-and-need constellation, an expanded radius of potential social interaction, and social institutions created to receive the growing individual within traditional patterns."[3] Great "philosophical and religious systems dealing with ultimate individuation seem to have remained," he concludes, "responsibly related to the culture and civilizations of their times. Seeking transcendence by renunciation, they remain ethically concerned with the maintenance of the world. By the same token, a civilization can be measured by the meaning which it gives to the full cycle of life. . . ."[4]

With remarkable concision in one brief chapter, Browning offers a nuanced analysis of Erikson on human drives and needs in terms of developmental goods and virtues, of traditional patterns of meaning in terms of encompassing moral narratives, and of the critical interplay between such traditional narratives and the life cycle in terms of the Golden Rule as a mixed-deontological principle of justice grounded in our phylogenetic need for "mutual recognition of and by another face."[5]

Erikson's moral psychology spans and synthesizes three models of ethical life in terms of principle, virtue, and narrative, which contemporary philosophical ethics conventionally advance as competing alternatives, according to Browning.[6] Those who advance an ethics of principle, such as the philosopher John Rawls, argue that conflicting communities and diverse individuals can no longer settle on the goods central to our lives together. Thus citizens of modern nations should instead work out procedural ethics of right conduct and mutual respect for one another as moral ends on the model of Kant's categorical imperative. Advocates of virtue ethics, such as Alasdair MacIntyre and Stanley Hauerwas, reply that such procedural principles need to be anchored, if not countered, by traditions of moral virtues and habits enacted and nurtured within communities of practice. Such communities of tradition share and seek to live

2. Don S. Browning, "Generativity, Ethics and Hermeneutics: Revisiting Erik Erikson," chap. 7 in *Christian Ethics and the Moral Psychologies* (Grand Rapids, MI: Eerdmans, 2006).

3. Erik Erikson, "Life Cycle," in *International Encyclopedia of the Social Sciences*, ed. David L. Sills (New York: Macmillan, 1968), 286.

4. Erikson, "Life Cycle," 291.

5. Browning, "Generativity, Ethics, and Hermeneutics," 8.

out narratives of the truth and goodness of human nature and destiny, rooted in the axial age of the world's religions and cultures yet still vital in modernity, insist many advocates of virtue ethics and diverse other thinkers such as Paul Ricoeur.[7]

Erikson brings together these perspectives within his own psychological framework attuned to the rhythms of biosocial development. He defines goods that are both moral and social, ontogenetic and phylogenetic, to make clear that "we need viable communities of tradition," says Browning, "but ones that actualize the goods of human development as well as exhibit the principle of respect for individuals as they struggle to grow."[8] First among these goods for Erikson are the goods of procreation and the actualization of the epigenetic timetable of human potentialities.

Browning infers from Erikson's basic definition of generativity "the concern in establishing and guiding the next generation."[9] Then come the goods of education and teaching as social practices to guide and pattern the goods that have been established. Generativity itself implies the cardinal virtue of care as "a quality essential for psychosocial evolution, for we are the teaching species."[10] Like other animals, humans instinctively encourage in our offspring what is ready for release. But as cultural, teaching animals, left unfinished by instinct, humans must also interpret, judge, and think about their desires dialectically. So Erikson focuses more on the modes, modalities, or biosocial patterns of human interaction, Browning notes, than he does on instinctual energies per se. He stresses the dialectic between biological drives, desires, or needs and their cultural meaning and evaluation in defining generativity within a theory of the epigenetic principle. It gives Freud's libidinal energy its due in place and time of origin but moves beyond the tension-reducing, pleasure-driven limits of libido conceived as a master instinct within a Hobbesian inner physics.[11]

Erikson's ethics of generativity resemble theories of kin altruism in contemporary evolutionary psychology and sociobiology, Browning points out, and these theories help ground Erikson's profound insight

6. Browning, "Generativity, Ethics, and Hermeneutics," 2-5.

7. Browning, "Generativity, Ethics, and Hermeneutics," 4.

8. Browning, "Generativity, Ethics, and Hermeneutics," 5.

9. Browning, "Generativity, Ethics, and Hermeneutics," 9, quoting Erik Erikson, *Young Man Luther* (New York: W. W. Norton, 1962), 267.

10. Browning, "Generativity, Ethics, and Hermeneutics," 10, quoting Erik Erikson, *Insight and Responsibility* (New York: W. W. Norton, 1964), 131.

11. Browning, "Generativity, Ethics, and Hermeneutics," 11.

that parents need their children as much as children need their parents. But Erikson's subtle symbolic and cultural elaboration of generativity reaches well beyond most evolutionary psychology, and its recourse to the exchange theory of reciprocal altruism, when it comes to accounting for cooperation and care among non-kin. Beyond the need to procreate and care for our offspring, Erikson recognizes relatively autonomous needs to know our world and our place within it, which lead us to identify and define ourselves in circles of social interaction and relationship far beyond the boundaries of basic kinship.[12]

This attention to finding meaning in life extends from parental care and love for our children to others in widening circles of community and concern to take in all of God's children. It reaches from the city to the society, from the neighbor to the stranger, from the creation to the redemption as expressions of God's love for all humans, made in God's image and to be loved as we love God. This vision of human meaning-making, says Browning, places Erikson in a long line of teleological moral thinkers from Aristotle through Aquinas to contemporary neo-Aristotelians.[13] Erikson shares their focus on virtue as realizing in personal character and social practice alike the teleological nature and destiny of human beings. He also shares their conviction that virtue builds on and fulfills natural inclinations, for example, by extending or checking certain inclinations or desires, while guiding and redirecting others. Much as it is for Aristotle and Aquinas, virtue for Erikson is a kind of mean between two extremes. It is a practical and dispositional congruence between a structured social environment and an active, interactive ego that seeks to synthesize developmental conflicts. Initially, for example, the conflict between trust and mistrust is synthesized by the virtue of hope bred by parental care of the needy, helpless infant.[14]

For Erikson, narrative envelops and valorizes all the desires and virtues of human life in their developmental unfolding, notes Browning, and it incorporates the moral principles this institutionalized development requires. As Erikson illustrates in his biographies of Luther and Gandhi, religious narratives underlie generativity by giving us faith in life's goodness through an "ontology of creation," as Browning puts it, to convey a basic trustworthiness to our own initiatives and the world's responsive-

12. Browning, "Generativity, Ethics, and Hermeneutics," 15.

13. Browning, "Generativity, Ethics, and Hermeneutics," 16; see, for example, Stephen Pope, *The Evolution of Altruism and the Ordering of Love* (Washington, DC: Georgetown University Press, 1994.)

14. Browning, "Generativity, Ethics, and Hermeneutics," 18.

ness to them.[15] It exercises a redemptive power to extend our sense of kinship beyond our own kind to take in all of humankind and all of creation.

Notwithstanding the centrality of ethics of virtue and narrative in Erikson's work, it also incorporates ethics of principle. Browning is at his most insightful in teasing out and filling in this least visible aspect of Erikson's moral synthesis. As a teleological thinker, Erikson emphasizes the need to actualize the human goods and potentialities that interact to sustain and renew the cycle of the generations. As a deontologist, he emphasizes that these goods must be universalized to include each and every present and future child, for example, by invoking a "universal sense of generative responsibility toward all human beings brought intentionally into this world."[16] By contrast to Kant's appeal to a universalizing reason in the categorical imperative, Erikson grounds this ethical demand for respecting all persons in the phylogenetic need for "mutual recognition of and by another face."[17] The universal justice of mutual recognition and regard to respect the intrinsic personhood and desert of the other pervades Erikson's ethic in theory and practice, Browning stresses, from his clinical commitment to it in good psychotherapy to his espousal of it in the nonviolent ethic of *satyagraha.*[18] It contains yet guides teleological perspectives on the good life, affirming our natural generative interest in the welfare of our own offspring yet checking the impulse of this interest to trump our universal obligation to the well-being of all children.

In this light, Erikson reformulates the Golden Rule, as follows:

> Truly worthwhile acts enhance a mutuality between doer and the other — a mutuality which strengthens the doer even as it strengthens the other. Thus the "doer" and "the other" are partners in one deed. Seen in the light of human development, this means that the doer is activated in whatever strength is appropriate to his age, stage, and condition, even as he activates in the other the strength appropriate to *his* age, stage and condition. Understood in this way, the Rule would say that it is best to do to another what will strengthen you

15. Browning, "Generativity, Ethics, and Hermeneutics," 21.

16. Browning, "Generativity, Ethics, and Hermeneutics," 8, quoting Erik Erikson, *Insight and Responsibility* (New York: Norton & Norton, 1964), 131.

17. Browning, "Generativity, Ethics, and Hermeneutics," 8, quoting Erik Erikson, *Insight and Responsibility*, 94.

18. Browning, "Generativity, Ethics, and Hermeneutics," quoting Erik Erikson, *Gandhi's Truth* (New York: W. W. Norton, 1969), 437-40.

even as it will strengthen him — that is, what will develop his best potentials even as it develops your own.[19]

This restatement does not reduce the Golden Rule to a simple, self-interested exchange, Browning makes clear, nor to a conditional contract on the conventional model of business or law. Instead it affirms a notion of "reversible mutuality" that applies equally to self and other to interweave and promote the fundamental goods of human development for all.[20] Such principles of justice must of necessity come to the fore, Browning argues by reference to Paul Ricoeur, when institutionally settled goods, practices, and virtues among one people, community, or group are surprised, overwhelmed, or brought into conflict with the quest for the good by other people.[21] We cannot live by either universal principles of justice or practical virtues alone, Browning points out. We need them both in the practical course of everyday life, and in the face of conflicting goods, practices, and ways of life. This is especially true when such conflicts arise between different communities, peoples, and nations. For their religious and cultural traditions require critique and dialogue in light of principles of justice grounded in the common human cry of our phylogenetic need for mutual recognition.[22]

The Institutional Dimension

What does not come through so fully in Browning's concise overview of Erikson as ethicist is Erikson's stage-by-stage depiction of the expanded radius of specific forms of social interaction in practices set within distinctive social institutions. These practices consist in the reciprocal process of forming virtues (and vices) that are at once personal and institutional, and as such serve as moral measures of both good character and a good society. Browning's focus is on generativity as the cardinal virtue of mature adulthood. He is less focused on the practical trajectory of character formation across all the sequential stages of the life cycle, set in widening concentric circles of institutionally arranged social relationships

19. Browning, "Generativity, Ethics, and Hermeneutics," 12, quoting Erik Erikson, *Insight and Responsibility,* 233.

20. Browning, "Generativity, Ethics, and Hermeneutics," 10-11.

21. Browning, "Generativity, Ethics, and Hermeneutics," 19, quoting Erik Erikson, *Insight and Responsibility,* 181.

22. Browning, "Generativity, Ethics, and Hermeneutics," 23.

and interactions centered around the family. Tracing out this trajectory in Erikson, however, allows us to weigh larger questions about the moral meaning of modernity crucial to Browning's concerns as well as Erikson's conception of the life cycle.

Erikson addresses "the challenges of modernity and the increased spread of social change, diversity, and social conflict that has come in its trail," Browning observes.[23] How much of the special relevance and powerful appeal of Erikson's moral psychology and its concept of generativity stems from his success in this encompassing effort? How much stems from Erikson's success in wedding a constellation of apparently universal human needs, drives, capacities, and functions to a constellation of very specific social goods, practices, and relationships institutionalized in middle-class American society in the decades following World War II?[24] What are the full implications of such social-historical specificity when it comes to different practical virtues formed in distinctive ways in particular institutions? Do they flow continuously over modern historical ground to meet the present and its moral challenges? Or do they take flight by sequenced and synthesized leaps of structural-functional faith to attain the integrity of a mature person able to "work and live" *("arbeiten und lieben")*, and then to provide the exemplary ideal of a caring and productive parent for responsible, public-spirited citizenship and wise guardianship of civilization itself?

Kohlberg and Critics: Moral Integrity Contested in Modernity

To weigh these questions let us examine Erikson's model of the life cycle by contrast to Lawrence Kohlberg's stage-and-sequence conception of moral development with an eye to key differences in their institutional analyses. Erikson places the family at the center of the society as a whole. He offers its moral ideals and narratives as exemplary for the wider institutional circles of the civic and political realms, with their republican and religious resonance of the polis and the Church as organic bodies. Thus persons develop through sequential stages of social practices and relation-

23. Browning, "Generativity, Ethics, and Hermeneutics," 2.

24. Cf. Ernst Mayr, *Animal Species and Evolution* (Cambridge, MA: Harvard University Press, 1963) and "The Evolution of Living Systems," *Proceedings of the National Academy of Sciences* 51 (1964): 934-41; Talcott Parsons, *The Evolution of Societies* (Englewood Cliffs, NJ: Prentice-Hall, 1977).

ships set in concentric circles of institutional arrangement marked by virtues that are at once personal and social. Parents nurture infants to create trust and to constitute hope in the image of providence, Erikson begins. Toddlers then learn to move, speak, and discriminate with increasing autonomy and a balanced sense of self-control without a shameful loss of self-esteem.[25] From the age of three or four, children learn to play within the family and beyond with age mates and older children, and to play out adult roles worth imitating with conscientious initiative. School-age children go on to learn the rules of disciplines, tasks, and tools in terms of competency and responsibility that anticipate the rule of law. Adolescents learn the languages of identity, ideological self-identification, and romantic love with more or less fidelity. Youths enter into adulthood through love and work that are ordered into a morally coherent, if not soteriologically significant, way of life within wider circles of social membership and loyalty. Thus they become productive and caring "generative" adults, who marry and raise families of their own. As adults age, they continue to take part in civic and religious institutions in ways that sustain their integrity and call on their practical wisdom to share responsibility for the society as a whole as ancestors of its future.[26]

By contrast to Erikson, Kohlberg stresses the socially situated boundaries of the family within a sequence of moral stages. He begins with behavioristic, egoistic models of "pre-conventional" morality that are aimed at avoiding punishment and obtaining pleasurable rewards.[27] Kohlberg construes ethics that stress caring relationship to others and responsibility for them as interdependent members of communities as "nice boy, nice girl" conformity to convention. Such caring relationships are localized within the home, linked to reference groups composed of other-directed individuals, and checked by the prescriptivist commands of law-and-order authority.[28]

Kohlberg's higher stages of morality begin with the kind of contractual exchanges and utilitarian cost-benefit analyses that mark both market economies and interpersonal transactions among mutually disinter-

25. Erikson, "Life Cycle," 286-92, here and below.

26. Erikson, "Life Cycle," 291-92.

27. Kohlberg, "Moral Development," 489-90.

28. Kohlberg, "Moral Development," 489-90. See Richard M. Hare, *The Language of Morals* (Oxford: Clarendon Press, 1952) on prescriptivist ethics; and David Riesman, with Nathan Glazer and Reuel Denney, *The Lonely Crowd: A Study of the Changing American Character* (New Haven, CT: Yale University Press, 1950) on inner-directed, other-directed, and autonomous types of personality.

ested adults. "Post-conventional" morality goes on to subordinate social relationships and practical virtues to rules, particularly in rule-utilitarian forms inherent in the bureaucratic regulation of modern work and public administration via standardized procedures and official functions taken to yield the greatest good consequences for all. It culminates in universalized principles of justice as fairness, on the Kantian contractarian model of John Rawls, which is grounded in a liberal logic of equality, reciprocity, and rights suited to the citizens of a liberal democracy.[29]

Precisely this moral logic is the object of John Meyer's pointed institutionalist critique in his essay on "Self and Life Course."[30] It resonates with post-modern protests against the dominating disciplines of late-capitalist bourgeois life, but it incorporates them into a systematic sociology of the bureaucratically administered, state-centered political economy of the United States today. Here the sovereign self of rights-bearing, freely choosing individuals as self-governing citizens is acknowledged in principle as both the ultimate source of liberal democratic society and its ultimate beneficiary. As actual members of rationalized modern societies, meanwhile, persons are distinctively organized in practice into carefully sequenced, pervasively age-graded systems of child rearing, education, occupational credentialing, career advancement, and retirement. They are bound by the hard-working duties and virtues of demonstrating disciplined capacities and skills specific to a given age, grade, or office — from reading at a fourth-grade level to writing for publication and tenure, to billing eighty hours a week to make partner in a corporate law firm.

By Meyer's account, however morally contradictory they may be, infinitely valuable and essentially equal sovereign selves — and more or less subordinated social members — are both highly institutionalized. That is why they can coexist so inconsistently, argues Meyer, because they are so stably uncoupled, within a structurally unified way of life. The expansion of modern administrative states since the eighteenth century, bureaucratically organized corporate economies since the nineteenth century, and extended schooling, credentialing, career sequencing, and official retirement systems in the twentieth century have combined to create modern individuals from persons once embedded in the kinship relations and roles of family, village, caste, and people — persons once

29. See John Rawls, *A Theory of Justice* (Cambridge, MA: Harvard University Press, 1971); also Rawls, *Political Liberalism* (New York: Columbia University Press, 1996) and Rawls, *Justice as Fairness: A Restatement* (Cambridge, MA: Harvard University Press, 2001).

30. Meyer, "Self and Life Course," esp. 243-44, 259-60.

bound by the duties and marked by the virtues inherent in these relations. Where once there were kith, kin, and the people of God, there are now individuals, not so much caged like cogs in a big industrial machine, as organized in the neatly staged and age-graded sequencing of a bureaucratic political economy. Here they are free to choose their spouse, their toothpaste, and their god, if not their president. Indeed they are obligated to choose in order to be good selves and good citizens within a bureaucratic grid that frames the market's bottom line of costs and benefits, the intersection of lawful ideals and group-interests in the public arena, and the consumerist castles of our romantic dreams.[31]

Who is left out of the middle-class life course by virtue of its sequencing and segregation? Women outside or at the bottom of the labor market, especially mothers, answers Meyer. Also left out are members of what he calls "off-track groups," the unemployed, uneducated, and unskilled. They are the least of these, in biblical terms; and not least they include "excluded minorities."[32]

This institutionalist account is deeply indebted to Max Weber in its conception of modern selves evolving in the West from religiously rooted notions of "sacred human souls," Meyer acknowledges, through historically structured processes "on the form of the rationalized society."[33] It follows Weber in positing that religiously organized notions of the individual soul in the West have led to subsequently rationalized organizations in the polity and economy as well as religion.[34] This rationalization stems from the decisive transformation of traditional kinship worked by the rise of salvation religions, as Weber argues in "Religious Rejections of the World."[35] He sees prophetic salvation religions that create congregational communities such as the Jewish synagogue, Christian church, or Buddhist *sangha* coming into conflict with the moral particularism and simple reciprocity of kinship relations. Soteriological faith runs thicker than blood, and it carries the faithful away from their natural kin and matrimonial community toward moral community with their savior, prophet, priest, brother, and sister in the faith as children of God, born again in the Word or made one and holy in the Law.

Members of the sib, village, and caste manifest the dualism of in-group and out-group morality, Weber thought, and the in-group reciproc-

31. Meyer, "Self and Life Course," 253-54.
32. Meyer, "Self and Life Course," 256-57.
33. Meyer, "Self and Life Course," 259.
34. Meyer, "Self and Life Course," 247.
35. Weber, "Religious Rejections of the World," 328-30.

ity of "As you do unto me, so I shall do unto you."[36] Religious congregations take ancient ethics of neighborliness and duties to aid kin and neighbors in distress, and they transfer these ethics to social relations among brethren in the faith. Then they universalize these ethics into the imperatives of all ethically rationalized world religions: to aid needy widows and orphans, to care for the sick, to give alms to the poor. From an ethic of reciprocity among neighbors in mundane need through a sense of the suffering common to all believers in a sinful world arose ethics of absolute ends and "acosmic love" for the universal neighbor, Weber thought, inspired by the experience of direct communion with God in shared worship and justified by the rationalization of ritual acts into an ethical way of life to answer the soteriological question of what we must do to be saved.[37]

Religious ethics of universal brotherhood and neighbor-love represent a perfect realization of the imperfection of all human doings, according to Weber, in perpetual conflict with the orders and values of this world. If everyone is our neighbor, he fears, then no one is. We live in a world of many gods and moral contradictions across separate social spheres, Weber concludes, and we cannot put it back together. We can only try to make the best of it by working as hard, loving as loyally, and engaging in political and civic life as responsibly as possible.[38]

By returning to Kohlberg's hierarchy of moral development and thinking institutionally about different modes of making moral meaning in modern society in this Weberian light, we can better appreciate the distinctiveness of Browning's more nuanced notion of the diversified integrity of modern moral virtues. Kohlberg's view of morality favors men over women and children, Carol Gilligan and others point out.[39] It does so by favoring individual legal rights and rules of fair play among individuals in bureaucratically regulated work and public life administered by a modern welfare state. It places these rules and rights above and beyond shared responsibility for nurturing care within the family and among friends, neighbors, and members of communities. It also ignores the moral ambiguity of the American polity, cultural critics charge, inso-

36. Weber, "Religious Rejections of the World," 329.

37. Weber, "Religious Rejections of the World," 330-40.

38. Weber, "Religious Rejections of the World," 329-30; cf. Weber, "Science as a Vocation," in Gerth and Mills, eds., *From Max Weber,* esp. 147-56; and Weber, "Politics as a Vocation," in Gerth and Mills, eds., *From Max Weber,* esp. 115-28.

39. Carol Gilligan, *In a Different Voice: Psychological Theory and Women's Development* (Cambridge, MA: Harvard University Press, 1982).

far as it sees there only a liberal constitutional democracy, and not a religiously resonant republic as well, thereby reducing public life to the procedural fair play of interests checked by rights.[40]

Such criticism casts doubt on stage theories of morality that claim to represent sequential levels of cognitive development or human growth per se across societies, cultures, classes, peoples, and historical epochs. But it justifies social and cultural construal of such theories to reveal the institutional contexts they assume and to show how these institutions are morally meaningful in distinctive ways. For example, the social experience of women who are chiefly responsible for parenting and homemaking supports a relational ethic of nurturing care, interdependence, and recognition of unequal needs as relevant to understanding moral desert. Institutional situation, then, not only the gendered interplay of culture and nature, figures in developmentalist findings that women commonly emphasize this outlook over ethics of equal rights, even exchange, and procedural justice that guide the modern marketplace and bureaucracy, which are disproportionately filled and controlled by men.[41]

The Moral Reintegration of Modern Society

Institutionalized differences in moral meaning do not exist only among persons of different sexes, social classes, races, regions, and religious, ethnic, or cultural backgrounds. They also exist for each individual, because she experiences different moral norms, values, and attitudes in different sectors of her own social life, and within each sector at different times in her life. Both authority and self-expression are relatively strong for *any* individual as a child, parent, and lover within the modern family. Consequentialism and the play of interests, at once cooperative and competitive, hold sway in business and bureaucratic life, circumscribed by law, appeals to rights, shared responsibilities, and minimal obligations not to injure. Among friends and lovers expressive feelings are the norm,

40. See, for example, Michael Sandel, *Democracy's Discontent* (Cambridge, MA: Harvard University Press, 1996); Robert Bellah et al., *The Good Society* (New York: Knopf, 1991); and Steven M. Tipton, "Republic and Liberal State: The Place of Religion in an Ambiguous Polity," *Emory Law Journal* 39(1) (Winter 1990): 191-202.

41. Steven M. Tipton, "Social Differentiation and Moral Pluralism," in *Meaning and Modernity: Religion, Polity, and Self*, ed. Richard Madsen et al. (Berkeley: University of California Press, 2002), 31-33.

while reciprocal responsibilities, duties, and householding calculations arise between spouses.[42]

Using Erikson's vision, Browning recognizes this institutionalized interplay of different modes of moral meaning within marriage and the family — and in their relations to religion, schooling, work, romance, law, politics, and civic life. He notes that this interplay honors both the possibility and challenge of the moral reintegration of modern society in all of its complexity and diversity, by contrast to its superordinate unification by universal principles of justice as fairness, as they define the highest stage of Kohlberg's theory. There these formal principles appear overgeneralized from the Kantian contractarianism of John Rawls, seen as an explicitly political ethic specifically suited in its procedural rationality to a modern liberal democracy of mutually disinterested, rights-bearing client-citizens of a regulatory welfare state. Instead Erikson relies on the interrelation of social spheres in taking the Golden Rule as a critical principle grounded in the need for mutual recognition, guided by norms of reciprocity, and aimed at a responsibilist analogue of universal neighbor-love. It owes much more to Aristotle than to Kant, Browning shows, and it coheres along lines that not only cross but blur the conventional boundaries of consequentialist and deontological ethics in favor of a teleology that is at once descriptive, normative and ritual-mythic in its anthropology.[43]

Erikson illuminates a kind of justice that is not chiefly distributive, commutative, or retributive, but primarily participatory across the actual practices and spirit of every institution that makes up the whole of society.[44] Such justice is a virtue that marks the moral integrity and harmony of society as a whole without obscuring or hindering its need for diverse virtues, and institutional arrangements for their practice, in order for society to flourish as a whole. By its absence or shortfall, conversely, such participatory justice marks a society's moral contradictions, conflicts, and corruption, including its justifiable subordination or unjustified hindering of other virtues in the name of justice. As Erikson sums up: "From the cycle of life such dispositions as faith, will power, purposefulness, efficiency, devotion, affection, responsibility, and sagacity (all of which are

42. Tipton, "Social Differentiation and Moral Pluralism."

43. Browning, "Generativity, Ethics, and Hermeneutics," 5-10, 17-19, with reference to William K. Frankena, *Ethics* (Englewood Cliffs, NJ: Prentice-Hall, 1973), 14-16.

44. Cf., for example, David Hollenbach, "Justice as Participation," in *Justice, Peace, and Human Rights: American Catholic Social Ethics in a Pluralistic World* (New York: Crossroad, 1988), 71-83.

also criteria of ego strength) flow into the life of institutions. Without them, institutions wilt; but without the spirit of institutions pervading the patterns of care and love, instruction and training, no enduring strength could emerge from the sequence of generations."[45]

Erikson synthesizes key elements needed for "guiding our ethical trajectories amidst the opportunities and threats of modernity in the 21st century," Browning concludes.[46] Every act of justice should seek to actualize the practical goods of the human life cycle, enabling us to affirm ethics of principles while overcoming their formalism and potential emptiness. Theories of moral virtue can likewise be affirmed yet substantiated in closer critical connection to the values they build on and actualize within the epigenetic timetables of the human species. With Erikson's aid, then, we can uphold the crucial importance of religious traditions of narrative, and the communities of practice that enact them, for shaping virtuous persons and social orders. And we can hold up these traditions for criticism insofar as they do violence to the cycle of human development or defy universal principles of mutual recognition and justice.

In these ways, Browning declares, Erikson's ethics of generativity enable us to draw into richer, clearer dialogue the modern world's vying religious traditions, philosophies, and ideologies to help provide the overlapping communities of meaning, moral character, and institutional arrangement we need to "create and maintain the future cycle of the generations."[47] Don Browning's gloss on the text of Erikson's theory of generativity turns out, in fact, to be an inspired and invaluable text in its own right, a revelation of the mutuality of ethical principles, practical virtues, and social institutions.

45. Erikson, "Life Cycle," 292.
46. Browning, "Generativity, Ethics, and Hermeneutics," 25.
47. Browning, "Generativity, Ethics, and Hermeneutics," 24.

3 The Place of Evolutionary Psychology in a Practical Theological Ethics of Families

Stephen J. Pope

Don Browning is one of only a few scholars who draw from evolutionary psychology in the development of a constructive theological position. This chapter offers an appreciative interpretation of Browning's effort in this regard. It will proceed first by noting some of the standard objections to evolutionary psychology and then argue that Browning's selective and critical appropriation of this body of literature manages to avoid its pitfalls while learning from its insights.

Evolutionary Psychology and Its Ambiguities

The phrase "evolutionary psychology" refers to a school of thought developed in the 1980s by Leda Cosmides, John Tooby, and Donald Symons, and popularized by Steven Pinker and Robert Wright. It has the ambition of explaining the deepest roots of human behavior in evolutionary terms, primarily through an understanding of the functioning of "evolved psychological mechanisms."[1] It was developed to offer a more acceptable evolutionary alternative to the "sociobiology" proposed by William E. Hamilton, Robert Trivers, and E. O. Wilson, and it was popularized by Richard Dawkins. Both schools of thought attempt to provide a comprehensive explanation of social behavior in terms of evolutionary

1. See Jerome H. Barkow, Leda Cosmides, and John Tooby, *The Adapted Mind: Evolutionary Psychology and the Generation of Culture* (New York: Oxford University Press, 1992).

theory.[2] The same is true of related approaches to human behavior such as "evolutionary ecology" and "behavioral ecology." The basic conviction shared by these perspectives is that human behavior can only be understood in the context of our evolutionary heritage and its impact on the basic biological, emotional, and behavioral tendencies that comprise "human nature."

Sociobiology was strongly criticized for promoting a radically reductionistic agenda. Instead of restricting itself to the methodological reductionism employed by all the sciences, sociobiologists went further in assuming that science alone provides the means for arriving at reliable knowledge (epistemological reductionism or "scientism") and that only what is discoverable by science is real (ontological reductionism or "ontological naturalism"). Without noting the difference between scientific judgments and metaphysical speculation, for example, Richard Dawkins, announces: "The universe we observe has precisely the properties we should expect if there is, at bottom, no design, no purpose, no evil and no good, nothing but blind, pitiless indifference. . . . DNA neither knows nor cares. DNA just is. And we dance to its music. "[3] Sociobiologists also naively ventured into the domain of morality and politics, proposing generalizations about the naturalness of certain gender roles, male aggression, dominance hierarchies, and more that evoked strenuous objections. Sociobiological writings in this vein failed to note the influence of culture on behavior and the pervasively cultural character of human nature. Its commitment to understanding human behavior in the same terms as the behavior of animals obscured human freedom and responsibility.

Evolutionary psychology, the next generation of the evolutionary approach to human nature, attempted to avoid all of these problems by constructing a theory of evolved "mental modules," acknowledging the power of culture on social arrangements and behavior, and avoiding extensive discussion of morality and politics. It has done so unevenly and with mixed success. The more technical writings of evolutionary psychologists have managed to accomplish some of these goals, but the popular writings of evolutionary psychologists like Steven Pinker, Robert Wright, and David Buss exhibit what philosopher Philip Kitcher calls "vaulting ambition. "[4]

2. See E. O. Wilson, *Sociobiology: The New Synthesis* (Cambridge, MA: Harvard University Press, 1975) and Richard Dawkins, *The Selfish Gene* (New York: Oxford University Press, 1976).

3. Richard Dawkins, *River Out of Eden* (New York: Basic Books, 1995), 133.

4. Philip Kitcher, *Vaulting Ambition: Sociobiology and the Quest for Human Nature* (Cambridge, MA, and London: MIT Press, 1985).

Evolutionary Psychology and Practical Theological Ethics

Given these problems, it is little wonder that most theologians keep their distance from these approaches to human behavior. I would like to argue that Don Browning's most important contribution to the discipline of theological ethics consists in his ability to use these evolutionary sources without accepting the unwarranted reductionisms with which they are often, but unnecessarily, joined. I will examine how he understands practical theological ethics as it relates to four topics: kin altruism, reciprocal altruism, parental investment, and religion.

Before turning to these evolutionary topics, it might help to begin with a description of Browning's "practical theological ethics." Browning believes that we need to think about how to live in the world as members of vital religious communities that are both instructed by rich traditions while at the same open to creative movements and insights emerging from contemporary experience and culture. Practical theological ethics is ultimately judged by its effectiveness and wisdom in shaping our conduct and policies.

Browning adopts the image of "levels" as a way of describing the central concerns of practical theological ethics. The visionary level is expressed in terms of narratives and symbols, such as the symbol of the Garden of Eden or the narrative of the passion story. The level of moral principles deals with ethical principles, rules, and obligations such as the "love commands." The third level pertains to fundamental human tendencies and needs, to what is sometimes and controversially called "human nature." The fourth level deals with the social and historical circumstances in which we are immersed, such as economic patterns. Finally, the concrete rules and roles in social practices and social institutions are applied through casuistic reflection within the context of concrete situations.

Practical theological ethics must consider all five of these levels and give proper weight to each. One cannot use one key level to explain the others — for example, by assuming that family life is determined by economics alone, or, conversely by assuming that appeals to religious ideals or norms will make unnecessary any rigorous reflection on marriage law or social welfare provisions. Browning rejects any attempt to argue that a single level is so important that it minimizes the significance of the others. I would even argue that his thoroughly non-reductionistic approach to these levels constitutes his major contribution to theological ethics vis-à-vis the issue of science. He proposes that sound moral judgments are best based in the careful attainment of a workable "reflective equilibrium" between these five levels.

Kin Altruism and Familial Love

The sociobiological theory of "kin altruism" holds that organisms can be expected to prefer to aid other organisms to the extent to which they share genetic similarity.[5] Sterile worker castes of insect societies evolved because their organisms could pass on copies of their genes through their fertile relatives within the colony. Human evolution also reflects a channeling of care to offspring, and it would be hard to imagine how the species could have survived without this inclination. Yet, there are evolutionary reasons why human beings tend to favor kin over non-kin and why it is easier to fear strangers than it is to trust them.[6] Human nature is constituted by relatively "open programs" rather than tightly scripted "closed programs."

Evolutionists argue that the earliest forms of reproduction-centered altruism were complemented by extensive periods of child-care. Human parents are unique among primates in the extent and length of time they spend rearing children. Altruistic behaviors were probably established in small kin groups before they were extended to others in the development of larger, multi-family groups. Kin altruism might also have contributed to the extension of altruistic behavior toward non-kin in communities within which kin were the primary beneficiaries, especially if one of the markers of kinship was long-term association.

Browning accepts the basic outline of "kin altruism" without reducing every component of family life to the logic of natural selection. He understands that evolution has shaped our emotional capacities and needs, but not in a way that makes culture and personality of little significance. Both culture and biology can make the family a place of imbalanced power and unhealthy competition. Browning recognizes as a descriptive matter both the positive benefits that can come from kin altruism to the family but also the potential for harm and injustice. Preferences can be nepotistic, morally biased, or otherwise ethically problematic, especially toward non-kin outsiders.

5. See W. D. Hamilton, "Innate Social Aptitudes of Man: An Approach from Evolution Genetics," in *Biosocial Anthropology*, ed. Robin Fox (New York: John Wiley and Sons, 1975), 133-35.

6. Richard D. Alexander, *Biology of Moral Systems* (New York: Aldine de Gruyter, 1987), 261.

Browning's normative framework takes this descriptive framework into account but is not derived from it. He proposes a kind of virtue-ethic model of familial relations based on his own synthesis of various interpretations of biblical *agape* — in particular those offered in Gene Outka's "equal regard," in Louis Janssens' personalist reception of the Thomistic order of goods, and in Christine Gudorf's and Barbara Hilkert Andolsen's feminist account of mutuality. The family moves in the direction of increased mutuality or friendship, and is always to be based in respect for every person within the family and in justice that promotes the well-being of each as an individual. Justice bounds relations outside the family as well, thus providing a hedge against unjust favoritism.

Some forms of family life can be harmful and even oppressive. Family is not the highest value, and a sound practical theology of the family must develop a balanced perspective that is both appreciate of the value of the family while not over-stating its significance or uncritically endorsing all forms of familial life. Browning's vision includes what he calls a new "critical familism," informed by feminist and other critical views of distorted interpretations of the family. "Critical familism" must be open to multiple perspectives and receptive to those who point to difficulties of family as well as to those who stress its values.

Reciprocal Altruism and Marriage

Robert Trivers' theory of "reciprocal altruism" holds that biologically unrelated individuals will trade beneficial acts under certain circumstances. The term "cooperation" refers to arrangements in which two or more individuals act at roughly the same time. "Reciprocal altruism" adds a factor of time to cooperation: individuals who interact only once will be rewarded for selfish behavior and penalized for altruistic behavior, since there is no opportunity in the future either to reciprocate for benefits or to punish for costs incurred. Over the course of repeated interactions, however, individuals can benefit by engaging in patterns of reciprocity.

The most detailed defense of the theory of "reciprocal altruism" comes from Robert Axelrod's analysis of the "prisoner's dilemma" game.[7] Axelrod argues that in a repeated series the best strategy for winning the prisoner's dilemma game is neither pure selfishness nor pure unselfishness, but a "tit-for-tat" strategy. Sometimes "nice guys finish

7. See Axelrod, *The Evolution of Cooperation* (New York: Basic Books, 1984).

last," but at other times they finish first. The most rational strategy is to cooperate with cooperators (do not exploit them) and punish cheats (do not let them exploit you).

The threefold rule of "reciprocal altruism" is that those who cooperate are rewarded with continued assistance, those who refuse to cooperate ("grudgers") are denied assistance, and those who defect ("cheats") are punished. The most stable evolutionary strategy is the grudger's. Cheats will take over and exploit suckers, but as cheats come to predominate, their strategy undercuts social order and makes any cooperation unlikely. Suckers are eventually eliminated, except when all players are suckers. A single cheat will eventually take over the game. A grudger employs the policy of cooperating with cooperators and not cooperating with cheats.[8] Nature thus encourages reciprocity and retaliation rather than the "sucker strategies" proposed by "turning the other cheek" or even following the Golden Rule.

Browning is critical of the underlying sociobiological model of the human person as essentially self-interested, but he is also appreciative of the fact that reciprocity is a fundamental feature of human social life. Reciprocity is fundamental to marriage. If the familial mother-infant bond is based in kin altruism, the marital bond is a reflection of reciprocal altruism. Browning's interpretation of neo-Darwinism allows for an interaction between genes and culture, and indeed for the abundant influence of cultural understandings of how we experience and understand our evolved biological tendencies. Marriage is different from "mating" and so cannot be understood on primarily biological or evolutionary grounds.

Browning interprets the normative significance of our evolved inclination toward reciprocal altruism in the context of the "equal-regard marriage." The moral ideal of the "equal-regard marriage" lies in deep interpersonal companionship and mutual love — an ideal captured most profoundly in Christian and other religious symbolism. This symbolism works to transform the emotions, needs, and tendencies that have evolved to be part of male and female sexuality into aspects of adult human life that can serve high moral and religious purposes.

He hopes that this model of marriage can be relevant across cultural and social settings. If it is to do so, he argues, it must be shown to be consistent with the major religio-cultural symbols of a given society. The tra-

8. See the mention of this axiom in Xenophon, *Memorabilia,* 2.6.21; Plato, *Lysistrata,* 221e; Aristotle, *Nichomachean Ethics,* 1169b16-22, 1162a16-19.

ditional Christian images of marriage as a sacrament or covenant can support reciprocity in the form of mutuality. He believes that our own society can continue to be enriched by Christian belief in the sanctity of the person, the goodness of creation, and the status of sex as a divine gift, all of which can lend support to the ideal of the "equal-regard marriage." His ideal, though, appeals beyond Christianity and even monotheism. He believes there are good public reasons, as well as a faith-inspired rationale, for embracing a family ideal based on commitment, permanence, equal justice, and public responsibility.

Before moving to the next topic, it is worth noting that Browning's account of marriage and family shows an interesting critical dependence on the theology of Thomas Aquinas. Browning appreciates Aquinas's realism about human emotions while he also rejects his Aristotelian teleological biology, the "physicalist" aspects of his natural law theory, and his patriarchal view of women. Ethics based on insights about human nature do not conform to the ordering of nature or to alleged intrinsic ends of biological functions (notably of reproductive sexuality, such that birth control would be ruled "intrinsically evil"). We do not have a moral obligation to regard our biological structures as sacrosanct. Browning's functional equivalent of natural law ethics makes the weaker claim that moral norms and virtues must be formulated in a way that acknowledges the value and significance of the central biologically based tendencies of human nature. Since some of these tendencies conflict with others, we face the moral task of selecting which should be acted upon and which should be denied or channeled. We do so by deliberating over which of these central tendencies are most important to us or more significant for our long-term good.[9]

Parental Investment and Male Commitment

The logic of "parental investment" holds that males will be more protective of their own children than of others, and accounts for why stepparents are more likely than parents to neglect or abuse children. If parents are inclined by nature to invest their limited resources in children who are most likely to themselves be reproductively successful in the future, then there seem to be evolutionary reasons for the practice of infan-

9. See Don S. Browning and Bernie Lyon, "Sociobiology and Ethical Reflection," *Theology Today* 36(2) (July 1979): 229-38.

ticide and child abandonment in many cultures.[10] Martin Daly and Margo Wilson argue that infanticide is found most often where paternity is unknown or inappropriate, or a newborn is deformed or otherwise compromised (rejection of an unfit newborn could be fitness-promoting), or there are insufficient familial resources, lack of paternal support, the mother is already overburdened by an older sibling, and the like.

The "parental investment" model is supported by the fact that individualized maternal love for an infant grows and deepens over the course of years, that younger children are at greater risk than older children and the latter tend to be more valued than the former, that mentally handicapped children are much more likely to be abused by their parents than other children, that women past their reproductive prime are less likely to harm a healthy, first-born child, and that stepchildren are at much greater risk of abuse and homicide than biological children.

Browning draws from this account of parental investment in his description of what he calls the "male problematic" — the estrangement of men from the women who have had their children and from the children themselves. He believes the "male problematic" is in part a reflection of human nature — our evolved animality — that is exacerbated by contemporary social mores and economic pressures. Here again his multivalent approach to human behavior allows for complexity and discourages any monolithic reductionism that forces us to choose "nature" or "nurture."

If the "male problematic" has complex roots, its solution must also be multi-layered. Browning here reaches back into the Christian tradition, which has remarkably helpful insights into this matter. Both Thomas Aquinas and Martin Luther recognized that fathers must be carefully and deliberately integrated into the institution of marriage, that men must consciously work to acknowledge and fulfill their responsibilities as fathers, and that male tendencies toward aggression and domination must be curbed by moral ideals and social norms. The support given by church, society, and economy to marriage and the family can build on the pro-social aptitudes resident in human nature, but they also resist other attributes of human nature.

Browning is nearly unique among Protestant theologians in his willingness to take seriously Aquinas's notion that the virtue of charity is in some ways bound to incorporate central aspects of the natural order of love. Aquinas's developed account of the order of charity has much to

10. See Martin Daly and Margo Wilson, *Homicide* (New York: Aldine de Gruyter, 1988), chap. 3.

teach us about the channeling of natural love into these social and affective relations. Browning appreciates Aquinas's recognition of the fact that we, like other animals, tend to care for our own offspring more than for others, that we have a special bond and felt responsibility for friends more than for strangers, and that paternal care is closely related to knowledge of paternity.

Browning relates this Thomistic account of natural care to various evolutionary theories. Informed by sociobiology while rejecting its reductionism, he enhances his Jamesian approach to human nature by drawing from Mary Midgley's Aristotelian and Wittgenstinian view of human motivation. This position recognizes that we have evolved to possess an array of biologically based needs and inclinations, but for a variety of reasons — especially those pertaining to the influence of culture — most people do not value reproduction as the highest good. Practical theological ethics faces the task of mediating between these and other levels of human nature and of striving to adjudicate conflicts by arriving at a reasonable and human order of priorities among them.

Browning proposes that we make use of the evolutionary psychological theory of parental investment in this non-reductionistic way. Parental investment theory holds that the human race was successful in reproduction because it evolved in a way that gave men a capacity to become bonded to women and to develop bonds with their children that would encourage them to expend their time and energy providing for them. Men are more prone to care for children whom they can recognize as their own than to care for the children of other men. Social, economic, and other large-scale forces can either encourage or discourage the formation of these bonds. In a broad sense, society can help children by promoting structures that build on our natural inclination to form bonds that can support the two-parent family, or so argued Browning and the team of authors that wrote *From Culture Wars to Common Ground.* If we want to do something about the threat to children presented by the deterioration of the family as a social institution in our society, our response ought to include the formation of policies that might encourage parental investment. But we must, at the same time, also avoid returning to gender-role stereotypes — the "female problematic" that ignores the needs and rights of mothers.

Browning and his coauthors show that there is no need to approach evolutionary psychology uncritically or in search of a simplifying monolithic reductive explanation for all things human. Evolutionary conceptions are necessary but not sufficient for theological ethics. They do not provide a normative framework. When sociobiologists write as if they do, they are merely smuggling their own unexamined moral presuppositions into their science and thereby doing a disservice to both. Browning takes the essential lines of his normative framework from his critical interpretation of major symbols of the Christian tradition (or, more broadly, the Judeo-Christian tradition), which he, in turn, interprets in light of the best scientific insights available.

This general approach to nature bears fruit in the ideal of marriage and the family. Evolutionary psychology indicates that we have not evolved to be disinterested or impartial with regard to our own well-being, but the moral ideal of gender equality and "equal-regard" love can be inculcated, at least to a certain extent, by careful training and education. Christian ethics provides a counter-weight to some of the less morally appealing aspects of our evolutionary heritage. Browning regards Ephesians 6:1-12 as breaking down the honor-shame code of antiquity that was supportive of patriarchy and male privilege, and he interprets 1 Corinthians 7 as inculcating male self-giving as well as female self-giving for the overall good of the family unit.[11]

Unfortunately, the forces of modernization tend to contribute to the worldwide tendency of males to drift away from their marriages and families. Browning, in response, argues that our need to re-establish conditions that support family formation can only proceed through pursuing a multi-dimensional agenda that includes political, economic, psychological, moral, and religio-cultural perspectives.

Religion and Public Theology

Evolutionary theorists who write about religion usually do so in a highly reductionistic way, and this topic offers a good example of the difference between Browning and his evolutionary interlocutors. As we have seen, sociobiologists begin with the premise that the proper understanding of all life comes from the natural sciences and that the most adequate explanation of human behavior is provided in evolutionary terms.[12] Presuming that all references to the transcendent are illusory, they argue that

11. See Don S. Browning, "Biology, Ethics, and Narrative in Christian Family Theory," in *Promises to Keep: Decline and Renewal of Marriage in America*, ed. Jean Bethke Elshtain and David Popenoe (Lanham, MD: Rowman & Littlefield, 1996), 119-56.

12. See Jerome Stone, "Varieties of Religious Naturalism," *Zygon* 38(1) (2003): 89-93.

religious practices, rituals, beliefs, and the like are widespread across time and space only because they speak to deep-seated emotional needs to belong to groups and to make sense of life and death. Science proves that the universe is purposeless, Dawkins holds, and those who affirm the existence of evolution are intellectually obliged to admit that religion is false. In nature, he says, one sees, "the total prostitution of all animal life, including man and all his airs and graces, to the blind purposiveness of these minute virus-like substances [that is, genes]."[13] Dawkins states confidently that "we no longer have to resort to superstition when faced with the deep problems: Is there a meaning to life? What are we for? What is man?"[14]

One would be hard-pressed to find a sharper contrast with Dawkins than Browning. Evolutionary treatments of religion suffer from a massive oversimplification of what in reality constitutes an extremely complex and sometimes very subtle array of activities, practices, and beliefs. Only a commitment to avoid reductionistic methodology will allow for the recognition of this complexity and diversity. What is referred to as "religion" is a vast range of highly diverse and often changing practices engaged in by people with quite varied motivations in different cultural contexts. Awareness of the multiple ways in which religion can be interpreted — and even religion understood as an array of natural human phenomena — requires something like Browning's multi-layered methodology.

Unlike the evolutionists in question, Browning does not presume a false dichotomy between religion and science because he neither equates religion with superstition nor mistakenly regards the notion of "God" as an explanatory hypothesis proposed by theology as an alternative to natural selection. Religion concerns the cultural and symbol level of human understanding, a sphere best approached through hermeneutics rather than the explanatory methods of the natural sciences. Unlike Dawkins, Browning recognizes ontological naturalism as a metaphysical and not a scientific position.

Browning pretends that science is neither value-free nor independent of metaphysical assumptions. He also holds that every comprehensive point of view contains implicit or explicit metaphysical assumptions concerning the ultimate framework within which human action takes place. He notes: "The basic difference between theological anthropology

13. Cited in Anthony O'Hear, *Beyond Evolution: Human Nature and the Limits of Evolutionary Explanation* (Oxford: Clarendon Press, 1997), 152.

14. Dawkins, *Selfish Gene*, 1.

and the anthropologies of other human sciences, it can be argued, is not that theology is morally and metaphysically freighted and the others are not. The difference is rather that theological anthropology takes responsibility for its moral and metaphysical judgments and many contemporary anthropologies do not."[15]

This understanding of practical theological ethics provides a rationale for an inter-religious as well as an interdisciplinary approach to families. Browning argues in *Marriage and Modernization* that Christian churches and other religious communities ought to participate in the ongoing interdisciplinary discussion about the family and reflect carefully about what might constitute a helpful and plausible normative understanding of the family. This awareness of complexity supports Browning's understanding of the multiple effects of globalization on the family and of a corresponding need to undertake a commitment to think deeply and carefully about marriages and families, and, Browning thinks, to "reconstruct" our ideals. Since we hold, globally, multiple ideals, the extent to which his reconstruction constitutes a radical change depends on the particular social and historical context within in which one is situated. If any such reconstruction wants to be persuasive, argues Browning, its research and reflection will have to be based on an appreciation of the importance of religion. Contending against the privatization of religion, he has repeatedly called for the development of public theology as a way of providing essential intellectual support for the public institutions of marriage and family.

Conclusion

This chapter has sought to develop an appreciative account of Browning's critical appropriation of evolutionary accounts of human behavior. This appropriation is made possible by Browning's appreciation of the ability of the sciences to provide an explanatory account of aspects of human behavior. The appropriation is made critical by his insistence that other dimensions of human understanding also shed light on the behavior in question — in this case, behavior related to marriage and the family. The fact that marriage and the family are both "natural" and "cul-

15. Don S. Browning, "Christian Ethics and the Premoral Good," in *Christian Ethics and the Moral Psychologies* (Grand Rapids, MI: William B. Eerdmans Publishing Company, 2006), 190-220.

tural" means that they cannot be reduced to one or the other category. The field of Christian ethics knows that marriage and family are historical and cultural realities that can only be understood if particular contexts are taken into account. Evolutionary theory, on the other hand, tends to think of marriage and family as rooted in our biology, genes, and phylogentic past. Browning rightly strives to show that since human nature is naturally both cultural and biological, we must bring both dimensions into focus if we are truly going to advance our understanding of marriage and the family.

4 Fatherhood, Feminism, and Family Altruism

M. Christian Green

Introduction: Fatherhood and Feminism

As a feminist in fatherhood studies, one gets used to querying expressions, somewhat along the lines of "What's a nice girl like you doing in a place like this?" One such expression came during a taxi ride to Boston's Logan Airport a couple of years ago. The driver, a ruddy, Irish-American who had attended college at Holy Cross, asked what I had been doing in town, which led to a discussion of my studies, which led to the inevitable question as to the subject of my dissertation. My driver, it turned out, was happily married and a devoted father, who was delighted to regale me with all manner of opinions and observations about fatherhood today. But when he asked enthusiastically whether I had read Dr. Laura Schlessinger's *The Proper Care and Feeding of Husbands*,[1] I struggled to stifle a burst of knee-jerk feminist revulsion. My driver's enthusiastic recommendation of Dr. Laura's advice recalled certain traditional views, encountered at various points in my inquiry into fatherhood, concerning the supposed need for wives to exert a "civilizing effect" on their husbands. Normally predisposed to teleological forms of ethical inquiry and the use of means to particular ends, I found myself in the midst a deontological moment. Visions of right, duty, and inexorable obligation filled my head. As we pulled into the terminal, I couldn't help bursting forth with the question, "Why can't men just be good fathers because it is

1. Laura Schlessinger, *The Proper Care and Feeding of Husbands* (New York: HarperCollins, 2003).

the right thing to do? Why do they need to be nagged and manipulated by women?" My driver just smiled patiently, as if I had missed the point. Then it was time for me to catch my flight.

The field of Fatherhood Studies was coming into its own when I entered into it and into an association with Don Browning in the mid-1990s. Movements like the Evangelical Christian Promise Keepers and the African American Million Man March were making the headlines. Influential books, such as David Blankenhorn's *Fatherless America* and David Popenoe's *Life Without Father,* were generating widespread cultural discussion. Indeed, one of the main points of these various fatherhood movements and publications was that fatherhood, apparently less biologically significant than motherhood, needed to be significantly reinvigorated by culture, and particularly by religion. As Blankenhorn put it:

> Because fatherhood is universally problematic in human societies, cultures must mobilize to devise and enforce the father role for men, coaxing and guiding them into fatherhood through a set of legal and extralegal pressures that require them to maintain a close alliance with their children's mother and to invest in their children. Because men do not volunteer for fatherhood as much as they are conscripted into it by the surrounding culture, only an authoritative cultural story of fatherhood can fuse biological and social paternity into a coherent male identity.[2]

From a feminist perspective, this paternal problematic was, indeed, a problem — particularly coming after a decade of feminist attention in the 1980s to an ethic of care largely derived from experiences of motherhood. Certainly the idea that fatherhood was not merely a matter of biological right, but rather needed to be lived out and embodied in relationships of care with their children was a welcome advance. *But why does fatherhood require such elaborate cultural constructions? Are men really such involuntary conscripts to this primary human relationship?* To reprise my question to the Boston cabbie: *Why don't men just care?* These were the nagging questions that remained in my mind.

The pursuit of a feminist understanding of fatherhood seems, to some, to have a certain oxymoronic quality, or even a sense of futility. Yet

2. David Blankenhorn, *Fatherless America: Confronting Our Most Urgent Social Problem* (New York: Basic Books, 1995). See also David Popenoe, *Life Without Father: Compelling New Evidence that Fatherhood and Marriage Are Indispensable for the Good of Children and Society* (Cambridge, MA: Harvard University Press, 1999).

this was the journey that I began under the wise and able mentorship of Don Browning. In this chapter, I sketch out the trajectory of that trip. First, I describe the genesis of the attention to fatherhood, both in Browning's work and in my own, in the field of developmental psychology, particularly in that field's delineation of an ethic of care with separate masculine and feminine instantiations. Second, I analyze Browning's understanding of the "male problematic" underlying fatherhood, as articulated in his recent and path-breaking, practical theological writings on marriage and family, situating that "male problematic" and its related "female problematic" in a long line of understandings about fatherhood in Western philosophy, theology, and political philosophy. Third, I say something about the implications of the male and female problematics in the field of family law and feminist ethics today. Finally, I offer a critical appraisal of the male and female problematics that will indicate the problems that these relational patterns continue to pose for family altruism and suggest that any revived masculine ethic of care must be accompanied by an ethic of justice for women.

Ethic of Justice, Ethic of Care

The need for a blended ethic of justice and care in both fatherhood and motherhood was, in fact, where my problem of fatherhood began. The problem first emerged for me in a course in feminist jurisprudence, taken during my second year of law school. The opening reading for that class was Carol Gilligan's *In a Different Voice,* a landmark study of women's moral development in which Gilligan contrasted a masculine ethic of justice, rights, and autonomy with a feminine ethic of care, responsibility, and relationship. The ethic of justice and the ethic of care were reflected in men's and women's "different voices" in moral reasoning. Gilligan prefaced her work with a disclaimer to the effect that these different voices were characterized by theme rather than gender, that the association of care uniquely with women was an "empirical observation" rather than an "absolute," and that no claims were made about the "origins of the differences" or their "distribution in a wider population, across cultures, or through time."[3] Most interesting to me, she maintained that her contrasts between male and female voices represented a "problem of in-

3. Carol Gilligan, *In a Different Voice: Psychological Theory and Women's Development* (Cambridge, MA: Harvard University Press, 1982), 2.

terpretation" rather than a generalization about the sexes, particularly since these differences, as she put it, "arise in a social context where factors of social status and power combine with reproductive biology to shape the experience of males and females and the relations between the sexes."[4] Despite the disclaimer, Gilligan's caution against conflating biology with culture, nature with nurture, was unheeded by many in the academy and in the wider culture.

Gilligan's dichotomy of justice and care became influential in a number of disciplines. The justice/care debate was particularly apparent in family law, which was engaged in a struggle of its own over how to understand and adjudicate family change. The feminist movement had had a major impact on family law in areas ranging from divorce reform, to reproductive rights, to the new emphasis on gender equality and neutrality in the difficult areas of parental rights and child custody. Into this climate of equality, neutrality, and rights between the sexes, came the new call in the post-Gilligan era for attention to gender difference. For some feminists, Gilligan's ethic of care came to be associated with a notion that mothers are the more natural and primary caregivers of children. Other feminists critiqued such associations as essentialist and traditionalist. But amid all the attention to women, mothers, and the valuation of care, the question to which I found myself returning was: *Where does Gilligan's theory leave men, particularly fathers, with respect to capacities for care and nurture?*

Decades before my own epiphany around the need for paternal care, Don Browning was plumbing the depths of developmental psychology for its possible contribution to a more adequate understanding of fatherhood and masculinity. Where Carol Gilligan was my entry point into these concerns, Gilligan's psychoanalytic predecessor, Erik Erikson, was Browning's focal point. Presciently titled for current fatherhood debates, Browning's early book, *Generative Man,* surveyed psychoanalytic perspectives on the "Good Man."[5] There, in a chapter on Erikson and his famous theory of generativity, under the subheading "Care and the Anthropology of Generative Man," Browning observed with Erikson, and with respect to the need *that men themselves have* for generative behavior and relationships:

> Something very fundamental happens to man when his needs for generativity are not met, something quite central to the direction of

4. Gilligan, *In a Different Voice,* 20.

5. Don S. Browning, *Generative Man* (New York: Delta Press, 1975).

> his energies and to his relationship to himself. Individuals who fail to achieve this delicate synthesis which generativity demands often become "stagnated" and "begin to indulge themselves as if they were their own — or one another's — one and only child." . . . Whatever the reasons, an inadequate capacity for generativity not only brings subtle diminishment to those who suffer from it, but passes itself on to succeeding generations. The sins of the fathers are indeed visited upon their children.[6]

As Browning observed, "the virtue that emerges when generativity is dominant over stagnation is care"[7] — and that care is achieved not merely through the bare act of procreation, but, interestingly as we shall see in surveying the Western fatherhood tradition, through teaching and various other forms of nurture of the next generation. In the manner of so many scholars in psychology and religion commenting in the aftermath of various horrors of the mid-twentieth century — Eric Erikson, Erich Fromm, Rollo May, Paul Tillich, Reinhold Niebuhr, and others — but in ways that are worth quoting and considering at some length again today, Browning connected this paternal problematic around generativity to a larger social and cultural diagnosis. In this regard, he observed:

> *For it is irresponsible creativity devoid of a quality of enduring care that is man's grandest temptation and greatest fault, not only through history but most specifically during modern times.* . . . The problem of man is his nongenerative mentality — his inability to care for what he creates, what he generates. . . . Buildings which are made to last no more than thirty years; the acres of urban rubble which witness to his unsteady creativity and impatient destructiveness; *his reckless tendency to produce more children than he can either educate or provide for;* his unwitting habit of building cities that are uninhabitable for families and children; his penchant for pursuing careers at breakneck speed and without regard to their effect upon his offspring; his knack for constructing societies so specialized and differentiated as virtually to segregate all children and young people from adult life; and finally his heartless capacity to conduct wars that call for no sacrifice to himself but that end in the sacrifice of his sons and daughters — all these things and many more testify to the nongenerative character of the modern mind

6. Browning, *Generative Man*, 163.
7. Browning, *Generative Man*, 164.

> and its strange proclivity for creating more than it can either care for or maintain.[8]

Reckless procreation in the absence of education and nurture will be one of the resounding themes of the analysis below, but Browning's other Erikson-inspired observations about non-generative creativity are clearly as pertinent today as they were three decades ago.

For those of us coming at the paternal problematic from a specifically feminist perspective — particularly one informed by feminist jurisprudence — the question of the peculiar blend of biology and culture in our notions of both motherhood and fatherhood is a central aspect of the problem. An additional dimension of the problem is the coalescence of biology and culture around understandings of care as involving altruism and self-sacrifice. This altruism aspect was actually my threshold question, as it came to me in an especially provocative quote in a then newly published appropriation of Gilligan's justice/care paradigm in *Caring for Justice,* a book by leading feminist legal theorist Robin West. There, in describing the harm that can accrue to women from rosy and naturalized assumptions of feminine altruism and self-sacrifice that color our understanding of motherhood, West observes:

> A mother who, for reasons of either biology or training or both, *will care* for a child is differently situated vis-à-vis the brute force of necessity than a father who may or may not engage in caregiving work. If a newborn is to be breast-fed, only the mother can do it. An older child must be not only fed, but clothed, sheltered, bathed, stimulated, entertained, and educated, and, if, for whatever reason, the father *will not* perform these tasks, the mother will. The mother feels the imperative dimension of that *must* as directed at her in a way the father does not. Necessity — whether biological or cultural — becomes, for the mother, a moral imperative.[9]

This question of the gendered division of caring labor between men and women in families, whether by virtue or necessity, has become, for me, a question of altruism — conventionally defined as the "unselfish regard for or devotion to the welfare of others."[10]

8. Browning, *Generative Man,* 164-65 (third emphasis added).

9. Robin West, *Caring for Justice* (New York: New York University Press, 1997), 117-18.

10. *Webster's Ninth New Collegiate Dictionary* (Springfield, MA: Merriam Webster, 1985), 76.

The question of who cares in the family has a long pedigree in feminist thought in law, theology, and other disciplines. Having animated many of the debates in the first wave of feminism — particularly concerning the divergence of separate spheres of work and family, and the emergence of the cults of "true womanhood" and "moral motherhood" in the nineteenth century — the question reemerged in robust form in the second wave of feminism in the 1960s and 1970s. In second-wave feminism, answers tended to fall into one of two camps of feminist thought. The first camp, which has come to be known as liberal or humanist feminism, followed an assimilationist model, emphasizing the sameness and equality of men and women, rather than gender-specific differences and disadvantages. The second camp, referred to variously as gynocentric feminism, cultural feminism, or relational feminism, has most of its origins in Gilligan's theory of difference, construed in a direction that emphasizes the practical necessity — and often the moral superiority — of women's caring capacities and commitments.

I shall take up the theories of the gynocentric theorists in a subsequent section of this chapter, but what was surprising to me in my examination of the liberal feminist legal theories of the family, in particular, was that there was more willingness to acknowledge and account for biological difference than is often conceded by their gynocentric feminist interlocutors. In a path-breaking article on equality and difference in the context of pregnancy, leading liberal feminist Herma Hill Kay, constructed what she called an "episodic analysis" of pregnancy, aimed at defending a vision of sex equality that would prohibit the use of sex and reproduction as a basis of classification, except where morally and legally relevant differences are involved. Indicating the merits of such a legal framework as a strategy toward gender justice and equality, Kay argued:

> Episodic analysis offers such a strategy by permitting mothers to recognize that their unique role in reproduction ends with childbirth. It allows fathers to see themselves as essential to the child's nurturance and development. With the help of this insight, *men, like women, should be able to draw an important aspect of their self-esteem and identity from their parental roles.* Women, like men, should be able to lead productive, independent lives outside the family.[11]

11. Herma Hill Kay, "Equality and Difference: The Case of Pregnancy," *Berkeley Women's Law Journal* 1(1)(1985): 84-85 (emphasis added).

Likewise, in another early article on sex equality, fellow liberal feminist, Sylvia Law, even while acknowledging the difficulties that accommodating sex differences poses within a strictly egalitarian framework, expressed concern about stereotypes of fathers as "absent, unknown, and irresponsible" and of mothers as having "unshakeable responsibility" for the care of their children.[12] Indeed, she argued:

> Men's lack of concrete connection with their young raises other, even more serious problems. Nurturing children — helping the next generation to stand on our shoulder — is one of the most noble tasks of any civilization. Yet few men ever have substantial day-to-day experience with young children. It seems plausible that intense relationships with young children encourage reverence for the future of the species and the planet. *It is deeply disturbing that so few men experience such relationships,* particularly those men who exercise the greatest power in government, business, and education.[13]

Far from wanting to assimilate women to a detached, non-nurturing, and putatively male model of parenting, these early liberal feminist theorists in law seemed concerned to articulate and defend a normative vision of the family in which both men and women would partake of nurturing activities in the home and public economic and political participation as workers and citizens outside the family. Otherwise, complaints about men's parenting foibles risk becoming self-fulfilling prophecies, with women picking up the parental slack. These liberal feminist legal theorists were insisting on a blend of justice and care in the ethics of both motherhood and fatherhood. Such feminist voices in developmental psychology and the law would be the jumping-off point for the fatherhood inquiry that I would pursue under Don Browning's able supervision.

The Long Tradition of Fatherhood and the "Male Problematic"

The question that overarched my reading of the Western tradition as a doctoral student in religious ethics at the University of Chicago Divinity School — where Browning has mentored so many of us in his long career

12. Sylvia A. Law, "Rethinking Sex and the Constitution," *University of Pennsylvania Law Review* 132 (1984): 993.

13. Law, "Rethinking Sex and the Constitution," 997-98 (emphasis added).

spanning psychology and religion, practical theology, and religious ethics — was whether there might be resources in the Western Christian tradition of philosophy, theology, and political theory that might contribute to a positive, normative vision of fatherhood, consistent with the liberal feminist call for shared parenting as benefiting men and women alike. This led me into a hermeneutical retrieval of fatherhood in two primary strands of that tradition — the Aristotelian-Thomistic strand and the liberal political strand.

Aristotle was the first stop on my intellectual journey through fatherhood traditions. Having been trained first in biology by his physician-father before moving into ethics and politics, Aristotle seemed a logical thinker to consult for insight into the interaction of biology and culture around fatherhood. In this, I was also informed by Browning, who had already begun plumbing the riches of Aristotelian thought in his own writings on what he called the "male problematic" of fatherhood and family attachment. Browning's primary writings on the Aristotelian-Thomistic arguments on fatherhood come in his contributions to the jointly authored family study, *From Culture Wars to Common Ground,* and in his more recent book *Marriage and Modernization.* These two volumes, products of the Religion, Culture, and Family Project, which Browning directed for over a decade, offer the most sustained discussions of the "male and female problematics" around fatherhood. In *From Culture Wars to Common Ground,* this comes in a chapter of the relevance of evolutionary psychology to Christian family theory and Christian understandings of love. There, in outlining the importance of Christian problems with and solutions to inadequate "paternal investment," as the evolutionary psychologists describe it, Browning and his coauthors argue:

> This means acknowledging how Christian love functioned throughout its history to counter what we call the *male problematic,* the tendency of men to drift away from families. But we speak as well of a *female problematic,* the tendency of females under some conditions to suppress their own needs and raise children without paternal participation, sometimes under great stress and a great cost. Neither male nor female problematics are sinful as such, but they become involved in sin when measured by historically emergent ideals of committed husband-wife relations, ideals that Judaism and Christianity have associated with the unfolding will of God. Understanding these problematics and the desires that motivate them shows

> why *eros* should be a fundamental part of an adequate definition of Christian love.[14]

Earlier in their argument, Browning and his co-authors attribute to Aquinas their insight into the "male problematic" as the "primordial male tendency to procreate but not to care for offspring or mate,"[15] the definition itself a hearkening back to Browning's earlier reflections on non-generative creativity in *Generative Man*. But Browning, like Aquinas, was eventually drawn back to an even earlier source in Aristotle.

From a feminist perspective, Aristotle, who famously characterized women as "misbegotten males," was something of a problematic source. My key task became to find insights in Aristotle that would shed light on contemporary questions of fatherhood, while also ensuring justice for women and mothers. The aspects of Aristotelian thought that became central to my analysis of fatherhood were: (1) his bio-psychological understanding of parenting, (2) his understanding of justice as equity and mutuality, and (3) his ethical and political emphasis on friendship between men and women in families. Aristotle's biological writings on human reproduction focus on the relatively long period of human infant dependency, and the "asymmetrical reproductive strategies" and patterns of "parental investment" — to invoke the terms used by contemporary evolutionary psychologists — as well as the age-old problem of "paternal certainty." Simply put, females are biologically inclined to adopt a strategy of heavy investment in early childhood care and nurture. Males are torn between the apparently evolutionarily advantageous option of spreading their seed widely or opting for a more culturally approved strategy of attachment to family — a choice that has been characterized as being between the "cad strategy" or the "dad strategy." In beginning my inquiry with an understanding of these bio-psychological phenomena, I was deeply indebted to Browning's introduction to these evolutionary psychological categories, as I was to his observation that "this simple anthropological insight . . . says much about why responsible fatherhood is precarious, difficult to achieve, and easy to dislodge and why the tasks of motherhood have sometimes expanded to undesirable limits."[16] But my analysis, like Browning's, only begins with biology — it does not end there.

14. Don S. Browning et al., *From Culture Wars to Common Ground: Religion and the American Family Debate* (Louisville, KY: Westminster John Knox Press, 1997), 106.

15. Browning et al., *From Culture Wars to Common Ground*, 22.

16. Browning et al., *From Culture Wars to Common Ground*, 69.

Biological essentialism and determinism may be thought to have free rein in Aristotle's theories and in their contemporary evolutionary psychological renderings. Yet Aristotle's take on these human biological tendencies still leaves plenty of room for cultural mediation. In fact, Aristotle provides an expansive three-phase definition of parenting as including not only begetting and its attendant task of meeting the immediate needs of infants and young children, but also nurture and education, which extend well into adulthood and can be the arena of fathers, as well as mothers. Moreover, procreation is not the only reason for men and women to partner up. Anticipating Augustinian discussions of the various goods of marriage, Aristotle tells us that human parents "live together not only for the sake of procreation but also for the various purposes of life" and "help each other by throwing their particular gifts into the common stock."[17] Later I shall say more about the connection of these biological theories to Aristotle's understanding of friendship. But it is worth noting that here, too, Browning's analysis is instructive, particularly his observation that "paternal investment was part of a wider reciprocal helpfulness between males and females. . . . It was a necessary, but not sufficient condition for the emergence of paternal care. Sexual exchange and reciprocal helpfulness were also necessary."[18]

As for the second of my Aristotelian themes, the concept of justice as equity and mutuality, in outlining his conception of justice in the *Nichomachean Ethics,* Aristotle tells us that, among the cardinal virtues of courage, temperance, wisdom, and justice — justice is the highest because it is relational. Indeed, foreshadowing the idea of Christian neighbor-love, Aristotle maintains that "it is the complete virtue in the fullest sense, because he who possesses it can exercise his virtue not only in himself but towards his neighbor also."[19] Even more provocatively, in the last chapter of the book on justice, Aristotle tells us that the highest form of justice is equity, a kind of corrective or remedial justice in which lawmakers engage when they find that a general or universal law may do an injustice in particular cases. In fact, equity turns out to be a kind of justice intended to address cases of differences in need and status that may make particular demands for redistribution and accommodation on those with greater power in a relationship. Indeed, Aristotle tells us that the "equitable man"

17. Aristotle, *Nichomachean Ethics,* in *Introduction to Aristotle,* ed. Richard McKeon (New York: Random House, 1947), Bk. 8, chap. 12.

18. Browning et al., *From Culture Wars to Common Ground,* 112.

19. Aristotle, *Nichomachean Ethics,* Bk. 5, chap. 1.

is one who is "*no stickler for his rights* in a bad sense but *tends to take less than his share* though he has the law on his side."[20] This is no mere ethic of formal equality or contractual reciprocity, but an ethic of mutuality that is attentive to the different needs of persons in relationship.

The conception of justice as equity is not problem-free from contemporary feminist and egalitarian perspectives, hinging as it does on conceptions of proportionality and status. As Browning observes of the lingering problem of Aristotelian "subordinationism," "Aristotle spoke of friendship and equity between husband and wife, but he meant by this a kind of proportional equity whereby the person with the greater honor (in this case the male) would receive greater goods and rewards."[21] Yet when read along with Aristotle's understanding of friendship as being not merely useful or pleasurable but, most important, virtuous, the notions of justice and equity can be interpreted, as some biblical and classical scholars have argued alongside Browning, as a profound, if at times not wholly complete, critique of the honor-shame culture of masculinity and paternity in Aristotle's time.[22] In this way, Aristotelian equity suggests critical uses that are highly congenial with and supportive of feminist critiques of gender subordination in philosophical and theological ethics, even though such an understanding of equity continues to be underappreciated in feminist legal theory.

Aristotelian friendship is, after all, problematically entrenched in the household code of masters over slaves, husbands over wives, and fathers over children — a code all too familiar to readers of the Pauline and Petrine epistles. Aristotle's critique of this paradigm is left rather deeply and unsatisfactorily implicit in his argument that there can, and should, be relationships of justice and friendship between unequals, as well as between equals — friendship of equals, meaning between men of virtue, being the prevailing norm of friendship in Aristotle's time. Yet, at one point, in a way that hints at a way around the problem of proportionality, Aristotle describes friendship as an "equalizing" force,[23] in a manner with affinities to the later Christian transformational message of Galatians 3:28. In his adherence to the household code, Aristotle arguably

20. Aristotle, *Nichomachean Ethics*, Bk. 5, chap. 10 (emphasis added).

21. Don S. Browning, *Marriage and Modernization: How Globalization Threatens Marriage and What to Do about It* (Grand Rapids, MI: Eerdmans, 2003), 69.

22. Carolyn Osiek and David L. Balch, *Families in the New Testament World* (Louisville, KY: Westminster/John Knox, 1997); Carolyn Osiek and David L. Balch, *Early Christian Families in Context* (Grand Rapids, MI: Eerdmans, 2003).

23. Aristotle, *Nichomachean Ethics*, Bk. 8, chap. 8.

overstates the case for fatherhood, but the larger point of his argument, constructive for a feminist theory of fatherhood, seems to be that the friendship between fathers and mothers is a mutual one — and one that is crucial for the survival of both the family and the wider society. At one point in the *Politics,* challenging his teacher Plato's call for sharing of wives and communal child-rearing, Aristotle praises paternal friendship, or paternal love, in a wonderful oenophilic metaphor as the "sweet wine" at risk of being diluted in the water of such a communal scheme.[24] At another point he describes parental love in a more pedestrian fashion as the glue that "holds states together."[25] Clearly, for Aristotle, much is at stake in the friendship of fathers and mothers in families. In fact, as we shall see, Aristotle's understanding of family turns out to be something of a template for many who follow in the Christian and liberal traditions.

Thomas Aquinas, Aristotle's foremost Christian translator, develops the themes of justice, equity, mutuality, and friendship in even richer theological ethical form. Aquinas builds on Aristotle's tripartite definition of parenting, relating it to the three precepts of natural law — preservation, propagation, and knowing God while living in society. He similarly preserves the Aristotelian notion of justice as equity, which figures prominently in his discussion of divorce. While Thomistic sexual ethics has sometimes been condemned as preoccupied with particular acts, there is an important ethic of relationality underpinning his discussions of sex and family. The most problematic effects of acts like fornication, incest, polygamy, and concubinage have to do with their impact on relationships, order, and social justice in families, including their effects on any children who may result from such unions. This emphasis on relationship carries over into Aquinas's understanding of marriage as a partnership and a "community of works,"[26] as well as one which, within a sacramental framework of permanence, operates as a vehicle of grace and redemption, particularly for men, ensuring that the "dad strategy" trumps the "cad strategy" amid the vicissitudes of male biological tendencies.

These relational and partnership dimensions of the Thomistic analysis of the male and female problematics correlate to the ethical and theo-

24. Aristotle, *Politics,* in *The Politics and The Constitution of Athens,* ed. Stephen Everson (Cambridge: Cambridge University Press, 1996), Bk. 2, chap. 4. See also Browning, *Marriage and Modernization,* 103 for a discussion of this remarkable metaphor for paternal affection.

25. Aristotle, *Nichomachean Ethics,* Bk. 8, chap. 1.

26. Thomas Aquinas, *Summa Theologica,* trans. Fathers of the English Dominican Province (New York: Benziger Brothers, 1947), III, "Supplement," Q. 65, a. 1.

logical arguments that Browning identifies, alongside Thomas's naturalistic account. The ethical argument is one based on "appeals to freedom, dignity, and the status of persons,"[27] particularly as these apply to women, in ways that may make Aquinas even more useful than Aristotle, though Aquinas is rarely recognized as such a resource, particularly outside of theology. Indeed, as Browning argues, "For Aquinas, because women are made in the image of God — although a little less perfectly — they enjoy a kind of equality with men. They are fit candidates for friendship with their husbands."[28] Of course, Aquinas, like Aristotle remains mired to some extent in the problematic model of household codes and proportional equity — a reality liable to result in his dismissal in the minds of many feminists — yet, as Browning observes, particularly in his understanding of the value of monogamy, "Aquinas brought into existence a new level of care and investment by males in their children and created greater equality and friendship between wife and husband."[29]

The theological-narrative argument that Browning identifies in Aquinas's discussion of marriage and the family contains the seeds of some even more important insights for feminist theory. This is particularly true of some of the points that Browning sees Aquinas deriving from the ethical arguments. First, there is Aquinas's understanding of dependency. This comes in the form of an assumption by Aquinas that women are necessarily dependent on men and thus should subject themselves to the wisdom of their male keepers. In a prototype of arguments in today's debate over "no-fault" divorce, Aquinas argues that neither spouse should be allowed to initiate a divorce, since this would deprive women of economic resources and male guidance. This is an issue that has actually occasionally brought feminist legal theorists, particularly those of the gynocentric type, into collusion with defenders of traditional marriage, though with markedly different motivations and rationales. Indeed, as Browning argues, in a manner that rankles some feminists and galvanizes others, "The contemporary slide of single mothers into poverty, in spite of their increased economic independence, suggests that his [Aquinas's] economic analysis had more merit than his assessment of women's need for male wisdom."[30] Second, there is Aquinas's argument about marriage as a sacrament and vehicle for supernatural grace. This is

27. Browning et al., *From Culture Wars to Common Ground,* 118.
28. Browning et al., *From Culture Wars to Common Ground,* 119.
29. Browning et al., *From Culture Wars to Common Ground,* 120.
30. Browning et al., *From Culture Wars to Common Ground,* 122.

an argument whose relevance is obviously felt more in theological than secular circles, and mostly in the Catholic and some Anglican traditions in which marriage remains sacramental. Yet it does correspond to a growing move in feminist theology in recent years to address the order of redemption alongside the order of creation — in ways that move beyond the strictly biological and natural toward normative, transformative, and redemptive arguments in the realm of marriage and family. This is, arguably, a welcome evolution away from more gynocentric formulations, which have occasionally become too mired in the "female problematic" and its assertions of feminine moral superiority based on maternal biology. The third and final dimension of Aquinas's theological argument that Browning usefully brings to the fore in ways that are helpful from a feminist perspective is the particular spin that Aquinas gives to the issue of sacrificial love. Consonant with his own theory of sacrificial love as a transitional ethic on the way to a love ethic of full equal regard, Browning argues that, for Aquinas, "the sacrifice is not an end in itself; it is a means for restoring friendship with spouse and parental commitment to children."[31] This concept, particularly in the form of male sacrificial commitment, is, as Browning observes, the theological counterpart of his naturalistic argument, largely borrowed from Aristotle, about male sexual ambivalence and detachment from family. But, as we shall see below in the discussion of family altruism, it also has the potential to liberate women from questionable forms of excessive self-sacrifice.

The liberal political tradition — the second strand that I explored alongside the Aristotelian-Thomistic tradition — has not been an explicit focus of Browning's work on the family, though he would likely admit to characterization as a "reconstructive" liberal in his understanding of religion, culture, and family in the American context and increasingly in the global context, as well. Three figures in that tradition stand out as worthy of special attention when it comes to fatherhood: John Locke, Jean-Jacques Rousseau, and John Stuart Mill. John Locke in many ways continues the Aristotelian-Thomistic tradition in his understanding of the natural and biological dimensions of the family, particularly in his expansive understanding of parenthood that includes a robust understanding of fatherhood. His theory of the nurturing father, like Locke's finding of a biblical equality of fathers and mothers in his *Two Treatises on Government,* sought to debunk the arguments of his patriarchal and absolute monarchy-supporting interlocutor, Robert Filmer. The

31. Browning et al., *From Culture Wars to Common Ground,* 123.

model of a father who shares power with a mother and treats his children in a nurturing manner is an apt analogue for the reined-in monarchy that Locke recommended. Locke was deeply concerned with life-or-death power that fathers could wield over children, and monarchs over their subjects. He remarked, at one point, that "they who say the *Father* gives Life to his Children, are so dazzled with the thoughts of Monarchy, that they do not as they ought, remember God, who is *the Author and Giver of Life*."[32]

Locke preserves the Aristotelian-Thomistic formula of fatherhood as involving a duty to "preserve, nourish, and educate" his children.[33] Consistent with the pre-nineteenth century assignment of moral responsibility to fathers, Locke emphasizes the importance to the child of having "some Body else guide him, who is presumed to know how far the Law allows a Liberty."[34] Locke further describes fatherhood as involving care, skill, affection, and love for the good of children, the family, and the wider society. Fathers and mothers are to provide one another, Locke tells us, with "mutual Support, and Assistance, and a Communion of Interest too, as necessary not only to unite their Care, and Affection, but also necessary to their common Off-spring who have a Right to be nourished and maintained by them, till they are able to provide for themselves."[35] Making nearly the same observations as Aristotle and Aquinas before him, Locke describes the socially and politically effective family in sociobiological terms in portions of his work that would be taken up, partially refuted, and culturally extended by another political theorist in the liberal tradition, Jean-Jacques Rousseau.

In his *Discourse on the Origin and Foundations of Inequality Among Men,* Rousseau takes issue with some aspects of Locke's naturalism, specifically his prescient, proto-evolutionary psychological extrapolations from the world of birds, observing at one point, that "it is no light undertaking to disentangle what is original from what is artificial in man's present Nature, and to know accurately a state which no longer exists, which perhaps never did exist, which probably never will exist, and about which it is nevertheless necessary to have exact Notions in order accurately to judge of our present state."[36] In these epistemological concerns regarding our ca-

32. John Locke, *First Treatise,* in *Two Treatises on Government,* ed. Peter Laslett (Cambridge: Cambridge University Press, 1988), 178.

33. John Locke, *Second Treatise,* in *Two Treatises on Government,* 307.

34. Locke, *Second Treatise,* 305.

35. Locke, *Second Treatise,* 319.

36. Jean-Jacques Rousseau, *Discourse on Origin and Foundations of Inequality*

pacity to know our nature and generally finding rather scant and fragile attachments in nature for fathers and mothers alike, Rousseau is particularly concerned to craft social and cultural solutions to our more problematic natural tendencies. In one such move — relevant again today in an era in which even some unmarried partners prospectively refer to one another as each other's "baby mamas" and "baby daddies" while they are planning, expecting, or raising children — Rousseau proposes temporally to expand the notion of fatherhood backward into the prenatal period, asking "If a woman is of no interest to a man through those nine months, if she even becomes unknown to him, why will he help her after the birth? Why will he help her rear a Child he does not even know is his, and whose birth he neither willed nor foresaw?"[37] If this proposal as seen as potentially leading to an equality between the partners, other proposals are more one-sided, as when Rousseau holds forth on the mother's role of "remembering" her children to their father, a concept that would seem to reduce motherhood to a purely instrumental role in the triadic relationship between the two parents and their offspring.[38] Rousseau seeks to shore up the emotional and cultural underpinnings for the bonds of love between men and women — most notably in the highly gendered programs of education that he prescribes for both boys and girls in *Emile,* his treatise on education that is perhaps his best-known work.

The short space of this chapter precludes detail on the full scope and nature of Rousseau's gender dichotomy in *Emile.* I will say that the inherent fragility of the arrangement seems to be one that Rousseau himself contemplated in a less well-known and fragmentary sequel to *Emile,* titled *Emile et Sophie: Les Solitaires.*[39] There, things fall terribly apart for Emile and Sophie, Rousseau's idealized husband and wife. In brief, the young couple moves to Paris with their infant son after the death of their infant daughter. Both are corrupted by city life and engage in adulterous

Among Men, in *The First and Second Discourses,* ed. Victor Gourevitch (New York: Harper & Row, 1986), 130.

37. Rousseau, *Discourse,* 224.

38. Jean-Jacques Rousseau, *Emile; or, On Education,* trans. Allan Bloom (New York: Basic Books, 1979), 361.

39. See Judith N. Shklar, *Men and Citizens: A Study of Rousseau's Social Theory* (Cambridge, MA: Harvard University Press, 1969), 234-35, and Susan Moller Okin, *Women in Western Political Thought* (Princeton, NJ: Princeton University Press, 1979), 168-72, for summaries and partial translations of this text, which has not yet been completely translated into English. For the French version, see Michel Launay, *Une grève d'esclaves à Alger au XVIIe siècle. Avec Emile et Sophie, ou Les Solitaires, de Jean-Jacques Rousseau* (Paris: J.-P. Rocher, 1988).

affairs, Sophie conceiving another man's child. After their separation, Emile schemes to get custody of his son, proclaiming at one point, "I would sooner see my son dead than Sophie the mother of another man's child!" This is the eighteenth-century version of those "Who's Your Daddy?" paternity revelation talk shows that proliferate today, enhanced by advances in DNA technology, but still revealing the fragility of fatherhood along with its inescapability. Rousseau's sequel also features an irredeemably autonomous and emotionally stilted understanding of masculinity — a failure of generativity in Browning's Eriksonian terms — that could benefit from a post-Gilligan gender analysis.

My historical survey of fatherhood continues in a comparison of liberal utilitarianism of John Stuart Mill with notions of fatherhood in the early papal encyclicals of Pope Leo XIII. What was striking in Mill was the way in which the Mill's famously untrammeled version of liberal autonomy expounded in the essay "On Liberty," is quickly constrained when one becomes a parent — particularly a father. Mill, like other thinkers in the Aristotelian-Thomistic and liberal traditions, subscribes to an expansive notion of paternal duty. Indeed, he remarks at one point that "if, either from idleness or from any other avoidable cause, a man fails to perform his legal duties to others, as for instance to support his children, it is no tyranny to force him to fulfill that obligation, by compulsory labor, if no other means are available."[40] The failure to educate, in particular, violates what Mill describes as "one of the most sacred duties of the parents (or, as law and usage now stand, the father)," constituting a "moral crime both against the unfortunate offspring and against society."[41] Pope Leo XIII construes fatherhood economically, as well as morally and politically. In early social encyclicals, such as *Rerum Novarum*,[42] Leo XIII defends a family wage for fathers and a mostly domestic sphere for mothers in ways that continued to shape papal teachings down through the family encyclicals of John Paul II in the twentieth century, though John Paul II eventually becomes enmeshed in some rather sentimentalized understandings of motherhood not altogether distinct from gynocentric feminist formulations.[43] The main point in considering Mill

40. John Stuart Mill, "On Liberty," in *On Liberty and Other Essays*, ed. John Gray (Oxford: Oxford University Press, 1991), 91.

41. Mill, "On Liberty," 116-17.

42. Leo XIII, *Rerum Novarum* [On Capital and Labor] (May 15, 1891).

43. See John Paul II, *Familiaris Consortio* [On the Role of the Christian Family in the Modern World] (November 22, 1981); John Paul II, *Mulieris Dignitatem* [On the Dignity and Vocation of Women] (August 15, 1988).

and the papal social encyclicals together, however, in a way reminiscent of Browning's argument about Aquinas's understanding of dependency, is to realize the key affinities between these two paradigmatically secular and theological formulations when it comes to fatherhood and family responsibility.

This long tradition of discourse and debate concerning fatherhood both confirms the existence of the male problematic and hints at solutions to it. The great importance of Don Browning's contribution to this discussion is, first, to identify and appreciate the significance of the biological and naturalistic dimensions of fatherhood as a basis for any further ethical and theological reflection. Biology is a necessary and fundamental component of fatherhood, but it is not sufficient. A second contribution of Browning's theory of both fatherhood and motherhood is the framing of these roles within ethical principles of equity, friendship, mutuality, and equal regard. These ethical frameworks for parental roles are a particularly rich repository for feminist ethics aimed at a mutually reinforcing and mutually critical relationship of justice and care in the family. The theological-narrative of Browning's contribution on fatherhood has been less a focus here than the other areas (though I shall say more about it in the conclusion), if only because it is more remote from the origins of the inquiry here in legal theory of the family — and *feminist* legal theory, at that. This is the area of the religion and theology of paternity, which turns out to play a large role in Browning's cultural argument for fatherhood. Indeed, through his critical reinterpretations of certain problem passages in the Christian tradition, most notably the Pauline letter to the Ephesians, Browning argues that classical religio-ethical traditions have played a central role in creating the necessary conditions for shared parental responsibilities between males and females through their interpretation, extension, and redirection of our fundamental natural tendencies. Thus, Browning's five levels of practical reason — tendency-needs, social-ecological, moral-obligational, practical-ethical, and visional-narrative — coalesce in his theory of fatherhood, as in other applications of his practical theology in an illuminating hermeneutical circle.

The Male and Female Problematics in Family Law Today

There is one area of Browning's practical theology of fatherhood that remains unsettled — at least from the feminist perspective of this writer. This has to do with the reception and resolution of the "male problematic" — particularly as accompanied by the "female problematic" — in family law and feminist ethics today. The "female problematic" around fatherhood manifests itself particularly in the continuing divide between liberal and gynocentric feminists around the issue of fatherhood. For, as indicated above, liberal feminist views have not been the only voices on fatherhood in feminist theory and family law. With the turn to difference in feminist thought, various gynocentric feminist voices emerged in family law. These gynocentric theorists were remarkably skeptical of the liberal feminist vision of sex equality — particularly when it came to enlisting men and fathers in the project. One of the leading articulators of the gynocentric vision of family in feminist legal theory has been noted family law professor Martha Fineman. Fineman has repeatedly characterized the liberal feminist attempt to bring fathers into responsible paternal practices as largely futile. She remarks succinctly: "Fathers, as a group, do not have an impressive record when it comes to continuing relationships with, or meeting responsibilities for, their children post-divorce."[44] In her provocative call for the abolition of marriage and defense of wider state and social support for the "mother-child dyad" as the *de facto* and *de jure* family unit, Fineman only occasionally turns attention to fatherhood, as when she argues with respect to new norms of nurturing fatherhood, "To be nurturing father is to concede the importance of mothering."[45] Fineman here gives away the goods on her argument about fatherhood — namely that fathers can be caregivers only so long as they engage in "mothering." At one point, she even calls for a "moratorium" on fatherhood, as traditionally construed, "so as to break the chain of indoctrination into masculinist culture."[46]

Fineman's views have earned wide circulation and comment in legal circles, and they are not atypical within the gynocentric strand of feminist legal thought. Another leading feminist legal theorist of the family, Mary Becker, argues for a maternal preference standard in cases of divorce and child custody. In a single article on the topic she uses the phrase "emotionally distant father" thirteen times, not counting the myriad other permutations and alternative expressions.[47] Indeed, Becker argues:

44. Martha Albertson Fineman, *The Neutered Mother, the Sexual Family, and Other Twentieth Century Tragedies* (New York: Routledge, 1995), 119.

45. Fineman, *The Neutered Mother,* 205.

46. Fineman, *The Neutered Mother,* 206.

47. Mary Becker, "Maternal Feelings: Myth, Taboo, and Child Custody," *Southern California Review of Law and Women's Studies* 1 (1992).

> As groups — on the average — unwed mothers and fathers differ in their interest in caring for their newborn children. Many unwed fathers do not know that their children exist, have not investigated whether or not a child was conceived. In our culture, as in others, it is overwhelmingly women who are responsible for children in general and newborns in particular, whether or not the parents are wed. Rare is the father, wed or unwed, who is willing to be the primary caretaker of a newborn.[48]

The frequency of Becker's repeated aspersions on fathers strikes this observer as raising the self-fulfilling prophecy problem, additionally reinforcing a view of fatherhood that may be unjust, even as a matter of law.

There is something of an irony here in that most of the fatherhood cases that come before courts involve fathers claiming a desire to be involved at some level in the lives of their children. Sadly, these claims by fathers are never entirely free from the suspicion that fathers are using custody as a bargaining chip to whittle down the level of their financial obligation. The place where the nature of fatherhood in law has been most clearly addressed is in cases of so-called "putative fathers," a legal term of art referring to unwed fathers who wish to claim paternity in cases where the mother wants to put the child up for adoption or to marry another man who will become father to her child. In the four key cases on this issue that have reached the United States Supreme Court,[49] the Court has articulated a "biology plus relationship" standard in which biology does not alone suffice for a paternity claim absent a showing of concrete relationship to the child. Thus, the law presumes that fathers are capable of care and should have relationships of care with their children.

One of the most productive aspects of working with Don Browning was the ongoing dialogue that we had over the relationship between law and religion in family matters. In recent years, consonant with his concern that theology be practical and public, Browning has engaged an ever-widening circle of professions and disciplines that deal with family issues.[50] In one notable engagement with the law, in which he situated his

48. Mary E. Becker, "The Rights of Unwed Parents: Feminist Approaches," *Social Service Review* (December 1989): 501-2.

49. *Stanley v. Illinois*, 405 U.S. 645 (1972); *Quilloin v. Wolcott*, 434 U.S. 246 (1978); *Caban v. Mohamed*, 441 U.S. 380 (1979); *Lehr v. Robertson*, 463 U.S. 248 (1983).

50. John Wall, Don S. Browning, William J. Doherty, and Stephen Post, eds., *Marriage, Health, and the Professions: If Marriage Is Good for You, What Does This Mean for Law, Medicine, Ministry, Therapy, and Business* (Grand Rapids, MI: Eerdmans, 2002).

"critical familism" within a broader critique of the market and civil society, Browning offered a critique of both liberal and gynocentric feminisms for their positions on the market-driven family of postmodernity. In relevant portion, he observed:

> Critical familism differs from liberal feminism that would give full access to the market but has few proposals to radically contain it other than government and business support for child care. Critical familism differs from gynocentric feminists who emphasize the elevated status of mothering before law and government but have few proposals to limit the demands of market rationality.[51]

In these remarks, as in the feminist theories he critiques, Browning may not seem to be saying anything explicit about fatherhood, but the very absence of fatherhood in these feminist legal theories is illustrative of that very important accompaniment of to the "male problematic" to which I have alluded above — namely the "female problematic" — which tends to elevate motherhood to the exclusion of fatherhood.

Motherhood, Fatherhood, and the Ethics of Family Altruism

To bring these themes of mothers, fathers, and the ethics of family altruism back into the picture, I return to the opening queries of this essay: *Why would a feminist write about fatherhood? Why should feminists care about fatherhood?* With respect to the first question, for some, it seems, there must be some ulterior motive — a standard critique of patriarchy, feminist conversion of fathers themselves, ultimate confirmation of the independence and self-sufficiency of women from any support that fathers might usefully provide? With respect to the second, I can only hope that I make the case now. For the truth is that I have learned as much from the research about motherhood and feminism as I have about fatherhood — not a surprising result in light of the inextricable links between the "male problematic" and the "female problematic."

Before Don Browning's writings on family gave such a concrete name to it, the first place that I had encountered the "female problematic" was in the kinds of questions that I asked about Carol Gilligan's work in *In a Different Voice.* A key phenomenon that Gilligan chronicled in her

51. Don S. Browning, "Critical Familism, Civil Society, and the Law," *Hofstra Law Review* 32 (2003-4): 325.

various studies of women's moral development was the move from a survival ethic focused on the self to an ethic that would gradually incorporate relations of care and responsibility to various others. Yet there was risk in this — risk that these women would be so concerned to overcome feelings and external accusations of selfishness that they would be led to sacrifice themselves for others in a way that would compromise their own self and its necessary autonomy and authenticity. This is clearly not the problem of men and fathers in the grips of the "male problematic"! But it is a serious problem for women struggling with the "female problematic." Another place where I encountered the "female problematic" in a way that continues to haunt is in feminist legal theorist Robin West's statement, quoted in full above, that the mother who "*will* care" is differently situated from the father who "*may* care" in a way that has significant moral and ethical implications for their sense of family obligation and family altruism.

Browning describes the "female problematic," first, in evolutionary psychological terms, as the "tendency for mothers to reenact the primordial mammalian family, i.e. to have children and raise them by themselves or with a coterie of close female relatives and friends."[52] He also describes it as "tendency to bond with the child to the exclusion of the father."[53] In the contemporary environment of decreased stigmatization of single motherhood, and to some extent greater economic support for it, as least in some advanced Western democracies, Browning describes the logical result of such social change: "Since for millions of years the successful mammalian family was the mother-infant dyad, there is reason to believe that if human males are not genuinely helpful and human mothers can find alternative support, the latter will work out their inclusive fitness (and inclinations to have and care for children) without the aid of a man."[54] Yet, even in reporting these social developments, particularly at the global level, Browning raises critical ethical questions about them, as when he argues and queries:

> This asymmetry of low investment on the part of males and high investment on the part of females leaves the latter, especially at the hu-

52. Browning, *Marriage and Modernization*, 94. It is worth noting that both this and the quotation below are italicized in the published versions, indicating Browning's considerable emphasis on them within the framework of his larger argument.

53. Browning, *Marriage and Modernization*, 94.

54. Browning, *Marriage and Modernization*, 111.

> man level, very vulnerable. It leaves human males with few reasons to become attached to a single female and their jointly produced children. So why, in the course of human evolution, did males become attached to their female consorts and invested in their children? And as we puzzle about how it came about, we should also ask, *is there worldwide evidence that this unique human phenomenon is coming undone? Could it happen that for a significant part of the population, procreation could become uncoupled from long-term mother-father bonding? And, if so, are we losing something in the process?*[55]

Indeed, it would seem that we should ask not only about the nature and effect of problems, but also, in the best practice of practical theology, about the strategies and resources toward their solution. In this regard, Browning sees considerable resources coming from religion.

In the early stages of my research on fatherhood, when I was focusing on the legal dimensions of the problem, I was occasionally asked another question, namely: *What does religion have to do with all of this?* Religion is certainly an important subtext of the work of all of the thinkers I consulted in my retrieval of long tradition of fatherhood in the West — though it is often hidden, on the liberal side of the ledger, in the ways that each liberal thinker grapples with the authority of religious tradition. Religion has more directly to do with the hermeneutical, or interpretive, dimension of my fatherhood project, particularly around the interrelationship of biology and culture. In reading the feminist legal theorists, in particular, I often found that there were three aspects of the family that were the subject of considerable ambivalence — biology, history, and religion — so much so that they are often strenuously avoided or omitted from the inquiry, as much if not more so by liberal feminists than their gynocentric counterparts. Each of these three influences on the family has tended to be seen as essentialist, determinist, and fundamentalist in much feminist thought. What has struck me in formulating the problem of fatherhood in the way that I did and in retrieving these various fatherhood traditions is the way in which each of these apparently foundational categories of biology, history, and culture is in fact highly interpreted and mediated to us by culture and by religion.

As noted above, Browning sees significant resources in Aquinas, as well as in a long line of later theologians in the Christian tradition, for his own interpretive resolution of the male and female problematics.

55. Browning, *Marriage and Modernization,* 109.

Browning sees classic religio-cultural symbols and traditions as having both created the necessary conditions for the cooperation of mothers and fathers in families and as powerful forces for restraining and redirecting natural tendencies and social pressures that would interfere with that cooperation. As endeavors that involve human imperfection along with divine aspiration, religious traditions have not always been free of their own tendencies to reinforce the both paternal problematic and patriarchy itself. Yet, significantly, for Browning, the failure of the Christian tradition to live out the Thomistic theological-ethical norms of paternal adequacy is not so much a question of the nature or ultimate validity of the norm — itself imperfectly realized in Aquinas's own questionable adherence to Aristotelian biology and misogyny — as it is a failure of expansive interpretation. With respect to the particular solution that Aquinas offers to the "male problematic," namely the counsel of *mutual* subordination by men and women in marriage and family, Browning argues that Aquinas's mistake was not so much in the prescription, but that "he failed to apply it to women as well . . . failed to include females in the grandness of [his] vision."[56] Browning's argument might be interpreted as requiring yet another measure of female self-sacrifice to offset the masculine — a regrettable piling on of yet another morally imperative "must" to the considerable burden of sacrifice that women already bear, whether by virtue or by necessity. But I believe that it need not be interpreted entirely or exclusively as such. As the ongoing feminist discourse of the gender of altruism and self-sacrifice in families attests, it may just be a call for feminists to continue the project of discernment about what an ethic of equity and mutuality, friendship and love, justice and care really requires — to find ways to ensure that an ethic of care is combined with an ethic of justice for both men and women.

Conclusion: Fatherhood in the Tales of Two Taxi Drivers

I had a more recent encounter with fatherhood in yet another taxi to Logan Airport. The day was wet and chilly, and my Haitian immigrant driver and I got into a discussion of the weather. The driver expressed an interest in getting a bit more schooling and then applying for jobs in Miami — where weather and thus life are good — but lamented that he had not been able to do it. When I asked what was holding him back, he re-

56. Browning, *Marriage and Modernization*, 93.

plied that it was his son, who resides in Boston with his ex-wife. He couldn't leave his son behind. Rather spontaneously, he then began to detail all of the risks inherent in "growing up as a black boy in America," as he expressed it. The bulwark against these risks was moral education, and he had to see that his son got this. A large proportion of his salary was going to private, religious school tuition for his son. When I asked what his ex-wife thought about all this, the driver said she just didn't get it. A few further emotive jabs at his ex-wife followed, but then he uttered something that seemed to be the real clincher for him, "You know, I need him as much as he needs me." Education, as he put it, was the "bridge between generations" and something that would make his son a "citizen of the world." This was a father, in a family decidedly on the margins of the stereotypical nuclear model, who clearly relished his paternal role. Moreover, he experienced that role as a moral imperative of care, quite independently of any "civilizing" female presence.

This paternal example would not seem to fit the Browning model. After all, Browning has been criticized for placing too great an emphasis on marriage as the solution to the male and female problematics in a way that may seem to exclude unmarried and divorced fathers from his vision. Yet components of the Haitian cab driver's story bear out fully the core principles of Browning's practical theology of fatherhood and attest to the ongoing significance of his contribution to fatherhood studies. First, the importance of the religio-cultural ideals for this father is clearly evident, even though the fact of the divorce also attests to his failure fully to live up to those ideals. The ongoing dialectic of ideal and real in everyday life is an important lesson of Browning's practical theology. Ideals have visional, narrative, obligational, and ethical weight, even — and perhaps especially — in the context of our ongoing struggle to embody them in everyday life. Second, the emphasis on mutuality, expressed so eloquently, in the words "I need him as much as he needs me," attest to the importance of Browning's argument that love must be mutual, as much and before it becomes equal. Finally, the expansive definition of fatherhood — extending here temporally across generations and geographically around the world — also embodies the crucial teaching function that Browning identified in Erikson and which is visible throughout the long tradition of fatherhood in the West, is clearly afoot in this story. In the context of this volume, it is probably not gratuitous to point out that Browning exemplified this role of teacher for many of us whose words are assembled in this volume.

5 Childhood Studies, Hermeneutics, and Theological Ethics

John Wall

The purpose of this chapter is to ask how, both methodologically and substantively, theological ethics should engage today in childhood studies.[1] More specifically, since there is now emerging an international interdisciplinary field of childhood studies, primarily in the social sciences, I ask both how theological ethics may contribute toward this broader field and how this field may in turn influence theological ethics. Don Browning's work significantly animates my discussion, both in its long-term investigation into the relation of religious ethics and the social sciences and in its shorter-term investigation of this relation through the lens of families. In relating this work to the field of childhood studies, I build on Browning's achievements but also take them into new areas. Through this somewhat shifted lens I conclude, in part, that Browning's groundbreaking methodological and normative ideas should also be pressed in new directions.

My argument is that, in an analogous way to women's and environmental studies, childhood studies should not only apply existing theological methods and norms, but also challenge and transform them. It should do so in new and distinctive ways. In analogy to terms like "feminism" and "environmentalism," I call this approach "childism." Christian ethics in particular has a long history of this kind of child-centered self-reflection: such as Jesus' placing a child "in the midst" of his disciples to explain the kingdom of heaven (Matt. 18:1-5), the early

1. A version of the present essay appeared in the *Journal of Religion* 86(4) (October 2006): 523-48.

church fathers using childhood to describe the ideal human image of God, Augustine's beginning his groundbreaking *Confessions* through his original sin in infancy and youth, and Friedrich Schleiermacher's exploration of the "feeling of absolute dependence" in relation to the notion of the child as gift.[2] The difference today is both a changed situation for children around the world and the possibility for greater empirical sophistication about the nature of childhood and its relations to families and society. The question for theological ethics is how to respond to the complex lives of children in the contemporary world in as sufficiently attentive and meaningful a way as to enrich, in turn, theological ethical understanding itself.

That a new ethical focus is needed regarding childhood today is evident from children's uniquely marginalized status under contemporary conditions of pluralism, individualism, and globalization. It is hardly news that children in rich and poor countries alike have become the poorest segment of the population, receive the least health care, face ever more complex challenges growing up, suffer the most from disintegrating families and communities, are the most vulnerable targets of mass media and advertising manipulation, and in various parts of the world are increasingly enslaved to sex trafficking, drugs, gang violence, and soldiering. What is more difficult to answer is why professional theological ethicists have played such a limited role in social debates on such issues.

Using the work of Browning, in conjunction with similar religious ethical thinkers like Paul Ricoeur, David Tracy, Sallie McFague, and Richard Kearney, I argue that the most promising methodological approach lies in theological ethical dialogue with the human sciences through a mutually transforming "hermeneutical circle." This hermeneutical circle allows theological ethics to make substantive critiques of the situation of children in today's world while at the same time learning from children's experiences in such a way as to deepen theological ethics itself. Substantively, the resulting "childist" theological ethics will demand a fundamental rethinking of the nature of human responsibility toward others.

2. Augustine, *Confessions*, trans. Henry Chadwick (New York: Oxford University Press, 1998), Bk. I; Friedrich Schleiermacher, *Christmas Eve: Dialogues on the Incarnation* (Lewiston, NY: Edwin Mellen, 1990) and *The Christian Household: A Sermonic Treatise* (Lewiston, NY: Edwin Mellen, 1991).

The Contemporary Field of Childhood Studies

Although the term "childhood studies" is relatively new, the interdisciplinary field of study that it describes has deep roots in the twentieth-century academy and continues to evolve. The center of gravity for this field lies in the human sciences, principally sociology, anthropology, developmental psychology, history, cultural studies, and law. It is these disciplines that, sometimes in contention with one another, have moved beyond isolated studies of children to found an increasing number of programs and centers for interdisciplinary childhood research, as well as scholarly journals devoted to childhood.[3] Much of this work is conducted on the analogy of women's studies and African American studies. It has also influenced public policy in many ways, including most visibly the formation and interpretation of the 1989 United Nations Convention on the Rights of the Child. Humanists in literature, the arts, philosophy, and other areas are by no means excluded from this field, even if they have not generally taken the lead. Important work is being done here, for example, on children's rights, children as philosophical thinkers, and children's voices and constructions in art and literature.

Within the current state of this field, one can detect two major methodological disputes. One dispute is over the usefulness of longer-standing developmental psychological approaches versus more recent approaches from social sciences like sociology, anthropology, and cultural studies. The issue here is whether childhood is better understood through generalized stages of individual, cognitive, emotional, and moral development or through wider diverse meanings and constructions of childhood in history, culture, and society. A second dispute is over the degree to which the well-being of children is bound up with the well-being of families. Some psychologists and social scientists believe families and marriage lie at the center of childhood studies while others do not. The result of these disputes is that "childhood studies" involves at least four major methodological approaches, which could be termed developmental-psychological,

3. Such research centers include the Centre for the Social Study of Childhood (Sheffield University, United Kingdom), the Chapin Hall Center for Children (University of Chicago), Childwatch International Research Network (University of Oslo), the Center for Children and Childhood Studies (Rutgers University), the Schubert Center for Child Development (Case Western Reserve University), and the Child Policy Research Institute (University of Florida). Major interdisciplinary childhood studies journals include *Childhood: A Global Journal of Child Research, Child: Care, Health, and Development, Children and Society,* and *Sociological Studies of Children and Youth.*

family-psychological, politico-sociological, and family-sociological. Let us briefly examine these in turn.

Developmental psychology ever since Sigmund Freud has set itself the fundamental task of looking beneath cultural and social variation to uncover general child development stages. Freud himself spoke of rather biologically determined phases of oral, anal, phallic (oedipal), latent, and genital (adolescent) development. Later psychoanalysts spoke more broadly of children's development in such areas as ego identity (Heinz Hartmann), object-relations (Melanie Klein and D. W. Winnicott), social identity (Erik Erikson), and sense of self (Heinz Kohut).[4] At the same time, psychologists have investigated the specifically "moral" development of children, including Jean Piaget's studies of children's internalization of social rules, Lawrence Kohlberg's stages of pre-conventional, conventional, and post-conventional moral reasoning, and Carol Gilligan's observations of growing capabilities for relationality and care.[5] These somewhat universalistic approaches to childhood have not been without internal disciplinary critique from the point of view of possible larger cultural differences, as we see in the writings of Margaret Mead, Sudhir Kakar, and Richard Shweder.[6] Nevertheless, they have produced powerful insights for education, therapy, law, and social policy in the United States and around the world.

More recently, and especially in the United States, psychologists such Salvadore Minuchia and Charles Fishman have developed a different kind

4. Sigmund Freud, *New Introductory Lectures in Psycho-Analysis,* German original 1933, trans. James Strachey (New York: W. W. Norton, 1965), 123; Heinz Hartmann, *Ego Psychology and the Problem of Adaptation,* German original 1939, trans. David Rapaport (New York: International Universities Press, 1958); Melanie Klein, *The Psycho-Analysis of Children,* German original 1932, rev. ed., trans. Alix Strachey (New York: Delacorte Press, 1975); Erik Erikson, *Childhood and Society* (New York: Norton, 1950); D. W. Winnicott, *Playing and Reality* (New York: Basic Books, 1971); Heinz Kohut, *The Analysis of the Self: A Systematic Approach to the Psychoanalytic Treatment of Narcissistic Personality Disorders* (New York: International Universities Press, 1971).

5. Jean Piaget, *The Moral Judgment of the Child,* French original 1924, trans. Marjorie Gabain (New York: The Free Press, 1965); Lawrence Kohlberg, *The Philosophy of Moral Development* (New York: Harper and Row, 1981); Carol Gilligan, *In a Different Voice: Psychological Theory and Women's Development* (Cambridge, MA: Harvard University Press, 1982).

6. Margaret Mead, *Coming of Age in Samoa: A Psychological Study of Primitive Youth for Western Civilization* (New York: W. Morrow and Company, 1928); Sudhir Kakar, *The Inner World: A Psycho-Analytic Study of Childhood and Society in India* (New York: Oxford University Press, 1981); Richard Jessor, Anne Colby, and Richard Shweder, eds., *Ethnography and Human Development: Context and Meaning in Social Inquiry* (Chicago: University of Chicago Press, 1996).

of "systems theory" approach that views children's well-being less individualistically and instead fundamentally bound up with the complex interactive context of their family.[7] Related to this family-centered approach is the field of "evolutionary psychology," in figures such as W. D. Hamilton, Martin Daly, and Margo Wilson, which links child outcomes to aspects of genetic natural selection through such things as paternal bonding and kin altruism.[8] Here also can be located the work of family psychologists like Judith Wallerstein, Sandra Blakeslee, and Mavis Hetherington who examine the impact on children of family disruption.[9] There is now a "marriage movement" in the academy and beyond that takes as one of its central concerns the impact of stable marriages for children, including most notably the "marriage education" work of psychologists such as Howard Markman, Scott Stanley, and John Gottman involved in the Coalition of Marriage, Family, and Couples Education.[10]

The greatest fault line in the childhood studies literature, however, comes from the critique made of psychological models overall by what has been termed a "social sciences" approach that arose primarily in Europe in the late 1980s. Instead of examining individual children or family systems, this approach investigates children as they participate in and are constructed by their diverse cultures and societies. The origins of this methodology can be traced back to the historian Philippe Ariès, who famously argued in his 1960 book *Centuries of Childhood* that experiences and interpretations of childhood have varied significantly across Western history (even if his narrower claim that childhood was invented only after the Middle Ages is generally rejected).[11] The seminal text in this new

7. See, for example, Salvadore Minuchin and H. Charles Fishman, *Techniques of Family Therapy* (Cambridge, MA: Harvard University Press, 1981).

8. W. D. Hamilton, "The Genetical Evolution of Social Behavior, II," *Journal of Theoretical Biology* 7 (1994): 17-52; Martin Daly and Margo Wilson, *Sex, Evolution, and Behavior* (Belmont, CA: Wadsworth Publishing, 1983).

9. Judith Wallerstein, Julia Lewis, and Sandra Blakeslee, *The Unexpected Legacy of Divorce: A 25 Year Landmark Study* (New York: Hyperion, 2000); E. Mavis Hetherington and John Kelly, *For Better or For Worse: Divorce Reconsidered* (New York: W. W. Norton, 2002).

10. Classic texts here include Howard Markman, Scott Stanley, and Susan L. Blumberg, *Fighting for Your Marriage: Positive Steps for Preventing Divorce and Preserving a Lasting Love* (San Francisco: Jossey-Bass Publishers, 1994); and John Gottman, *What Predicts Divorce: The Relationship Between Marital Processes and Marital Outcomes* (Hillsdale, NJ: Lawrence Erlbaum Associates, 1994).

11. Philippe Ariès, *Centuries of Childhood*, French original 1960, trans. Robert Baldick (New York: Vintage Books, 1962). Those who contest Aries' claim of child-

social sciences paradigm is the 1990 interdisciplinary volume edited by the British sociologists Alan Prout and Allison James, *Constructing and Reconstructing Childhood.*[12] Here the argument is advanced that childhood — or rather "childhoods" — cannot be understood apart from how children interact with a range of diverse social variables such as poverty, class, gender, race, culture, and ethnicity. As James puts it elsewhere, "to see children as social actors is core to childhood studies. From that perspective, one sees children both as individuals who participate in a social world and as members of a social category defined by particular social, historical, and ideological processes."[13] This new methodology has spawned a worldwide explosion in childhood studies across disciplines as varied as sociology, anthropology, law, medicine, cultural studies, media studies, education, economics, and public policy. Figures here include Chris Jenks, Myra Bluebond-Langnor, Paul Willis, Jens Qvortrup, Irene Rizzini, and Richard Shweder, to name but a few.[14]

A final method in the study of childhood can be found in some of the ways that sociology and other social sciences have been applied to children in the United States, where the focus is again more frequently around the

---

hood's invention — though not his claim of childhood's variation — include Linda Pollack, *Forgotten Children: Parent-Child Relations from 1500-1900* (New York: Cambridge University Press, 1983).

12. Allison James and Alan Prout, eds., *Constructing and Reconstructing Childhood: New Directions in the Sociology of Childhood* (New York: Falmer Press, 1990).

13. Allison James, "Understanding Childhood from an Interdisciplinary Perspective: Problems and Potentials," in *Rethinking Childhood,* ed. Peter B. Pufall and Richard P. Unsworth (New Brunswick, NJ: Rutgers University Press, 2004), 36.

14. See, for example, Chris Jenks, *Childhood* (New York: Routledge, 1996); Allison James, Chris Jenks, and Alan Prout, *Theorizing Childhood* (Cambridge: Polity Press, 1998); Myra Bluebond-Langnor, *The Private Worlds of Dying Children* (Princeton, NJ: Princeton University Press, 1978); Paul Willis, *Critical Education in the New Information Age* (Lanham, MD: Rowman & Littlefield, 1999); Pam Foley, Jeremy Roche, and Stanley Tucker, eds., *Children in Society: Contemporary Theory, Policy and Practice* (New York: Palgrave/Open University Press, 2001); Flemming Mouritsen and Jens Qvortrup, eds., *Childhood and Children's Culture* (Odense: University Press of Southern Denmark, 2002); Irene Rizzini, *From Street Children to All Children: Improving the Opportunities of Low Income Urban Children and Youth in Brazil* (New York: Cambridge University Press, 2002); Kathleen Marshall and Paul Parvis, *Honoring Children: The Human Rights of the Child in Christian Perspective* (Edinburgh, Scotland: Saint Andrews Press, 2004); and Peter B. Pufall and Richard P. Unsworth, eds., *Rethinking Childhood* (New Brunswick, NJ: Rutgers University Press, 2004). A large international and interdisciplinary conference on this paradigm of childhood studies, including over a thousand papers, took place at the University of Oslo in 2005 titled "Childhoods 2005 Oslo: Children and Youth in Emerging and Transforming Societies."

specific arena of marriage and families. Beginning around the same time in the late 1980s, as the above Europeans model, American sociologists like Sarah McLanahan, Gary Sandefur, David Popenoe, Alan Wolfe, William Goode, and Linda Waite have investigated the impacts of marriage and divorce on children in terms of broad social outcomes like poverty, education, health, and general social capital.[15] Some of this research is partnered with the above "marriage movement." However, it focuses less on what it takes therapeutically to create strong marriages and families and more on the consequences of marriage and its disruption on children's broad social well-being (as well as the resulting well-being of society). Unlike the European politico-sociological model, this family-sociological model places less emphasis on children's agency and diversity than on their social vulnerability and their dependency on families for social mediation.

Emerging Theological Ethics of Childhood

Despite the obvious ethical questions raised in all four major areas of this field, and despite its own long and complex traditions of reflection on childhood, theological ethics today has not, as a field, approached childhood with the same disciplinary focus as it has approached, for example, women, race, medicine, the environment, business, or war. Theologians have tended to engage issues of children, if they have done so at all, around specific and isolated questions like abortion, health insurance, and spiritual formation. Nevertheless, several scholarly voices have recently emerged, especially in the United States, that are rethinking childhood as an important Christian ethical concern in its own right. These voices are asking new — and sometimes re-asking very old — questions about the larger aims and purposes of child rearing and the obligations toward children of families, churches, communities, and the state. Let us examine how this conversation is developing and how it varies both normatively and methodologically.[16]

15. Sarah McLanahan and Gary Sandefur, *Growing Up with a Single Parent: What Hurts, What Helps* (Cambridge, MA: Harvard University Press, 1994); David Popenoe, *Disturbing the Nest* (New York: Crown Publishers, 1993); Alan Wolfe, *Whose Keeper? Social Science and Moral Obligation* (Berkeley: University of California Press, 1989); William Goode, *World Changes in Divorce Patterns* (New Haven: Yale University Press, 1994); and Linda Waite and Maggie Gallagher, *The Case for Marriage* (New York: Doubleday, 2000).

16. I have also examined this conversation in "Animals and Innocents: Theological Reflections on the Meaning and Purpose of Child-Rearing," *Theology Today* 59(4)

The earliest such work on the Christian ethics of childhood goes back to the 1980s in what I will call the "communitarian" approaches of figures like Stanley Hauerwas, Jean Bethke Elshtain, and Gilbert Meilaender.[17] Drawing chiefly on pre-modern thinkers like Aristotle, Augustine, Thomas Aquinas, and John Calvin, this approach generally opposes itself to modernity and its perceived betrayal of children through moral and expressive individualism. It argues that children fare poorly in the contemporary world primarily because they lack strong families, traditions, and social narratives under which to develop civilized and meaningful social values. Children are not just individual or autonomous agents, but need to be socialized into the larger values and virtues of coherent moral communities. As Meilaender puts it, "parents commit themselves to initiating their children into the human inheritance and, more particularly, into the stories that depict their way of life. In so doing they shape, mold, and civilize their children."[18]

Methodologically, communitarianism can be described as taking a "top-down" approach in which children's lives are to be formed in accordance with traditional norms and values. Similarly, child rearing itself places children under the disciplinary tutelage of normatively grounded adults, particularly parents. The strength of this model is that it manages to break through the virtual silence of Christian ethical voices on childhood in the late twentieth century by demonstrating the importance of substantive child rearing aims and communities. It also questions a profound individualism within especially the psychological (but also frequently the sociological) sciences of childhood. At the same time, however, communitarianism has generally approached the human sciences as an object of critique and not a source of new insight. This arguably op-

(January 2003): 559-82; "The Christian Ethics of Children: Emerging Questions and Possibilities," *Journal of Lutheran Ethics* (electronic journal) 4(1) (January 2004); "'Let the Little Children Come': Child Rearing as Challenge to Contemporary Christian Ethics," *Horizons* 31(1) (Spring 2004): 64-87; and "Fallen Angels: A Contemporary Christian Ethical Ontology of Childhood," *International Journal of Practical Theology* 8(2) (Fall 2004): 160-84.

17. Stanley Hauerwas, *A Community of Character: Toward a Constructive Christian Social Ethic* (Notre Dame, IN: University of Notre Dame Press, 1981); Jean Bethke Elshtain, "The Family and Civic Life," in *Rebuilding the Nest: A New Commitment to the American Family,* ed. David Blankenhorn, Steven Bayme, and Jean Bethke Elshtain (Milwaukee: Family Service America, 1990), 119-32; Gilbert Meilaender, "A Christia View of the Family," in Blankenhorn et al., *Rebuilding the Nest,* 133-48.

18. Gilbert Meilaender, "A Christian View of the Family," in Blankenhorn et al., *Rebuilding the Nest,* 143.

poses much of the very Christian tradition on which it stands, which has frequently learned a great deal from the scientific observations of the time, such as in Thomas Aquinas's use of medieval stage developmental theory and Aristotelian sociobiology.[19] This approach arguably also underestimates the impact on children's lives of larger economic, political, and global conditions, so that a starving child in sub-Saharan Africa, for example, may need more than initiation into moral values. It is also not clear from this perspective how (indeed if) one would view children as having their own moral agency or voice.

In part in response to such problems, a more recent view of the Christian ethics of childhood has emerged in the writings of Kathleen and James McGinnis, Cornel West, Herbert Anderson, Susan Johnson, Pamela Couture, and Adrian Thatcher, who take what I term a "liberationist" approach.[20] Rather than opposing modernity and critiquing the contemporary human sciences of childhood, this approach learns a great deal from them. Methodologically, it shares what could be called a "bottom-up" approach that starts in children's own actual lives, voices, agency, and experiences. The reason to engage theologically with childhood is that, as Thatcher puts it, children "are often the ones with no voice, the unconsulted and sometimes undeserving victims of oppression."[21] Similarly, in terms of guiding norms, these modern liberationist scholars claim — much as the father of modern liberal theology, Friedrich Schleiermacher, claimed — that children should be appreciated not just as recipients of adult values but more important as gifts of God and

19. Thomas Aquinas, *Summa Theologica* (New York: Benziger Brothers, 1948), Supplement, Q. 43, a. 2. Thomas here adopts a theory of development in which in the first seven years a child "neither understands by himself nor learns from another," in the second seven years "can learn from another but is incapable by himself of consideration and understanding," in the third seven years becomes "both able to learn from another and to consider by himself," and finally in the fourth seven years (that is, starting at twenty one!) can reason about not only "things concerning one's own person" but also "the things outside one's person."

20. Kathleen and James McGinnis, *Parenting for Peace and Justice: Ten Years Later* (Maryknoll, NY: Orbis Books, 1990); Sylvia Ann Hewlett and Cornel West, *The War Against Parents: What We Can Do for America's Beleaguered Moms and Dads* (New York: Houghton Mifflin Company, 1998); Herbert Anderson and Susan Johnson, *Regarding Children: A New Respect for Childhood and Families* (Louisville, KY: Westminster John Knox Press, 1994); Pamela Couture, *Seeing Children, Seeing God: A Practical Theology of Children and Poverty* (Nashville, TN: Abingdon Press, 2000); and Adrian Thatcher, *Marriage After Modernity: Christian Marriage in Postmodern Times* (New York: New York University Press, 1999).

21. Thatcher, *Marriage After Modernity*, 152.

bringers of divine goodness and wisdom into the world.[22] Couture argues, for example, that "shared responsibilit[ies] become words of liberation when they result in practices that contribute to the resilience of children and those who care for them, the kind of resilience that continues to share responsibility despite overwhelming odds, gains, and disappointments, a resilience that is tenacious because it arises from God's grace."[23]

The result, methodologically, is that theological ethics not only learns a great deal from the empirical study of children's contemporary lives, but also uses the experiences of children to transform theological ethics' own understanding of the kingdom of God. Liberationist childhood studies is thereby significantly patterned on Christian feminism, black theology, and other movements that start with experiences of social marginalization and move from there to a deepened interpretation of the Christian message. Such an approach is arguably closer than communitarianism to Jesus' holding up childhood as a theological model of the kingdom of heaven. At the same time, however, it is not altogether clear how far childhood studies can in fact be patterned on feminist and other liberationist methods. Unlike other marginalized groups, children do not, as children, have sufficient capacities to enact their own grassroots liberation for themselves. They will never, for example, organize their own communities of resistance or hold university faculty positions in which to challenge ethical hegemonies. As vulnerable beings they may in fact rely, more than women and minorities, on substantive guidance and support from others. While liberationism does frequently call for children's social and political protection, its bottom-up methodology may ultimately leave unclear what *unique* form of responsibility children in particular demand from adults and society.

Don Browning's contribution to this discussion has inspired still a third methodological and normative possibility. Starting in the mid-1990s, Browning and other figures like Lisa Sowle Cahill, Mary Stewart Van Leeuwen, and Bonnie Miller-McLemore developed what some have termed a "progressive familism." All of these Christian thinkers have close ties to liberationism and feminism (hence the term "progressive"), but they also believe that the well-being of children is uniquely dependent on others and particularly on parents (hence "familism"). Significantly,

22. For a detailed discussion of Schleiermacher on childhood, see Dawn DeVries, "'Be Converted and Become as Little Children': Friedrich Schleiermacher on the Religious Significance of Childhood," in *The Child in Christian Thought*, ed. Marcia Bunge (Grand Rapids, MI: William B. Eerdmans Publishing Company, 2001), 329-49.

23. Couture, *Seeing Children, Seeing God*, 16.

progressive familists are deeply engaged with the fields of developmental and evolutionary psychology, partly because these fields offer empirical insight into families, but also, and perhaps even more important, because they help describe how children *become* — rather than how they just already are — competent social agents. In other words, children's social agency is not just a given but also a developmental task falling first and foremost on families. Thus, for example, Browning and Van Leeuwen use developmental psychology to argue for the importance of marriage in the "attachment" of fathers in particular to their child-rearing responsibilities. Cahill blends psychological insight into how children form compassion with insights from Catholic natural law theory to argue for the family's unique role in educating children to grow into active participants in the larger common good. And Miller-McLemore uses feminist psychology to articulate a Christian theology of parenting centered on developing children's agency in relation to their larger world.[24]

This third approach has arguably a more complex relation to the human sciences than the other two. It self-consciously strives to form a clear balance of both ethical critique and empirical learning. Browning, in particular, has developed a sophisticated hermeneutical methodology for theological engagement with the human sciences based on the work of Paul Ricoeur.[25] From this perspective, the human sciences never achieve complete independence from historical values and ethical assumptions, out of which their investigations and animating questions arise. But at the same time, historical values are themselves enriched through the capacity of the human sciences to provide critical reflection upon them. The human sciences should be viewed (from a theological ethical point of view) as infusing theological ethics with what Ricoeur calls a "moment of distanciation" or "critical test."[26] That is, they provide linguistically

24. See Don S. Browning, Bonnie J. Miller-McLemore, Pamela D. Couture, K. Brynolf Lyon, and Robert M. Franklin, *From Culture Wars to Common Ground: Religion and the American Family Debate,* 2d ed. (Louisville, KY: Westminster John Knox Press, 2000); Don S. Browning, *Marriage and Modernization: How Globalization Threatens Marriage and What to Do About It* (Grand Rapids, MI: William B. Eerdmans Publishing Company, 2003); Lisa Sowle Cahill, *Family: A Christian Social Perspective* (Minneapolis, MN: Augsburg Fortress Press, 2000); Mary Stewart Van Leeuwen, *Gender and Grace: Love, Work, and Parenting in a Changing World* (Downers Grove, IL: InterVarsity Press, 1990); and Bonnie Miller-McLemore, *Let the Children Come: Reimagining Childhood from a Christian Perspective* (San Francisco: Jossey-Bass, 2003).

25. Don S. Browning, *A Fundamental Practical Theology: Descriptive and Strategic Proposals* (Minneapolis, MN: Fortress Press, 1991), 80-82, 182-83.

26. Paul Ricoeur, *Hermeneutics and the Human Sciences: Essays on Language, Ac-*

structured empirical observations in relation to which ethical values may be rendered more complex, tested in relation to practices and reality, shown their limits, and critiqued from points of view such as gender and race. Theological ethics questions the ethical presuppositions that animate the human sciences, while the human sciences in turn test historically settled ethical ideals against the complexities of human reality.

This "hermeneutical circle" or "hermeneutical realism" is similar, Browning claims, to Tracy's "critical correlational" theological method, but applied more specifically to the human sciences. Tracy himself revises Paul Tillich's method of correlation (which has had a profound influence on liberationism) so that not only does the contemporary world put new questions to historical traditions (as for Tillich) but also, in a more circular way, traditions are also used in turn to question contemporary ontological and moral assumptions. Thus a *critical* correlation or genuine hermeneutical circle involves theological ethics and the human sciences in a two-way and mutually enriching "dialogue" or "conversation."[27]

The advantage of this circular methodology for childhood studies is that it combines the strengths of both a communitarian top-down injection of robust traditions and a liberationist bottom-up attention to children's actual situation and experiences. Christian ethics is able to make central use of the human sciences while retaining an independent critical voice of its own. The disadvantage, as I will shortly suggest, is that it remains too narrowly focused on the relation of children to families. As the name "progressive familism" implies, childhood studies is here understood as a subset of family studies, as if the ethics of childhood is reducible to how families should function and how society should support them. This is why this approach has gravitated toward engagement with psychological and sociological models that have the same family focus. This centering of childhood studies around families in the North American academy needs to be questioned. As the above-referenced European "social sciences" approach to childhood studies has shown, children's lives are also related to larger social structures *directly,* not just indirectly through the mediating functions of marriage and parenting. While family is central to how children experience society, it does not exhaust all that may be said about children's interactions with such factors as mass me-

---

tion, and Interpretation, ed. and trans. John B. Thompson (New York: Cambridge University Press, 1981), 87-100, 131-44, and 203-9.

27. Browning, *A Fundamental Practical Theology,* 44-47; David Tracy, *The Analogical Imagination* (New York: Crossroad, 1981).

dia, culture, education, rights, class, gender constructions, economics, health care, and politics. A truly child-centered theological ethics will build on this third way but also press beyond "familism" to a broader "childism" — that is, to placing children themselves at the center of inquiry in all their family, cultural, economic, gender, historical, and social complexity.

A Postmodern Hermeneutical Circle of Childhood Studies

In order to develop a revised hermeneutical circle that can respond to the unique challenges of studying childhood, it is worth recalling that "hermeneutics" itself has a complex developmental history. Not coincidentally, Schleiermacher is the founder of both the modern theology of childhood and modern hermeneutics. No other major theologian has written as much on childhood as Schleiermacher. And, in the early nineteenth century, he moves hermeneutics beyond mere techniques for the exegesis of classic texts (especially scripture) into a general method of human social understanding. Schleiermacher adapts Kant's critique of pure and practical reason to argue for a new hermeneutics as the practice of "divining" behind human linguistic expressions the mysterious "genius" or "subjectivity" of the individual author.[28] Childhood, for Schleiermacher, serves among other things as a divine gift from God to the world that epitomizes this subjective hermeneutical mystery. Hermes, as the messenger of the gods, takes his purest and most complete form in each new baby that enters the world. Hermeneutics divines the kind of inner natural wisdom or intuition that each of us still in some way retains from childhood despite the inevitable corruptions and distortions of language and society. Thus, childhood becomes a vital hermeneutical concern in part because it embodies the kind of sacred human inwardness that hermeneutical understanding seeks to approach. It may not be going too far (though I cannot defend it here) to make the argument that Schleiermacher's early writings on childhood deeply influence his later theology and hermeneutics.

While I do not share Schleiermacher's romanticism about either hermeneutics or childhood — his valorization of subjective purity — I do

28. Friedrich Schleiermacher, *Hermeneutics: The Handwritten Manuscripts*, ed. Heinz Kimmerle, trans. James Duke and Jack Forstman (Missoula, MT: Scholars Press, 1977). For Schleiermacher's writings on childhood, see note 1.

believe we can profit from once again rethinking hermeneutics in relation to children. This possibility has been obscured by subsequent developments in hermeneutics itself. In the early twentieth century, Wilhelm Dilthey insists against Schleiermacher that the proper object of hermeneutical interpretation is not the hidden subject behind language, but rather *language itself,* as the means by which humanity expresses itself in history.[29] Because history and language are dominated by adults, however, the relation of hermeneutics to childhood becomes that much more difficult to establish. On this account, children will never have the same hermeneutical agency or voice as adults, but rather, insofar as they are not yet linguistically competent, remain outside the hermeneutical circle. Subsequently, Martin Heidegger argues that hermeneutics should *oppose* empirical inquiry by describing *Dasein*'s pure phenomenological "being-in-the-world."[30] His student Hans-Georg Gadamer interprets this to mean that the proper object of hermeneutics is "historically effected consciousness" or human understanding as it is always already constituted by historical traditions.[31] These developments, however, obscure the relation between hermeneutics and childhood. While children share historical being-in-the-world with adults, they do not share the same historically effected capabilities for its deliberate hermeneutical interpretation.

Fortunately, as Browning has shown, Paul Ricoeur develops a more complex hermeneutical theory. While Ricoeur never addresses the study of childhood, his hermeneutical circle involving "distanciation" proves significantly more useful for childhood studies. This is because, in Ricoeur's view, the historically effected interpretation of human being-in-the-world cannot be carried out apart from larger circular dialogue with the empirical tests of actual experience. Such distanciation occurs whenever one enters what Ricoeur calls the linguistically structured world of a "text," whether that text is a literary classic or an empirically informed human scientific observation. The psychological and social sciences therefore provide one important means for gaining a critical or self-reflective "distance" on one's historically engrained values and assumptions.[32]

29. Wilhelm Dilthey, "The Development of Hermeneutics," in *Selected Writings*, ed. and trans. H. P. Rickman (New York: Cambridge University Press, 1976).

30. Martin Heidegger, *Being and Time*, German original 1926, trans. John Macquarrie and Edward Robinson (New York: Harper & Row, 1962), 30, 31, and 62.

31. Hans-Georg Gadamer, *Truth and Method*, German original 1960, 2d rev. ed., trans. Joel Weinsheimer and Donald G. Marshall (New York: Crossroad, 1992), 265-307.

32. Ricoeur, *Hermeneutics and the Human Sciences*, 43-62 and 131-44.

Such a critical hermeneutical circle has two advantages for childhood studies. First, it includes both "child" and "adult" perspectives as sources of meaning: pre-reflective historical horizons that shape adults' and children's worlds alike, and reflective textual and scientific modes of reflection that are more distinctively adult and toward which children only gradually develop. Children may even, as Ricoeur has suggested for Jerome Berryman, be able to explore this pre-scientific world *more* authentically than adults through their deep capacities for symbolism and play.[33] But only adults (at least in principle) are *fully* capable of making arguments about their tradition-constituted values by subjecting them to cultural and scientific critique and, as a result, taking ultimate responsibility for their own moral perspectives and actions. It is these kinds of critically self-reflective capabilities that make it meaningful to distinguish the terms "child" and "adult" in the first place. Yet the distinction is a matter of degree rather than kind and does not eject children from the hermeneutical circle itself.

Second, a critical hermeneutical circle of this kind shows, methodologically, how children may be studied as at once participants in their shared social worlds and distinctive objects of empirical inquiry. For adults, these two sides of the hermeneutical circle can operate as one: we belong to a moral history that we can also interpret critically for ourselves. But for children this relation or tension of belonging and reflection is relatively undeveloped. Children bring their own interpretive perspectives to their worlds. But the younger the child, the less she or he brings to this interpretation socially *distanciating* capabilities such as scientific observation, falsification of assumptions, cultural comparison, testing against experience, or accounting for others' points of view. As a result, children's well-being depends to a particularly high degree on empirical understanding and response from adults. The younger the child, the more she or he needs adults to stand in, as it were, to provide for them the critical and empirical dimensions of the hermeneutical circle.

The hermeneutical circle of Ricoeur and Browning requires further modification, however, if it is to answer to the full challenge of childism. This modification reflects my own and others' sympathetic revisions of Ricoeurian hermeneutics in a more "postmodern" direction. Childhood raises to an especially sharp degree the problem of what Emmanuel Levinas, Jacques Derrida, John Caputo, Sallie McFague, and Richard

33. Jerome W. Berryman, *Godly Play: An Imaginative Approach to Religious Education* (Minneapolis, MN: Augsburg Fortress, 1991).

Kearney have called the interpretation of "otherness" or "difference." In my view it is possible, indeed necessary, to recognize otherness without (as some have claimed) abandoning the notion of a hermeneutical circle. "Otherness" does not mean "othering" — the marginalization of those who are different. Rather, it refers to the sense in which each singular human being is ultimately *irreducible* to any understanding, narration, or construction of them whatsoever. Levinas claims that no other is fully reducible to anything "said" about them, but is always also its own transcending or infinite "saying" beyond language and meaning (indeed, as a "face" of the Wholly Other).[34] Or as some have argued, a little differently, each "other" person continually escapes interpretation as a linguistic object by virtue of their utter and mysterious *différance* (their difference as endlessly deferred).

A similar modification to our hermeneutical circle is suggested by certain forms of feminism which argue that critique of traditional assumptions needs to be radicalized into critique also of who controls the hermeneutical circle itself by which traditions are interpreted. As Sallie McFague has said of feminist theology, the interpretation of traditional worldviews should be viewed as "metaphorical" in the sense that "good metaphors shock, they bring unlikes together, they upset conventions, they involve tension, and they are implicitly revolutionary."[35] The hermeneutical circle must be performed with an eye to understanding who is being marginalized from participation in the hermeneutical circle itself. It should seek to become ever more responsive to the shock of "others" whose participation has historically been excluded.

Such is especially, if not most profoundly of all, the case with children. Children perhaps more than any other group are prone to having their "saying" capabilities overshadowed by what is "said" by others about them. They are the most easily marginalized segment of society. The fact is that the study of children is of necessity originated and conducted not by children themselves but by adults. Such is the case even in the laudable efforts of social scientists to include children's participation in research, since this participation is still initiated, guided, and interpreted ultimately by grown-ups. The underlying problem is not how to make children equal research participants. It is how to interpret the

34. Emmanuel Levinas, *Otherwise than Being, or Beyond Essence,* French original 1974, trans. Alphonso Lingis (Pittsburg, PA: Duquesne University Press, 1981), 46.

35. Sallie McFague, *Metaphorical Theology: Models of God in Religious Language* (Philadelphia, PA: Fortress Press, 1982), 17.

meaning and status of children in their "otherness" when children more than any other group cannot fully interpret their own otherness for themselves.

The hermeneutical circle of childhood studies should therefore include what I would call a decentering or asymmetrical moment. It should, perhaps, be a hermeneutical *ellipse* orbiting not one point but two: the interpreter and the interpreter's irreducible other. The problem of interpreting childhood in society makes the need for an asymmetrical hermeneutical circle especially evident. Children's experiences must be allowed to disrupt and constantly open up even the interpretive assumptions adults bring to them. Ricoeurian "distanciation" must be radicalized into a hermeneutical "decentering" in which traditional ethical assumptions are open-endedly tested through dialogue with empirical, textual, and moral difference. Oddly enough, such a task returns us in a certain sense to Schleiermacher's divination of the child (and humanity) as gift. Children demand from adults an interpretation of not only their sameness to adults but also their irreducibility and even mystery. However, through a more sophisticated hermeneutical circle based on Browning and Ricoeur, this gift need not become romanticized — which is itself a form of marginalization. Rather, children's gifts of meaning to the world may be provided concrete interpretive responses by adults and society through the hard, tireless, and ultimately endless work of better understanding children's distinctive voices and experiences.

The Theological Ethics of Childhood

Theological ethicists, from this perspective, should seek to engage in the field of childhood studies through the fullest possible dimensions of such a hermeneutical circle. Top-down ethical critique of the social sciences and bottom-up experiential learning from them should be placed in dynamic and critical tension with one another. In this way, theological ethics may more readily function, as it frequently has in history, in a genuinely creative and transforming way: responsive to new understandings and situations but also productive of new insight and debate.

Allow me to illustrate this theological ethical role by discussing perhaps the most important claim of the new childhood studies literature in the social sciences: namely that children should be understood as social "agents." Children's agency has taken a central place in the sociology, anthropology, history, law, and other studies of childhood in Europe and now increasingly in the United States. According to a recent interpretation, children's agency means that "children's actions affect their worlds and especially their social worlds," so that childhood studies "emphasizes children's quest to make sense of their world and to construct a good fit with it."[36] The study of children's agency is the study of how children participate in creating their social environments, exercise their own social competencies, act diversely rather than stereotypically, construct independent ideas and meaning, and help to interpret their own cultures, communities, and identities. Agency also includes "voice," which "puts the focus on children's commitment to *make known* their own ability to act on their own behalf, whether to ensure their own interests or to modify the world that surrounds them."[37]

The appeal of this language of children's agency is twofold. First, it helps the social sciences distinguish themselves from the otherwise dominant methods of developmental psychology, which, it is argued, start from the point of view of what children *are not yet*, namely developed adults, rather than what they are and can do in and of themselves, as well as in their full cultural and individual diversity. While some would argue this critique is unfair, nevertheless a stand is taken that you cannot understand childhood without understanding children as competent and diverse social actors. Second, and more important for our purposes, the notion of children's agency is appealing because it suggests an alternative to how children have generally been understood throughout history. Children actively participate in their social worlds rather than being passive recipients of adult socialization. This claim expands and further develops the Enlightenment view, beginning in the work of John Locke and Jean-Jacques Rousseau, that "unenlightened" practices of child rearing ignore children's distinctive human capabilities.[38] What is added by the new social sciences perspective, however, is both an empirically precise method of stripping away easy adult preconceptions about childhood and, most important, a resulting and perhaps even unprecedented appreciation for children's own social agency in all its fullness and complexity.

To the ear of a theological ethicist, however, this emphasis on children's agency raises significant questions. The notion that agency defines what it means to be human has profound problems even when it comes

36. Peter B. Pufall and Richard P. Unsworth, "Introduction: The Imperative and the Process for Rethinking Childhood" in *Rethinking Childhood*, ed. Peter B. Pufall and Richard P. Unsworth (New Brunswick, NJ: Rutgers University Press, 2004), 9.

37. Pufall and Unsworth, "Introduction" (emphasis added).

38. See further chapter by M. Christian Green herein.

to adults. Postmodern ethics of various kinds has shown that human life in society is fundamentally conditioned by a number of *non*-agential factors. These include historical and cultural traditions, shared social narratives, systems of power, commitments to common goods, biological and evolutionary needs, intersubjective norms of dialogue and relationship, transcending sources of social meaning, and needs for receptivity and responsiveness toward persons and cultures that are other. Jürgen Habermas argues that since ethics confronts human life with a "pluralism of ultimate value orientations," it must be grounded ultimately not in the expression of subjective agency but in procedures of larger "intersubjective discourse" that allow for mutual dialogue to arise and flourish *between* diverse points of view.[39] Ricoeur has criticized one-sided ethics of agency as masking the mere utilitarian pursuit of self-interest in which the powerless silently lose out.[40] More emphatically, Levinas has shown how the ethics of agency can be used to justify social violence (Levinas himself was a Jewish survivor of the Holocaust) in permitting those with the greatest social agency to "totalize" shared moral worlds. Ethics should begin, according to Levinas, in agency's very opposite: the otherness of the other calling the self to "a passivity more passive still than the passivity of matter."[41]

From the hermeneutical point of view developed above, persons are both agents and patients at once, capable of interpreting their social worlds but also in turn always interpreted by those social worlds and by others within them. As Ricoeur has argued (in a way that I view as more complex than in either Habermas or Levinas), moral, intellectual, and affective life are everywhere voluntary and involuntary at once, both constituting from within and constituted from without, so that agency is but one point in a larger hermeneutical circle necessary for forming social meaning.[42] The Christian tradition supports such a view by qualifying human agency or freedom by humanity also being primordially fallible

39. Jürgen Habermas, *Moral Consciousness and Communicative Action,* German original 1983, trans. Christian Lenhardt and Shierry Weber Nicholsen (Cambridge, MA: The MIT Press, 1990), 66 and 76.

40. Paul Ricoeur, "Love and Justice," French original 1990, in Ricoeur, *Figuring the Sacred: Religion, Narrative, and Imagination,* ed. Mark I. Wallace, trans. David Pellauer (Minneapolis, MN: Fortress Press, 1995), 329.

41. Levinas, *Otherwise than Being,* 15.

42. Paul Ricoeur, *Freedom and Nature: The Voluntary and the Involuntary,* French original 1950, trans. Erazim V. Kohák (Evanston, IL: Northwestern University Press, 1966).

and, hence, ultimately dependent on sources of meaning larger than itself. For Ricoeur this means that love for others is not just an autonomous act (as in the classic Enlightenment ethics of Immanuel Kant) but also the placing of ultimate faith in an already given goodness of creation. As he puts it, moral agency takes place within the context of an "economy of the gift" in which the reception of a sense of one's own "given" human goodness makes it possible in turn to imagine resisting one's own participation in evil and "giving" a more superabundant love to others.[43] Or, as Richard Kearney has similarly put it, moral life should involve neither pure agency nor pure prostration before the other — each of which he calls a form of "idolatry" — but rather a constantly self-transforming "practical wisdom" that seeks through love of others ever broader "interlacings of alterities."[44] If the Christian tradition has sometimes moved too far away from agency by emphasizing self-sacrifice, a hermeneutical perspective reminds us that love is ultimately interactive, mutual, responsive, and productive of new social relations.

On these grounds, theological ethics may make at least two important forms of critique of the recent social science emphasis on children's agency. First, one can argue for a more complex view of children in and of themselves. As full human beings, children do not simply act on their world but rather interact in a passive-active way with a world that itself shapes and influences their interpretations of their experiences. As well as conditions like history, culture, power, and community, children also face the moral condition of having to learn to respond in an active-passive way to others. Respecting children's full humanity involves recognizing their fullest dimensions as both actively participating in and passively belonging to larger moral worlds. Indeed, few adults would, in the end, welcome being treated one-dimensionally as agents alone. Overemphasizing children's agency is just as simplistic and therefore dehumanizing as overemphasizing their need to be molded and socialized.

Second, a more interdependent understanding of childhood demands more complex thinking about the responsibilities owed children by adults. It is true that adults need to better appreciate children's own agential competencies. However, adults and society should also recognize the special depths of children's human vulnerability. For example,

43. Ricoeur, "Love and Justice," 315-29.

44. Richard Kearney, *Strangers, Gods, and Monsters: Interpreting Otherness* (New York: Routledge, 2003), 12.

mass media advertising does not simply confront children with a potential loss of social agency but, more important, can take advantage of children's market passivity or receptivity in a more profound way than it may adults'. The younger a child, the easier it becomes to manipulate his or her wants and desires for independent or harmful adult ends. Failing to see children as not just agents in but also patients of their larger social worlds ironically obscures their being influenced by adult ambitions and exposes them to greater rather than lesser manipulation.

Such a critique of the one-sidedness of talk of children's agency could also be carried forward into a similar critique of the social sciences' adoption of the language of children's "rights," although we can only touch on this question briefly here. From a hermeneutical point of view, children require both "negative" rights to protection and appropriate participation and "positive" rights to state and social aid. This point is lost on those in the United States, particularly as informed by the above-referenced form of communitarianism, who largely reject rights language as such or who view children only through the lens of family life. Children in this country would be significantly better off in many ways with stronger rights to health, economic well-being, and a social voice, as outlined in the 1989 United Nations Convention on the Rights of the Child (which the United States is only one of two countries in the world not to have ratified). If rights language has limitations it also sets a basic groundwork for treatment with full human dignity that too many children clearly lack.

However, as Browning has emphasized, rights language when it comes to children should also be balanced with languages of adult responsibility.[45] This can be seen by considering such children's rights in the U.N. Convention as "freedom of expression" (Article 13), "freedom of thought, conscience and religion" (Article 14), and mass media "access to information" (Article 17). Expression, conscience, religion, and mass media information are issues, for children more acutely than for adults, not just of freedom and access — norms grounded in human agency — but also of nurturance, dependency, and guidance. The special relation of children's rights to adult responsibilities was more clearly recognized in earlier international agreements in 1924 and 1959 on which the 1989 Convention is partly based. Here one finds significantly more central language of adult and societal "duty" toward children, "responsibilities" for "special safeguards and care," and children's needs for "special protection" and extra

45. Don Browning, "The United Nations Convention on the Rights of the Child: Should it be Ratified and Why?" *Emory International Law Review* 20 (2006): 157-83.

"love and understanding."[46] The language of adult responsibility, while not absent in the 1989 Convention, in earlier agreements provides a clearer recognition that children are not just little adult agents deserving the same rights as all, but also profoundly vulnerable, relational, conditioned, and in need of special care from others. My own view, which I cannot defend here, is that "rights" in light of children are not expressions of individual autonomy but mark distanciating second points of otherness in a hermeneutical moral ellipse that demand society's self-creative attention.

In these and many other ways, the contemporary field of childhood studies would be greatly enriched by more complex ethical inquiry. Theological ethics could play a vital role in bringing its diverse languages and traditions to this task. Its special expertise in this area does not qualify it to dominate all social debate, but it does provide the occasion for a much needed critique of the contemporary world's child-related ethical assumptions. Social scientists, psychologists, and society at large cannot avoid using ethical language concerning children because children's lives have important ethical dimensions. What is more, childhood studies as a discipline contains inherent ethical aims and ambitions, such as the improvement of children's lives and respect for their diverse experiences. A full hermeneutical circle of childhood studies suggests that theological ethics has a significant responsibility — both to the childhood studies field and to children themselves — for assessing and helping to shape such underlying normative understandings.

How Childhood Studies Should Transform Theological Ethics

The question remains how consideration of childhood may or should in turn transform theological ethics. Here, one might say, is the disciplinary pay-off, the chance to rethink ethical methods and norms so as to reimagine not only childhood but also ethics itself. There are many possible ways in which this might happen. At a minimum, including childhood challenges theological ethics to involve a greater sense of what I call "creative responsibility."[47] Such a norm mirrors substantively what I have been

46. See the "Geneva Declaration of the Rights of the Child" adopted by the League of Nations (the precursor to the U.N.) in 1924; and the U.N.'s "Declaration of the Rights of the Child" of 1959.

47. See my *Moral Creativity: Paul Ricoeur and the Poetics of Possibility* (New York: Oxford University Press, 2005), chap. 3.

arguing for methodologically. Childhood shows in the strongest possible terms that human beings are responsible for one another. But it also presses ordinary understandings of moral responsibility toward their received and radically creative dimensions, dimensions in which *those responsible* are called to the decentering, disruption, and asymmetrical transformation of their received and assumed moral horizons. Beyond closely related feminist and liberationist norms of inclusive participation, what may be called a "childist" theological ethics requires the ever new creation of one's own moral worlds in a way inclusively responsive to others.

What the psychological and social sciences of childhood truly reveal is not just children's distinctive capabilities and agency, important though these are, but, in a more complex way, the kinds of *tension* that exist between children's agency and their larger surrounding worlds. Let us take, for example, the issue of children's poverty in the United States. Children in this country have the highest rates of poverty in the developed world for a number of interlocking reasons: lack of government assistance, massive economic inequality, racism, high rates of divorce and teen parenthood, the economic marginalization of mothers, a culture of extreme individualism, children's commodification and sentimentalization, and much more. Such social conditions, certainly beyond the control of children themselves (not to mention to varying degrees the adults around them), create the "perfect storm" for children to become (as they did in the 1970s, surpassing the elderly) the poorest group in society, with the youngest of the children statistically the poorest.[48]

Empirical studies of these multiple conditions do in fact suggest ways in which children exercise social agency, such as through resilience to poverty's effects, awareness of family situation, support of parental employment, self-limitation of wants, and capabilities to adapt and grow even under the severest conditions. However, they also reveal a massive failure of American society to respond to the needs of its most vulnerable members, and indeed to respond to human vulnerability as such. The problem faced in children's poverty is not just children's lack of social participation. The problem, more fundamentally, is that "social participation" in the United States today is defined in primarily adult, individualistic, market competitive, and utilitarian ways, so that children are bound to lose out. As Barbara Bennett Woodhouse has argued, American

48. Statistics on child poverty can be found, among other places, at the United States Census Bureau, www.census.gov, P60-210, and the Annie E. Casey Foundation's "Kids Count Data Book" at www.aecf.org.

"rights" language tends to emphasize this kind of state-free autonomy over state support for needs and dignity.[49] Or, as Jürgen Habermas would put it, the life-world of children (both within and outside families) has been thoroughly "colonized" by the values of the marketplace, values which happen to be chiefly agential and adult.[50]

Through various techniques of careful observation, the human sciences stand in a unique position, methodologically, to dig beneath assumptions and stereotypes and explain what makes American child poverty so problematic. This is the case in at least three important respects. First, they can explain how poverty plays into children's underlying developmental vulnerabilities. For example, the younger a child is, the fewer basic capabilities he or she is likely to possess for such things as securing social capital, supporting parents leaving home to work, resisting mass media exploitation to sell toys, or making heard his or her plight. Second, the human sciences can describe the unique conditions that contribute toward poverty in contemporary families. For example, families in the United States bear significant burdens for children's health and economic well-being so that high rates of family and marital disruption represent a major cause of children's economic hardship. And third, the human sciences can map the multiple and diverse ways in which children's poverty is related to larger social structures. These include inequalities in the job market, impacts of mass media, and access to political power. The human sciences are particularly well suited to understanding such experiences from the point of view of children because empirical methods can test and disrupt the ordinary assumptions by which adults so easily oversimplify children's lives. Somewhat like in environmental ethics, the theological ethics of childhood relies deeply on empirical observation for fully understanding the complexities of its subject.

Substantively, such observations help theological ethicists see, among other things, that ordinary adult conceptions of moral responsibility toward one another may not be adequate to the kind of responsibilities owed to children. The theological ethics of love, for example, may look different when confronted with children's being trained by mass media into a culture of consumerism. Love in this case is not served well by either treating children as equal to adults or initiating children into

49. Barbara Bennett Woodhouse, "Re-Visioning Rights for Children," in *Rethinking Childhood,* ed. Peter B. Pufall and Richard P. Unsworth (New Brunswick, NJ: Rutgers University Press, 2004), 229-43.

50. Jürgen Habermas, *The Theory of Communicative Action,* vol. 2, *Lifeworld and System: A Critique of Functionalist Reason,* German original 1981, trans. Thomas McCarthy (Boston: Beacon Press, 1987), 325, 355, and 367-73.

anti-market moral values. Love may require instead a middle approach in which children are nurtured to engage with increasingly critical and creative capabilities their pervasive media and market surroundings. It may also need to confront market distortions of love into an ethic of "giving children what they want." As Daniel Cook and others have shown, the marketing industry believes it is doing good for children by responding to children's "agency" in this way.[51] The empirical work of the social sciences shows that ignoring the reality of the situation is just as problematic as ignoring the special problem it raises for children.

A more adequate interpretation of social responsibility may be developed also by bringing a childist perspective on children's experiences to the Bible. For example, the very first command from God to humanity is the Genesis 1:28 injunction to "be fruitful and multiply." As having just been created "in the image of God," humanity is asked to understand itself somewhat like its own Creator as, primordially, a generative, reproductive, creative being. Most obviously this command implies reproduction of a biological kind, making it inherently related to children. But it can also suggest — as thinkers like Henri Bergson, Martin Buber, Gustavo Gutiérrez, Philip Hefner, and Elizabeth Johnson have variously shown[52] — a broader responsibility for *social* reproduction, so that responsibility for offspring offers a symbol or model for human responsibility overall. Responding to children's poverty, for example, can be placed in the light of a broader human responsibility for meaningful social reproduction. Just as God created the world, so also is humanity as

51. See Daniel Thomas Cook, in *Commodification of Childhood* (Durham, NC: Duke University Press, 2004).

52. Henri Bergson, *Creative Evolution,* French original 1907, trans. Arthur Mitchell (Westport, CT: Greenwood Press, 1944), 10, 27, 271, 274, 287-88, and 292; Martin Buber, *On the Bible: Eighteen Studies by Martin Buber* (New York: Schocken Books, 1968), 72 and 87; Gustavo Gutiérrez, *A Theology of Liberation: History, Politics, and Salvation,* Spanish original 1971, 15th anniversary rev. ed., trans. Sister Caridad Inda and John Eagleson (Maryknoll, NY: Orbis Books, 1988), 168; Philip Hefner, *The Human Factor: Evolution, Culture, and Religion* (Minneapolis, MN: Fortress Press, 1993), 239; and Elizabeth A. Johnson, *Women, Earth, and Creator Spirit* (New York: Paulist Press, 1993), 38. Classical sources for an interpretation of Genesis 1:27-28 include Mathetes, *Epistle of Mathetes to Diogenes,* in *The Apostolic Fathers* (Grand Rapids, MI: William B. Eerdmans Publishing Company, 1975), chap. 10; Clement of Alexandria, *Stromateis* (Washington, DC: Catholic University of America Press, 1991), Bk. II, chap. 19; Origen, *Contra Celsum,* trans. Henry Chadwick (New York: Cambridge University Press, 1953), Bk. VIII, chap. 18; and Moses Maimonides, *A Guide for the Perplexed,* trans. Michael Friedländer (New York: E. P. Dutton, 1904), chap. 54.

God's image obliged to create or co-create its own social world ever anew, on a paradigm of parental and social fruitfulness and multiplication through care, love, and nurturance of the next generation.

Other biblical groundings of morality are also significantly shaped by considerations of childhood. These include the original "innocence" of Adam and Eve as symbolic of ultimate human goodness; Abraham's social covenant as building a nation around future offspring; Jesus' incarnation in this world as an infant; the blessedness in the beatitudes of the meek; the gospel symbolism of becoming "children of God"; and, as mentioned before, Jesus placing a child in the midst of his surprised disciples to explain who enters the kingdom of heaven. While the Bible certainly also marginalizes children, there is nevertheless a strong vein of ancient Jewish and Christian moral teaching that suggests that a less fallen society calls for responsiveness to the nature and meaning of children's lives. This child-centered moral possibility has been taken up throughout Christian theological history.[53]

My own interpretation of the significance of childhood for theological ethics — in all of children's empirical, religious, and social dimensions — reflects normatively the kind of postmodern hermeneutical perspective I have been advancing. That is, childhood calls society to be "fruitful and multiply" in a circular, self-disruptive, asymmetrical, and ongoingly self-transforming sense. From a child-centered point of view, human moral responsibility includes responding to the vulnerabilities of others — such as their poverty, incapacity, or powerlessness — in a self- and socially creative way. What must be disrupted or re-created most of all is the world of those who hold social opportunities and power. Marginalized members of society such as children are not only "other" in the negative sense of demanding *not* to be oppressed but also "other" in the positive sense of requiring a different and new response from those who influence their lives.

In the case of children in particular, this responsibility is deeply circular. What is required is both the social self-creativity of the adults around them and the gradual development of social self-creative capabilities within children themselves. These have their beginnings in children's play and imagination, but they also need to be nurtured into competencies for engaging with and changing society. All of us to one degree or another

53. Marcia Bunge, ed., *The Child in Christian Thought* (Grand Rapids, MI: Eerdmans, 2001); and O. M. Bakke, *When Children Became People: The Birth of Childhood in Early Christianity* (Minneapolis, MN: Fortress Press, 2005).

desire not only to participate in society for ourselves but also to have society respond in turn to our own incapacities, vulnerabilities, and dependencies. Moral responsibility involves, in this case, not just reciprocity and equality but also a moment of ethical distanciation that opens the worlds of those responsible to surprising and disruptive transformation. This moment of distantiation may be called a "right" in a postmodern sense. From a childist point of view, moral responsibility is neither equally reciprocal nor authoritarian but asymmetrical or decentering. It involves what Augustine in his *Confessions* calls "distension":[54] the creative "stretching out" *(distensio)* of comfortable moral horizons in response to what they exclude, as well as a continuing effort to draw others and oneself into mutually creative social participation.

Such an endlessly self-creative social responsibility arguably articulates something profound in the Christian ethical message. The dependency of humanity on God should open each of us to the important ways in which human beings are radically dependent upon one another. Responsibility for children as "the least among us" shines a particularly strong light on what it means to love fellow creatures of God overall. A sense of responsibility to human vulnerability is suggested in the gospel meaning of the Golden Rule: "Do to others as you would have them do to you" (Luke 6:31). As Ricoeur and others have argued, this formulation implies a double substitution: you are asked to imagine yourself as a *recipient* of another's actions so as to understand your own moral *agency* from another's point of view.[55] The Golden Rule puts you in the position of the one responsible, but from the point of view of the one you may potentially victimize. It demands two moral centers at once: yourself and the other. This decentering function of the Golden Rule is further radicalized by its immediately following Jesus' extreme love command: "Love your enemies, do good to those who hate you, bless those who curse you, pray for those who abuse you" (Luke 6:27-28). The juxtaposition of such an asymmetrical or radical love command on the Golden Rule protects the latter from being reduced to any easy reciprocity or exchange. It renders moral responsibility a demand for superabundance toward others in the service of realizing a more fully common humanity.

From this angle, the child may be viewed as contemporary morality's greatest test. The work of the human sciences shows the diversity of

54. See Augustine, *Confessions,* Bk. 11.

55. Ricoeur, "Love and Justice," 324; and "Ethical and Theological Considerations on the Golden Rule" in Ricoeur, *Figuring the Sacred,* 301.

ways in which children's lives are disenfranchised but also deeply resilient. It can map the complex contours of problems like children's persistent poverty or relations to mass media. But theological ethics must step in to help imagine how to make children a creative new response. To do to a child as you would have done to yourself is to respond to the profoundest possible depths of human otherness and marginality with a radically self-transforming love and hope. It is to open oneself and one's social world to reversing ingrained exclusions and oversimplifications through ever more other-inclusive moral horizons. Responsibility for children in both families and society reveals the extent to which moral life is not just a fixed reality but also a transcending journey of creative response and renewal.

Conclusion

Whatever normative conclusions may be drawn, theological ethicists ignore the unique situation of children and childhood at their own peril. Neglecting marginalized groups like women and racial minorities weakened the voice of theological ethics in the past, both by silently playing into larger social wrongs and by failing to learn and grow from those silenced. Childhood in the United States and the world presents theological ethics today with a new and different but just as acute social challenge. Don Browning's work in theological hermeneutics and family ethics has opened up fresh new horizons for child-centered methodologies and norms. The next step is to press theological ethics in a fully childist direction, one that not only studies childhood and its contexts, but also takes the perspectives and experiences of children as grounds for rethinking theological ethics itself. This gesture of responsiveness and self-critique has already begun to animate the human sciences. How much more, then, should it be welcomed and deepened further by Christian ethicists who in one way or another trace a transformed world to the possibilities incarnated in an infant's birth.

6 Judge William and Professor Browning: A Kierkegaardian Critique of Equal-Regard Marriage and the Democratic Family

Timothy P. Jackson

Introduction: The Priority of Agapic Love to Natural Justice

Don Browning forgets in a day more about sex, marriage, and the family than I will learn in my lifetime. Moreover, he writes on these matters with striking intelligence and grace, always including in his work charitable summaries and fair criticisms of a wide range of opposing views. Indeed, Professor Browning is akin to Søren Kierkegaard's wise pseudonym, "Judge William," who would defend marriage against its sophisticated detractors and thereby call modern (and modernized) aesthetes to a more ethical existence. I myself am moved by the moral seriousness of Browning's "critical familism" and convinced by many of its concrete prescriptions for the reconfiguration of relations between husbands, wives, and children. My main thesis, nevertheless, is that Browning's account of marital love as "equal regard" is inadequate for his purposes. In accenting "mutuality" between spouses, it puts the cart before the horse, seeing a fruit or secondary accompaniment of love as its heart and soul. It thereby risks reducing sacramental covenant to contractual justice, something that Browning himself has repeatedly warned against.

Browning is well aware that there are competing views of marital love. Alone and with co-authors, he dedicates several volumes to exploring the cultural assumptions and consequences of three models of love: mutuality, self-sacrifice, and self-fulfillment. Browning and colleagues document contemporary "struggles over how to define and balance sacrifice, mutuality, and individual fulfillment," but they defend what they call "the ideal of the equal regard, mother-father, public-private partnership."[1] They explain that they "use 'equal regard' to describe a relationship between husband and wife characterized by mutual respect, affection, practical assistance, and justice — a relationship that values and aids the self and other with equal seriousness."[2] Equal regard has its place, to be sure, and I certainly do not want to endorse *un*equal regard or *in*justice between spouses. But, in the spirit of Kierkegaard, I offer a contrasting picture of marriage and the family based on *agape,* a love that is not really about reciprocity or the lack of it. Such love accents three things that Browning's ideal deemphasizes: the primacy of the God-relation, the unconditional character of the marital bond, and openness to sacrifice for the sake of the other rather than for the sake of the relation.[3]

I begin the body of this chapter by looking carefully at an *un*ethical (but not uncommon) perspective on marriage and the family, represented by Kierkegaard's pseudonym "A." I then turn first to Judge William's and next to Kierkegaard's appraisal of marital and familial relations, showing the strengths and weaknesses of both. Against this background, I am at last able both to appreciate and to criticize Don Browning's work at length. My critique of Browning is recognizably "Kierkegaardian" in inspiration, but by no means do I agree with all of Kierkegaard's main theses. The moral of my story is that, as high an ethical achievement as is mutuality in marriage, it is not sufficient to save the modern family, religious or secular. Christ came into the world to reveal a divine agapic love that transcends natural justice, and Christians ought never to conflate the two or confuse their proper ordering. Such moves are to be avoided not only because you cannot have justice without love, but also because agapic love is itself the highest good in any sphere of life. Equality and respect are worth championing, especially in "political" contexts that involve conflict but including the supposedly "personal" domain of companionate marriage. These values remain subordinate, however, to the grace Christians believe is captured by the *imitatio Christi.* The personal may be the political, as some feminists ar-

1. Don S. Browning, Bonnie J. Miller-McLemore, Pamela D. Couture, K. Brynolf Lyon, and Robert M. Franklin, *From Culture Wars to Common Ground: Religion and the American Family Debate,* 2d ed. (Louisville: Westminster John Knox Press, 2000), 18 and 7.

2. Browning et al., *From Culture Wars to Common Ground,* 2.

3. My perspective on love is very close to that of Mary Murphy, one of Browning et al.'s interviewees. Browning and his colleagues have some sympathy for Ms. Murphy's views, but they explicitly reject them in favor of Maria Taylor et al.'s celebration of mutuality and equal regard. See Browning et al., *From Culture Wars to Common Ground,* esp. 104-5.

gue, but the political and the personal must both bow in Christians to the prophetic.

Two Pseudonyms on Love, Marriage, and Equality

"A"

In *Either/Or,* Part II, Kierkegaard's "Judge William" responds in a series of letters to a young man who is determined to live his life on purely aesthetic terms. The youth, known initially merely as "A," lives for the sake of personal pleasure and passing amusement. He is no crude sensualist, since he seeks primarily intellectual distraction and social intrigue, rather than physical gratification. But, for him, existence is without moral point and choice does not finally condition the chooser: one remains free to skim along the surface of life unencumbered by the past.

A is a connoisseur of music and literature — especially such erotic classics as Mozart's "Don Giovanni" and Goethe's "Faust" — as well as an astute psychologist. But, for him, cultural beauty and the soul itself are but shallow and transitory things. Time is a collection of vanishing moments that have no real significance, so the challenge of life is to keep it "interesting" by "rotating the crops." One must love nothing devotedly and commit to no one permanently, for this would inevitably become tawdry and tedious. One must not be weighed down by past memories or even buoyed up by future hopes, for this would imply that some action or event can define you. Sublime detachment in an ether of pure possibility is the order of the day: "No part of life ought to have so much meaning for a person that he cannot forget it any moment he wants to; on the other hand, every single part of life ought to have so much meaning for a person that he can remember it at any moment."[4] Approached in this way, every instant of time is like every other: a thought experiment without lived continuity or purpose.

In short, A is the perfect anti-Kantian. He is moved by mood and inclination, rather than by reason and will; not the ethical performance of duty, but the poetic avoidance of boredom, is the maxim of his action. Other people, especially women, are to be used for their entertainment value. Woman is especially vulnerable to dalliance and abuse, according to A, because she is more devoted and self-sacrificial than man. Being

4. Søren Kierkegaard (A/Johannes the Seducer), *Either/Or,* Part I, trans. Howard V. Hong and Edna H. Hong (Princeton: Princeton University Press, 1987), 293.

physically weaker than man and more prey to emotions like fear, she is simultaneously more charming and less dignified, more coy and less self-aware. As A puts it, woman is "the weaker sex" whose "essence is a devotedness that takes the form of resistance."[5]

Above all, marriage is to be shunned as a bourgeois custom that saps a man's world of its romance. A insists, "Never become involved in *marriage.* Married people pledge love for each other throughout eternity. Well, now, that is easy enough but does not mean very much, for if one is finished with time one is probably finished with eternity."[6] To vow to remain with, and limit oneself sexually to, one woman[7] is the very image of unlovely ennui. "Even friendship is dangerous; marriage is still more dangerous, for the woman is and will be the man's ruination as soon as he contracts a continuing relationship with her. Take a young man, spirited as an Arabian horse; let him marry and he is lost. At the outset, the woman is proud, then she is weak, then she swoons, then the whole family swoons."[8]

I find in A's unsystematic remarks three related, but distinguishable, objections to marriage: (1) it involves an insupportable view of temporal constancy: the wife's appeal will eventually fade, and the husband's attention will inevitably lapse; (2) it entails a destruction of masculine freedom and achievement: the wife is needy and dependent, if not dishonest, and the husband will be domesticated by her "swoons"; and (3) it is simply an enemy of the erotic: male desire craves novelty and numbers, both of which are precluded by conventional matrimony. There is clearly an underlying misogyny in much of this. A goes so far as to say that "a woman's love is only pretense and weakness."[9]

This is not to say that A offers a principled defense of bachelorhood as a superior state; he is too elusive and ambivalent for such an earnest conviction. His being oscillates between tragic skepticism and comic aloofness, a flight from actuality that is tinged with not a little self-pity. As A writes,

> Marry, and you will regret it. Do not marry, and you will also regret it. Marry or do not marry, you will regret it either way. Whether you marry or you do not marry, you will regret it either way. . . . Trust a

5. Kierkegaard, *Either/Or,* 339 and 388. These quotations are from "The Seducer's Diary," but, as I note below, I believe A to be the author of these pages too.

6. Kierkegaard, *Either/Or,* 296.

7. A is assuming a norm of heterosexual marriage, of course, and he writes from an unabashedly male point of view.

8. Kierkegaard, *Either/Or,* 297.

9. Kierkegaard, *Either/Or,* 297.

> girl, and you will regret it. Do not trust her, and you will also regret it. Trust a girl or do not trust a girl, you will regret it either way. Whether you trust a girl or [you] do not trust a girl, you will regret it either way. . . . This, gentlemen, is the quintessence of all the wisdom of life.[10]

A's depiction of reflective aestheticism, presented in Part I of *Either/Or,* comes to a climax in "The Seducer's Diary." In these pages, also largely a series of letters (with commentary), we watch one "Johannes" ruthlessly manipulate "his Cordelia." He toys with both her soul and her body, so orchestrating things that she is the one who first proposes the overstepping of social convention and moral propriety. It is Cordelia, that is, who suggests a tryst in which she will give herself to Johannes physically, as well as emotionally. Johannes makes it clear that he has no real longing to possess her carnally; it is "the interesting" — the thrill of the hunt, the will to power — that engages him. As A says, "the enjoyment consists not in what I enjoy but in getting my own way."[11] After Johannes has bedded her, he wants nothing more to do with Cordelia:

> But now it is finished, and I never want to see her again. When a girl has given away everything, she is weak, she has lost everything, for in a man innocence is a negative moment, but in a woman it is the substance of her being. . . . I shall not bid her farewell; nothing is more revolting than the feminine tears and pleas that alter everything and yet are essentially meaningless. I did love her, but from now on she can no longer occupy my soul.[12]

The editor of A's aesthetic papers, "Victor Eremita," believes that "Johannes" the seducer is actually A himself, and I assume as much in my own analysis. More to the point, I read "The Seducer's Diary" as Kierkegaard's pseudonymous effort to write the tale of a roué who is more "Faustian" than Faust. Goethe's Johannes Faust is a brilliantly complex fellow, having degrees in law and theology, but he still needs the supernatural help of Mephistopheles to win his Gretchen. Moreover, Faust "desires immediacy [in the form of the young woman] not spiritually but sensually,"[13] according to Johannes. Perhaps most important,

10. Kierkegaard, *Either/Or,* 38-39.
11. Kierkegaard, *Either/Or,* 31.
12. Kierkegaard, *Either/Or,* 445.
13. Kierkegaard, *Either/Or,* 207.

Faust ultimately repents and is saved. Kierkegaard's Johannes, in contrast, pulls off his "intensive" schemes all by himself with a cold-blooded and unapologetic efficiency that puts the German seducer in the shade. As noted, he wants not sensual gratification with an innocent young girl but aesthetic entertainment from a Cordelia at the height of her female powers. Typical of Johannes is his declaration: "I own nothing; I desire to own nothing; I love nothing; I have nothing to lose."[14] We can only guess what becomes of SK's seducer in the end, but his salvation seems unlikely.

"Judge William"

In opposition to A's aestheticism stands Kierkegaard's pseudonymous ethicist, Judge William. William accuses A of loving "the accidental" and of wanting to be always merely an observer of existence, living in an "aimless fantasy."[15] As a result, A's life has no abiding meaning, no concrete reality. At the heart of William's alternative view is the theme of willing continuity for one's personality by respecting others, keeping promises, and generally doing one's duty. "Above all, he writes, "have a little more respect for woman."[16] In doing one's duty, one determines to make one's past words and deeds binding on one's future actions and desires, thus one revolutionizes the experience of time. Temporal moments are no longer simply fleeting instants, vanishing without a trace into the past, but rather the present context of ethical decisions that deeply qualify the self. The central ethical decision that defines a man, according to William, is that of marriage to one woman. The marriage vow is the quintessential example of committing oneself over time to a particular identity and relationship. With the performative utterance "I do," an eternal resolve is brought into the flux of time, thereby infinitizing it and one's own spirit.

William, a married man, does not simply set marital fidelity at odds with aesthetic enjoyment; on the contrary, he spends a great deal of time defending what he calls "the esthetic validity of marriage." He seeks to convince A that "the eroticism of first love," which the bachelor prefers to commitment, is not denied or lost but rather deepened by marriage. Wil-

14. Kierkegaard, *Either/Or*, 327.
15. Kierkegaard, *Either/Or*, 7.
16. Kierkegaard, *Either/Or*, 207.

liam "fights," as he puts it, for "the enormous task of showing that marriage is the transfiguration of the first love and not its annihilation, is its friend and not its enemy."[17] For him, Christian spirituality is against, not "the joy and fullness that are in the sensuous in its innocence," but rather "the selfish," the egotism that often characterizes erotic relations governed only by "mood."[18]

In short, Judge William is the perfect Kantian. He would lift A out of his aesthetic self-absorption, which William equates with "despair," and into "the ethical," understood as "the universal" and "the abstract."[19] The universal is all persons and one's duties to them, duties that are the categorical dictates of conscience rather than contingent and mutable preferences. "The ethical takes the form of law,"[20] William avers, and one notes that, in good Kantian fashion, this law is self-legislated. Even a married couple ought to transform and ennoble their relationship by "making love an obligation, an obligation they impose upon themselves face to face with a higher power."[21] At the heart of duty, in turn, is radically free choice: one is to will oneself into ethical existence by affirming one's dignity as a free agent, a dignity that transcends accidents of time and place. An individual is impacted by actions and events in the spatio-temporal world, but he can still express "his sovereignty over himself" by seeing his concrete life as a "task."[22] In William's words:

> A human being's eternal dignity lies precisely in this, that he can gain a history. The divine in him lies in this, that he himself, if he so chooses, can give this history continuity, because it gains that, not when it is a summary of what has taken place or has happened to me, but only when it is my personal deed in such a way that even that which has happened to me is transformed and transferred from necessity to freedom.
>
> As a product [of a specific environment] he [the individual] is squeezed into the forms of actuality; in the choice he makes himself elastic, transforms everything exterior into interiority. He has his place in the world; in freedom he himself chooses his place — that is, he chooses this place. He is a specific individual; in the choice he

17. Kierkegaard, *Either/Or*, 31.
18. Kierkegaard, *Either/Or*, 49.
19. Kierkegaard, *Either/Or*, 255.
20. Kierkegaard, *Either/Or*, 255.
21. Kierkegaard, *Either/Or*, 56.
22. Kierkegaard, *Either/Or*, 251.

> makes himself into a specific individual: namely, into the same one, because he chooses himself.[23]

The inner ability to choose oneself in freedom, to legislate moral laws for oneself, is also what Kant identified as the source of human dignity.

Given his analysis of marriage, one might wonder how William thinks about men and women more generally. Does he represent an advance over A in this regard? Representative early comments from the Judge include:

> the other sex [woman] . . . is both the more religious and the more esthetic. [Woman] is man's conscience. [Man's] proud ebullience is dampened by his constant returning to [woman]; her weakness is strengthened by her leaning on him.[24]

Near the end of his correspondence with A, the extreme romanticism of William's perspective becomes fully manifest and is worth quoting at some length:

> A woman comprehends the finite; she understands it from the ground up. That is why she is exquisite, which every woman essentially is; that is why she is lovely, which no man is; that is why she is happy, happy as no man can or ought to be; that is why she is in harmony with existence as no man can or ought to be. . . . She is more perfect than man, for surely the one who explains something is more perfect than the one who is hunting for an explanation. Woman explains the finite; man pursues the infinite. . . . Woman is not supposed to know the anxiety of doubt or the agony of despair. . . . That is why I hate all that detestable rhetoric about the emancipation of women. God forbid that it may ever happen. . . . Could there really be one woman simple and vain and pitiable enough to believe that within the definition of man she would become more perfect than man, not to perceive that her loss would be irreparable?[25]

Clearly, William does not subscribe to a modern theory of gender in which sex does not fundamentally determine various social roles and psychological sensibilities. Instead, he endorses a traditional picture of sexual complementarity, with all the political implications this usually entails.

23. Kierkegaard, *Either/Or*, 250-51.
24. Kierkegaard, *Either/Or*, 66-68.
25. Kierkegaard, *Either/Or*, 311-12.

According to William, woman's life "is supposed to be hidden and secret," i.e., confined to the private and familial. What he seems to resist, not to say fear, most of all is women adopting the sexual mores typical of men. This would make them "half men," in his estimation, and even more subject to the predatoriness of male seducers (like Johannes). Notice, however, that most of the hierarchies implied or announced in the foregoing quotes put women on top. There is more than a little patronizing in this — no liberal feminist he — and William evidently embraces the (pseudo-)Pauline view that a wife is to be "subservient to her husband."[26] Still, for all his celebration of sexual dimorphism, William also vigorously affirms basic aspects of equality and mutuality between the sexes, including in marriage. Women are capable of "the highest," which is religious faith, perhaps even more capable than men. Moreover, William proclaims of his own spouse,

> My wife is not the slave woman in Abraham's house, whom I banish with the child, but neither is she a goddess with whom I wheel around in amorous capers. . . . She was independent and, what is more, so contented that she did not need to let herself be sold; she was sound, sounder than I, even though more intense. . . . Truly she owes me nothing, and yet I am everything to her.[27]

Speaking more universally, William says, "the Church certainly does not make woman a mere slave; it says: 'And God said I will make a companion for Adam,' an expression that has just as much esthetic warmth as it has truth."[28] In apparent tension with his previous remark that "woman is not supposed to know the anxiety of doubt or the agony of despair," he even writes the following:

> "Woman is weak," it is said. "She cannot bear troubles and cares — the frail and the weak must be dealt with in love." Falsehood! Falsehood! Woman is just as strong as man, perhaps stronger. And do you really deal with her in love when you humiliate her in this way [by keeping secrets from her]? Or who gave you permission to humiliate her, or how can your soul be so blind that you regard yourself as a creature superior to her? Just confide everything to her. If she is weak, if she cannot bear it — well, then she can lean on you; after all, you

26. Kierkegaard, *Either/Or,* 91.
27. Kierkegaard, *Either/Or,* 81.
28. Kierkegaard, *Either/Or,* 92.

> have strength enough. But you cannot tolerate that; you do not have the stamina for that. Therefore, it is you who are lacking in strength and not she.[29]

In short, the woman is "simultaneously more perfect and more imperfect than the man."[30] With this, William accepts some of A's assumptions about gender complementarity, but he would celebrate difference rather than mocking or exploiting it. One continues to worry about an overly romanticized, even patronizing, image of woman, but A's brutal misogyny is left behind in favor of a decidedly more egalitarian picture.

In all that he writes, Judge William is not merely contrasting an aesthetic lifestyle with an ethical one and saying, arbitrarily, choose! A's and William's perspectives are discontinuous in several respects, and to move from one to the other cannot be necessitated by some objective argument, or even by divine grace. Any such existential transition requires a free "leap," an uncoerced paradigm shift, wherein a new form of being is embraced. But here is no utter incommensurability between points of view; in fact, there are *internal* reasons why a person may find aestheticism, say, unsatisfactory. To become an ethical individual, an aesthete must choose choice, so to speak; he or she must take good and evil seriously as applicable to his or her actions and intentions, and this requires a conversion away from wantonness.[31] Conversions can be plausibly motivated, however, without being logically or causally compelled. A major aim of Kierkegaard's authorship as a whole, I believe, is to illustrate that to live merely for pleasure and amusement, with no ethically binding decisions, is to frustrate a spiritual potential inherent in all human beings. The quest for perpetual distraction without commitment comes to smash, *even on its own terms,* in boredom. As A himself writes,

> My soul is dull and slack; in vain do I jab the spur of desire into its side; it is exhausted, it can no longer raise itself up in its royal jump. I have lost all my illusions. In vain do I seek to abandon myself in joy's infinitude; it cannot lift me, or, rather, I cannot lift myself. . . . My soul has lost possibility. . . . Pleasure disappoints; possibility does not exist.[32]

29. Kierkegaard, *Either/Or,* 113.
30. Kierkegaard, *Either/Or,* 92.
31. Kierkegaard, *Either/Or,* 168-69 and 219.
32. Kierkegaard, *Either/Or,* Part I, 41.

A's fate awaits anyone who tries to embody a thoroughgoing egotism, even the imperial voluptuary who can command all the resources of Rome to placate desire. William pities A and judges him likely to come to a bad end. A is voluble but cold, brilliant but untruthful. Good Lutheran that William presumably is, he considers any man like A who so masterfully belittles marriage to be "dangerous,"[33] both to himself and to others.

Søren Kierkegaard on Love, Marriage, and Equality

Exposition

There are several affinities between Judge William's defense of marriage and Søren Kierkegaard's praise of Christian charity in *Works of Love.* They both speak of the need to make *eros* (indeed, all love) "a matter of conscience,"[34] for example, rather than a volatile emotion or a prideful choice. In addition, they both explore the ways in which one's enacted conception of freedom and moral responsibility determines one's experience of time. Kierkegaard's phrase for the needed transformation of marital love is that God becomes "the middle term"[35] between husband and wife, such that the spouses love one another first as neighbors and only second as specific marriage partners. When God becomes the intermediary in this way, eternity enters time, and I can well imagine William applauding this terminology.

The chief difference between William and Kierkegaard consists, I believe, in their relative weightings of will and grace and in their relative distrust of *eros* and other preferential relations. William mentions the importance of gratitude to God and the close connection between the ethical and the religious dimensions of life. He even discusses the ubiquity of sin and the need for repentance and forgiveness before God and other people. Nevertheless, quite often he sounds astonishingly Promethean in his valorization of the human will and its freedom. He writes, for instance:

> Not until I absolutely choose myself do I absolutely infinitize myself because I myself *am* the absolute, because only I myself can choose absolutely; and this absolute choice of myself is my freedom, and

33. Kierkegaard, *Either/Or,* Part II, 79-80.

34. Søren Kierkegaard, *Works of Love,* trans. Howard V. Hong and Edna H. Hong (Princeton: Princeton University Press, 1995), 139.

35. Kierkegaard, *Works of Love,* 107.

> only when I have absolutely chosen myself have I posited an absolute difference: namely the difference between good and evil.[36]

The *summum bonum* for William sounds remarkably like Kantian autonomy, sovereignty over self, even as the *summum malum* seems like heteronomy, being governed by objects or inclinations outside of your control. For all its noble accent on dignity and respect for persons, this Kantian perspective carries with it some familiar problems: (1) What do we do with humans who are not autonomous noumenal beings but dependent embodied creatures? This includes children, the mentally handicapped, and the senile, but it also encompasses normal adults in many (if not all) moments of their lives. (2) Even among currently autonomous persons, what are we to make of weakness of will and consistent perversity of will? Kant himself worried a good deal over "radical evil" and the limits of abstract consistency as a moral principle.

As I read Kierkegaard's *Works of Love,* it is partly a corrective of Judge William's overly optimistic Kantianism. In spite of William's panegyric on shared duty and enduring commitment within marriage, he proves too Kantian to capture the radically other-regarding nature of the marital bond and the grace necessary to fulfill it, as these are understood by Kierkegaard. William himself eventually senses that his heroic accent on human volition has largely left God out of the picture and that it comes to smash on weakness and guilt. We cannot (or at least do not) always do our duty or otherwise live up to our commitments, so we must appeal to religious categories like redemption and forgiveness, categories that transcend any merely rational ethic. Even as I assume that A wrote "The Seducer's Diary" that concludes his pages, so I assume that William wrote the sermon on "In Relation to God We Are Always in the Wrong" that concludes his. In any case, enter Kierkegaard *in propria persona* and his emphasis on Christ-like love and the profound need for divine grace. Instead of autonomy, self-rule, Kierkegaard foregrounds theonomy, being ruled by God; indeed, eschewing "the freedom that is 'without God in the world,'" he insists that "every person is God's bond servant."[37] Furthermore, Kierkegaard emphatically ties such servanthood to the grace of Christ and the Holy Spirit.

Whereas William puts marriage at the center of his work as an ethical paradigm, Kierkegaard displaces it in his by noting the ways in which

36. Kierkegaard, *Either/Or,* Part II, 237-40.

37. Kierkegaard, *Works of Love,* 115 and 107.

it can be a temptation to forget God. If Judge William sounds at times like Martin Luther in his championing of the marital estate, Kierkegaard himself sounds like Saint Paul in his lukewarmness about it. Even when transformed by obligation, marriage is still founded on "preferential love" *(eros)* and is not itself to be identified with "true love" *(agape)*. Both the human will and marriage are deflated, then, in the Dane's later work. This is perhaps partly a result of his being further away from his own break with Regina Olsen, which he could not patch up, and more aware of the unlikelihood of his own wedding. Kierkegaard is never so Gnostic, not to say bitter, as to call marital love and other preferential relations evil. He declares explicitly: "The Christian may very well marry, may very well love his wife, especially in the way he ought to love her."[38] But the key point is that the marriage (like friendship and love of country) is to be subordinated to and governed by God. The same goes for self-love: "To love God is to love oneself truly."[39] Even as William "dethroned" the aesthetic without simply rejecting it, so Kierkegaard dethrones the ethical without violating it. The ethical "universal" (relations to other people, one's spouse, and one's self) is secondary to "the highest," the God-relation. A mature religious faith appreciates that we can neither make nor save ourselves by our own will power, and that all human goods (including gender justice and self-respect) depend on the gratuitous love of God.

Critique

I have noted that Judge William is a traditionalist with respect to gender roles yet still affirms a fundamental equality between the sexes. On the question of relations between the sexes, Kierkegaard writes under his own name,

> What abominations has the world not seen in the relationship between man and woman, that she, almost like an animal, was a disdained being in comparison with the man, a being of another species. What battles there have been to establish in a worldly way the woman in equal rights with the man —

These are moving words, and they seem far more open to the full emancipation of women than was William. Yet the quoted passage continues with

38. Kierkegaard, *Works of Love,* 145.
39. Kierkegaard, *Works of Love,* 107.

> but Christianity makes only infinity's change and therefore quietly. Outwardly the old more or less remains. The man is to be the woman's master and she subservient to him; but inwardly everything is changed, changed by means of this little question to the woman, whether she has consulted with her conscience about having this man — as master, for otherwise she does not get him. Yet the conscience-question about the conscience-matter makes her inwardness before God absolutely equal with the man.[40]

Inward or spiritual equality is affirmed here, at least in name, but the inegalitarian externals are left basically the same. Marriage and family remain deeply hierarchical institutions for Kierkegaard, as for William. Surely this hyper-spiritualizing of values like equality and liberty will not do, however, for it denies the importance of embodied social relations.

Kierkegaard's *Works of Love* is the greatest work of Christian ethics since the Reformation, I believe, its signal contribution being its exploration of the priority of love of God and neighbor over *eros, philia,* and self-love. That achievement is marred, however, by a failure to take incarnate love seriously enough. The inner and the outer just are not as separable as Kierkegaard implies — materially, morally, psychologically, or politically. Self-image and self-respect cannot be so completely untied from communal reputation and bodily treatment. Kierkegaard's comments on "the conscience-matter" are rather like telling a runaway slave that he is as good as the master, spiritually speaking, but that he is to continue to endure his physical shackles and social degradation. Lest one think that Kierkegaard is singling out gender relations for special insulation, he avers quite broadly that "Christianity does not want to make changes in externals . . . it wants only to make infinity's change in the inner being."[41] This seems to me badly mistaken, even offensive. It is certainly incompatible with the teachings and example of Christ. Jesus took bodily disease, social alienation, and institutional (especially religious) tyranny quite seriously. He did not directly assault the Roman Empire as such, and for good prudential reasons, but he did heal the sick, have table fellowship with publicans and sinners, drive the moneychangers out of the Temple, and imply that the emperor's power was not divine ("render unto Caesar what is Caesar's, but unto God what is God's"). These were all publicly

40. Kierkegaard, *Works of Love,* 138.
41. Kierkegaard, *Works of Love,* 139.

provocative acts, threatening to both religious and secular authorities. Crucifixion was, after all, the Roman punishment for subversion of imperial hegemony.

One might argue that inner liberation is *more important* than outer and/or that spiritual freedom must precede *chronologically* the more political kinds. Given the hazy dividing line between inner and outer, this would be a tough case to win, but it makes some intuitive sense. What is close to moral madness, in contrast, is the suggestion that Christianity is not interested in physical bodies and collective organizations, i.e., "externals." As Kierkegaard himself observes, "in Christ perfection looked down to earth and loved the person it saw. . . . Therefore if you want to be perfect in love, strive to fulfill this duty, in loving to love the person one sees, to love him just as you see him, with all his imperfections and weaknesses."[42] To love the neighbor "just as you see him [or her]" is to care for a real person with both soul and body, both individual wants and needs and group affiliations and vulnerabilities. Kierkegaard's acceptance of female equality remains ambivalent at best, then, and this must qualify our appreciation of what is, otherwise, a beautiful and compelling depiction of love and marriage. That said, I believe that, suitably corrected, Kierkegaard's analysis of love suggests a cogent critique of Don Browning on marriage and the family. Let me now turn to Professor Browning.

Don Browning on Love, Marriage, and Equality

Like Judge William, Don Browning wants to defend the aesthetic validity of marriage. His attention to the divergent reproductive (i.e., erotic) strategies of men and women, together with his analysis of kin altruism, resembles William's call for a proper "balance between the aesthetic and the ethical."[43] There are universal duties of justice applicable to both husbands and wives, and these are crucial; but, like Thomas Aquinas, Browning teaches us that we must also incorporate the sexes' embodied natural desires into the goods of marriage. Generally speaking, a father will only consent to be grafted into the family dyad of mother and child, for instance, if his paternity of that child is guaranteed. He will only stand by the mother and see to the care and education of the child if he is

42. Kierkegaard, *Works of Love,* 174.
43. Kierkegaard, *Either/Or,* Part II, 155ff.

confident that his legitimate erotic needs are met, including having exclusive sexual access to his wife. Browning displays considerable courage in taking the body and gender differences seriously in this way, and considerable originality in trying to synthesize evolutionary psychology with Christian ethics. Moreover, he is far better than Kierkegaard at translating his moral proposals into concrete prescriptions for social reform. He avoids the Dane's overemphasis on the inwardness of the single individual and even provides a helpful corrective to this tendency in more contemporary authors.

For all his bold defense of gender equality amid gender difference and respect for marital dignity amid threats to same, however, I fear that Professor Browning labors under some of the same limits as Judge William. He, too, makes marriage sound at times quite Kantian, like a willed association of autonomous persons for reciprocal advantage. (Kant himself notoriously saw marriage as a joint contract in which husband and wife give each other exclusive right to one another's bodies, a kind of corporate property agreement.) Browning is sensitive to the danger here: he and his colleagues note that "love as mutuality, unless carefully defined, can drift into individualistic forms of reciprocity — 'I will do good to you *if* you do good for me.'"[44] But not even a careful definition can blunt the contractarian implications when "mutuality" is given center stage. An emphasis on mutuality inevitably puts reciprocal justice first and makes an unconditional *agape* handmaiden to that end. Browning and his colleagues never forget the occasional need for self-sacrifice for a fully functional relationship, but self-sacrifice is a "*subordinate moment of love that is mainly in the service of equal regard.*"[45] "Self-giving," as they sometimes call it, performs the tactical function of renewing or restoring mutuality, but it is "not an end in itself."[46] How this is distinct from "individualistic forms of reciprocity" is very hard to see, however. If self-giving is not productive or preservative of equal respect, then presumably it is indeed to be abandoned as folly.

Following Aquinas, Browning sometimes construes marriage as a species of "friendship," and this is a genuinely touching evocation of the communion possible between husband and wife. Even so, we Kierkegaardians resist any effort to replace *agape* with either *jus* or *philia;* John Rawls and liberal feminism notwithstanding, neither reciprocal justice

44. Browning et al., *From Culture Wars to Common Ground,* 47.

45. Browning et al., *From Culture Wars to Common Ground,* 23.

46. Browning et al., *From Culture Wars to Common Ground,* 24.

nor mutual friendship can supplant *agape,* either inside or outside marriage. We defend a view of marriage, that is, in which the spouse is loved first of all unconditionally, as a neighbor before God, and then as a cooperative partner, close friend, or erotic bedmate. If the search for reasonable "common ground" leads to equal-regard marriage and the democratic family, then better to fight the good fight in the "culture wars" in the name of Christian charity. Mutuality and democracy are very great goods, but the profound truth behind biblical *agape* is that these goods emerge best when they are not aimed at too directly or valued too highly. ("Don't let the left hand of social justice know what the right hand of agapic love is doing.") Christ-like love has priority, with justice and respect for personal dignity having second place as fruits of the vine, rather than the other way round. *Pace Browning, self-giving is not mainly in service of mutuality but, rather, in imitation of Christ and in the service of the neighbor.*

Like Browning and many feminists, I want to defend against any conception of self-sacrifice that would make it masochistic. I hold, for instance, that any sacrifice of legitimate interests must be both consensual and constructive. Coercion, profligacy, and self-loathing are no virtues. There are many sham offers of, and manipulative appeals for, self-sacrifice — the martyred mother, the domineering father — and these give the ideal a bad name. But the genuine article has been seen at least once in the world — in the Incarnation. Less pessimistically, I am confident that real self-giving is practiced by countless individuals of all genders, races, faiths, and sexual orientations, in and out of wedlock. As a Christian, I also hold that these humble acts are empowered by the Holy Spirit, however anonymously. It is surely a mistake, nonetheless, to see such sacrifice as mainly instrumental to common benefit or personal happiness. For, again, this implies that if there is no reciprocation — no "pay off" for me — then all bets are possibly, even probably, off. "For better or for worse, for richer or for poorer, in sickness and in health" — these familiar covenantal words make no mention of *mutual* advantage. In the marriage vow, each party voluntarily pledges to surrender self-interest and to serve the other. *Both* parties make this pledge, of course, but Browning of all people knows that it is a modern heresy to see this as a tit-for-tat bargain between two human beings. The vow is most basically a promise *to God,* thus it does not hold individual compliance hostage to any fellow creature's performance — as though, if my wife does not care for me when I am sick, then I am not obliged to care for her when she is sick. The primacy of the God-relation is what makes it a religious sacrament rather than a civil contract.

As noted, for Kierkegaardians, duty to God is ideally the "middle term" in all human loves. The God-relation governs and sustains romantic love and friendship, for instance; it keeps them from going over into their opposite, hatred, by making them a matter of conscience before God rather than of personal gratification in community. If *eros* and *philia* (preferential desire and friendship) are pursued because mutually engaging or beneficial, then what happens when they cease to be such? Popular literature and tabloid journalism are full of stories of love affairs gone wrong that end in resentment and even homicide. *Agape* does not vilify or reject the lesser loves, as though Christ-like love is simply opposed to sexual pleasure and friendly fellowship. Such world-hatred is approximated by Anders Nygren in his still-influential *Agape and Eros,* and Browning properly takes him to task for over-statement. But *agape* does show up the poverty and instability of *eros* and *philia* in isolation; it "dethrones" them, to use Kierkegaard's term, and puts them under the shadow of the cross. *Agape* is not embraced in order to make preferential desires or interpersonal relations more effective or satisfying, but rather as its own reward. *Agape* loves the other in obedience to God and for the other's own sake . . . end of story. To instrumentalize the unconditional and kenotic character of Christ-like love is to make it decidedly less than it is. This is akin to recommending nonviolence because it "works" — i.e., is politically expedient — rather than because it is ingredient in the kingdom of God.

The instrumentalizing of *agape* is also manifest in evolutionist defenses of altruism that equate it with an aid to social cooperation and reproductive success. By acting self-sacrificially, or even merely *appearing* to act self-sacrificially, one acquires a reputation that secures others' empathy and assistance, and so one is more likely to get one's genes into the next generation. So the socio-biological argument runs. Browning himself is often an astute critic of sociobiology, preferring to use the phrase "evolutionary psychology" or "evolutionary ecology" to distinguish his views from more reductionist forms.[47] I fear, nevertheless, that he cedes too much to neo-Darwinian and other naturalistic takes on familial virtue and related cultural phenomena. He contends, for instance, that a key response to "the male problematic" of fathers drifting away from their families is to draw on affection for one's own flesh and blood *(storge)* to induce fathers to support their children. Biological affinity can be appealed to in order to bond a male to his progeny and, in turn, to the female who

47. Browning et al., *From Culture Wars to Common Ground,* 106-11.

bears them — "the primordial mammalian mother-infant family."[48] I have nothing against parental instincts, but if a central reason to care for one's children is that they carry one's own genes, and if a central reason to care for one's wife is that she is the vehicle of your own procreative ambition, then a kind of narcissism has been allowed into the core of familial love. *Storge* need not be denied, but it does need to be baptized and thus sanctified by Christian charity; it can no more replace or provide the inspiration for *agape* than can *eros, philia, jus,* or *amor sui.* Quite generally, when peaceableness, kindness, and fathering become chiefly instrumental to something else — whether political stability, survival of the fittest, or mutuality in marriage — they stop being themselves. Thus a kingdom ethic says, "Away with all tactical pacifism, tactical altruism, and tactical marriage!"

Consequences matter morally, and Kierkegaard dwells far too exclusively on motivational "inwardness" in his evaluation of social hierarchies. As I have indicated, he writes as though acknowledging the "spiritual" equality of masters and slaves, men and women, for example, were enough, independently of abolishing slavery and establishing gender justice in the real "outer" world. There is no denying that Kierkegaard was a monarchist in politics and a traditionalist (not to say chauvinist) in matters sexual and that he tended to depict Christianity as leaving temporal "externals" unchanged. *Pace* Kierkegaard, though, some "worldly distinctions" are tyrannical and to be publicly overthrown in the name of faith, hope, and love themselves. Still, Kierkegaard offers a needed corrective to a creeping utilitarianism that would sap Christian ideals of their meaning and power. The Kierkegaardian alternative to the modern domestication of Christianity is explicitly biblical and, when properly construed, promotes gender equality and communal democracy. It also outstrips and limits these goals, however, by pointing to something more fundamental: Christ-like love.

Christ-like love must be understood along two axes or dimensions. Along the vertical axis, the direct God-relation, such love participates in the holiness of the heavenly Father and Mother and obediently subordinates all human volition to divine commands. Along the horizontal axis, interpersonal relations, it embodies three main features: (1) unconditional willing of the good for the neighbor, (2) equal regard for the well-being of the neighbor, and (3) passionate service open to self-sacrifice for the sake of the neighbor. It is crucial to realize that, as I use the phrase

48. Browning et al., *From Culture Wars to Common Ground,* 111.

"equal regard," it is primarily *non*-self-referential. It refers first of all and most of the time to a refusal to draw invidious distinctions *between others,* a universal and even-handed concern for all people — whether they are rich or poor, male or female, black or white, gay or straight, etc. As a person oneself, one is included in the egalitarian mix, in a sense: *every* human life bears the image of God and so can either give or receive *agape.* But the accent is not on affirming self but on not denigrating others. When Browning speaks of "equal regard," in contrast, he usually means parity of respect between self and other, especially between husband and wife. For neither Browning nor myself does equal regard necessarily mean identical treatment;[49] we must meet people where they are, with all their context-specific wants and needs. For Browning, however, "equal regard" connotes mutuality between self and other, whereas for me it connotes absence of prejudice between an other and another other. Similarly, the equality in "equal-regard marriage" takes its measure from the husband and wife as specific male and female, while the equality in Christian marriage takes its measure from the neighbor in relation to God. Rather than saying "I am equal to you and you are equal to me," Christian spouses say "We are all equally the neighbor before the Lord." In the latter case, as Kierkegaard puts it, "the presence of God makes the two essentially equal."[50] Prudence is a virtue, but rather than building self-interest and self-preservation into the heart of Christian love, my reading leaves them largely to the office of God or to the byproduct of that love. Equal regard, in Browning's sense, is more characteristic of courtship, in my view, than of marriage proper.

Of the two axes described above, the vertical, the God-relation, has priority, in as much as it expresses the "first and greatest" love commandment of Matthew 22. The Creator alone is to be loved with all one's heart, mind, and strength; unreflective obedience shown to a creature is the model of idolatry. Of the three interpersonal features, the first is predominant, in as much as it entails the other two, while the other two do not entail it. Unconditional willing of the good for the neighbor implies equal regard for all, for instance, since the neighbor is anyone and everyone, and everyone is equally the neighbor. Moreover, you cannot qualify the unconditional, as though it were contingent, and you cannot subdivide the good, as though it were a limited resource. Equal regard, on the other

49. For more on this crucial distinction, see Gene Outka, *Agape: An Ethical Analysis* (New Haven: Yale University Press, 1972).

50. Kierkegaard, *Works of Love,* 342.

hand, does not imply unconditional willing of the good for the other. Such regard is quite compatible with, even suggests, a calculated reciprocity that does unto others as they have done unto you. Moreover, formal equality makes no mention of "the good" as such; it may mean equivalent disdain or vindictiveness toward another.

Browning is surely right to attend to feminist critiques of any ethic of self-sacrifice that unfairly burdens women or that would make them complicit in tyranny. *Agape* is an equal opportunity employer, applying to both men and women. In addition, self-sacrifice must be "critical," as Browning and his co-authors argue, lest it merely pander to evil or encourage patriarchy in men or self-loathing in women. Christ himself prudently picks his spots, so to speak, and does not always run headlong to a proffered cross. I express these truths by referring to "openness" to self-sacrifice, under the right conditions. So long as it is consensual and constructive, self-giving may be an admirable (even required) expression of Christian charity. Nevertheless, Browning and his coauthors go wrong, I believe, in holding that self-sacrifice is mainly aimed at sustaining or restoring mutuality. Forgiveness, for example, is sacrificial in that it involves a letting go of ill will and of "just" retaliation, but it need not seek or accept an ongoing relationship with the other. Think of a woman who forgives her drunken and abusive husband but still gets herself and the children out of the house, perhaps permanently. (Such physical separation does not necessarily mean formal divorce, of course.) The point is that I can surrender a legitimate interest for the sake of someone, including my spouse, without tying this to future intimacy. I may do this first for God's sake, second for her sake, and even third for my own sake. But none of the above turns on or translates into mutuality. Indeed, I can sacrifice for another whom I know will never return the favor — as with an enemy or in "the work of love in the remembrance of one dead" that Kierkegaard famously praises.

Kierkegaardians can learn much from Browning about the importance of spousal respect and friendship, but the Dane remains unsurpassed in highlighting the trumping importance of unconditional *agape* and individual accountability before God. I myself believe that in calling true love "essentially sacrifice,"[51] Kierkegaard (like Nygren) overstates

51. The quoted phrase is from an older translation in Kierkegaard, *Works of Love*, trans. Howard and Edna Hong (New York: Harper and Row, 1962), 247. The newer Princeton translation reads "Love is a giving of oneself" that "does not seek its own" (264), which is less punchy but also invites the question of the limits of appropriate self-giving.

the case and risks severing *agape* from critical judgment. Not all acts of Christian charity must or should take one to the cross. There is no denying (at least by Christians), however, that *openness* to the cross, *under appropriate circumstances,* is an unavoidable part of all human relations that would be faithful and redemptive. Though important, equal regard and mutuality are neither primary nor sufficient in marriage; they are frequently the *consequences* of marital love, but they are not the central *aim* or inspiration. Mutuality is not the exclusive, nor even the main, measure of what is "constructive" sacramentally; and the same is true of justice and friendship. Self-fulfillment is still more decentered by a Kierkegaardian understanding of marriage and family, though it too can take its rightful place as an upshot of proper love of God and neighbor. Browning sees the need for attention to externals and to social justice better than Kierkegard does, but Kierkegaard better sees the need for sacrifice and the unconditional. My solution is to see equal regard as part of marriage, but not the only or even the most important part.

Browning and his colleagues painstakingly document the "family changes" afoot in the 1960s, 1970s, and 1980s — "divorce, out-of-wedlock births, stepfamilies, single parenthood"[52] — and they plausibly argue that these changes have not been conducive to true freedom and have harmed both children and parents. Ironically, however, Browning and his colleagues seek to support their normative case by taking the pulse of the very *Zeitgeist* that is failing us: "*Our society is undergoing a profound revolution in its image of good marital and family love.* Mutuality is being perceived more positively; self-sacrifice is being perceived more negatively."[53] They do not uncritically reduce morality to a matter of taking polls, but they write as though it is a virtue of their views that they resonate with the increased public affirmation of mutuality. My misgiving is obvious: the same statistics that Browning cites about the contemporary breakdown of the family ought to make us wary of the contemporary focus on mutuality. There seems to be an empirical correlation between the erosion of the family that Browning laments and the theory of the family that Browning champions. *Putting it bluntly, equal-regard marriage was tried in the latter half of the twentieth century, and Don Browning among a select few has helped us see that it didn't work.*

In *Marriage and Modernization,* Browning elaborates, exclusively under his own name, a further defense of "a 'critical' love ethic of equal re-

52. Browning et al., *From Culture Wars to Common Ground,* 21.
53. Browning et al., *From Culture Wars to Common Ground,* 20.

gard"[54] within marriage, paying particular attention to how globalization threatens the family. He reiterates some of the key theses of *From Culture Wars to Common Ground,* including that "husbands and wives do not sacrifice for one another as an end in itself but as a step toward restoring love as mutuality."[55] He again embraces the Kantian goods of respect for all persons as ends in themselves over individualistic and corporate forms of utilitarianism. But the crucial points of contention remain. To embrace sacrifice for its own sake is masochistic, but to see sacrifice as merely to enhance or repair mutuality is to miss the ineliminably tragic dimension of finitude. Some human needs can be met only by an unreciprocated gift. Treating "persons as ends," including husband and wives, is admirable in many contexts, but it is not synonymous with treating them as "children of God, as *imago Dei,* and as people for whom Christ died."[56]

Browning writes that his "argument will not pit modernization *against* marriage but will be about having both modernization *and* marriage."[57] I must confess, nevertheless, that I am among those he predicts will say "it must be one or the other."[58] In my view, marriage as mutuality and equal regard is not suffering *because of* modernization and individualism but rather *as* modernization and individualism. Browning has a highly sophisticated understanding of "modernization," informed by Max Weber and an impressive list of contemporary sociologists (such as William Goode, David Popenoe, and Alan Wolfe). If modernization means emphasizing "the naturalistic base"[59] of marriage and the family over the supernatural origin and end, however, then we Kierkegaardians will indeed perceive an either/or. I myself have defended Christianity's affinity with democratic values,[60] but it is imperative that *agape* retain its controlling status in any political equation. More to the point, *agape* must precede, restrain, and reform liberty and equality, not merely affirm or translate them. Moving equal regard and democracy to the core of marriage and the family threatens this priority.

54. Don S. Browning, *Marriage and Modernization* (Grand Rapids, MI: Eerdmans, 2003), 44.

55. Browning, *Marriage and Modernization,* 98.

56. Browning, *Marriage and Modernization,* 53.

57. Browning, *Marriage and Modernization,* 5.

58. Browning, *Marriage and Modernization.*

59. Browning, *Marriage and Modernization,* 88.

60. Timothy P. Jackson, *Political Agape: A Defense of Prophetic Liberalism* (manuscript).

Browning highlights the ways in which early Christianity aimed at "extending to families the equal regard implied by the second half of the Great Commandment — 'You shall love your neighbor as yourself' (Matthew 22:39)."[61] But I fear that this fails to appreciate the radicality of Christ-like love. Jesus' *final* love command in John suggests that we do not know how to love ourselves properly, that just as preferential desires are unstable and must be brought under the rule of charity, so self-love readily turns into masochism without the grace of God. Who in fairly judging himself could escape self-loathing, thus leading to an equality of despair? Unlike Matthew 22's "love your neighbor as yourself," we are commanded in John 13:34 to "love one another," not based on a natural self-love, but based on Christ's own cruciform life: "as I have loved you." This Christocentric criterion radically subordinates all other forms of love — including, to repeat, *eros, philia,* and *amor sui.* Jesus' final love command, then, goes beyond the Golden Rule, the Kantian categorical imperative, and even the second love command of Matthew.

To repeat, this is not to say that equality and mutuality are unimportant values, much less intrinsic evils; it is to say, rather, that they are limited goods that cannot bear the weight that many (Christians and non-Christians) have sought to place on them. A due commitment to equal regard can combat a lingering patriarchy, but when equality and mutuality become the *summum bonum,* they generally aggravate the individualism, economic commodification, and governmental bureaucratization that Browning so wisely wants to resist.[62] What are no-fault divorce, out-of-wedlock births, abortion-on-demand, the harvesting of fetal tissue, state-warehousing of orphans, and the like but the rotten fruit of putting the dignity of autonomous persons above the sanctity of life and love? Women and men can be equally callous and self-interested — what is unreasonable about that? — and democratic equality ungrounded in religious compassion is but a glittering vice.

I hasten to add that Browning is well-aware of "the great theme of *agape* — Christ's sacrificial love for the church,"[63] and that he repeatedly avers that "love as equal regard . . . does not omit a place for sacrificial love and the cross."[64] Moreover, he and his coauthors in *From Culture Wars to Common Ground* clearly recognize that

61. Browning, *Marriage and Modernization,* 43.

62. See Browning, *Marriage and Modernization,* 239; Browning et al., *From Culture Wars to Common Ground,* 21.

63. Browning, *Marriage and Modernization,* 70.

64. Browning, *Marriage and Modernization,* 45.

> The new twenty-first-century equal-regard family will not be *the* Christian family. . . . The intact, equal-regard, public-private family is consistent with Christianity and reflects certain Christian values, but it will *be* fully Christian only if additional themes of Christian love, forgiveness, and grace surround this family and are acted out within it.[65]

But the question is whether one can have the bloom of Christian marriage and family life without the roots. Again, equal regard is an upshot or secondary implication of Christ-like love, but it is not the governing heart and soul. That heart and soul is an *agape* that unqualifiedly promotes the well-being of the other, even as Christ as bridegroom is faithful servant to the church even unto death. I appreciate the fact that Browning is writing for a wider secular audience, not just for the Christian community, and I, too, am a critic of theologians who offer a sectarian retreat from the profane world and its trite opinions and corrupt institutions. To call an unbelieving public, lost in hedonism and despair, to ethical standards of fairness and respect is a real achievement. (We shall always need a Judge William or Professor Browning to challenge our cultural aestheticism.) Yet the ethical, so understood, is but an unstable "stage" without the religious. The oft-discussed danger of accommodation looms large here, and I do not believe one can begin with Kantian equal regard and arrive at Christian families by addition — any more than one can begin with biblical *agape* and arrive at respect for persons by subtraction. No matter how much one adds seriatim to a finite sum, it will remain finite; and the only way to subtract from an infinite sum is to collapse it to zero all at once, which is to void it altogether. The latter is what happens, I fear, when "Christian love" is "defined as equal regard."[66]

To put the point yet one more way, whereas Browning would construe mutuality as a kind of "middle" road between *agape* and *eros*,[67] I would give decisive pride of place to *agape* over both *eros* and mutuality.[68] ("For the gate is narrow and the road is hard that leads to life" [Matthew 7:14].) Browning has a most impressive forbearer in St. Augustine in trying to synthesize *eros* and *agape* into some third thing: *caritas* in Augustine's case, "equal regard" in Browning's case. But, some Roman Catholic

65. Browning et al., *From Culture Wars to Common Ground,* 7.

66. Browning, *Marriage and Modernization,* 45.

67. Browning et al., *From Culture Wars to Common Ground,* 101.

68. See Timothy P. Jackson, *The Priority of Love: Christian Charity and Social Justice* (Princeton: Princeton University Press, 2003).

scholars notwithstanding, Augustine's Latin *caritas* is *not* an adequate translation of New Testament Greek's *agape*.[69] (Kant's *"Respekt vor Personen"* fares no better.) To begin with *eros* as preferential desire, as in the Bishop of Hippo and the neo-Platonic eudaimonists, is to end with *eros* as preferential desire, as in Professor Browning and the neo-Darwinian evolutionists. Augustine would school *eros* into *caritas* by directing it at the truly excellent and beneficial, i.e., God, even as Browning and his coauthors think that "*eros* should be a fundamental part of an adequate definition of Christian love."[70] In both cases, however, love still depends, un-biblically, on the merit or profitability of the loved object rather than on the grace and dedication of the loving subject. Only *agape*, following Christ's lead, is steadfast and unconditional in imitation of God's own covenant fidelity. Browning and his colleagues aver that "love as equal regard, as we use it, includes elements of *eros* and sacrificial self-giving, although it subordinates both to equal concern for other *and* self."[71] But this is the theological equivalent of wanting to have your cake and eat it too. If equal concern for self and others trumps, then one has surrendered *agape* and is preaching another Gospel.

I no doubt display my Protestant sensibilities when I argue that one cannot get, via dialectical ascent, from natural law to supernatural love. Rather, the supernatural must stoop to convert the natural. For example, rather than "love for the neighbor, stranger, and enemy" being "an analogical extension of natural family love," as Browning maintains,[72] Christ himself apparently saw natural family love as having to be *transformed* by the *super*-natural virtue of self-denial. "If anyone comes to me and does not hate his own father and mother and wife and children and brothers and sisters, yes, and even his own life, he cannot be my disciple" (Luke 14:26). Jesus encouraged his followers to "not worry about tomorrow" (Matthew 6:34), but instead to "deny themselves and take up their cross daily and follow me" (Luke 9:23). It is a question of priority, of what has pride of place: agapic love in obedience to God or social justice in the name of mutuality? To practice Christ-like love is to participate in God's own holiness, eternal life here and now, and this is to reconfigure all temporal human relations, including marriage and parenting, *away from* economies of exchange and personal fulfillment and *toward* spontaneous

69. See Timothy P. Jackson, *Love Disconsoled: Meditations on Christian Charity* (Cambridge: Cambridge University Press, 1999), 11 and 61-70.

70. Browning et al., *From Culture Wars to Common Ground*, 106.

71. Browning et al., *From Culture Wars to Common Ground*, 101.

72. Browning et al., *From Culture Wars to Common Ground*, 23.

gratitude and service. To repeat, nothing is more egalitarian and democratic than "no fault divorce," the assumption that both parties can initiate a dissolution of the union, for whatever reason, regardless of the impact on children, one another, and the wider society.

Conclusion: Second Immediacy and Second Marriages

Akin to the Kantian Judge William, Don Browning challenges the aestheticism of our day by uncovering its inconsistency and destructiveness. He would combat the alarming collapse of Western marriage and family life by finding common ground between conservative and liberal, religious and secular, moralists alike. Again like the wise William, he addresses us as we are but would prompt men and women to move from seduction and abandonment to respect and fairness. This is a real and rare achievement. I fear, even so, that just as the Judge's humane vision comes to smash on human dependency and guilt — as William vaguely sees at the end — so Professor Browning's model is insufficiently attentive to the limits of equality and the human will. We need self-kenosis and theonomy more than mutuality and autonomy.

Only through an agapic love open to grace can one achieve the "second immediacy"[73] of passion and responsibility that Judge William and Professor Browning want. By letting go of equal regard and mutuality as central concerns, a kind of teleological suspension of the ethical, one is liberated to be a dedicated husband, wife, or parent before God. One looks first to the sanctity of the other and then lets personal dignity take care of itself. Paradoxically, one is even more likely to realize true democratic equality when this is ancillary to the doing of God's will. To paraphrase Jesus in Mark 8:35, "whosoever will save his (family) life shall lose it; but whosoever shall lose his (family) life for my sake and the gospel's, the same shall save it."

If Browning allowed that equal-regard marriage and the democratic family are volatile and incomplete but generally the best we can do in a pluralistic culture, I would understand. I would demure, but I would understand. What is troubling, if well intentioned, is his suggestion that rec-

73. In Kierkegaard's lexicon, a "second immediacy" or a "later immediacy" after reflection refers to a spontaneous religious faith that redeems the aesthetic and ethical stages or dimensions of life. See, for instance, Kierkegaard (Johannes de Silentio), *Fear and Trembling*, trans. Howard V. Hong and Edna H. Hong (Princeton: Princeton University Press, 1983), 82.

ognizably Christian marriage — even love *simpliciter* — can be fundamentally identified with mutuality. To identify the core of Christian love with equal regard — or even the Golden Rule — is "to sell one's birthright for a pot of message."[74]

All this having been said, I must end with a disclaimer. Søren Kierkegaard was, and I am, unmarried and childless, while Don Browning is a faithful husband and admired father. Both Kierkegaard and I may well be suspected of a kind of naiveté, even hypocrisy, in advocating a rigorous *agape* as the foundation of marriage and family. Kierkegaard jilted his fiancée Regina Olsen, after all, and I am divorced. How can I extol what might be called "cruciform familism," in opposition to Browning's "critical familism," when I am neither spouse nor parent? I feel the force of this question, and I can only respond by pleading two points. First, to lift up Christ-like love as an ideal is primarily to indict oneself and others, rather than to boast. As Kierkegaard observes in his *Works of Love* and *For Self-Examination,* Christ is a model that simultaneously builds up and crushes: he is both impossible prototype and indispensable Redeemer. Second, I still hope one day to have a wife and children and thus to bear, by God's grace, the very burdens I perhaps too glibly celebrate. May God help me to achieve a second immediacy, but may God deliver me from too much mutuality in my second marriage!

74. I lift this pun from Paul Ramsey's *Speak Up for Just War or Pacifism* (University Park: Pennsylvania State University Press, 1988).

7 Why We Should Revise Browning's Model of a 60-Hour Workweek for Parents

Rebekah Miles

Of all the proposals set forth in the work of the Religion, Culture, and Family Project, the one that has received the most public attention is the recommendation that married couples with children have a combined workweek of no more than 60 hours.

THE RELIGION CULTURE AND FAMILY PROJECT ELECTRONIC NEWSLETTER[1]

The proposal for a combined 60-hour workweek for couples with children is the Religion, Culture, and Family Project's most celebrated idea, and it is also the proposal that leaves me the most ambivalent. Don Browning and his colleagues put forward this model both to encourage parents to balance work at home and on the job in a way that is healthier for their families and also to prompt business, civic, religious, and other leaders to support policies and practices that will make part-time employment a better option for working parents. Browning and his colleagues have been extremely successful in garnering support for this model. As Browning put it, "[This proposal] is the one people always

1. "Combined 60-Hour Workweek," Religion Culture and Family Project (RCFP) Electronic Newsletter, July 11, 2001. The genesis of this chapter (along with several pages of text) was in an online exchange I participated in with Don Browning and Amy Laura Hall. See "A Response to Don Browning's 'Critical Familism, Civil Society, and the Law,'" June 2003, The Religion and Culture Web Forum, The Martin Marty Center, The University of Chicago, found at: http://marty-center.uchicago .edu/webforum/062003/response_miles.shtml.

pick up on and want to talk about."[2] The popular press, business magazines, and national think tanks have taken up this idea.

More to the point, it has been embraced and enacted by many couples with young children. For example, when my husband and I decided after our daughter Anna was born that we would not continue with two full-time jobs, this 60-hour proposal and the rationale behind it were pivotal in our deliberations. We give the 60-hour model a lot of the credit for that decision and for the good things that followed in its wake — including a more sane life, a happier marriage, and even the birth of our second child, Katherine. We ultimately decided, however, that the 60-hour model did not go far enough for us. Len subsequently quit his job as a hospital chaplain and is now without paid employment, but with an abundance of unpaid highly rewarding work as a father, spiritual director, and active churchman. My criticism and reformulation of the 60-hour model grows out of our life as a family and our appreciation for the 60-hour model.

This 60-hour model workweek for parents is just one small part of the Religion, Culture, and Family Project. Like the 60-hour model, the project itself has been astonishingly successful. Led by Browning and funded by the Lilly Endowment, the project set off an explosion of interest and research in the field of religion and family studies. It directly launched dozens of books, and the aftershocks of that first wave of books will likely lead to dozens more books on marriage, children, divorce, and related topics. Browning has continued to play out the implications of this research in his subsequent writing and project leadership. Throughout these many works on marriage and family, Browning combines the roles of scholar and social reformer, eager not only to foster religious reflection on marriage and family but also to reform and revive actual marriages and families.

I challenge here the best-known proposal of the Religion, Culture, and Family Project — the 60-hour combined workweek for parents — not because I object to the project or the aims of the 60-hour model itself, but precisely because I embrace them. I see my challenge of the model as one small part of this process of family reflection and transformation that Browning has led so ably.

Browning's 60-hour model is not without benefits. It has served several worthy purposes (in addition to the benefits it brought to my household). It has given policymakers and business leaders a model

2. Pamela Mendels, "Should Working Parents Work Less?" *Business Week* (December 27, 2000), http://www.businessweek.com/smallbiz/content/dec2000/sb20001227_601.htm (accessed May 23, 2007).

around which to rethink how jobs are structured. The model has also offered parents with young children a simple tool to help them reflect on how much time they give to employment and to more direct care of their families. Standing over and against the temptation of parents to work too many hours outside the home or to be limited only to the home, this model encourages both parents to be fully engaged in the life of the family as well as in professional market activities beyond the family, and it gives theological and other justification for women's participation in the workforce. The 60-hour model helps moderate the tendency of some families and the larger culture to capitulate to market encroachment, but for all its usefulness, the 60-hour model does not go far enough.

I am convinced that while the 60-hour model sets helpful limits on some extreme aspects of market encroachment in the family, it also reflects and even furthers the very market encroachment it seeks to hinder. The 60-hour model is not simply a barrier or a hedge against the encroachment of the market but also a partial capitulation to it.

Let me say more about the 60-hour model. Don Browning, along with other colleagues in the Religion, Culture, and Family Project, proposed an ideal or model workweek for couples with children. In this model workweek, a husband and wife would divide 60 work hours in, for example, a 30-hour/30-hour or 40-hour/20-hour pattern. Both should be involved in the challenges of paid employment. In his writings and in private conversation, Browning has reiterated the importance of paid employment for both mother and father.[3] Volunteer activities outside the home, although valuable, are not included in the 60-hour workweek.

In addition, both the mother and father should also have time to invest deeply in their marriage and in the lives of their children. For single parents, who face much greater strain as they combine employment with care for children, they recommend a 30-hour workweek. Moreover, they

3. For more on the 60-hour workweek, see Don and Carol Browning, "Better Family Values: A New Paradigm for Family Policy Can Bridge the Partisan Gap," *Christianity Today* 39(2) (February 6, 1995): 29-32; Don Browning, Bonnie Miller-McLemore, Pamela Couture, Brynolf Lyon and Robert Franklin, *From Culture Wars to Common Ground: Religion and the American Family Debate* (Louisville, KY: Westminster John Knox, 1997, 2000), 327-28; Browning, "The Task of Religious Institutions in Strengthening Families," 11, accessed at http://marty-center.uchicago.edu/research/rcfp/communitarianpolicy.htm; Don Browning and Gloria Rodriguez, *Strengthening American Families: Reweaving the Social Tapestry* (New York: The American Assembly, 2000), 11-15; Browning, "Families and the Sixty-Hour Workweek: What Does it Mean for Church, Society, and Persons?" (unpublished ms.).

propose ways that governments and businesses can support this move toward 60- and 30-hour models by, for example, creating more part-time jobs with benefits. According to Browning, the 60-hour mother/father model or 30-hour single-parent model would limit the market's encroachment on family life and benefit mothers, fathers, children, and the larger society. (I sometimes use the mother/father language because most of the studies focus on two-parent, heterosexual families. I look forward to a time when we have more data from a wide array of families.)[4]

Browning and his co-authors offer the 60-hour model as a partial remedy to a well-known and much discussed tension in American culture between the growing number of hours that many working parents spend in the labor force and the ever-present and pressing needs of their family — particularly the need to care for young children and to nourish a healthy marriage (which is, in turn, good for both children and parents.) Over the last thirty years, as many U.S. workers have increased their work hours and as many more women — including mothers of young children — have entered the workforce, couples have struggled to fulfill the responsibilities of these two realms along with their other forms of family, civic, and religious engagement. Scholars, pundits, and prophets observing these changes have generated a steady stream of books, articles, and news shows trying to make sense of them. You do not have to spend much time in this stream to notice that while there is general agreement that we have problems, there is widespread disagreement about the causes, extent, and appropriate remedies for them.[5]

4. Much of the literature around work/family balance has focused more on the roles of mothers than fathers and more on intact two-parent heterosexual families — often those in the middle class. I have seen only a few studies on gay and lesbian families (including a study suggesting that gay and lesbian couples tend to have a much more equitable balance of work in and outside the home).

5. See, for example, my article "That's All a Mule Can Do: The Ethics of Balancing Work at Home and on the Job," Maguire Center Occasional Papers (Maguire Center for Ethics: Dallas, 2003); Juliet Schor, *The Overworked American* (New York: HarperCollins, 1992); Rosalind Barnett and Caryl Rivers, *She Works/He Works: How Two-Income Families Are Happier, Healthier, and Better Off* (New York: HarperCollins, 1996); Arlie Hochschild, *The Time Bind: When Work Becomes Home and Home Becomes Work* (New York: Henry Holt and Company, 1998); John Robinson and Geoffrey Godbey, *Time for Life: The Surprising Way Americans Use Their Time,* 2d ed. (University Park: Pennsylvania State University, 1999); Francine Deutsch, *Halving it All: How Equally Shared Parenting Works* (Cambridge, MA: Harvard University Press, 1999); and various documents on work/life balance at The Families and Work Institute website, accessible at: http://www.familiesandwork.org.

To ground this 60-hour dual earner workweek, Browning offers theological justification drawn from Genesis 1:28 and Phyllis Trible's commentaries on this passage. When Adam and Eve are told to "be fruitful and multiply and to have dominion," they receive a "religiocultural mandate that gives equal opportunity and equal responsibility to male and female in both reproductive and economic activity." Thus the demand for both men and women to engage in reproductive and economic activity is "established by God's will." It "has got the weight of the divine" behind it and is a part of our being. Browning uses this idea — which he calls an "ontology of equality" — to ground the claim that both husbands and wives should participate in care of home and children and in paid economic activities beyond the family.[6]

Browning and his colleagues support the 60-hour model with the claim that it benefits marriages and family life.[7] As backing for this model, Browning cites most often a single study that is reported to show that families with one parent employed full-time and the other part-time have higher levels of martial happiness and other advantages than either families with both spouses employed full-time or families with one spouse employed full-time and the other "non-employed."[8] (For simplicity's sake I will normally refer to these options as the "dual full-time earner model" and the "full-time earner/non-employed parent model.")

6. Browning, "Families and the Sixty-Hour Workweek." Browning draws on Phyllis Trible's *God and the Rhetoric of Sexuality* (Philadelphia, PA: Fortress, 1978).

7. Most of the studies I address and the studies that Browning cites deal with the happiness and satisfaction of the husband and wife. There have been many interesting studies about the effects of parental employment on children. The impact of maternal employment on young children is disputed. See for example, Jane Waldfogel et al., "The Effects of Early Maternal Employment on Child Cognitive Development." *Demography* 39(2) (May 2002): 369-92; Barnett, *She Works/He Works;* Sylvia Hewlett, *When the Bough Breaks: The Cost of Neglecting our Children* (New York: HarperCollins, 1991); Ellen Galinsky, *Ask the Children* (New York: William Morrow and Company, 1999). Even though there are still disputes, the findings on effects for children are more consistent than the findings for spouses. Some studies show no differences, others show slight increases of negative behaviors, and still others show slight increases of positive behaviors.

8. See Jacqueline Olds et al., "Part-Time Employment and Marital Well-Being: A Hypothesis and Pilot Study" (Belmont, MA: Department of Psychiatry, Harvard University McLean Hospital, 1993). In at least one place, Browning also mentions Rosalind Barnett and Caryl Rivers, *She Works/He Works: How Two-Income Families are Happier, Healthier, and Better Off* (New York: HarperCollins, 1996). The Olds study is the primary, or often sole, study generally cited in Browning's writings on the 60-hour model cited in note 3. See Browning and Browning, "Better Family Values."

The primary study on which they rely has several limitations. The pool for the study, as Browning acknowledges, was small and, as its authors emphasize, was limited by the "socioeconomic homogeneity" of the couples interviewed. The research team, all members of the Department of Psychiatry at Harvard Medical School, initially identified five couples "through personal contacts of the investigators." Then these five couples were asked to provide names of other couples they knew who had at least one child over one but under five years old. This process was "repeated" until the researchers had identified thirty couples.[9] In all thirty households the fathers were employed full-time. Ten of the mothers were also employed full-time. Ten were employed part-time. And another group of ten were full-time mothers and not employed. These couples were, on average, much older, richer, and better educated than most American couples with preschool children. The mean average age of the parents was 37.5, the mean average family income was almost $90,000 (more than double the average family income at that time — both nationally and in Cambridge where the study originated),[10] and all of the participants had college or graduate degrees. The full-time moms did not fit the "traditional" profile. Most of them had paid childcare. The researchers describe the typical full-time mom in their study as a "nonworking but part-time housewife."[11] This is not your typical U.S. working family. The authors readily acknowledge the limitations of the study, describing it as a "pilot study" producing data that "at this point are only suggestive."[12]

Although the study does, indeed, show that the ten couples in the full-time/part-time model reported greater marital satisfaction in several areas, the study also shows some advantages for the full-time earner/non-employed parent model.[13] The husbands whose wives worked part-time reported greater mutuality in their marriages, and these husbands also spent more time caring for their children when their wives were not

9. Olds et al., "Part-Time Employment and Marital Well-Being," 6.

10. The median family income in the U.S. around the time of this study was about $35,000. Joint Economic Committee of the U.S. Congress, "Money Income of Households, Families and Persons in the US: 1990," Consumer income, Series P — 60, No 174, Issued August 1991, and a Cambridge city government webpage entitled, *Frequently Asked Questions About Cambridge Demographics,* Department of Cambridge Community Development. Accessed at: http://www.cambridgema.gov/~CDD/data/datafaq.html#12.

11. Olds et al., "Part-Time Employment and Marital Well-Being," 9.

12. Olds et al., "Part-Time Employment and Marital Well-Being," 14.

13. Olds et al., "Part-Time Employment and Marital Well-Being," 7-8.

present. (The study does not indicate that they actually spent more time caring for their children *overall*, simply more time without the wife present.) And for the couples where the wives were employed (either full- or part-time), life was more exciting than for the couples where the wives were not employed. At the same time, there were disadvantages for both groups of dual earner couples. For the couples with employed wives (both full- and part-time), stress was a bigger factor than for the couples where the wives were not employed. Moreover, among the husbands of "at home wives" almost half reported that their relationship with their wives was "the most satisfying feature of their life." In contrast, only 10 percent of the husbands in full-time/part-time couples and none of the husbands in dual full-time earner couples said that their relationships with their wives were "the most satisfying feature of their life."

Looking at the overall study as reported by the researchers, the most significant finding may not be that the full-time/part-time model has the advantage, but that the dual full-time earner couples faced additional challenges. They reported lower levels of mutuality and intimacy and higher levels of worry and conflict than the other two groups. Because the sample for the study was so small, so homogeneous, and so unlike average U.S. working couples, it is hard to know what this study might tell us about the population at large. Moreover, because the results show some advantages and disadvantages for all three categories, it is difficult to say for sure which model worked best even among these thirty well-heeled couples on the northeastern seaboard.

Although Browning, in several articles, cites only this small study in support of the 60-hour dual earner workweek, he could now draw on a much larger and more compelling study designed to test his 60-hour model. In an article in the May 2006 issue of *The American Behavioral Scientist*, the researchers describe how they intentionally set out to "explore the 60-hour hypothesis of Browning et al."[14] The title of the article, "Researching the 60-Hour Dual Earner Workweek: An Alternative to the 'Opt-Out Revolution,'" indicates another angle on their findings. Given recent reports about the slight rise in the number of highly educated professional women leaving the workforce to be full-time mothers (specifically Lisa Belkin's controversial *New York Times Magazine* piece, "The Opt-Out Revolution"),[15] the research-

14. Jeffrey Hill et al., "Researching the 60-Hour Dual Earner Workweek: An Alternative to the 'Opt-Out Revolution'" *American Behavioral Scientist*, 49(9) (May 2006): 1187.

15. Lisa Belkin, "The Opt-Out Revolution," *The New York Times Magazine* (October 26, 2003).

ers were also interested to find that, at least in their study, the 60-hour model led to the greatest family satisfaction.

The researchers examined the responses of 1,565 IBM employees (all of whom had spouses and children eighteen years old or younger) from the "2001 IBM Global Work and Life Issues Survey." The employees fell into several categories — full-time/part-time couples (representing the 60-hour model), dual full-timer earner couples, and full-time earner/non-employed parent couples. (The spouses of the employees, unless they were also IBM employees, were not included in the study.) According to its authors, their study "reveals that . . . the 60-hour workweek for dual-earner professionals appears to be a more advantageous alternative than either opting out altogether by leaving the workforce or opting in to the arrangement where both partners work full-time with high career aspirations." The IBM employees in the 60-hour full-time/part-time combination reported higher levels of "family satisfaction" than either of the other groups as well as better "work/family fit," lower levels of "work/family conflict," and higher levels of job flexibility.[16]

Not all of the advantages were associated with the 60-hour dual earner model. The IBM employees in the 60-hour model reported lower levels of commitment to their jobs at IBM and lower performance ratings on their last job evaluations than employees in the other two groups. In addition, employees in the full-time earner/non-employed parent model reported the highest levels of job performance and job satisfaction (higher than employees in either the 60-hour or the dual full-time dual earner model).

Although family satisfaction was lowest among employees in the full-time earner/non-employed parent model and highest among those falling in the 60-hour model, it is hard to know how to interpret those findings. Employees responded to one question under the heading "family satisfaction." The IBM work/life study asked how they would rate their "personal and/or family life," and they were given the following choices "1 — Extremely successful, 2 — Very successful, 3 — Successful, 4 — Neither successful nor unsuccessful, 5 — Unsuccessful, 6 — Very unsuccessful, 7 — Extremely unsuccessful."[17] One can easily imagine that many people, especially more traditional people (including some full-time employees whose spouses care for the home and family full-time) might believe that their family life was very happy and satisfying but

16. Hill et al., "Researching the 60-Hour Dual Earner Workweek," 1196.
17. Hill et al., "Researching the 60-Hour Dual Earner Workweek," 1199.

would hesitate to say that their "personal and/or family life" was "extremely" or "very successful" because it could conceivably sound boastful. The success language is more commonly used in relationship to the marketplace than our family lives.

Unlike the Harvard Medical School study of thirty couples, the IBM study used a much larger and somewhat more diverse sample. Even so, it was, like the Harvard study, somewhat homogenous. The participants were mostly professionals who had, on average, an annual individual income (not family income) of almost $90,000, and "the average level of education" was an undergraduate degree.[18] Again, this is not your average U.S. working family. Moreover, there were, as I described above, advantages and disadvantages associated with each of the categories.

There are other studies confirming the claim that mothers and fathers who are both employed report greater levels of family satisfaction and marital happiness. Some studies show greater advantages for the full-time/part-time model and others do not. On the other side, some researchers disagree with the claim that dual earner models (of whatever combination) are better for marriages and families. Among that group, some argue that it is basically a wash. Others see greater advantages for the couples where only one partner is employed.[19]

For example, Lina Guzman, drawing on data from the National Survey of Families and Households, found that "women's employment is associated with lower levels of marital happiness and increased levels of marital conflict among wives."[20] The husbands of employed wives and the husbands whose wives were not employed did not differ significantly in their reports of marital happiness (although husbands of employed wives did report slightly "lower levels of marital happiness and higher levels of marital conflict)."[21] Overall, Guzman concluded from this study that "employment significantly lowers the marital quality of wives."[22]

This study avoids some of the problems of the Harvard Medical School and IBM studies described previously. The National Survey of Families and Households, which was run by researchers out of the Uni-

18. Hill et al., "Researching the 60-Hour Dual Earner Workweek," 1191.

19. See note 5.

20. Lina Guzman, "Effects of Wives' Employment on Marital Happiness," Working Paper # 85, *National Survey of Families and Households* (October 2000), 15. Available at: http://www.ssc.wisc.edu/cde/nsfhwp/nsfh85.pdf.

21. Guzman, "Effects of Wives' Employment on Marital Happiness," 15.

22. Guzman, "Effects of Wives' Employment on Marital Happiness," 23.

versity of Wisconsin at Madison, drew on a much broader and more representative national sample that was conducted in three "waves" in the late 1980s and the early 1990s, and at the beginning of this decade. The first wave included over 13,000 responses. For Guzman's research, which relies on the first two waves, she limited the pool to the couples that had participated in all the interviews of the first two waves and who were in intact first marriages and had children at home under the age of nineteenth. That limited the pool to just under 1,200 couples.

Other researchers used the same data from the National Survey of Families and Households and came up with a different headline: "Full-time work for wives decreases the likelihood of divorce but does not improve marital happiness." When this researcher team compared the data from the different waves of the study, they found that women in unhappy marriages were more likely than those in happy marriages to have entered or remained in the workforce full-time between the waves of the study, but that once in the workforce, these unhappy marriages were more likely to stabilize and were less likely to end in divorce.[23] This study suggests, then, that women's employment can be a stabilizing factor for marriages.

Although the National Survey of Families and Households has many advantages over the IBM and Harvard Medical School studies described above, it has hardly settled the matter. Many different researchers using different methods and different subjects have come up with different and inconsistent findings. In fact, reviews of the literature often mention the inconsistencies among the various studies. Jacqueline Olds writes of the "extensive literature with many competing claims," and she quotes another article that describes the work/family studies as "complex and occasionally contradictory."[24] Rosalind Barnett, a well-known scholar and advocate for employed parents, notes that the findings from these various studies are "quite inconsistent."[25] It is hard to make sense

23. Robert Schoen et al., "Wives' Employment and Spouses' Marital Happiness; Assessing the Direction of Influence Using Longitudinal Couple Data," *Journal of Family Issues* 27(4) (2006): 506-28.

24. Olds et al., "Part-Time Employment and Marital Well-Being," 3, quoting E. M. Rallings and F. I. Nye, "Wife-Mother Employment, Family, and Society," in *Contemporary Theories about the Family,* ed. W. R. Burr et al., 2 vols. (New York: The Free Press, 1979).

25. Rosalind Barnett, "Toward a Review and Reconceptualization of the Work/Family Literature," *Genetic, Social, and General Psychology Monographs* 124(2) (May 1998): 125-84.

of these varying and sometimes contradictory findings. I am not taking one side or the other, but simply noting that the research on employment and marital and family happiness is disputed. It is not at all clear that the 60-hour model has the greatest advantages.

The findings are inconsistent at least in part because there are so many mitigating factors that are tied up with people's assessments of employment and family life. Consequently, findings vary depending on what mitigating factors — if any — are considered. For example, some scholars suggest that surveys should include questions about the husband's and wife's preferences for employment. It is no great surprise to learn that if both husband and wife want to be employed, want their spouse to be employed, and are, in fact, both employed, they tend to be happier about their employment and their work/family balance. Moreover, gender expectations can be a factor. If, for example, a woman is employed of necessity, but neither the husband nor the wife believes that women should be employed outside the home, then they are less likely to be happy about the situation.

Other mitigating factors in assessing employment and work/family balance may include the following:[26]

- Is the employment by choice or of necessity? People who are employed by choice tend to be happier about it.
- Does the job offer the employee much autonomy? People holding jobs that offer little autonomy in decision making tend to be less satisfied.
- Is the work stressful or the work environment highly competitive? In some studies highly competitive work environments were linked with higher levels of marital conflict.
- If both father and mother are employed outside of the home, how do they divide the work of caring for home and children? Women tend to be happier about their employment and work/family balance if their husbands do an amount of home/child care that they think is fair. The wives' happiness does not appear to be tied to the actual divisions of household tasks — which tend to fall heavily on the side of the wife even when both are employed full-time — but to the wives' perception of fairness.
- How many traditionally female chores does the husband do around

26. For summaries of these mitigating factors, see Guzman, Olds, Barnett, and Hill.

the house? In one study, when husbands were more involved in typically female households tasks, the marriage had greater conflict. Researchers suggest that perhaps the couple is in transition and is still having conflict about what tasks the husband should be doing around the house.

- How much flexibility does the employee have during work hours to take care of family needs such as tending sick children or going to parent-teacher meetings? Some studies suggest that greater flexibility is associated with a better sense of work/family balance.
- How many hours does the employee work and how many hours does the employee want to work? Is shift work required? Shift work tends to be hard on the employee's health and sense of well-being, but it does have its advantages. In families were the mother and father work different shifts, the father tends to be more actively involved in the care of home and children.
- In addition, some researchers have also suggested that people's perceptions of employment and work/family balance may be influenced by factors such as socio-economic status, education level, gender, and ethnicity.

In many cases, when some of these variables are accounted for, the differences in work/family tension and marital satisfaction diminish or even disappear. Guzman, for example, found that much of the negative effect of wives' employment on their reports of marital quality could be accounted for by the wives' work stress, their perception of the fairness of the division of labor in the household (not so much the actual division itself), and to a lesser extent by the wives' and husbands' work preferences.[27] As Guzman notes, the impact of women's employment may be negative in the general pool but is much less so for those women who experience lower levels of stress on the job and who feel good about the division of labor at home. Guzman's findings about which mitigating factors are most significant differ from the findings of some other studies (which, in turn, differ from each other). So, on top of all of these mitigating and complicating factors listed here, we have an additional complicating factor, that researchers disagree about which of these factors are most significant.

My point in laying out these contrasting and even inconsistent findings from studies on employment and work/family balance is not to

27. Guzman, "Effects of Wives' Employment on Marital Happiness," 23.

show that the 60-hour model is bad or good for families, but simply to note that given the data we have now, it is hard to say that one model is significantly better than another. Given the inconsistencies in the data as well as the effect of other mitigating factors, why lift up the 60-hour dual earner workweek as the single model? Why offer one model as the ideal, when it appears that the best configuration of time on the job and at home may vary significantly from family to family depending on an array of factors?

Instead of privileging one formula or model for configuring parents' time on the job, why not highlight a few guiding principles and then point to several models noting the difficulties or temptation that go along with them? First, for all the disagreements in the studies, there is widespread agreement that children do better when both parents are actively involved in their care. Second, researchers generally agree that women's satisfaction with employment is linked to a division of household labor that seems fair to them. Third, there is a general consensus that excessive work hours by parents are linked with an overall decline in the well-being of the family as a whole. Fourth, parents, on average, seem to be happier when they have responsibilities both in the home and beyond the home in service to others. Whether or not this last point can be proven statistically, the claim is still at the heart of Christian notions of vocation and the active love of God and neighbor. Thus, this claim is compelling even if it is not proven to lead to the greatest immediate happiness. Other principles could be added.

As couples try to discern how best to configure their work on the job, in the home, and in the wider community, they can reflect, then, on these guiding principles and perhaps others:

- Children need care from both mothers and fathers.
- Husbands and wives (especially wives) are happier if there is a division of household labor that they (especially wives) perceive to be fair.
- Parents are called to serve others both in the home and beyond it.
- When either or both parents work excessive hours, the family often suffers.
- Parents are responsible to provide for themselves and their families and, as earlier Christians often noted, to give to the poor.[28]

28. See, for example, John Wesley, Sermon 29, "Upon Our Lord's Sermon on the Mount: Discourse the Ninth," §16, in *The Works of John Wesley,* ed. Thomas Jackson, 14

If parents choose (and are able) to follow the full-time earner/non-employed parent model, then the couple can intentionally plan so that the employed parent makes time to be with the children and that the non-employed parent has areas of service outside of the home. If, on the other hand, a couple chooses or is compelled to use the model where both are employed (whether full-time or part-time), then they can look to these principles and others. They can work out rules for living that fit their family and community. They can make sure that they come to an agreement about a fair division of household labor and that, where possible, they limit employed work enough to be fully involved in the lives of their children and spouse. Parents can attend to these various factors whatever their configuration of paid and unpaid work.

Although I do not want to uplift one model as primary, I do think that the 60-hour model could still be used to point to an advisable upper limit of combined employment hours for many dual-earning couples with children at home. There is precedent for this move. The Institute for American Values did not privilege the 60-hour model over the full-time earner/non-employed parent model but still picked up the 60-hour model and used it as a goal that dual earner couples could aim for as an upper limit for their combined work hours. The primary authors, Jean Bethke Elshtain and David Popenoe, advise: "For married couples with children at home, aim for an overall commitment to paid employment that does not exceed 60 hours per week."[29] If business leaders and policymakers took this model seriously, they could encourage the provision of more part-time jobs with benefits. This would make the 60-hour model more of a possibility for dual earner parents as well as the 30-hour workweek for single parents.[30]

But even as an upper limit, I do not think the 60-hour model is necessary or advisable for all dual earner couples. Although some studies

---

vols., CD-ROM edition (Franklin, TN: Providence House, 1994) 1:640 and Thomas Aquinas, "Whether Religious are Bound to Manual Labor," *Summa Theologica,* I-II, Q. 187, a. 3. Wesley offers another reason to earn money, one that might be particularly applicable today — to avoid debt.

29. Jean Bethke Elshtain and David Popenoe, *Marriage in America: A Report to the Nation* (New York: Council on Families, Institute for American Values, 1995), accessed at http://www.americanvalues.org/html/r-marriage_in_america.html.

30. Although many of the studies and, consequently, the primary focus of this chapter, have been on the activities, decisions, and perceptions of parents, these family decisions are not made in a vacuum. Alongside the principles for parents' discernment described above, we also need similar principles for shaping public policy.

suggest that the dual full-time earner model brings greater risks for marriages and families, other studies show that many dual full-time earner families do well.[31] It may depend on some of the mitigating factors reviewed above. In their discernment, couples can include reflection on these mitigating factors and on the potential risks of spending too many hours on the job. They can develop a rule of life that takes into account these factors and risks. Of course, many couples in low wage jobs must have two paychecks to cover the minimal needs of their families for food and shelter. They do not have the luxury of choosing a different model.

There could be other exceptions to the 60-hour recommended goal. Some fathers and mothers are engaged in full-time ministries or other callings that are extremely costly in time and energy. In my seminary classes, when the subject turns to self-care and the need for pastors to have a 40- or 50-hour workweek, the children of missionaries and activists are scandalized. "Are we not called," they ask, "to give our whole lives to Christ and the mission of the church? How could we put that commitment on hold after 40 or 50 hours and still be faithful to the command of Christ?" They have a point. It is hard to imagine advising Martin Luther King, Jr. to limit his work as a pastor and civil rights leader to 40 hours a week. His absences must have been hard on his family, but those absences from his family were necessary for King to be a catalyst in changing American culture and improving the lives of so many other families.

These decisions about how to configure hours of work on the job, in the home, and in our communities are matters of discernment. Parents look at the many variables in their home lives (including their finances), at their own gifts and limits as individuals, and at their jobs and job possibilities and then make decisions given their assessment of their particular circumstances. Christian and other religious couples can also pray and be open to God's spirit as they explore and discern God's will and ongoing call in their lives. This process of discernment takes time, which is precisely what many American working couples feel they lack. I am convinced that their best chance for living well and faithfully comes as they, no matter how hard it seems, find time to reflect together about their lives, their goals, their faith, and how they

31. See Barnett and Rivers, *She Works/He Works;* Barnett, "Toward a Review and Reconceptualization of the Work/Family Literature"; and the writings of Ellen Galinsky, many of which are available at the Families and Work Institute at: http://www.familiesandwork.org.

want to live in the time that is available.[32] The research reviewed here does not warrant lifting up only one model, but it does suggest that people's happiness about work/family balance may often depend on attentiveness to and thoughtful reflection on the particular circumstances of their households.

But even if the studies yielded clear evidence that the 60-hour model generally led to greater marital happiness, would that be a sure reason to support the 60-hour model? If it turns out that couples are happier when both husband and wife are employed, I would want to know why happiness is linked to employed work as opposed to unpaid volunteer work caring for others.

Perhaps some people are happier with a paying job than with non-paid community and family service, because we live in a culture that often values people not by the depth of their commitment to God and neighbor but by the numbers on their monthly paycheck. We live in a culture that often values our quantifiable contribution to the GNP over our unpaid contribution to the Kingdom of God. Perhaps having absorbed the values of our culture, we value others and ourselves by the standards of money, status, and paid employment. And we like the extra money. This is very American, very middle-class, and perhaps even very human; it is certainly not very Christian (although, many Christians, including me, are guilty of these tendencies). In a culture that places a premium on making money, it would be no surprise if people — including many Christians — were happier when they were making money. If those who could afford to forgo wages are happier with part-time employment than with part-time service without pay, the proper response of the church is not to encourage people to get jobs so that they will be happier in this money-driven, work-obsessed culture; the proper response of the church is to challenge that system of values and, indeed, to encourage people to live in opposition to those values — whether they are working with or without pay, full-time or part-time.

If families can afford it, I see no compelling advantage for the 60-hour model over the full-time earner/non-employed parent model. As long as both partners have enough time with their children and with each other and as long as their financial needs are met (including the long-term financial security of the non-employed partner) and as long as they

32. Dorothy Bass, *Receiving the Day: Christian Practices for Opening the Gift of Time* (San Francisco: Jossey Bass 2000) and Tilden Edwards, *Sabbath Time* (Nashville: Upper Room Books, 1992).

both find meaning in their work — paid or unpaid — I see no reason to privilege one model over the other.

Clearly, not all families can afford to live on one salary. For parents making low wages, one 40-hour-a-week job will not cover the necessities for a family; the additional employment hours are necessary until we enact a living wage or provide greater social supports. But if a family can afford to live on one salary and to have one parent that is not employed, then the opportunities for ministry and service are extraordinary. The person freed from paid employment may be able to do things in the community that would never have happened otherwise — starting a tutoring program in a poorer school or offering services to homeless families, for example. Just thinking through my own extended family, I can think of many examples of service to public schools, churches, synagogues, and local communities that would never had been rendered if both parents had been employed. There are many crucial tasks in our society for which no pay is given. In light of the recent decline of community and community service detailed in Robert Putnam's *Bowling Alone* and in light of the recent budget cuts in services for the poor, children, and the elderly, the need for volunteer service is particularly great in our time.[33] Both paid and unpaid work can yield great benefits.

I affirm Browning's "ontology of equality" that grounds male and female responsibility for family and for the world beyond the family, and I see warrants for this idea throughout scripture. I am not at all convinced, however, that the divine command to be fruitful and have dominion provides much support for a model that calls for both parents in a household to engage in employment that yields a paycheck.

Browning and his colleagues propose the 60-hour model to combat market encroachment into the family. I am simply arguing that they could take the fight against market encroachment one step further by refusing to privilege paid over unpaid work. This is no minor point. By privileging paid work over unpaid service to community, Browning underemphasizes a crucial part of Christian family life — the vocation of the family and its members to transform the world through sacrificial love and service. There is much more to public life outside of the home than employment. The vocation of family members extends beyond the

33. Robert Putnam, *Bowling Alone: The Collapse and Revival of American Community* (New York: Simon and Schuster, 2000). See also Commission on Children at Risk, *Hardwired to Connect: The New Scientific Case for Authoritative Communities* (New York: Institute for American Values, 2003).

family to care for others — especially those others who are poor. And service to and with the poor rarely pays well; indeed, it rarely pays at all. It is costly.

The job of churches and other civic institutions is not simply to promote the work/family formula or formulae that lead to reports of greater happiness but to question the prevailing understandings of happiness. Churches at this juncture can encourage parishioners to pray, reflect, and talk with others about ultimate human happiness and satisfaction as it relates to the love of God and neighbor.

The key question in this discernment is not about the best form or formula for the family's configuration of work hours. The key question is about the ultimate purpose of the family. There are many ways of framing this deeper purpose of the family in relation to the responsibilities of paid employment and other responsibilities in the home and beyond. One could ask: what configuration will help the family and its members to grow in the love of God and neighbor and in service to them? What life patterns and arrangements will best promote holiness, righteousness, the restoration of the Image of God in the lives of the members of a family and, through their service, in the lives of others beyond that family?

In her book *Family: A Christian Social Perspective,* Lisa Sowle Cahill questions the tendency in some quarters of the American family debates to privilege a particular form of the family with both a mother and a father in an intact marriage. Cahill seeks not simply to broaden the understanding of family forms, but also to change the focus from family form to family function. She writes: "The ideals of Christian family life should focus more on function (fostering gospel informed commitments and behaviors) than on regularity of form." Cahill's "socially transformative family" seeks to move beyond care for the needs of the family to include the needs of the larger community.[34] Cahill draws the readers' attention to African American families as models for altruistic service. While Euro-American families often focus on the survival and fulfillment of the immediate family and its members, according to Cahill, African American families are more likely to find meaning in service to and relationship with those outside of the immediate family — extended family, neighbors, church community, and others.

This is an important corrective for much of the recent American discussion about families. We have tended to focus on what family forms

34. Lisa Sowle Cahill, *Family: A Christian Social Perspective* (Minneapolis: Augsburg Fortress, 2000), xi.

and behaviors produce well-adjusted children, better marriages, happier parents and children. Our arguments about parents' employment, about two-parent homes, about single parenthood, and about divorce tend to focus on the question: how will this family form or behavior affect the happiness and well-being of the members of the family, especially the children? This is, of course, extremely important. We need to know, for example, that excessive employment hours for mothers or fathers are often bad for the well-being of the family and its members. But if we stop there, we are shortchanging the family and the larger society. One of the great gifts of the Religion, Culture, and Family Project is that, at its best, it has helped to push the discussion beyond a primary focus on the individual family to consider other families and the larger social systems as well.

As middle-class and upper-middle-class families decide what configuration of employment and other unpaid work is best for their families, they should also consider what is good for other families. Much of the research and some of the recommendations from family/work studies assume that parents have a choice about how to configure their hours. But many parents who have low wage jobs need two incomes to provide the bare necessities for their household. (I suspect that many middle- and upper-middle-class workers who insist that they have to have two full-time salaries to afford the necessities have an inflated notion of what is necessary to sustain a family. Many middle-class parents do have some choice.) How can families with greater economic prosperity and greater choice work toward a society that is more just for poorer families?

One small but significant way to nourish justice for the poor can begin close to home. As middle-class parents work longer hours at their employment, not only do they have less time for service to neighbor, including the poor, they also come to rely on the low wages and hard work of poorer workers to make their own longer hours and prosperity possible. When middle-class parents are employed longer hours outside the home, low wage workers often take up the slack — cleaning the homes of middle-class families and caring for their children. These workers rarely make a living wage, and they often usually receive no benefits.[35] Sometimes what seems to be best for the immediate well-being of middle-class families may not be best for poorer families, or even, in the end, for the true well-being of

35. See Barbara Ehrenreich, *Nickel and Dimed: On (Not) Getting By in America* (New York: Henry Holt and Company, 2001) and Christine Firer Hinze, "U.S. Catholic Social Thought, Gender, and Economic Livelihood," *Theological Studies* 66 (2005): 568-91. For a controversial reflection, see Caitlin Flanagan's "How Serfdom Saved the Women's Movement," *Atlantic Monthly* 293(2) (March 2004): 109-28.

those middle-class families. If we are all one body, then the well-being of the individual members is dependent on the health and well-being of the whole. More prosperous families, while working to enact a living wage and better working conditions in the larger society, also have an obligation to pay a fair, living wage to poorer people in their employ.

My larger point is that the family discussion is often focused on the happiness of the individual family and that many families in our culture are inward focused to their own peril. It is good for family members (and their happiness and well-being) to remember that the family has a larger purpose than its own survival, well-being, and happiness. And, more important, even if it were not good for their immediate well-being and happiness to remember that larger purpose, it would still be good. It would still be the right thing to do.

Our forgetfulness of the larger focus of the family may be rooted in our forgetfulness of Christian language and worldview. It is difficult to understand this argument — that family members have a larger purpose beyond the family — without knowing something about Christian notions of vocation, sacrificial love, service, and righteousness. These particular, confessional claims are crucial for understanding the arguments that Christians make about human purpose, responsibility, and even the nature of families.

One of the crucial categories for understanding family is the concept of vocation, including the relationship between various vocations as parents, as spouses, as workers, as community members, and primarily, of course, as Christians.[36] The category of vocation has helped me to reflect on Browning's 60-hour model. Our primary vocation as Christians plays itself out in these various callings. A common Christian claim is that the ultimate vocation is the love of God and neighbor which is expressed in the various activities of our lives — including parenthood, marriage, friendship, prayer, service, employment, and innumerable other activities. The idea of vocation can provide a lens for families as they discern which configuration of work on the job, in the home, and in the wider community is best given their circumstances.

John Wesley observed that some Christians of his time made vocational decisions about their employment and their marriages for the wrong reasons — out of concern for "the things on earth, rather than the things above." Wesley was not at his most charitable in his response: "Re-

36. For more on Christian claims about vocation, see my article "That's All a Mule Can Do," note 5 above.

pent, repent of your vile earthly-mindedness: Renounce the title of Christians, or prefer, both in your own case and the case of your children, grace to money, and heaven to earth!"[37] Wesley recommended that people discern God's will for their employment or their marriage by asking what choices will offer the greatest opportunity for *"being and doing good."* He wrote:

> Suppose, for instance, it were proposed to a reasonable man to marry, or to enter into a new business: In order to know whether this is the will of God, being assured, "It is the will of God concerning me, that I should be as holy and do as much good as I can," he has only to inquire, "In which of these states can I be most holy, and do the most good?" And this is to be determined, partly by reason, and partly by experience. Experience tells him what advantages he has in his present state, either for being or doing good; and reason is to show, what he certainly or probably will have in the state proposed. *By comparing these, he is to judge which of the two may most conduce to his being and doing good; and as far as he knows this, so far he is certain what is the will of God.*[38]

Christian parents today who are trying to find the best configuration of work on the job, in the home, and in service to the wider community can use this advice from eighteenth-century England. Couples can seek to discern God's will about their employment by pragmatic deliberation, looking for the configuration that will offer the greatest opportunity to "be most holy and to do the most good" or, more simply put, to be and to do good.

The church needs to remind Christians of this larger vocation to be and to do good, countering the tendency to forget about the larger purpose of the family and to focus instead on the well-being of individual members inside the family. Our forgetfulness of Christian language and worldview is at the heart of the problem. We have become so proficient at the public discourse of the market and our shared language of capitalism, that we have grown deaf or indifferent to the claims of the faith that stand over and against the values of the market. Only through the critical reinvigoration of our Christian tradition and its ideas about marriage and family, and only through more faithful living in relation to that critically

37. John Wesley, Sermon 118, "On a Single Eye," in *Works of John Wesley*, 7:303-4.

38. John Wesley, Sermon 37, "The Nature of Enthusiasm," in *Works of John Wesley*, 5:474 (emphasis added).

reappropriated tradition, will Christians have a chance to form and maintain authentically Christian families that have a radical vision of service and transformation that goes beyond their own well-being and beyond the values of the market.

This is exactly what Browning and his colleagues are trying to do — to limit the encroachment of market forces into the family and into our ideas about family and critically to reinvigorate Christian traditions concerning marriage and family. One of the primary reasons that the Religion, Culture, and Family Project has been so successful is that Don Browning sets up groups and discussions to foster critical engagement. He seems more interested in creating the conditions for further reflection and new arguments to emerge (and then to be engaged and reengaged) than he is in nailing down the one best argument. I raise these questions about the 60-hour model not to oppose Browning and his colleagues, but to join in their efforts. My questions and arguments are not a fundamental challenge to Browning and his colleagues but are, in the end, an extension of their arguments.

8 Teaching Equal Regard to the Abandoned Generation: Case Studies from a Psychology of Gender Class

Mary Stewart Van Leeuwen

Participation in the decade-long Religion, Culture, and Family Project (RCFP) has been a highlight of my three decades-plus academic career. Much of that project's success was due to the fact that its director, Don Browning, was uniquely skilled at keeping various team members — scholars from Mainline, Reformed, Evangelical, and other Protestant traditions as well as Catholics and Jews — talking to and learning from each other without sacrificing their religious distinctiveness. Don's unfailingly gracious manner, eagerness to learn from other disciplines and religious traditions, and stellar background in practical theology combined to make our annual seminars and work-in-progress meetings during the 1990s events to be anticipated beforehand and savored long after.[1]

Those meetings were never without controversy. Team members differed on the relative importance of cultural versus structural explanations for current problems affecting North American families, on market forces as primarily the friend or foe of covenant relationships, and on the relative weight to be given to the sciences, the social sciences, and religious traditions in the understanding and solution of family-related challenges. There were some topics (such as homosexuality) that we agreed to sideline in order to keep the focus of the project clear and manageable, and other questions (for example, those concerning abortion and contra-

1. As an academic psychologist, my first introduction to Don Browning's scholarship was in his work *Religious Thought and the Modern Psychologies* (Minneapolis: Fortress Press, 1987). See also Don S. Browning and Terry D. Cooper, *Religious Thought and the Modern Psychologies*, 2d ed. (Minneapolis: Augsburg Fortress, 2004).

ception) that infrequently appeared on our radar screens because for many of us they were considered settled.[2] Yet we kept talking to each other, kept writing, and in the end had two book series totaling more than twenty volumes, plus a nationally broadcast PBS video documentary on the history and meaning of marriage. I can only conclude that the age of miracles is not past.

In this chapter, I shall apply some insights from the Religion, Culture, and Family Project to some experiences in teaching Psychology of Gender to upper-level undergraduates in Christian liberal arts settings. My first two examples, which focus on the topics of divorce and co-parenting, have clear ties to previous RCFP writings by Don Browning and others. The third example extends the RCFP conversation somewhat, as it focuses on the topic of contraception, and my (mostly evangelical Protestant) students' surprising embrace of the (mostly Catholic) theory and practice of Natural Family Planning. What links my students' interest in all three topics seems to be their desire to find a third way between the larger culture's promotion of hedonism and so-called rational self-interest, and the stereotypical gender roles — often accompanied by a doctrine of male headship in church and family — that many have experienced in their churches.[3] Don Browning's treatment of the rational-choice model is seen in his critique of economists Milton Friedman, Gary Becker, and Richard Posner, and their questionable extension of rational-choice microeconomic theory (often with some socio-biological additions) to other spheres of life, including mate selection and family dynamics.[4] His critique of the male headship model appears constantly in his advocacy of the "equal-regard" family as an extension of the second great commandment. As he wrote in 1995:

> "To love your neighbor as yourself" . . . [means] that we are to love our neighbor, be it friend or spouse, with the same seriousness as we naturally love ourselves. To love the other with equal seriousness as our-

2. An exception to this is Catholic theologian Lisa Sowle Cahill's book in the first RCFP series, *Sex, Gender and Christian Ethics* (New York: Cambridge University Press, 1996), about which more below.

3. By hedonism I refer not to the simple affirmation of personal pleasure, but to the elevation of personal pleasure as the chief motive and end of human striving, and the attempt to reduce all other motives to it.

4. See, for example, Don S. Browning, "Egos Without Selves: A Critique of the Family Theory of the Chicago School of Economics," in Don S. Browning, *Equality and the Family: A Fundamental Practical Theology of Children, Mothers, and Fathers in Modern Societies* (Grand Rapids, MI: Eerdmans, 2007).

> selves is a strenuous ethic, far more strenuous than either ethical egoist or utilitarian perspectives. But to love or regard the other as ourselves means we are entitled to love or regard ourselves equally to the others. This ethic does not allow us to regard ourselves more, but neither does it permit us to take the masochistic stance of regarding ourselves less. This is a rigorous and highly demanding ethic of mutuality.[5]

What follows is, first, a description of the larger context — social and religious — in which my teaching of the Psychology of Gender is done, and, second, a consideration of the three more specific topics dealt with in that course, each of which overlaps with and extends the concerns of the Religion, Culture, and Family Project.

Teaching the Abandoned Generation

As one of the core team members of the RCFP, I found it both interesting and challenging to be in a distinct minority on three fronts simultaneously: as a social scientist (rather than a theologian or biblical scholar), as a neo-Calvinist with Evangelical leanings (rubbing shoulders with a plurality of team members schooled in the mainline church heritage of the University of Chicago Divinity School), and as an academic primarily involved in the teaching of undergraduates (rather than graduate students or seminarians). Duke University chaplain Will Willimon and his co-author economist Tom Naylor have called today's American undergraduates "the abandoned generation," in part because universities have become places where the most ambitious and erudite professors often aspire to teach as little as possible. Moreover, even when they do teach, many professors abdicate responsibility for the moral formation of their students under the cover of a putative — though actually impossible — value-neutrality. Willimon and Naylor concluded that such attitudes and practices have contributed to the escalating problems of substance abuse, indolence, and excessive careerism among American undergraduates. Supplied with fewer and fewer avenues for exploring the bigger questions of purpose and meaning, many college students have settled for the acquisition of lucrative career skills and/or the pursuit of short-term gratification.[6]

In terms of raw percentages, Evangelical colleges and universities

5. Browning, "Egos Without Selves."

6. William H. Willimon and Thomas H. Naylor, *The Abandoned Generation: Rethinking Higher Education* (Grand Rapids, MI: Eerdmans, 1995).

do not face to the same degree the problems of student substance abuse and sexual acting out as can be found in allegedly secular or more loosely church-related institutions. Nor to the same extent do they face the opposing problems of excessive personal ambition and passive resistance to learning. But face them they still do, as can be seen by the number of conferences and workshops offered in recent years by the Council for Christian Colleges and Universities and the Christian College Consortium, aimed at faculty and student development staff in close to two hundred member institutions. The topics of these initiatives have run the gamut from post-adolescent cognitive and sexual development to the challenges faced by professors as they undertake spiritual formation, intellectual mentoring, and relating faith to learning in the classroom.[7]

How responsibly yet sensitively to guide young adults' sexual and relational choices is in many ways no less challenging for the predominantly baby-boomer generation of Christian college professors than for their contemporaries at neighboring institutions of higher learning. For one thing, the students in their classrooms are overall no less likely to be children of divorce than at the nearby state university. George Barna's 2001 U.S. random national survey found that 33 percent of born-again adults (as having made an individual commitment to Jesus that is still personally important to them, and expecting to go heaven as a result of this commitment) had gone through a divorce — not statistically different from the 34 percent rate among those who rejected the born-again label. Moreover, close to 90 percent of those divorces had taken place after — not before — the time of their conversion.[8] In response to these figures, David Gushee, a theological ethicist at Baptist-related Union University in Tennessee, bluntly asserted that defining Christian commitment as Barna did — in terms of "one past experience, one current feeling and one belief about the future" — is theologically inadequate because of its disconnect from ongoing behavioral responsibility. "The problem, however, does not rest with the research firm," Gushee concluded. "It rests with the churches themselves. . . . 'Christianity' is all too often a cultural phenomenon that reflects and fully participates in American culture, rather than standing in any way apart from it."[9]

7. For further details on such initiatives, consult the web sites of the Council for Christian Colleges and Universities (www.cccu.org) and the Christian College Consortium (www.ccconsortium.org).

8. "Born-Again Adults Less Likely to Co-Habit, Just as Likely to Divorce," *The Barna Update,* August 6, 2001, accessible at: http://www.barna.org.

9. David P. Gushee, *Getting Marriage Right: Realistic Counsel for Saving and Strengthening Relationships* (Grand Rapids, MI: Baker, 2004), 228-29.

Gushee would not be surprised to learn that the pedagogical challenge rests not just with born-again students, but with those trying to teach them. For example, at a recent conference on "Gender Identity and Human Sexuality" attended mainly by student development professionals in the Christian College Consortium (representing some of the oldest confessionally Christian institutions in the U.S.) participants agreed that it was often challenging to counsel students — and even their own children — against the sexual excesses of contemporary culture when they and their generation had helped to launch the sexual revolution of the 1960s and 1970s.[10] And the forty-something Episcopalian pastor who led the conference's worship services confessed that he never speaks to young people about sex without first apologizing for the legacy of sexual anarchy that he and his generation have bequeathed to them.[11]

Aspects of that legacy showed up in the analysis of a 2005 whole-population survey of undergraduate sexual behavior at my own university.[12] In this well-crafted study, 98 percent of male and female students classified themselves as born again, following the first part of Barna's definition. Yet large percentages of both sexes reported having engaged in

10. Nationally representative research on American sexual behavior shows that by age twenty-one, approximately 85 percent of males and 80 percent of females have had vaginal intercourse, and that these figures are not much lower when only college-attending groups are sampled. The corresponding percentages for men and women at Christian colleges are closer to 50 percent, and for all types of sexual behavior, only the rate — not the presence of a given behavior — differs, and that not as much as might be expected. See, for example, William D. Mosher, Anjani Chandra, and Jo Ann Jones, *Sexual Behavior and Selected Health Measures: Men and Women 15-44 Years of Age, United States, 2002,* Advance Data from Vital and Health Statistics, vol. 362 (Hyattsville, MD: United States Department of Health and Human Services, Centers for Disease Control and Prevention, National Center for Health Statistics, Sept. 15, 2005). On the impossibility of so-called worldview neutrality in any classroom, but especially those in which the social sciences are taught, see, for example, Mary Stewart Van Leeuwen, "Scuttling the Schizophrenic Student Mind: On Teaching the Unity of Faith and Learning in Psychology," in *Teaching As an Act of Faith: Theory and Practice in Church-Related Higher Education*, ed. Arlin C. Migliazzo (New York: Fordham University Press, 2002), 21-40.

11. Christian College Consortium Conference on Gender, Identity, and Human Sexuality, June 15-18, 2005, Gordon College, Wenham, Massachusetts. Mindful of their own limitations as mainly middle-aged and older boomers, the conference planners also listened to the edgy and hip musings of Lauren Winner, a twenty-something convert from Orthodox (though by her own admission hardly chaste) Judaism, and the author of *Girl Meets God: A Memoir* (New York: Random House, 2003) and *Real Sex: The Naked Truth About Chastity* (Grand Rapids, MI: Brazos Press, 2005).

12. Wendy Steinberg, "Report to the Eastern University Administration on the Spring 2005 Sexual Behavior Survey," Eastern University, September 2005.

mutual masturbation (49 percent of males, 41 percent of females), oral sex (46 percent and 44 percent), and genital sex (25 percent and 29 percent). These figures are still substantially lower than in nation-wide surveys of young adults, for whom the prevalence of both oral and genital sexual activity is closer to 80 percent for both sexes. But they are still troubling, especially given that four times as many women as men cited partner pressure as the main reason for their first sexual experience (oral, genital, or anal), and more than three times fewer cited sexual arousal. At the same time, 44 percent of all respondents reported that they were unhappy about their past level of sexual experience, and the vast majority of *both* sexes in this group said that they wished they had not done what they had already done.[13] And fully 88 percent of male and 85 percent of female respondents indicated that they had made a conscious decision to remain sexually abstinent until marriage — regardless of prior sexual experience — or were seriously considering such a decision — even though 17 percent of males and 24 percent of females also indicated that they were still sexually active! It thus seems that many Evangelical students are in a state of internal conflict. They are or have been involved in casual sexual relationships, but often sense them to be less than healthy, despite the barrage of cultural (and occasionally even religious) messages assuring them that sex is no big deal and that whatever feels good in the context of mutual consent and adequate protection against disease and pregnancy is just fine.

Also between Two Worlds: Evangelical Children of Divorce

It is against such a backdrop that I teach an undergraduate course each year on the Psychology of Gender. Along with the standard research and theoretical issues related to gender[14] the topics of divorce, marriage education, communication and conflict resolution between spouses, and the benefits of co-parenting are a regular part of the curriculum, and my treatment of them overlaps with the accumulated thinking of the RCFP team of scholars.[15] What Don Browning and other authors of *From Cul-*

13. Fifty-four percent of the entire sample indicated satisfaction with their past level of sexual experience, with the vast majority of these (both sexes) indicating that they had very little experience, and wanted to remain so.

14. As surveyed by Hilary M. Lips' excellent text, *Sex and Gender: An Introduction*, 5th ed. (New York: McGraw Hill, 2005).

15. See in particular Don S. Browning, Bonnie J. Miller-McLemore, Pamela D. Couture, K. Brynolf Lyon, and Robert M. Franklin, *From Culture Wars to Common*

ture Wars to Common Ground somewhat awkwardly called "the committed, intact, equal-regard, public-private family" figures prominently as a goal to be considered. If course evaluations are any indication, it is an ideal that my largely Evangelical students come to regard as a refreshing "third way" between the doctrine of gendered separate spheres with which many of them have grown up and the individualistic hedonism that surrounds them in American culture at large. Browning and his co-authors write:

> By "intact" we mean a family in which mother and father are parenting their own children in a lifetime marriage. . . . We use "equal regard" to describe a relationship between husband and wife characterized by mutual respect, affection, practical assistance, and justice — a relationship that values and aids the self and other with equal seriousness. . . . We use "public-private" to characterize families in which husband and wife have privileges and responsibilities in both the public and private spheres of life.[16]

In light of Barna's documented divorce rate among "born-again" Americans, it should come as no surprise that the yearning for an intact marriage (and the realization that it is far from guaranteed) is as strong among Christian undergraduates as anywhere else. Indeed, I have been

Ground: Religion and the American Family Debate (Louisville, KY: Westminster John Knox, 1997). See also Mary Stewart Van Leeuwen, "Reinventing the Ties That Bind: Feminism and the Family at the Close of the Twentieth Century," in *Religion, Feminism and the Family*, ed. Anne Carr and Mary Stewart Van Leeuwen (Louisville, KY: Westminster John Knox, 1996), 33-52; Mary Stewart Van Leeuwen, *My Brother's Keeper: What the Social Sciences Do (and Don't) Tell Us About Masculinity* (Downers Grove, IL: InterVarsity Press, 2002); Christine Firer Hinze and Mary Stewart Van Leeuwen, "Whose Marriage? Whose Health? A Christian Feminist Ethical Response," in *Marriage, Health, and the Professions: If Marriage Is Good for You, What Does This Mean for Law, Medicine, Ministry, Therapy, and Business*, ed. John Wall, Don Browning, William J. Doherty, and Stephen Post (Grand Rapids, MI: Eerdmans, 2002), 145-66, and David Blankenhorn, Don S. Browning, and Mary Stewart Van Leeuwen, eds., *Does Christianity Teach Male Headship: The Equal-Regard Family and Its Critics* (Grand Rapids, MI: Eerdmans, 2004), chap. 4.

16. Browning et al., *From Culture Wars to Common Ground*, 2. The authors also note that "intact family" includes children who enter the family through adoption or assisted reproduction, and that the "ethic of equal regard" has significance for parent-child as well as inter-spousal relations. See further Don S. Browning, "Adoption and the Moral Significance of Kin Altruism," in *The Morality of Adoption: Social-Psychological, Theological, and Legal Perspectives*, ed. Timothy P. Jackson (Grand Rapids, MI: Eerdmans, 2005), 52-77.

teaching Psychology of Gender long enough to have followed some of my former students as they journeyed through both marriage and divorce, sometimes with parenthood along the way. One of them — now teaching at her former undergraduate institution — was brave enough to go public about that journey, describing the way that it both tested and strengthened her faith. Realizing that most of her students expected both to get and stay married, she reflected on the fact that twelve years previously she "had sat in exactly the same classroom (at one of those very desks as a matter of fact), firmly believing both those things about myself." Although coping well — with welcome help from church and family — as an academic and a single parent, she confessed that

> I used to absolutely hate the idea of being divorced, in part because it carried with it that unspeakable burden of guilt and shame. The week before the divorce was finalized I even harbored a tiny, terrible wish that my husband would die (quickly and painlessly!) in a car accident so that I could be widowed instead of divorced. It just sounds so much less sordid. I don't care that roughly half of the marriages in the United States end in divorce — mine wasn't supposed to. This was not part of my life plan.
>
> It still isn't. But it is part of my life, and it doesn't need to change for me to become the person God wants me to be. One of the most important things I've ever learned is that we don't really have control over our own lives. We fight and fret and rage, we weep and beg and try again, but for all our efforts we simply can't control people and events outside ourselves. I'm not living the life I thought I would . . . but that doesn't keep me from responding to God's call at least as well as I could have in the life I idealized. God doesn't call us to live perfect, bright shiny lives. All God asks of us is to live in grace with honesty and integrity. [And] there's a reason even beyond simple honesty for Christians not to cover up our brokenness. Our failures and heartaches provide God powerful ways through which we can reach out to hurting people around us. . . . [As the Leonard Cohen song says] "There are cracks, cracks in everything, that's how the light gets in." . . . [And] cracks aren't just how light gets in to us in our misery and darkness — they're how light shines through us to other people.[17]

17. Christina Van Dyke, "The Beauty in Brokenness," *Perspectives: A Journal of Reformed Thought* 20(3) (March 2005): 8-11.

Those "cracks" also show up in the young adult children of divorce who land in my Psychology of Gender course. In recent years the first inkling I've had about who they are comes when they read Elizabeth Marquardt's 1999 essay on "The Moral and Spiritual Lives of Children of Divorce." This paper, originally written by one of Don Browning's students (and also a RCFP intern), was seen by him to be breaking such new ground that it was added to the reading list of RCFP team members.[18] Indeed, in his desire to extend practical theology to issues of public policy, Browning, while not necessarily advocating a return to fault-based divorce, had already proposed that religious institutions should back certain revisions to divorce laws. In 1998 he wrote:

> Since the advent of no-fault divorce in the late 1960s and early 1970s, the marriage contract has become weaker than most business contracts. In many states, it can be broken unilaterally, and the dissenting partner has little recourse. From both a philosophical and theological perspective, we hold that marriage agreements should be more like covenants, i.e., binding agreements between a husband and wife, between them and the wider society, and, for the religious, between these two individuals and a transcendent power as they conceive it. Such multi-dimensional agreements should not be broken with ease. . . . [Family scholars] do not agree as to whether the present system of no-fault divorces should be rejected completely. . . . We do agree, however, that in cases where couples with children want divorce by mutual consent, they should undergo required counseling on parenting after divorce, and on the potential impact of the divorce on children. Furthermore, couples should be required to develop a long-term financial plan to cover the needs of children until they are 18 and in some cases older. This plan would have to be accepted by the court before the divorcing couple could begin to divide property between them.[19]

In my class, Marquardt's paper is one of several articles whose discussion is student-led, and I have learned to expect that it will be children of divorce who volunteer — yea, compete — to lead that discussion. In the

18. Elizabeth Marquardt, "The Moral and Spiritual Lives of Children of Divorce," University of Chicago Divinity School, Religion Culture and Family Project, 1999.

19. Don S. Browning, "The Task of Religious Institutions in Strengthening Families," in *Equality and the Family*, 240-41.

process of coming out of the divorce closet to their peers (who usually had no more idea of their status than I did) most identify strongly with one or more of the experiences that Marquardt explored in this preliminary paper, then later documented more thoroughly in a larger empirical study, *Between Two Worlds,* published in 2005.[20]

Like Marquardt's national-sample subjects, and Marquardt herself, my students from divorced families admit to having felt like exiles from the parental homes between which they had to commute. They remember seeing these homes as conflicting moral spaces with competing expectations. They often felt pressure to take sides and keep secrets in parental conflicts. Many felt they had to assume the role of parent toward one or the other of their own parents in the continuing emotional upheaval of the divorce, and they admit to being ambivalent about taking the risk of marital commitment as a result of such experiences. And while most seem to have a strong faith or at least a continuing openness to developing one, they often admit to having shared Marquardt's ambivalence toward God at various times in their lives:

> "Where is God in all this?" I asked, and still do. I've struggled with anger at God for many years. In one sense anger at God is not a bad thing. Many of the great prophets and theologians spent most of their lives shaking their fist at God. But anger has also kept me distant from God. Too often I've embraced a false sense of control, moving through the day checking items off a list so that I could avoid having to feel. . . . [Children of divorce] are child-sized old souls. When we come of age and leave home, we are less likely overall to be religious. We long for spirituality as much as our peers from intact families do, but loss, suffering, lack of trust in and anger at our parents, and even anger at God, are more defining qualities of our spiritual journeys.[21]

Marquardt's preliminary paper (and her larger empirical study) also explored her respondents' understanding and application of the Old Testament injunction to honor one's parents, as well as their appropriation of

20. Elizabeth Marquardt, *Between Two Worlds: The Inner Lives of Children of Divorce* (New York: Crown Publishers, 2005). Marquardt's study included a survey of 1,500 young adults (ages 18 to 35) from both divorced and intact families, in addition to in-depth interviews with a subset of seventy. All of the respondents from divorced families had stayed in contact with both parents and had experienced their parents' divorce before the age of fourteen.

21. Marquardt, *Between Two Worlds,* 138, 139.

the New Testament parable of the prodigal son. Not surprisingly, my students who are Evangelical children of divorce often focus their attention on these themes. "Honor is a two-way street," one of them wrote in a course reflection paper. "It's hard to honor a parent who isn't living up to his responsibilities as a father, and I don't think God would honor him if he tried to play that card with me."[22] Others point out that the parable of the prodigal son is relevant to themselves only inasmuch as they share the son's feelings of having been "in exile" from their respective homes. Otherwise, many believe, it is one or both of their parents who were more like (unrepentant) prodigals — for example, by failing to make child support payments even when they were able, by making promises to stay in touch that they did not keep, or by putting their post-divorce desire to pursue new sexual relationships above the needs of their children.

For well-educated conservative Christian youngsters, divorce may still be shrouded with more shame than is the case for their peers at large. For some, like my former student and her child, its effects may be mitigated by the support of churches and other family members, and by a sense of participation in the larger biblical meta-narrative, in which God finally "works all things together for good" (Romans 8:28). But in many respects, its risks for the adult children of divorce are the same. As Marquardt and other scholars of divorce have pointed out, just because such young people function well publicly — indeed, often *over*-function — doesn't mean they remain emotionally unscathed.[23] My students from divorced families routinely express the relief they experience in reading Marquardt's paper. Finally, they say, someone is "telling it like it is" for us, rather than treating divorce as a minor bump on the developmental landscape of the children who go through it, or smothering their sense of domestic bifurcation and truncated childhood with what Marquardt calls "happy talk," in the form of divorce-romanticizing children's books and even greeting cards. Herself the child of a so-called good divorce (one in which both parents shared her care, both physically and financially) Marquardt concluded from her research that, absent very high conflict in a family, there really is no such thing as a "good" divorce for children. On the contrary, divorce is an experience that can deeply affect those who go through it, even when as adults they appear to be functioning successfully.

22. Quotations from students are moderately edited when necessary to protect the identities of their authors.

23. See also Judith Wallerstein, Julia M. Lewis, and Sandra Blakeslee, *The Unexpected Legacy of Divorce: A 25 Year Landmark Study* (New York: Hyperion, 2000).

Nor are my students generally impressed by critics who point out that studies like Marquardt's do not compare conflict-ridden families that have undergone divorce with similar families that stayed together "for the sake of the children." Surely, these critics argue, children in the latter families would show the same range and quantity of problems as children of divorce, thus demonstrating that the operant factor is not divorce per se, but the miserable homes children lived in *prior* to the divorce.[24] But this is a questionable assumption, as my students discover when they read about a mammoth, thirty-three-year longitudinal study involving virtually all the British children born during the first week of March 1958. In subsequent years, interviews were conducted with the children's mothers, fathers, and teachers and (eventually) with the children themselves, of whom over two-thirds were still in the study at age thirty-three. During that time, of course, some of their parents had divorced and others had not, thus allowing the researchers to examine ongoing conflict similarities (and differences) between the two groups. The authors of the study found that only about half the problems suffered by children of divorce could be attributed to pre-divorce conflict in the home. Significantly, only about a third of divorces in America occur in what are defined as high-conflict marriages, and it is only such divorces that leave children, on the whole, better off than they would be in an intact family.[25]

24. For example, Constance Ahrons, *The Good Divorce: Keeping Your Family Together When Your Marriage Comes Apart* (New York: HarperCollins, 1994); Stephanie Coontz, *Marriage, A History: From Obedience to Intimacy, or How Love Conquered Marriage* (New York: Viking Penguin, 2005); Vicki Lansky, *Divorce Book for Parents: Helping Your Children Cope With Divorce and Its Aftermath*, 3rd ed. (Minnetonka, MN: Book Peddlars, 1996); Vicki Lansky, *It's Not Your Fault, Koko Bear: A Read-Together Book for Parents and Young Children During Divorce* (Minnetonka, MN: Book Peddlars, 1998).

25. Andrew Cherlin et al., "Longitudinal Studies of Effects of Divorce on Children in Great Britain and the United States," *Science* 252 (1991): 1386-89. Other critics have argued that it is not divorce per se but simply post-divorce economic strain on single-parent families that accounts for the problems in children of divorce. However, the negative effects of divorce have been shown to persist even when income is controlled for — for example, when generous child support is paid or when children's economic status is raised by the custodial parent's remarriage. At best only half the variance associated with the children's problems is attributable to the economic stresses that accompany single parenthood. See David Blankenhorn, *Fatherless America: Confronting Our Most Urgent Social Problem* (New York: Basic Books, 1995), chap. 10, for a review of the pertinent literature.

From the Great Chain of Being to the Doctrine of Separate Spheres

But even well-parented students from intact homes are aware — both from national statistics and personal experience with friends and family member — that their own risk of being divorced in the future is considerable. As a result, many are anxious to explore models of family life that they believe will contribute to both marital longevity and marital happiness. In the twenty-years-plus I have taught Psychology of Gender, I have found that for many conservative Christian audiences the least threatening — indeed, most beguiling — way to introduce Don Browning's ideal of "the committed, intact, equal-regard, public-private family" is through a critical examination of the doctrine of separate spheres for men and women, beginning with some Western-world social history then going on to contemporary social psychological studies of families in both Western and non-Western societies.

Students are often surprised to learn that from the classical era through the early modern period in the West, women and men were almost never referred to as "opposite sexes." Rather, both were considered "human," but in differing degrees. According to Aristotle's *scala naturae* (which in the Greek/Christian synthesis of the medieval era became the "great chain of being") women were rational beings, but to a lesser extent than men. And since rationality was what separated humans from brutes, it followed that *all* the human virtues — courage, autonomy, appreciation of beauty, capacity for friendship, even sexual self-control and the ability to teach children — were assumed to be more developed in men than in women. In Dorothy Sayers' memorable phrase, women were in effect "the human-not-quite-human."[26] But paradoxically, it was in part just because of this doctrine that most women and men had roles that overlapped greatly. It was generally assumed that women could do most of the same things that men did — just not as competently, and (in patriarchally run society) certainly with less authority. Thus, for most families right up to the dawn of the Industrial Revolution workplace, dwelling place, and childrearing space largely coincided, making the household a locus of fairly self-sufficient production — not just repro-

26. Dorothy L. Sayers, "The Human-Not-Quite-Human," in *Are Women Human?* (Downers Grove, IL: InterVarsity Press, 1975), 37-47. See also Prudence Allen, *The Concept of Women: The Aristotelian Revolution, 750 B.C.–A.D. 1250* (Grand Rapids, MI: Eerdmans, 1997).

duction — and a place in which, although some gendered division of labor existed, there was substantial overlap between men's and women's work.

It would be hard to exaggerate how much this state of affairs changed as the Industrial Revolution gained momentum in the Western world toward the end of the eighteeenth century. Subsistence farming more and more gave way to mechanized commercial agriculture. With steadily cheaper consumer goods available, adult women — at least if they were middle-class or above — were less occupied with traditional tasks such as spinning, weaving, soap making, and poultry raising, and gradually went from being co-producers with their husbands to being mainly purchasers and consumers of household goods. Increasing numbers of men exchanged the family shop or farm for waged labor in factories or offices, which greatly reduced the amount of time they spent interacting with wives and children. As capitalism and commerce expanded, this increasingly gendered division of labor was more and more portrayed as both natural *and* biblical, and the language of "opposite sexes" began to replace the earlier idea of women as "incomplete" or "less well-developed" men. To give them some sense of purpose to replace the economically productive roles they were rapidly losing, women were now idealized as the *morally superior* and self-sacrificing "angels of the home." Men, by contrast, were to become social-Darwinist-driven "captains of industry," even though in practice this extreme bifurcation of gender roles (and virtues) was a luxury beyond the reach of most poor urban families — not to mention those still working on family farms — whose survival continued to require shared economic and nurturing activities from *all* family members, regardless of age or sex.[27] Thus was born the nineteenth-century doctrine of gendered separate spheres, according to which masculinity — at least in its hegemonic or socially dominant form — was characterized by instrumental calculation and individual self-promotion in public arenas such as the marketplace, the academy, and the political forum. Moreover, with the decline of adult control over courtship in supervised settings, and the corresponding advent of public dating paid for by young men, masculinity also became more stereotypically connected to sexual predation — or at least to the idea

27. See, for example, Carl Degler, *At Odds: Women and the Family from the Revolution to the Present* (New York: Oxford University Press, 1980) and Gail Bederman, *Manliness and Civilization: A Cultural History of Gender and Race in Nineteenth Century America* (Chicago: University of Chicago Press, 1996).

that whatever a young man spent on a date should be repaid with corresponding sexual favors. And since men were now assumed to have far less control over their sexual urges than young women, the latter (rather than parents and other community adults, as in earlier times) were designated as the sexual gatekeepers.[28] Femininity thus became associated with economic dependence, sexual purity, and piety. In a partial reversal of the earlier, Aristotelian-influenced portrait of gender relations (namely "anything women can do, men can do better") women were now seen to be *superior* as educators of children, models of sexual restraint and self-sacrificing love, as well as providers of emotional respite to their husbands and sons from the increasingly individualistic world of profit and competition. In effect, the cultural mandate of Genesis 1:28 ("Be fruitful and multiply; fill the earth and subdue it") was now divided by sex and location. Women were to be the reproductive specialists (physically and emotionally) at home, while men subdued the earth elsewhere. In historian Gail Bederman's words, "pious women would keep their sons and husbands moral; productive men would work to become successful entrepreneurs . . . and together they would forge godly homes, the epitome of Christian Progress."[29]

The Case for Co-Parenting

It is this set of ideals — clearly more historically constructed than biblically warranted — that many Evangelical undergraduates have grown up with. Granted, it is a set of ideals often honored more in the breach than the observance, and one about which many students are ambivalent, even if they have been trained to accept it as the "biblical model" of gender and family relations.[30] Many are thus both surprised and relieved to learn about the demonstrated benefits — for children of both sexes — of

28. Beth L. Bailey, *From the Front Porch to the Back Seat: Courtship in Twentieth-Century America* (Baltimore, MD: Johns Hopkins University Press, 1989).

29. Gail Bederman, "'The Women Have Had Charge of the Church Work Long Enough': The Men and Religion Forward Movement of 1911-1912 and the Masculinization of Middle-Class Protestantism," *American Quarterly* 41(3) (1989): 432-65 (quotation from p. 436).

30. See for example Sally K. Gallagher, *Evangelical Identity and Gendered Family Life* (New Brunswick, NJ: Rutgers University Press, 2003) and W. Bradford Wilcox, *Soft Patriarchs, New Men: How Christianity Shapes Fathers and Husbands* (Chicago: University of Chicago Press, 2004).

nurturing, equally involved parenting by fathers alongside mothers. They are equally intrigued to learn that those benefits are different from what one would expect under the doctrine of separate spheres. For example, Freudian and functionalist theorists classically believed that boys needed to have interaction with their fathers in order to cement "essential" masculine attitudes, behaviors, and roles after spending so much of their early lives with their mothers. And indeed there is a wealth of research — in both industrialized and pre-industrial cultures — showing that the more nurturantly involved fathers are with their sons, the more secure those sons are in their gender *identity* — which is defined simply as the sense of being comfortable and secure as a male. But nurturantly fathered sons are in general less likely than the sons of more-typically absent or distant fathers to be concerned about adopting stereotypically masculine *behaviors,* in particular "hyper-masculine" behaviors such as antisocial aggression, the sexual exploitation of girls, or misogynist attitudes and actions.

For example, sociologist Scott Coltrane's complex analyses of almost two hundred pre-industrial societies (using the data bank known as the Ethnographic Atlas) has shown that nurturant fathering of children is the *single best predictor* of reduced abuse of women, low levels of hostility among adult men, and the economic and social empowerment of women in cultures where such fathering is commonplace.[31] Coltrane's indices of women's empowerment included the extent to which they had a voice in domestic and political decision making; whether formal positions of influence were open to women; the extent to which women featured favorably in cultural origin myths; whether they could challenge husbands' decisions; and the extent to which they could inherit property, own or control dwellings, and have a say about the use of the products of their own — and men's — labor. His measures of father involvement with children included the amount of time men spent in proximity to their young children, the degree to which they shared in children's routine caretaking, and ratings of the culture's overall degree of paternal affection. Coltrane also included behavioral measures based on competing theories about the origins of male dominance and women's relative lack of power in pre-modern cultures,[32] but in the end

31. Scott Coltrane, *Family Man: Fatherhood, Housework and Gender Equity* (New York: Oxford University Press, 1996).

32. For example, some anthropologists theorize that men's involvement in warfare exaggerates existing physical sex differences and thus leads to male-dominated social structures. Others say that male preoccupation with war limits their involve-

confirmed that the strongest empirical predictor of high female status was nurturant fathering:

> In those societies with high levels of father-child proximity, women tend to be active participants in community decision-making. Similarly, societies with significant paternal involvement in routine childcare are more likely than father-absent societies to include women in public decision and to allow women access to positions of authority. Societies that couple frequent father-child contact with high levels of father-child affection are the most likely to exhibit significant female public authority and status.[33]

The benefits of co-parenting also accrue to nurturantly fathered girls, who are more likely to show independent achievement and less likely to engage in premature sexual and reproductive activity than girls with low father involvement. Why is this so? Here some of the neo-psychoanalytic insights of feminist object-relations theorists are helpful.[34] In cultures and subcultures where fathers are absent or uninvolved, boys tend to define themselves in opposition to their mothers and other female caretakers, and thus are at risk of engaging in misogynist and hyper-masculine behaviors as a way to shore up a fragile gender identity. And girls who are not sufficiently affirmed *as persons* by available and nurturing fathers are

---

ment with childcare and thereby promotes behaviors aimed at shoring up insecure male gender identities. Others argue that men in hunting cultures are more apt to bond with each other, ignoring children and excluding women from their shared non-domestic activities. Still others assert the opposite: that hunter-gatherer cultures, by virtue of their small size, nomadic existence, and lack of material accumulation tend toward gender egalitarianism, whereas settled populations that farm and trade food surpluses begin to differentiate gender roles more sharply and allow men to take control of resources, to the detriment of women. Still others argue that it is certain male-oriented social structures, such as patrilocal residence and patrilineal kinship and inheritance systems that disadvantage women.

33. Scott Coltrane, "Father-Child Relationships and the Status of Women: A Cross-Cultural Study," *American Journal of Sociology* 93(5) (1988): 1060-95 (quotation from p. 1085). See also his "Micropolitics of Gender in Nonindustrial Societies," *Gender and Society* 1 (March 1992): 86-107.

34. See, for example, Dorothy Dinnerstein, *The Mermaid and the Minotaur: Sexual Arrangements and Human Malaise* (New York: Harper and Row, 1976); Nancy Chodorow, *The Reproduction of Mothering: Psychoanalysis and the Sociology of Gender* (Berkeley: University of California Press, 1978); and Jessica Benjamin, *The Bonds of Love: Psychoanalysis, Feminism and the Problem of Domination* (New York: Pantheon, 1988).

at risk of developing a mindset that sees their sexuality and reproductive potential as the main criteria of feminine success. The bottom line appears to be this: children of both sexes need stable, nurturant, and appropriately authoritative parents of both sexes to help develop a secure gender identity. But such co-parenting also allows children to relate to each other primarily as human beings, and not as reduced, gender-role caricatures: ironically, those who are most concerned to display rigidly stereotypical masculinity and femininity are apt to have the *least* secure gender identities.

I have come to call this "the paradox of nurturant co-parenting,"[35] and have seen it resonate often with Psychology of Gender students, men as well as women. A male student from North Africa, writing about Scott Coltrane's work, affirmed that it was "quite adventurous reading for me because of the cultural background I come from." He went on to observe that in his country

> men still live in a fantasy world where they want to be dominant both in public and domestic realms. The history of family life has reinforced this notion that men are superior to women. But as a Christian reader I found [Coltrane's work] to be very rational and realistic. Love is the very core of Christian values, and yet we find it being misused and misinterpreted both in Christian and secular contexts. When we read the gospels, we find Jesus laboring to help his disciples understand the magnitude of the love he was offering. . . . It is very clear to me that Christ loved the church so much that he was willing to make the ultimate sacrifice. He was a great example of servant leadership, as opposed to what people think of headship in our society today. The point I would like to make here is that if a man is to be a family man, he needs to understand that love is at the center of his deeds, not our society's distorted norm of power. If a husband loves his wife, he will do whatever it takes to make sure she is getting rest. He will share the burden of the family and become considerate.

A woman student was equally intrigued by the work of Yale child psychiatrist Kyle Pruett, who for almost two decades has followed families in which fathers were the primary caregivers. Pruett found that both boys and girls in such families were cognitively precocious, enthusiastic nurturers (of plants, animals, and/or younger siblings), and uncon-

35. For a more extended discussion and literature review, see Van Leeuwen, *My Brother's Keeper,* esp. chaps. 5 and 6.

cerned about adhering to narrow gender stereotypes, even as they approached adolescence.[36] This particular student chose to look at Pruett's work since, as she wrote, "my mom basically raised me because my dad was not in a healthy psychological state, so I have always wondered how I would be different as a person today if I had had a stable father." She noted that

> Pruett talks about how fathers are so important for a child's upbringing, and how they can help their children become emotionally, physically and psychologically healthy, just by fathering well and by being there. . . . My parents divorced when I was in my early teens. Since my dad was not the greatest person I have ever known, whenever he had visitation I would dread it. He never fulfilled his role as a father when he lived at home, so I did not expect him to after he left. My father definitely did not follow Pruett's guidelines for nurturing children and setting age-appropriate challenges and limits. He had no idea how to handle the situation and neither did I. The result was a weak relationship between my father and me as I grew older. Pruett was right when he said that a father has to stay in his child's life, or they will lose each other.

This student's observations were doubly poignant because she was in a cohabiting relationship about which she was very ambivalent. She sensed that a dearth of adequate fathering in her past might have been one factor leading her to jump unreflectively into her current living arrangement. Reviewers of the relevant social science literature generally agree that such vulnerability is common to under-fathered women, regardless of class or ethnic background. From her qualitative research among African American women, journalist Jonetta Rose Barras found that under-fathered adult women were more apt to regard themselves as unworthy and unlovable, to fear rejection, abandonment, and commitment, and to be susceptible to anger and depression. "Too often," Barras observes, "women who are wounded by the loss of their fathers go from man to man, from bed to bed, calling sex 'love' and hoping to be healed by the physical closeness. Sometimes," she notes, "sex is not enough. Fatherless girls can develop an obsession with having a baby [as] a last defense against loneliness, against abandonment. . . . At least when he leaves we will have someone — we won't be

36. Kyle Pruett, *The Nurturing Father* (New York: Warner, 1987) and *Fatherneed: Why Father Care Is as Essential as Mother Care for Your Child* (New York: The Free Press, 2000).

alone. In fact, we'll still have him, because we have his baby. It is ludicrous, but nevertheless we cling to this reasoning."[37]

Another scholar summarized the relevant literature on underfathered girls this way: "Deprived of a stable relationship with a non-exploitative adult male who loves them, these girls can remain developmentally 'stuck,' struggling with issues of security and trust that well-fathered girls have already successfully resolved."[38] Ironically, for girls as for boys, the steady presence of nurturant and appropriately authoritative (as opposed to authoritarian or permissive)[39] fathers results *not* in rigidly gendered behaviors — including, *in extremis,* premature heterosexual activity and childbearing — but in a secure gender identity that allows sexual behavior and heterosexual relations to take a balanced place alongside other adult developmental tasks that emerge under the rubrics of work, love, and the articulation and practice of a transcendent worldview. This "paradox of nurturant co-parenting" is seen by most of my students as eminently compatible with a biblical anthropology that begins with the creation of *both* man and woman in the full image of God, and with the cultural mandate of Genesis 1:26-28, whose dual call to "love and work" (". . . fill the earth and subdue it . . .") is given to *both* members of the primal pair — not divided by sex, as it was under the questionable (and historically recent) doctrine of separate spheres.

Contraception and Gender Justice

Thus far I have described how my Psychology of Gender students have appropriated and identified with writings on divorce and co-parenting

37. Jonetta Rose Barras, *Whatever Happened to Daddy's Little Girl? The Impact of Fatherlessness on Black Women* (New York: Ballantine, 2000), 70.

38. Blankenhorn, *Fatherless America,* 47.

39. "Authoritarian" parenting is defined as the unilateral imposition of rules by parents and the expectation of obedience, with little regard for developmental stage and little resort to explanation or mutual discussion. "Permissive" parents, at the other extreme, defer to their children's wishes, make few demands, and rarely use any kind of punishment. In contrast to both these extremes more effective, "authoritative" parents (of both sexes) are both demanding of *and* responsive to their children. Such parents exert their control not just by setting and enforcing rules in a consistent and age-appropriate manner, but also — especially with older children — by explaining the rationale behind the imposed rules, by encouraging two-way communication, and by allowing exception to rules for a given developmental stage.

that have emerged from the Religion, Culture, and Family Project. My final example concerns a topic that surfaced less frequently in RCFP discussions — namely, contraception and family planning. When it did, one of the project's most articulate analysts was Catholic feminist theologian Lisa Sowle Cahill of Boston College. In her RCFP volume *Sex, Gender and Christian Ethics,* Cahill traced the official Catholic teachings on marriage and family from Pius XI's rejection of the Anglican acceptance of birth control in 1930 to John Paul II's personalist philosophy and its related "theology of the body."[40]

The "personalism" of John Paul II grew out of the nineteenth- and twentieth-century phenomenological writings of philosophers such as Edmund Husserl, Max Scheler, and Maurice Merleau-Ponty. It emphasized that the quality of individual experience and intersubjective spousal relations was at least as important as magisterial definitions of what constitutes valid Christian marriage and marital sex. Personalism has thus enabled recent Catholic thinkers to place as much stress on the mutually loving relationship of spouses as on "the idea that an act of [marital] consent creates an ontological bond which cannot disappear, no matter what the real circumstances of the relationship which it supposedly grounds."[41] Cahill wrote that in recent years

> the Roman Catholic teaching authority, [while] as committed as ever to absolute norms, has come to see sex as essentially constitutive of personal identity, has adopted the language of the couple's intersubjectivity to express sex's moral meaning, and has dimmed the lights once beamed on procreation. According to John Paul II, "sexuality, by means of which man and woman give themselves to one another through acts which are proper and exclusive to spouses, is by no means something purely biological, but concerns the innermost being of the human person as such" and is a sign of "a total personal self-giving."[42]

40. See Pius XI, *Encyclical of Pope Pius XI on Christian Marriage (Casti Connubii)* (December 31, 1930); John Paul II, *Veritatis Splendor* (August 6, 1993). See also Mary Shivanandan, *Crossing the Threshold of Love: A New Vision of Marriage in the Light of John Paul II's Anthropology* (Washington, DC: Catholic University of America Press, 1999) and Christopher West, *Theology of the Body for Beginners: A Basic Introduction to Pope John Paul II's Sexual Revolution* (West Chester, PA: Ascension Press, 2004).

41. Cahill, *Sex, Gender and Christian Ethics,* 195.

42. Cahill, *Sex, Gender and Christian Ethics,* 6. The quotation from John Paul II is from his *Apostolic Exhortation On the Role of the Christian Family in the Modern World (Familiaris Consortio)* (November 22, 1981), Par. 11.

Nevertheless, Cahill was ambivalent about this turn in Roman Catholic sexual ethics. On the one hand, it emphasizes that "total personal self-giving" requires openness to procreation, and therefore that any means of birth control other than abstinence is still to be regarded as sinful. But in a world where many women remain economically, physically and sexually vulnerable (particularly in poorer countries) Cahill rightly asserts that such language can become dangerously romantic nonsense: "The personalist potentials of sex and marriage," she wrote, "are in fact being destroyed for poor women because the biological meaning of sex as reproduction is culturally not only primary, but often a means of constraint and even oppression. . . . The Christian social message of reciprocity and inclusion must begin by transforming the family — and women's sexual roles as mothers and wives — if it is to be a genuine school of Christian values."[43] On the other hand, she agreed that "the defenders of official Catholic teaching are not wrong in their uneasiness about the prevalence of social attitudes toward sex which, in divorcing sex from procreation also seem to divorce it from commitment and responsibility." The latter attitude is particularly widespread in the developed and increasingly secularized nations on both sides of the Atlantic:

> The status of women worldwide has certainly improved since [Pope Paul VI wrote against birth control in] 1968, partly due to increased access to education, health care, and family planning measures. Yet, at the same time, continuing permissiveness towards men's sexual behavior, combined with a greater social expectation that women will trade sex for relationship even without commitment, and the effective cultural dissociation of sex from responsibility for procreation, has contributed to widespread use of abortion as a means of birth control, and to the destabilization of families in industrialized nations. . . . The connection between sex, love, and babies cannot be apprehended, much less advocated, in any individualist or act-oriented concept of sex. . . . A strength of Catholic tradition is its strongly social vision of these realities.[44]

My students are exposed to both sides of this critique. In the unit on gender justice, they read about Amartya Sen's worldwide calculations of some fifty million "missing women" due to selective abortion, perinatal health risks, and inadequate attention to girls' and women's nutrition,

43. Cahill, *Sex, Gender and Christian Ethics*, 215.
44. Cahill, *Sex, Gender and Christian Ethics*, 206.

healthcare, and education.[45] They learn about the U.N.'s Human Development Index (HDI) and Gender-Related Development Index (GDI), which rank nations' quality of life not according to the more crude measure of gross domestic product, but on how well the social goods of literacy, health, and basic income are distributed by class and gender.[46] Although the gap is certainly variable, the U.N.'s annual statistics show that even today, no nation in the world treats its women as well as its men, all of which seems to make the official Catholic resistance to contraception myopic at best, and downright sexist at worst.

Marital Chastity: Oxymoron or Expression of Equal Regard?

But thanks to the presence of two of its adherents among our faculty (philosopher Randall Colton and his wife Kristen) my students also learn about the Catholic-inspired practice of Natural Family Planning (NFP).[47] I include this topic — as well as a class visit by the Coltons — not, as I am careful to explain, because I think it is the only Christianly defensible way to space children. Nor do I do so because I adhere to the natural-theological rationale behind the Catholic embrace of NFP (I am, after all, a Calvinist who is reflexively suspicious of natural theological arguments) but because NFP is a arguably a uniquely *just* form of birth control, inasmuch as it requires symmetrical attention, effort, and empathy

45. For example, Amartya Sen, "The Many Faces of Gender Inequality: When Misogyny Becomes a Health Problem," *The New Republic* (September 12, 2001): 35-40.

46. For an explanation of these indices, see the United Nations Development Programme's *Human Development Report, 1995* (New York: Oxford University Press, 1995), esp. chap. 3.

47. The assigned reading includes Richard Fehring, Stella Kitchen, and Mary Shivanandan's "Introduction to Natural Family Planning" (Washington, DC: United States Conference of Catholic Bishops, Diocesan Development Program for Natural Family Planning, 1999), at http://www.usccb.org/prolife/issues/nfp/intronfp.html. It should be noted that although NFP has been developed largely by Catholics, by the mid-1990s only about 4 percent of Catholics were using it, while approximately 75 percent were contracepting, including around 30 percent who had undergone sterilization — about the same percentage as the rest of the U.S. population. By contrast, Evangelical Protestants, who have no doctrinal reasons to avoid contraception in marriage, are ironically becoming more interested in NFP. See, for example, Jenell Williams Paris, *Birth Control for Christians: Making Wise Choices* (Grand Rapids, MI: Baker Books, 2003).

on the part of both spouses. Rather than assuming that the goal of birth control is to accommodate women's bodies to men's schedule of sexual desire, or treating women's fertility as a nuisance and its physical manifestations as sources of disgust and pollution (still a strong cultural subtext, even in "enlightened" Western settings), NFP calls for mutual attunement to — and respect for — the complementary aspects of female and male fertility, and mutual participation in a rhythm of marital sex alternating with "marital chastity."

My decision to include this topic in the course beginning a few years ago was in part serendipitous. The Coltons — both Southern Baptists — had embraced Natural Family Planning originally by default, due to health issues that made the use of birth control pills too risky. But in the process of doing so, they became convinced — both theologically and psychologically — that NFP was a potential source of great blessing to Christian (and indeed any) marriage, and they became writers about, and teachers of, the method, also to my class.[48] Although initially skeptical, many of my students end up convinced that NFP is a positive practice both sexually and psychologically, and (when consistently practiced) a reliable indicator of fertility, and not a biological version of Russian roulette practiced only by Catholics who should know better. Physically, NFP works by treating each menstrual cycle as unique, and calculating fertile and infertile periods by a combined index that includes changes in the woman's daily-recorded basal body temperature and changes in the quality and quantity of cervical mucus. Psychologically, NFP encourages and enhances couple communication and mutual respect. One group of writers and teachers on NFP summarized these benefits as follows:

> Couples using NFP accept their fertility not as a nuisance or even a disease, but as a gift. When the physical pleasures of sexual intercourse are a couple's primary focus, the woman can feel used. NFP treats the woman not as a sexual object, but as the unique person she is. NFP does not downplay the importance of sexual union and sexual pleasure; but through the practice of periodic abstinence NFP helps couples to find other ways in which to be attentive to each other in each cycle. [It] can re-ignite the romance of courtship for a married couple. As couples who use NFP often say, "Every cycle we have a

48. See Gregory R. Beabout and Randall Colton, "If You Want Justice, Work for Chastity," presented at the conference "From Death to Life: Agendas of Reform," University of Notre Dame, September 27, 2002.

> wedding night." When couples love one another enough to abstain and be more considerate of each other, both become more secure in their relationship. . . .
>
> Periodic abstinence is difficult at times. It also brings its own reward. Men find that they can direct sexual desire in the service of love and not be controlled by it. . . . NFP instruction puts the emphasis on a couple's shared responsibility not only for having children, but also for managing their combined fertility; both spouses accept the challenge of abstinence during the fertile phase if they wish to avoid pregnancy. NFP requires couples to communicate. It helps them to talk about many things that may have been difficult to talk about before. Through charting their fertility, they have a starting point for discussing the intimate aspects of their life, such as their sexual feelings and desires, their hopes or fears about pregnancy . . . [and] their faith in God. Good, substantive interpersonal communication strengthens a marriage.[49]

Why are my mainly Evangelical students so receptive to this topic? In the same way that today's students do not romanticize divorce because they understand — both academically and experientially — the decades of research exposing its unanticipated consequences, so, too, they are disinclined to romanticize the rhetoric of the sexual revolution bequeathed to

49. Fehring et al., "An Introduction to Natural Family Planning," 11 and 12. Orthodox Judaism also requires the alternation of sexual abstinence with sexual enjoyment according to the woman's menstrual cycle — though for reasons of ritual purity, rather than for family planning. Thus couples are called to abstain from sex for a full week after the cessation of the woman's menstrual flow, at which time she undergoes ritual purification by immersion in the water of the *Mikvah* as a condition of returning to sexual activity. Indeed, even non-observant Jewish couples have been known to continue this custom just because "it can re-ignite the romance of courtship" and strengthen interpersonal communication. But although men use the *Mikvah* by custom under certain circumstances, none of these (with the exception of immersion upon conversion to Judaism) is required by Jewish law, so its mandated monthly use by women seems to affirm — whether intentionally or not — that their bodies are somehow polluted to a degree that men's are not. For further details about this practice, see, for example, Aryeh Kaplan, *Waters of Eden: The Mystery of the Mikvah* (New York: Union of Orthodox Jewish Congregations of America, 1976) and Michael Kauffman, *Love, Marriage, and Family in Jewish Law and Tradition* (Northvale, NJ: Jason Aronson, 1992). For one revisionist approach, see, for example, Charlotte Elisheva Fonrobert, "A Mikvah for Feminists," (European Conference of Women Rabbis, Cantors, Scholars and All Spiritually Interested Jewish Women and Men, 2001), http://www.bet-debora.de/2001/jewish-family/fonrobert.html.

them by their baby-boomer predecessors. They have learned that, far from decreasing the number of abortions and out-of-wedlock births (as its promoters confidently predicted it would half a century ago) the rise of contraception has been correlated with an increase in both. Many women students also know — both experientially and intellectually — that instead of simply equalizing women's sexual freedom and happiness with men's (the standard mantra half a century ago), the widespread use of contraception has also encouraged male irresponsibility and a reductionistic view of women's bodies by both themselves and their partners.[50] If fear of pregnancy is the "only" reason for remaining chaste, and if women now have easy access to contraception, then every woman should, it seems, be always available for sex, since there is no longer any reason to say no. (On this note, recall that in the sexual behavior survey of students at my university, *four times* as many women as men cited partner pressure as the main reason for their first sexual experience.)

Moreover, this mindset is actually promoted among Evangelicals, subject only to the legalism that you should first be married, and then confine sex to the person you're married to. All of the major Protestant denominations — Mainline and Evangelical — had endorsed contraception by the late 1970s (even Billy Graham disagreed with Pope Paul VI's 1968 anti-contraception encyclical, *Humanae Vitae*) and Evangelical "sex guides" have subsequently promoted contraception as a way to elevate the meaning of sex above mere procreation.[51] In their best-selling book, *The Act of Marriage* (of which two and a half million copies were in print by 2000), Evangelical superstars Tim and Beverly LaHaye recommended the pill to newly married women as the preferred method of birth control, supposedly because of its safety and simplicity: "Then, after she and her husband have learned the art of married love, she may decide on some other method."[52]

50. It is a seldom-acknowledged fact that almost all first-wave American feminists — including Susan B. Anthony and Elizabeth Cady Stanton — campaigned for the criminalization of abortion (which was widely available and widely used in the 19th century) precisely on the grounds that it allowed men to separate sex from responsibility for both the resulting children and the women who bore them. See, for example, Serrin M. Foster, "The Feminist Case Against Abortion," *American Feminist* 11(2/3) (Summer 2004): 28-33.

51. Lara V. Marks, *Sexual Chemistry: A History of the Contraceptive Pill* (New Haven, CT: Yale University Press, 2001); Andrea Tone, *Devices and Desires: A History of Contraceptives in America* (New York: Hill and Wang, 2001).

52. Tim and Beverly LaHaye, *The Act of Marriage* (Grand Rapids, MI: Zondervan, 1976; rev. 1998), 64.

Aside from the implicit assumption that birth control is solely the woman's concern, these authors also seem to be underscoring what many of my women students recall as the main message of their own Evangelical sex education: before marriage, cross your legs and just say no; after marriage, uncross your legs and just say yes. Or as the fiancé of one of my students put it when he dismissed her attempts to discuss NFP as a possibility, "Being married allows for sex whenever I want it." Not surprisingly, many young Evangelical women are looking for something a little less unilateral. One of them, reflecting on the assigned reading on NFP, wrote:

> I was skeptical about NFP, even after reading the article on it, but I understand it relatively well now, and was even presented with the opportunity to defend it to my friend Chris, who will be marrying his girlfriend soon. Chris apprehensively mentioned that his girlfriend does not morally support the use of birth control, so I told him about NFP. He was skeptical about both its effectiveness and its practicality. His primary concerns were the periods of abstinence and what NFP would do for sexual interaction. He said something along the lines of "'Hey, baby, I'm ovulating — No way!' Mucus? No thanks. Not sexy." As if male ejaculate isn't like mucus, but something women will just take in stride, or even think is wonderful. I agree that talking about a woman's cycle is not sexy, but I do think it's still very intimate, like being comfortable enough around someone to fart and not feel self-conscious about it. I still do not know if I will be using NFP if and when I marry, but I now think it is a valid option.

Male students also have misgivings about the sexual double standards described above. In the same way that women can use food as a way of coping with depression or anxiety, men can be addicted to sex, even within marriage: demanding it as their right, but in reality using it as a way to mask depression, the quintessential "female" disorder to which men in our culture are not supposed to be vulnerable, but in fact are.[53] Therapist Alon Gratch notes further that for most of his male clients, "everything is about sex, except sex, which often enough is about shame, emotional absence, masculine insecurity, self-involvement, aggression, and self-destructiveness. . . . The sexual arena is where men play out

53. See, for example, family therapist Terrence Real's volume, *I Don't Want to Talk About It: Overcoming the Secret Legacy of Male Depression* (New York: Scribner, 1997), esp. chap. 3. See also Van Leeuwen, *My Brother's Keeper,* chap. 11.

emotional conflicts which, ultimately are not about sex at all."[54] Having learned about — and sometimes identified with — such therapeutic issues in other parts of the course, male students can be just as attracted as women by the discipline, the psychological benefits, and the gender-symmetrical responsibilities inherent in NFP. One of them, single and finishing his degree after a stint in the armed forces, wrote:

> In my experience, no one ever talks about anything like NFP. In a society where casual sex is common, there is not much appeal in such a careful, restrictive method. The quick fix is found in more invasive methods of contraception. But Dr. and Mrs. Colton presented a very compelling basis for employing NFP. It is a method that honors and loves God's creation by letting it be all it was created to be. Dr. Colton characterized the marital act as something signifying the total self-giving of spouses to each other. The point he made about sexuality being an entire dynamic including chastity, periodic abstinence, and honored fertility was very poignant. Chastity is not merely the control of sexual desires and/or behavior outside of marriage. It finds its expression in heterosexual marriage, where sexuality is to be selfless, patient, symbolic of Christ's covenantal commitment to the church, and respectful of fertility. Having these specific and express ideas about what sexuality should look like gives me more confidence and excitement about marriage. Learning about NFP is a large piece in my development toward becoming a responsible Christian spouse, and it's quite exciting.

Conclusion

In their 1997 volume *From Culture Wars to Common Ground,* Don Browning and other RCFP scholars enumerated and clearly appreciated the contributions that biology, economics, history, and psychology have made to our understanding of sex, marriage, and families. Yet they cautioned against accepting reductionistic explanations based on theory and research in any or all of these disciplines. "Modern Christian thinkers should consider the following strategy," they wrote. "They should use [these disciplines] last, not first. They should begin with the scriptures of the communities of faith that form them, with the Genesis ordinances

54. Alon Gratch, *If Men Could Talk, Here's What They'd Say* (Boston: Little, Brown, 2001), 18.

about male and female leaving their families of origin and becoming one flesh. These scriptures contained intuitive wisdom. . . . The eyes of faith [should place other] explanations within a theology and ethic that find a place for the hand of God."[55]

My experience as an RCFP scholar teaching the Psychology of Gender to undergraduates affirms the rightness of such a conclusion: whether dealing with the topics of marriage, divorce, sex, or child rearing, Christian young adults are far from being unreflective hedonists. They are certainly influenced to no small degree by the sex-saturated and materialistic culture that surrounds them. But in spite (or perhaps because) of this, most are hungry for transcendence and for the challenge of living out a worldview that affirms both individual needs and communal responsibilities, that has both creational and eschatological meaning. The books and other resources that have flowed from Don Browning's leadership of the Religion, Culture, and Family Project have increased their confidence that such a worldview is both wonderful and workable.

55. Browning et al., *From Culture Wars to Common Ground,* 125.

9 Family Faith Formation at the Nexus of Practical Theology and Christian Education

Richard Robert Osmer

In this chapter, I enter into a dialogue with the work of Don Browning to explore some of the ways Christian congregations might strengthen the faith formation of families. Research indicates that many parents today look to congregations for help in raising their children, especially in the area of morality.[1] They believe that their children face issues that are more difficult and, potentially, more deadly than they faced while growing up. Parents also believe they receive less support from other institutions in raising good children than did their own parents.[2] Congregations that forge a strong partnership with families in this task, thus, are responding to a felt need of parents with children and youth. This may strengthen the loyalty of these members to the congregation and may even attract new members. But this partnership may also reach beyond the congregation to address social conditions and public policies that impact the well-being of families. When this is done, the congregation moves beyond simply meeting the needs of its own members and plays a role in shaping the common good.

I have no doubt that congregational leaders, particularly pastors and Christian educators, are one of the keys to forging a stronger partnership between congregations and families. This chapter, thus, proceeds in two steps. First, it examines the sort of theological education that pastors and educators need to receive if they are to address issues of this sort. Second, it imagines a course taught in a seminary or divinity school that

1. Dean Hoge, Benton Johnson, and Donald Luidens, *Vanishing Boundaries: The Religion of Mainline Protestant Baby Boomers* (Louisville: Westminster/John Knox, 1994).

approaches this partnership from the perspective of practical theology. In both steps, I draw on the thinking of Don Browning, who has proposed a new model of theological education and carried out the most extensive program of research and reflection on the family among contemporary practical theologians.

Toward a New Model of Theological Education

Most Protestant seminaries and divinity schools today continue to educate their students in ways determined by the encyclopedic paradigm of theology. By this, I mean a vision of theology forged during the modern period that focuses on specialized academic disciplines organized around the fourfold theological encyclopedia: biblical studies, church history, dogmatic theology, and practical theology.[3] Theological schools are organized into departments based on each of these fields, and students are required to take courses in each department.

The encyclopedic paradigm was a response to the rise of the modern research university and the important role science played in this setting. Scholarship was no longer viewed as a matter of handing on the cultural and religious heritage of the past but as engaging in original research that yielded new knowledge in the present. If theology was to have a place in the research university, then it had to demonstrate that it too carried out research along these lines.

Friedrich Schleiermacher and others responded to this challenge by reconceptualizing theology along the lines of the theological encyclopedia, with two central features.[4] First, theology was differentiated into specialized academic disciplines with their own particular methods, language, and theories. These were patterned after the specialized research programs of cognate fields prominent in the university. Second, a clear

2. Don Browning, Bonnie Miller-McLemore, Pamela Couture, Brynolf Lyon, and Robert Franklin, *From Culture Wars to Common Ground: Religion and the American Family Debate* (Louisville: Westminster/John Knox Press, 1997), 9.

3. For the history of the theological encyclopedia, see Edward Farley, *Theologia: The Fragmentation and Unity of Theological Education* (Philadelphia: Fortress Press, 1983).

4. Friedrich Schleiermacher, *Brief Outline on the Study of Theology: Philosophical, Historical, Practical* (Richmond: John Knox Press, 1966). See also his *Christian Caring: Selections from Practical Theology*, ed. James Duke and Howard Stone (Philadelphia: Fortress Press, 1988).

demarcation was made between theoretical research and practical application, patterned on the distinction between objective, "disinterested," scientific research, on the one hand, and technological application, on the other. Within the theological encyclopedia, this pattern was embodied in the distinction between the fully "scientific" (i.e., research-oriented) scholarship of biblical studies, church history, and dogmatic theology and the practical application of practical theology.

To a large extent, this encyclopedic paradigm continues to structure contemporary theological education in North America and Europe. Students take courses in different departments that focus on the specialized scholarship of a particular field. It is left to practical theology or the "practical field" to help students integrate and apply what they have learned to their work in congregations or other forms of ministry. Increasingly, however, this paradigm is being called into question. Indeed, theological schools that continue to educate their students along these lines might be characterized as "shell institutions" in the sense of the sociologist Anthony Giddens.[5] From the outside, "shell institutions" look the same as they have in the past, but internally they are no longer capable of carrying out the work they need to perform. Let us see why this is the case with regard to educating leaders prepared to address the partnership between families and congregations.

If the family shows up at all in the curriculums of theological schools, it is likely to appear in the "practical field" in courses like "Ministry with Families" or "Ministry with Children and Youth," where the family is a small part of a course structured around developmental issues and congregational programs. Pastoral care courses sometimes give extensive attention to family systems theory with an eye to pastoral counseling. In the encyclopedic paradigm, such courses are expected to focus primarily on "how to," that is, on practical programs and guidelines that pastors and educators can apply as soon as they enter ministry. Indeed, students who have been socialized into the encyclopedic paradigm come to such courses with this strong expectation in mind. They want relief from courses in other fields that are theory-heavy and seem remote from their future work. They grow impatient when such courses have a strong theory component, assigning reading, for example, which interprets the family sociologically or historically. Occasionally, the family is studied in courses on Christian ethics or systematic theology, usually to illustrate a

5. Anthony Giddens, *Runaway World: How Globalization is Reshaping Our Lives* (New York: Routledge, 1999), 36-37.

moral or doctrine framework or as a form of special ethics. In such courses, the family is addressed almost exclusively in terms of normative theoretical issues.

What we see here is the way specialization in the encyclopedic paradigm undercuts the possibility of integration and conversation across disciplinary lines. Dogmatic and ethical matters are treated in some courses and practical issues and programs in others. There is little interaction between normative, contextual, and action-oriented reflection. Moreover, a clear distinction between theory and practice continues to structure departmental offerings and approaches. Some courses focus primarily on theory and academic research; others, on practice. There are, of course, many exceptions to the scenario I have just laid out. These take the form of interdepartmental courses or courses in which Bible scholars or dogmatic theologians include practical issues (such as, write a sermon on the basis of your exegesis; interpret an issue like alcoholism in terms of the doctrines of *imago Dei,* sin and grace). But such courses run up against the larger institutional patterns shaping education in their theological school, which include such matters as distribution requirements, course prerequisites, and the need for professors to cover prescribed departmental offerings. However well-intentioned, such initiatives are something like putting a band-aid on a broken arm. They do not really treat the underlying problem.

It is precisely to address this underlying problem that Don Browning has proposed a new paradigm of theological education, based on a new way of organizing the theological enterprise as a whole.[6] His proposal constitutes nothing less than a shift beyond the encyclopedic paradigm. This proposal is based on a broader shift in the academy, the recognition of the hermeneutical and practical dimensions of *all* scholarship. The intellectual currents flowing into this shift are many, including thinkers like Ludwig Wittgenstein, Martin Heidegger, Jürgen Habermas, Richard Rorty, Richard Bernstein, and many others. Browning's key dialogue partner is Hans-Georg Gadamer, who brings together hermeneutic philosophy's understanding of the hermeneutical circle and Aristotle's understanding of *phronesis,* or the practical wisdom of moral

6. My discussion of Browning's proposal draws on his *A Fundamental Practical Theology: Descriptive and Strategic Proposals* (Minneapolis: Augsburg Fortress, 1991) and his "Toward a Fundamental and Strategic Practical Theology," originally published in 1991 and now appearing as chapter 1 of Don S. Browning, *Equality and the Family: A Fundamental Practical Theology of Children, Mothers, and Fathers in Modern Societies* (Grand Rapids, MI: Eerdmans, 2006).

reasoning.[7] In effect, Gadamer undercuts the very notions of science and rationality to which the older, encyclopedic paradigm was a response.

Two key dimensions of Gadamer's work are important to Browning's proposal. First, Gadamer reworks the notion of the hermeneutical circle to underscore the temporality of all understanding, including the understanding of scholarship. It is not disinterested objectivity that advances scholarship. Rather, it is the dialectical interplay of understanding and interpretation, in which pre-understandings, grounded in the "effective history" of past interpretations and traditions, are put at risk in order to interpret a subject matter anew in the present and to open up new possibilities for living and understanding in the future. Gadamer spells this out in terms of his important idea of a *hermeneutical experience,* portrayed in terms of a hermeneutical circle that includes pre-understanding, the experience of being brought up short, the interplay and fusion of horizons, and the emergence of new understanding which is applied to contemporary life.

This part of Gadamer's thinking is widely known and quite influential. It is a second dimension of his work to which Browning calls special attention, the "Aristotelian" insight of Gadamer. Interpretation leading to new understanding does not merely end in practical application; rather, it is practical throughout. As Gadamer puts it: "Application is neither a subsequent nor a merely occasional part of the phenomenon of understanding, but co-determines it as a whole from the beginning."[8] This interplay of practice and interpretation is quite similar to Aristotle's concept of *phronesis* in which moral judgments in the sphere of *praxis* are not a matter of applying universal principles but of determining what is going on and how best to respond in particular situations. Reflecting on this important point, Browning writes: "Gadamer sees hermeneutics as a broadly moral and practical enterprise that emerges out of the situations of our traditions or practice. When these practices become problematic, we try to orient ourselves by reexamining the classic sources that have shaped our present practices."[9] Broadly speaking, thus, all forms of interpretation involve *phronesis* or practical reasoning in which application suffuses the whole.

Both dimensions of Gadamer's work are important to Browning's

7. Browning, *Fundamental Practical Theology,* 37-42. Hans-Georg Gadamer, *Truth and Method* (New York: Crossroad, 1982).

8. Quoted in *Fundamental Practical Theology,* 39.

9. *Fundamental Practical Theology,* 39.

proposal about theological education, which is based on his reconceptualization of the entire enterprise of theology. He describes this reconceptualization as the development of a *fundamental practical theology,* defined as follows: "I find it useful to think of fundamental practical theology as critical reflection on the church's dialogue with Christian sources and other communities of experience and interpretation with the aim of guiding its action toward social and individual transformation."[10] The basic structure of theology in this approach is practice-theory-practice, and it includes four distinct "moments," which represent different forms of theological reflection within a larger whole.

Descriptive theology develops an account of "theory-laden religious and cultural practices" and the tension, problems, and questions embedded in these practices.[11] It sets in motion the process of theological reflection, articulating the contemporary problems and possibilities that theology must address. Browning sometimes describes this as a form of "thick description," but it is clear from his research in the Religion, Culture, and Family Project that descriptive theology involves a wide range of empirical research methods and includes elements of interpretation and even explanation, as well as simple description.

Historical theology takes its bearings from the findings of descriptive theology and asks: What do the normative texts and practices that already are a part of the effective history of the Christian community imply for present practice when they are confronted as honestly as possible?[12] This sort of theological reflection encompasses scholarly approaches to the Bible like literary, historical, and cultural criticism, as well as the historical methods commonly used in church history. But these specialized forms of scholarship are not ends in themselves, taking their bearings from the academic guild. Rather, they are grounded in and oriented toward the practical questions and issues facing the contemporary church and society.

Systematic theology seeks a fusion of horizons between the vision implicit in contemporary practices and the vision implied in the practices of normative Christian texts.[13] It is systematic in that it seeks to explore large, encompassing themes running across particular situations and contexts in the present in dialogue with general themes in "the gospel."[14]

10. Browning, *Fundamental Practical Theology,* 36.
11. Browning, *Fundamental Practical Theology,* 47.
12. Browning, *Fundamental Practical Theology,* 49.
13. Browning, *Fundamental Practical Theology,* 51.
14. Browning, *Fundamental Practical Theology,* 57.

By "the gospel," I take Browning to mean God's self-communication in Christ, within the history of Israel, which has been the subject of a history of reflection in church doctrine, ethics, and Christian philosophy. The key point is the way constructive work in systematic theology remains connected to present practice. While its themes are broad, they are formed in response to contemporary issues, insights, and questions.

Strategic practical theology focuses on particular situations, striving to understand them in all their concreteness, to determine appropriate norms that can guide responses to their specific problems and possibilities, and to form strategies of action that support or reform present practices. My own model of practical theology is quite similar to Browning's, with two closely related differences.[15]

First, I broaden the scope of practical theology to include episodes, situations, and contexts, extending the scope of this field beyond particular situations. An episode is an incident or event that emerges from the flow of everyday life and evokes explicit attention and reflection. A situation is the broader and longer sequence of events, patterns of relationships, and life circumstances of which an episode is a part. It often is best understood in the form of a narrative, placing a particular incident within a longer story. A context is composed of those social structures and cultural patterns that make up the field in which a situation unfolds. Contexts also have histories that can be interpreted in terms of narrative analysis. But their histories are longer and their patterns are more enduring.

Second, I create a stronger link between descriptive and strategic practical theology than is implied in Browning's proposal. I recognize that it may be necessary to distinguish these moments of theological interpretation in order to clarify their different purposes. Within the academy today, however, practical theologians are the one group of *theologians* who are carrying out this sort of empirical work in the form of ongoing research programs. Browning's own work in the Religion, Culture, and Family Project is a case in point. But we could also note the empirical research of James Fowler, Johannes van der Ven, Friedrich Schweitzer, Kenda Dean, and my own as examples of practical theologians involved in empirical research. I realize there are many social scientists who carry out research on congregations and religion that has much to offer descriptive theology, like Robert Wuthnow, Nancy Tatom Ammerman, Penny Edgehill Becker, Christian Smith, Michael Emerson,

15. I have described this model in Richard Osmer, *The Teaching Ministry of Congregations* (Louisville: Westminster John Knox Press, 2005), introduction and epilogue.

and Stephen Warner. Their perspective, however, is that of social science, not theology, which influences the issues they investigate and their willingness to address normative issues.

These two caveats lead me to describe practical theology as overlapping the interpretive tasks Browning outlines as descriptive and strategic practical theology. Accordingly, I believe this field carries out four primary tasks: (1) the *descriptive-empirical,* which seeks to explore empirically what is going on in particular episodes, situations, and contexts; (2) the *interpretive,* which seeks to place research findings in broader interpretive and explanatory frameworks; (3) the *normative,* which interprets theologically the patterns discovered through research and develops ethical norms to guide appropriate forms of response; and (4) the *pragmatic,* which focuses on strategies and models of action and supports a reflective dialogue with situations and contexts as these strategies are enacted.

On the surface, it would appear that I have incorporated *all* of the elements of Browning's fundamental practical theology within a single field. In a sense, this is true. Yet, I believe I am simply drawing out something that is largely implicit in his overview of fundamental practical theology and apt to be overlooked. Each moment of theological interpretation is a kind of circle within the larger circle of the whole. While focusing on a distinctive task, the interpretive procedures used in each form of theology recapitulate the larger whole in ways appropriate to this task. This is what I have done above with regard to practical theology.

We find something similar in Richard Hays's description of New Testament ethics.[16] Hays focuses on a key task of historical theology, the interpretation of Christian scripture. He portrays this task as including four moments: (1) the *descriptive,* which focuses on the exegesis of texts; (2) the *synthetic,* which involves placing particular texts in their canonical context; (3) the *hermeneutical,* which acknowledges the temporal distance between the text and present life and explores analogical and metaphorical relations that bring them into conversation; and (4) the *pragmatic,* which explores ways that new understanding might be embodied in contemporary Christian communities.[17] Hays's proposal, like my own, represents a circle within the larger circle of a fundamental practical theol-

16. Richard Hays, *The Moral Vision of the New Testament — Community, Cross, New Creation: A Contemporary Introduction to New Testament Ethics* (San Francisco: HarperSanFranscisco, 1996).

17. Hays, *The Moral Vision of the New Testament,* 3-10.

ogy. Something like this is necessary if the interpretation of each form of theology is to retain its character as *phronesis* in which application suffuses the whole.

Moreover, Hays's description of the interpretive tasks of New Testament ethics raises an additional point, also implicit in Browning's proposal: the importance of dialogue across different forms of theology. Hays calls attention to this issue by noting the sorts of problems that occur when the members of other fields take shortcuts in their use of Scripture to warrant their proposals. He offers a devastating critique of the use of the New Testament in the ethics of Reinhold Niebuhr, Karl Barth, John Howard Yoder, and Stanley Hauerwas. Rather than entering into a dialogue with the interpretive procedures and findings of biblical studies, these ethicists often use Scripture selectively, by-pass careful exegesis, and fail to place particular texts in their canonical context. They would have done better to enter into a sustained dialogue with biblical scholars who could offer help in these tasks.

But a similar point can also be made with regard to Hays's own proposal. In his description of the hermeneutical and pragmatic steps of biblical interpretation, there is no mention whatsoever of the importance of entering into a dialogue with the empirical and contextual forms of analysis offered by practical theology. Biblical scholars simply take an "imaginative leap" in order to discern analogies between texts and present life.[18] But what sort of interpretation of the present context are they assuming? Would they not do better to enter into a sustained dialogue with practical theologians who might help them deepen their understanding of this context?

One final comment about Browning's proposal is in order. The understanding of present practice informing this proposal is highly contextual. Practices are embedded in communities; communities are embedded in larger social systems and cultural patterns, which have histories. This means that the theological enterprise as a whole and its specific "moments," or forms of theology, are necessarily interdisciplinary. Why is this the case? When theology reflects on the practices of the Christian community, it must strive to understand the ways they are responsive to the social and historical contexts of which they are a part. This involves engaging the intellectual resources of the contemporary world, which throw light on these contexts. When theology focuses on cultural practices beyond the church, it recognizes that such practices inevitably pro-

18. Hays, *The Moral Vision of the New Testament*, 6.

ject a normative and, even, quasi-religious horizon, which theology must assess. Browning's critical assessment of the practices of therapeutic psychology is a case in point.[19] His preferred way of conceptualizing this interdisciplinary task is in terms of the revised method of correlation in which the questions and answers of the Christian tradition are brought into a mutually critical conversation with the questions and answers of contemporary culture.

Beyond the Encyclopedic Paradigm: Families and Congregations in Partnership

There are many signs of dissatisfaction with the older encyclopedic paradigm in theological schools today, and Browning's proposal is only one of several that have received attention in recent years.[20] What would it take to implement Browning's proposal? At least four things would be necessary.

Redefining the Endstates of Theological Education

The term "endstates" is taken from the educational theory of Howard Gardner.[21] It describes knowledge, attitudes, and skills that are valued by a particular community and are necessary for its adult members to carry out certain roles or to create certain products. These endstates guide the selection of knowledge, attitudes, and skills included in education, which typically are general during childhood and adolescence (for example, the ability to read, write, use math, think critically, etc.) and become more

19. Don Browning, *Religious Thought and the Modern Psychologies* (Philadelphia: Fortress Press, 1987).

20. Joseph Hough and John Cobb, *Christian Identity and Theological Education* (Atlanta: Scholars Press, 1985); Charles Wood, *Vision and Discernment: An Orientation in Theological Study* (Atlanta: Scholars Press, 1985); David Kelsey, *To Understand God Truly: What's Theological about a Theological School* (Louisville: Westminster/John Knox Press, 1992).

21. Howard Gardner, *Frames of Mind: The Theory of Multiple Intelligences* (New York: Basic Books, 1983); *The Unschooled Mind: How Children Think & How Schools Should Teach* (New York: Basic Books, 1991); *Multiple Intelligences: The Theory in Practice — A Reader* (New York: Basic Books, 1993); *The Disciplined Mind: What All Students Should Understand* (New York: Simon & Schuster, 1999).

specific during college and graduate school (for example, as determined by people's majors and career aspirations).

In Browning's model, the endstates of theological education would be described in terms of the capacity to engage in the sort of theological interpretation needed to provide leadership for a Christian community and to guide this community in carrying out its mission in the world. The key insight here is that theological interpretation as a scholarly enterprise and the theological interpretation of congregational leaders share the same basic structure. They both involve descriptive, historical, systematic, and strategic "moments" or tasks. The purpose of education in theological schools, thus, is to cultivate the knowledge, attitudes, and skills that pastors and others will need to carry out theological interpretation in its varied forms in concert with their leadership of congregations.

An activity as basic as preaching, for example, involves all four forms of theological interpretation Browning has identified. It involves the knowledge and skills of responsible textual interpretation. Preaching on particular texts, moreover, is deepened when informed by a dogmatic framework (in the background) and by prior study of ethical issues. Preaching involves strategic thinking and performative skills, the ability to fashion a sermon for a particular congregation and to communicate in ways that are effective. Pastors who have explored the culture of their congregations through the research strategies of congregational studies will be in a much better position to forge language, address issues, and effect change through their preaching.

In short, the descriptive, historical, systematic, and strategic "moments" of Browning's fundamental practical theology are not only interrelated within the enterprise of theology and theological education, but also hang together in the actual work of congregational leaders. The overarching endstate of theological education, thus, is to cultivate a *habitus* of theological interpretation — habits of reflection and skillful action — appropriate to leadership of congregations.

Reorganizing the Curriculum

A second key task is organizing the curriculum in ways that are no longer structured around the offerings of departments which mirror the specialized branches of the theological encyclopedia. This requires developing *educational pathways* that allow students to acquire over time the capacities of theological interpretation and skillful action necessary for leadership. The idea of educational pathways takes account of the fact that everything cannot be learned all at once in a curriculum and that more complex knowledge and skills are built up in a cumulative fashion.[22] The key is designing clear trajectories within the curriculum that allow students gradually to deepen the interpretive competencies and skills necessary to carry out the descriptive, historical, systematic, and strategic tasks of leadership. These will no longer be identified with specific departmental offerings.

In my school, for example, some biblical scholars make use of cultural forms of interpretation that take account not only of the cultural context of biblical texts but also of the cultural context of contemporary interpreters. It is quite conceivable that such scholars might make an introduction to empirical research and interpretation an important part of their course. Or, they might assume an introduction to empirical research methods in another course and take students deeper into a particular method like ethnography. Developing deeper competence in the descriptive task of theological interpretation, thus, could follow a variety of educational pathways, which are not located in one department alone. All that would be needed is a way of identifying what competencies will be learned in a particular course and at what level (introductory or advanced). Faculty would need to be clear about the desired endstates of the curriculum and to articulate the contribution of a particular course to some aspect of these endstates. Course offerings would no longer be listed as departmental offerings but in terms of the weight they give to the descriptive, historical, systematic, or strategic dimensions of theological interpretation.

Institutionalizing the Practice-Theory-Practice Relationship

The concept of institutionalization is taken from a body of research that assessed the highly influential book on college and university education by Ernest Boyer, *Scholarship Reconsidered.*[23] Institutionalization is defined as "the point at which an innovative practice loses its 'special project' sta-

22. For a discussion of the concepts of endstates and educational pathways, see Osmer, *Teaching Ministry of Congregations,* chaps. 5, 6.

23. Ernest Boyer, *Scholarship Reconsidered: Priorities of the Professoriate,* A Special Report of The Carnegie Foundation for the Advancement of Teaching (New York: Jossey-Bass, 1990).

tus and becomes part of the routine behavior of the system."[24] Browning's proposal that the theological enterprise as a whole take the form of practice-theory-practice would initially take the form of "innovative practices" as the curriculum of a theological school began to move beyond the encyclopedic paradigm and professors experimented with new ways of organizing their courses and redesigning the curriculum as a whole.

For these innovations to become a part of the "routine behavior of the system," institutionalization must take place on three levels.[25] At the *structural* level, change is conceptualized as faculty engagement of the knowledge and skills associated with this innovation, ongoing assessment of individual performance, and the organizational alterations needed to administer and support these changes. At the *procedural* level, behaviors and policies associated with the innovation become standard operating procedures for departments and the entire curriculum. At the *incorporation* level, values and norms associated with the innovation become a part of the educational institution's culture.

When institutionalization of the practice-theory-practice pattern is conceptualized as involving these three levels, it goes far beyond window-dressing. It involves shifts in pedagogical practices and the organization of course requirements, departments, institutional research, and the reward system of a school of theology. This would take leadership on the part of the administration and key members of the faculty.

Cultivate and Reward Interdisciplinary Work

Congregational leaders interact all of the time with professionals in other fields when visiting hospitals, referring members to therapists or recovery groups, advocating school reform, involving members in social service organizations, and working with lawyers or business women and men in church committees. Moreover, if they are to develop a deeper understanding of historical events, cultural trends, and the social context of their congregation, they will need to read literature other than theology over the course of their ministerial careers. It is very important, thus, that

24. John Braxton, William Luckey, and Patricia Helland, *Institutionalizing a Broader View of Scholarship Through Boyer's Four Domains*, Ashe-Eric Higher Education Report, vol. 29, no. 2 (San Francisco: Jossey-Bass, 2002), 5.

25. Braxton, Luckey, and Helland, *Institutionalizing a Broader View of Scholarship*, 5-7.

they acquire the knowledge and skills of interdisciplinary thinking. Browning's proposal describes all forms of theological interpretation as inherently interdisciplinary along the lines of the revised correlational approach.

It is not necessary to follow Browning's particular interdisciplinary model to see the importance of his point. Interdisciplinary work is important to virtually every profession and field today, from city planning to research on the human genome. Acquiring the capacity to bring theology into conversation with other fields and professions, thus, must be a central goal of theological education. It is one of the most obvious ways the older encyclopedic paradigm of theological education is no longer adequate. Specialized disciplines working in relative isolation are largely a thing of the past.

When the curriculum of a theological school is no longer structured around departmental offerings, interdisciplinary courses become more likely and more valuable. In such courses, professors with different scholarly backgrounds can help students learn the ways their particular fields interact, supporting integration across the four tasks of theological interpretation. I regularly teach with a philosophical theologian, for example. His interest in the science-theology dialogue interacts with my interest in teaching youth and young adults how to engage science from the perspective of faith, rather than viewing it as a competitor to faith. Our strengths are complementary. Over the course of the semester, students explore broad themes like evolution and theological anthropology (the systematic moment of theological interpretation) and how they might use what they are learning to teach in congregations (the strategic moment). This course is interdisciplinary to the core, involving the theology-science dialogue, the Christian education-general education dialogue, and the dialogue between philosophical theology and practical theology. It teaches and models interdisciplinary work within theology and in relation to other fields.

Students who participated in a curriculum organized along these lines would be well prepared to provide leadership to congregations in forging a stronger partnership with the family. It is likely that they would have studied the family in some of their courses, given the high profile of the debate over family values in contemporary American politics. But even if they had not, they would have learned the competencies of theological interpretation and skillful action needed to provide leadership on this issue in their congregations and community.

I shall conclude this chapter with a kind of thought experiment in which I imagine a new course, "Parent Education," designed to teach students how to provide leadership in forging a stronger partnership between families and congregations. The imaginary context of the course is a theological school with a curriculum designed along the lines of Browning's proposal.

Four assumptions guide my thinking about the course within this curricular context. First, the purpose of the course is to help students learn the knowledge, attitudes, and skills necessary for a particular form of theological interpretation. In this case, I shall focus on the descriptive and strategic tasks of interpretation, which includes an introduction to empirical research methods. Second, this frees me from the drive for coverage: the need to cover every important book on this topic. Too often, students read book after book in their many courses, leaving them little time to reflect on and integrate what they are learning. In contrast, my primary goal is to teach a style of theological interpretation, which they can enrich at later points through further reading. Third, I hope to offer them a sense of the whole, while focusing in depth on one of its parts. Forging a stronger partnership between the congregation and family is multidimensional. By the end of the course, I hope students will have a sense of these various dimensions. But they will only deal with one dimension in depth: the ways congregations might engage in parent education. This allows me to teach them the entire "circle" of practical theological interpretation in relation to this one issue: the descriptive-empirical, interpretive, normative, and pragmatic. Having learned this in relation to parent education, they will be in a position to bring this style of reflection to bear on other dimensions of the family-congregation partnership. Fourth, I use teaching approaches that are appropriate to my goal. The lecture method will sometimes be used but so will methods like discussion, case study, action/reflection, and role-play. Peer learning also will be an important. Congregational leadership involves learning from and working with others. In my own leadership of the course, I want to model this attitude and give students the opportunity to reflect on the possibilities and problems of collaborative learning.

With these four assumptions in mind, I shall outline the flow of the course over a twelve-week semester in which classes end before Christmas vacation, followed by a reading period and exams during the first weeks of January. The course will be taught in a two-hour plenary and one-hour precept. The plenary will be held in a large room with movable chairs and will include a short break at the end of the first hour.

Week One — Course Overview

This week is designed to accomplish two goals: to provide an overview of the four tasks of practical theological interpretation and to go over the course syllabus. The first hour will consist of a lecture on practical theology, providing examples of each task taken from the debate over family values. This lecture will be posted on blackboard and will be discussed in the precept later in the week. Walking them through the syllabus in the second hour, I shall then explain how the course is designed to teach them each of the tasks of practical theology. Students need to identify another student in the course with whom they would like to work on their research project: conducting two focus groups with parents in the same congregation. Assignment for next week: Write a three- to five-page reflection paper on the ways their family shaped their values and religious identity. Before leaving class, they are placed in groups of four. They are to email their reflection paper to the other members of this group at least twenty-four hours before the next plenary and are to come to class having read each other's papers.

Week Two — The Descriptive-Empirical Task of Practical Theological Interpretation

Reading: Chapters 1, 4-6, *Research Design: Qualitative, Quantitative, and Mixed Methods Approaches* by John Creswell. The goal of this class is to introduce students to the role of empirical research in practical theological interpretation. The class begins by having students gather in their group of four and identify common themes appearing in their papers. They are to group these themes into analytical categories that capture at least four ways parents influence the values and religious identities of their children. These categories are to be written down and handed to me at the end of the class. Later that week, I shall attempt to consolidate the categories and then post them on blackboard. The end of the first hour will be a brief discussion of what they have discovered. The second hour will focus on the assigned reading to introduce the topic of empirical research, noting that the task of gathering, comparing, and categorizing data, carried out in the first hour, is a basic pattern of such research. The last ten minutes will be used to allow students to form research teams. The precept will focus on a family issue in a short case study, exploring the sort of empirical research that might called for to better understand what is going on in this case and how this might be conducted on the basis of Creswell's model.

Week Three — Empirical Research on Children of Divorce

Reading: *Between Two Worlds: The Inner Lives of Children of Divorce* by Elizabeth Marquardt. The goal of this class is to teach the art of asking good questions, which is important to the discussion method of teaching and empirical research. After briefly explaining this topic, I shall then attempt to model it by using the discussion method to explore Marquardt's book. In the second hour, the class will reflect on my teaching in small groups and the strengths/limits of the discussion method generally. The class will regather and look closely at the questions used in Marquardt's research. The precept will introduce the idea of a questioning route in focus groups, leading the students in a focus group discussion during the first half of the meeting.

Week Four — Focus Groups as a Method of Research

Reading: Chapters 1, 3-6, *Focus Groups: A Practical Guide for Applied Research,* 3d edition, by Richard Krueger and Mary Anne Casey. The goal of this class is to introduce students to focus groups as a way of gathering data. In the first hour, I shall lecture on the assigned reading. The second hour will focus on the task of the task of forming good research questions and developing a questioning route for focus groups that elicits data relevant to their research questions. The basic research question informing their projects is: What sort of help do parents want from their congregations in raising good children? Assignment: Research teams are to meet before their precept and write a questioning route that might be used in their focus group research. These will be discussed in the precept. I shall gather what they have come up with and use them to form a questioning route that will be followed by all research teams. This will make it possible for the research teams to compare and combine their data.

Week Five — Is the Family Declining or Changing? The Interpretive Task of Practical Theological Interpretation

Reading, Part 1, *From Culture Wars to Common Ground,* by Don Browning, et al. The first hour will be a lecture on the assigned reading and highlight a key claim of the book: "The fundamental family issue of our time may be how to retain and honor the intact family without turning it into an object of idolatry and without retaining the inequalities of power, status, and privilege of earlier forms"[26] In the second hour, I shall present the questioning route for their focus group research and give the class the opportunity to critique its language and questions. The end-result will be posted on blackboard. Assignment: In the next two weeks, research teams are to conduct two focus groups of parents with children or youth still living in the home. The parents are to be members of the same congregation. One person will lead the group and the other will use a laptop computer to record a rough transcription of comments and themes (which should be added to immediately following the focus group). They will switch roles for the second group. Following their focus group research, they are to reflect on their rough transcriptions, identifying important themes and comments that are grouped into analytical categories. They are to write up what they have learned in a five- to seven-page paper, answering the question: What sort of help do parents want from their congregations in raising good children? No precept this week: Students are to begin setting up focus groups.

Week Six — An Ethic of Equal Regard: The Normative Task of Practical Theological Interpretation

Reading, Parts II and IV, *From Culture Wars to Common Ground.* The goal of this class is to introduce an ethic of equal regard and to allow students to practice using this ethical principle to assess different situations. The first hour will offer a mini-lecture on equal regard which offers biblical grounds for this ethic not covered in the assigned reading. In small groups, the class will then focus on several family issues written up in the form of brief cases: a family with an alcoholic father; a dual-career family in which one spouse has been offered a promotion that requires the family to move; an adolescent daughter who is unwilling to do her part of the family chores. Their task is to explore the issues brought into focus when each scenario is viewed through the normative lens of equal regard. The precept focuses on the strengths and limits of this normative perspective.

Week Seven — Parenting as a Form of Moral Education: The Pragmatic Task of Practical Theology

Reading: Parts 1 and 3, *Raising Good Children* by Thomas Lickona. The goal of this class is to introduce strategic thinking about parent education

26. Browning et al., *From Culture Wars to Common Ground,* 71.

by exploring an approach to parenting based on an ethic of equal regard. I shall speak to the limits of Lawrence Kohlberg's theory of moral development, which guides Lickona's proposal, and the ways Lickona's approach to parenting might be reconceptualized to incorporate elements of an ethic of care. In the second hour, students are placed in small groups and asked to recall their reflection papers for the second week of class. In what ways did their parents embody an ethic of equal regard in their relation to one another and to their children? The precept will focus on the developmental dimensions of Lickona's proposal, introducing the idea of perspective taking and considering its role in other regard.

Week Eight — Embodying an Ethic of Equal Regard: Family Meetings

Reading: Chapters 12-16, *Raising Good Children.* The goal of this class is to explore Lickona's idea of family meetings as a way of setting family rules and cultivating perspective taking and other regard. Using the fishbowl method, groups of students will role-play three family meetings that deal with issues appropriate to children of different ages. Students will receive their roles in advance. Discussion will follow each role-play. The precept will focus on Lickona's approach to discipline. Assignment due: Research teams are to turn in their projects, written together. Part 1 — A brief description of the congregational context of their focus groups and a summary of what they have found. Part 2 — Drawing explicitly on course reading, they are to interpret their findings in terms of broader trends characterizing the contemporary family. Part 3 — A critical evaluation of an ethic of equal regard as a norm that might guide contemporary families. Students will have a chance to revise their papers on the basis of my feedback. Also, I shall take seriously the data generated by the class as a whole and report to them some of the findings to emerge out of their focus group research.

Week Nine — Recovering Worship Practices in the Home

Reading: *Family, the Forming Center: A Vision of the Role of the Family in Spiritual Formation* by Marjorie Thompson. The goal of this class is to introduce the idea of spiritual formation and the practices needed to make families "centers" of this process. Using the discussion method, I shall focus on four key practices Thompson identifies: prayer, family worship, service projects, and story-telling. The second hour and precept will invite students to begin strategizing how they might teach these practices in parent education.

Week Ten — Designing a Curriculum for Parent Education

Reading: *Teaching Teachers to Teach* by Donald Griggs. I shall begin this class with a power-point presentation that summarizes the findings to emerge out of the research of the entire class. This presentation will be posted on blackboard, and students are encouraged to draw on it when revising their papers. Following this presentation, I turn to the goal of teaching students how to design a curriculum for parent education. Their final project, handed in during the exam period, will consist of a revision of their earlier paper (Parts 1-3) and a new Part 4, which consists of a curriculum for parent education. This is designed for an eight-week, Sunday morning series in the congregation of their focus groups. In this class, I shall teach them how write lesson plans. Assignment: Working in project teams, they are to write up the lesson plan for the first class of their curriculum and bring it to the precept, where it will be discussed.

Week Eleven — Teaching Methods and Curriculum Design

Reading: Chapters 1, 4, 5, 9-11, *Creative Teaching Methods* by Marlene LeFever. In this session, the class will explore different teaching methods that might be used in their parent education curriculum. These are covered in the assigned reading, and many have been modeled in this course. The class will reflect on the sorts of skills and preparation that are needed to use these teaching methods successfully. The precept will focus on their lesson plan for the second class of their curriculum on parent education.

Week Twelve — Reflection on the Course and Evaluation

Reading: None. Students are asked to bring their course syllabus to class, and I shall lead them through it as a way of recalling the learning activities designed to teach them the knowledge and skills of practical theological interpretation. I have found that if I have established trust with the class and present this sort of evaluation as a way I can improve the course, then students are honest in their feedback. I also will ask them to evaluate the possibilities and difficulties of peer learning, embodied in their research projects and the collaborative learning activities used in the course. This sort of evaluation of the course as a whole is a way for students to name what they have learned and to view the different readings and activities of the course as interrelated dimensions of practical theological interpretation.

Let me conclude with a final comment. I have never taught this course so it truly is a thought experiment. It is likely that I shall do so in the future. I offer this thought experiment, however, to make a larger point. This sort of course would have its greatest impact if the sort of practical theological interpretation it teaches is deepened in other courses by different professors who share a common vision of practical theology. And these courses would be effective if they were part of a curriculum designed to teach theological interpretation in its diverse, but interrelated forms. This is the value of a comprehensive proposal like Don Browning's, and for his willingness to tackle this difficult task we are all in his debt.

10 The Carnal Knowledge of History: Practical Historical Theology and the Past and Future of Intimacy

Garrett E. Paul

A carnal knowledge of history yields nearly as many improbable perplexities as promising resources for a practical theology of families. But it is unavoidable if we are to overcome the contradiction of our family history. "Carnal knowledge," of course, is that civil if not altogether genteel term for sexual intercourse, here taken to signify knowledge of the material (including sexual, but also economic, reproductive, etc.) infrastructure of marriage and family. "Family history" usually denotes a fascination with one's family tree (sometimes to the seventh generation or more), but can also connote the psychotherapeutic interest in a client's "family of origin" (though usually not that far back). Here I use it to signify not only the history but also the historiography and historicity of families and the family institution. A practical theology of marriage must embrace carnal knowledge and family history in all these senses (though personal family trees may possibly be disregarded). This history is a source of many difficulties but also many resources, and the purpose of this chapter is to identify constructive ways to deal with both.

This work here is deeply indebted to the achievements of Don Browning and his colleagues in both method and content — not least simply for having put marriage and families back on the theological and ethical agenda along with gender and sexuality. I am also in complete agreement with eliminating the division between practical and historical theology. But rather than engage Browning's work directly at the outset, I will focus initially on how historiography as well as history itself can inform a practical theology of families. Only after that, near the midpoint of the chapter, will I articulate some of the consequences this has for Browning's theological method.

That said, this chapter has two theses. The first is that any practical theology of marriage, family, and sexuality[1] must be informed not only by a critical social theory, but also by a critical historical theory. This historical theory entails a knowledge of the formal logic of history and historical causality, and particularly an understanding of how meaning is extracted from history, that is, the philosophy of history.

The second thesis follows from using this critical historical theory in an actual analysis — necessarily speculative — of the contemporary historical situation. Using much the same evidence as Browning, I shall argue that the history of carnal knowledge itself has reached a contradiction between the human need for interpersonal, intergenerational, and intersexual intimacy and a global infrastructure that increasingly destroys the very structures required to fulfill that need. This, like the house divided against itself, cannot long endure.

The question is not *whether,* but *how* it will be transformed, and how the Church must respond. I propose elements of both a public and, what I will call, a semi-public or sect-like theology.

Carnal Knowledge in History: The Formal Logic of History and Family History

> *"Those who do not study the past are condemned to repeat its mistakes."*
>
> George Santayana

> *"History repeats itself."*
>
> Adage

> *"It is not important to study history. What is important is to make it."*
>
> Attributed to Otto von Bismarck

1. I more frequently use the phrase "marriage, family, and sexuality" rather than "families." This choice — carnal knowledge more broadly construed — is meant to underscore the connections and tensions between all three. This is by no means contrary to the spirit or letter of Browning's work.

"History is bunk."

Henry Ford

"Good old days," "The Golden Age"

Commonplaces

"Decline of the West"

Book by Oswald Spengler

"Progress is our most important product"

Slogan for General Electric

Each of these is a common saying, and each embodies a more or less inadequate and even cracker-barrel perspective on history, though such perspectives are not foreign to a few scholarly books as well. Some are negative views — including Santayana's famous remark (at least taken out of context), since it implies that only negative lessons are to be learned — some are positive, and some dismissive, like the jibes of Ford and Bismarck. But they all illustrate that history is approached with certain presumptions about its significance or lack thereof, and is subject to some kind of hermeneutical circle. The interpreter looks back to history with certain conceptions of what will be found there, and comes "back" to the present having found certain things that may or may not change the interpreter's mind about the present and the future. Many German readers of Spengler's *Decline of the West*[2] "returned" from their reading with their pessimistic views of the Weimar Republic confirmed and deepened.

Historical accounts of sexuality, the body, and gender have flourished for the last third of a century. They tell us much about the concerns of the historians and their own times. For those historians that represent the past or its dominant narratives chiefly as the source of contemporary problems (patriarchy, shame, sexual repression, etc.), the clear implication is that solutions must come chiefly or completely through a break with the past, or at least with received interpretations of it. They perform the important task of deconstructing misconceptions of the past and imparting a healthy distrust of sources.[3] Browning and his colleagues inter-

2. Oswald Spengler, *The Decline of the West,* 2 vols., trans. Charles Francis Atkinson (New York: Knopf, 1926-28).

3. Sigmund Freud, of course, is the textbook case of an interpreter of the history of sexuality as a history of repression. A more recent highly influential interpretation is

pret the past with a different set of deconstructions, arguing that Christianity did not merely perpetuate ancient patriarchy. They identify textual[4] and material[5] evidence that testifies to a break with Greco-Roman honor-shame codes and to an improved status for women, even if the movement did not eliminate patriarchy.

The age-old frustration for the interpreter and the practitioner alike is, How can different people presented with ostensibly the same evidence come to such different explanations? The facile conclusion that it makes little difference is suitable in some contexts, but not when one is confronting patriarchy, domestic violence, or a family crisis. Which brings us to some formal considerations of the logic of history and historiography, and then to the philosophy of history.

History must be studied according to a different logic than nature, and operates with a different causality than nature. Understanding this distinction properly is crucial for a practical theology of families. This does not mean that history is unnatural, nor that it is not subject to the "laws" of nature. However, it has proved impervious to all attempts to reduce it to predictable laws, and it is safe to predict that it will remain so. Human sperm and ova behave in predictable if not deterministic ways within certain biological constraints, yet the human ability reliably to impede fertilization of our ova while continuing to engage in sexual intercourse throughout the female cycle was achieved only once in history. If we forget that ability and re-create it later, it will happen differently next time, with somewhat different results. There was only one Napoleon and one Luther, and even though neither could fall up nor be unconstrained by mammalian tendencies toward territoriality, each still had only one Waterloo and one Worms, and neither will ever happen again. Historical events are unique, unrepeatable, and almost completely unpredictable.[6] And historical *causality,* likewise, is contingent or non-deterministic. It is not random in the sense of being uncaused nor subject to the laws of probability, but remains contingent and individual.

Michel Foucault, *The History of Sexuality,* trans. Robert Hurley (New York: Pantheon, 1978).

4. Don S. Browning, *Marriage and Modernization* (Grand Rapids, MI: Eerdmans, 2003), 68-76; Don S. Browning et al., *From Culture Wars to Common Ground* (Louisville, KY: Westminster John Knox, 1997), 129-50.

5. Carolyn Osiek and David L. Balch, *Families in the New Testament World* (Louisville, KY: Westminster John Knox, 1997), 5-36, 213-14.

6. Also see Andrew Porter, "Material Differences Between History and Nature," *International Philosophical Quarterly* 44 (174) (2004): 185-200.

Historical agents act with intentions; sometimes those intentions are achieved, often they are not, and frequently enough the exact opposite comes to pass. In this sense history is both intended and ironic. This is of the utmost importance when we consider how we will respond to our own historical situation. We will unquestionably develop more control over human reproduction in the future; can and will we take the consequences of our actions into account any more than did the first people to make use of reliable contraception in the twentieth century? Development of affordable contraception for women in the mid-twentieth century was promoted, in part, as a way for families to limit the number of children, although its appeal was also surely due to women gaining more control over reproductive decisions. Some opponents feared the end of marriage while some advocates predicted better functioning families or greater sexual freedom and fulfillment, or both. Neither could have foreseen what actually happened — more reproductive control for women, declining fertility rates, weaker families, less nurtured children, greater sexual freedom and exposure, a pandemic of fatal sexually transmitted disease, and serious predictions that marriage will cease to exist as an institution. The inability to foresee the future is not a weakness, but it is a serious failure to consider the *possible* consequences.

One more element of history must be included, and this is the importance of historical infrastructure. This is best expressed in the Marxist-inspired (but better formulated by Max Weber) doctrine of infrastructure and superstructure. In its crude form this holds that the superstructure of society — ideas, intimate relations, family forms — is fully determined by the material infrastructure, chiefly the control of the means of production. In its more sophisticated form (present in Browning) it is understood as the ways in which the material infrastructure, particularly the institutional differentiation of social tasks, both determines and influences human action.[7] One simple yet easily overlooked element of infrastructure is transportation: the rapid growth in the length of a day's journey from 1800 to 2000 has had revolutionary effects on the family. Decreased infant and maternal mortality gave women greater potential equality with men, fueling demands to realize that equality in political

7. See, e.g., Browning's use of Alan Macfarlane's analysis of the interaction of theology and economic infrastructure to understand the emergence of nuclear families prior to the development of early capitalism: Browning, *Marriage and Modernization,* 58, citing Alan Macfarlane, *Marriage and Love in England, 1300-1840* (Oxford: Blackwell, 1986), 335-42. But see also Browning's criticisms of excessive reliance on infrastructural explanations, *Marriage and Modernization,* 68-71.

and economic institutions. Infrastructure and superstructure have a dynamic relationship.

To sum up: marriages and families are subject to natural causes, and are yet unpredictable, unique, intentional, and ironic. The institutions of family and sexuality change over time and space, and while the change is not random, it is not wholly predictable either. It is contingent, not in the sense of being purely accidental, but in the sense of being affected by unpredictable and contingent causes.

The hermeneutical circle is nowhere more evident than in the history of marriage, family, and sexuality. There is no one single place to start the task of interpreting families; the task is circular, going from natural causality to historical causality, from intentional events to ironic ones, from infrastructure to superstructure and back again. There are better and worse places to begin, but no one right place. Moreover, historical events are already interpreted as they happen; the mere selection of what is thought to be worth recording, or what is accidentally preserved, begins the process. Which families' lives are documented, and whose artifacts happen to be preserved? Why is one topic chosen rather than another? Historians choose the topic of "family" or "domesticity" or "women's history," and the perspective rapidly becomes concrete.

Carnal Knowledge in History: A Historical Theology of Family History

If questions are inevitably put to history, what shall they be? How can we avoid crude ideology and idle chatter? And, more important, which questions shall history put to us? This enterprise which seeks to extract meaning from history is usually called the philosophy of history. I say "extract" to exclude any sense that meaning is merely "constructed" in the sense of using history as an inert building site, and equally to exclude any sense that the meaning of history is simply out there, waiting to be discovered. *Extracting* the meaning of history here means confronting the questions of marriage, human sexuality, family arrangements, and reproduction. And if, as we consider these questions, we are concerned with the will of God and the church's responses, we are then engaged in historical theology and not only the philosophy of history. Historical theology continues to be informed by the philosophy of history and an awareness of history's characteristics.

A brief return to the aphorisms quoted earlier illustrates both the difficulty and ubiquity of trying to draw lessons from history. Each carries a bit of truth: some things were better in the past (the Mississippi and Rhine were cleaner), some worse (child and maternal mortality were higher), and Santayana was right about the avoiding past mistakes (the Third Reich should teach us many lessons). But even the wittiest of these sayings is shallow, inadequate, and misleading. They are bad enough to provoke that most beloved and tedious of current student clichés, "who's to say?" But we need to say something.

This is both easier and harder than it seems. Two important facts about history are so near to us that we easily overlook them. One is that history tells us much about ourselves, and we are therefore part of it. It tells us what nature and history have made of us, and what our choices have intentionally and ironically made of us. With marriage and mating, sexuality and family, it tells us what evolution, psychology, culture, and religion — and God, ultimately — have made of us, and what we have made and unmade of ourselves. The second fact is that history, including the present, presents us with a variety of possibilities from the past and for the future, or possible futures. Which of these are realized depends, in part, on choices we make in the present. Or, perhaps better expressed, it depends on how we respond to the possibilities history presents to us in the present. History is, quite simply, unavoidable

The chief difficulty is that criteria for these decisions must be developed for a moving target, and they must come from a moving target. Moreover, the outcome of these decisions is sure to be ironic. Indeed, this is one reason decisions of this kind are not likely to be made in confidence without a degree of faith in some sort of providence, whether natural, dialectical, or divine.

A clearer understanding of the character of these decisions comes from understanding that the line between the past, present, and future is largely arbitrary (even if expedient). We are immersed in history; it is not separate from us. The past is still subject to change, because the events of the past are not finished; and the future is already here, because its events have begun. *History must be understood dynamically.* The feudal, bourgeois, and peasant marriages of the past continue to live on in their present effects; future forms of sexuality have begun to arrive, and discerning the multiple directions in which marriage and family are moving is one of the chief tasks of an historically informed practical theology. Moreover, present-day interpretations and decisions and guesses must always be done with an eye toward what the likely consequences of these decisions will be ten, twenty, and even five hundred years from now. This is true of historiography as well — what we choose to describe from the past influences our future. If Bismarck said it wasn't important to write history, he was wrong. Describing the past influences the future, and is one way history *is* made.

But if Bismarck is wrong because the boundary between past and present is not fixed, then both he and Ford must be granted a partial concession: those who do not study the mistakes of the future are condemned to repeat them. That is, we should seek to avoid the mistakes of the future that already have their seeds in the present. Thus the warnings sounded by Don Browning,[8] among others, point to how the continued rationalization of sexual and family relations in terms defined by their place in the economic infrastructure signify a future which, in some senses, is already here. That is, the way in which the very conditions which make for the successful raising of children are being undermined in "developed" societies foreshadows the globalization of these conditions and the devastating consequences that may ensue in economic terms alone, quite apart from the sheer human cost. One need look no farther than the role played by disruption of family structures in the HIV/AIDS crisis in Africa.[9]

At this point it will surely be objected that this involves us in that most risky and imprudent of historical pursuits, prediction. How can we avoid looking foolish in light of the unpredictability of historical causality? One need only look at 1930s predictions of what the world would look like in the 1960s to be convinced of the futility of such endeavors. Yet such predictions as space travel, electronic banking, and — more to the point — "test-tube babies" — demonstrate that prognostication does not entirely deserve its tarnished reputation, and even helps to *create* the future. Even if ridiculous predictions like personal helicopters outnumbered accurate ones like home computers by 1,000 to 1, every correct insight makes the effort worthwhile.

Reading out of the past and into the future, where we have come and where we are going and how we should respond, is *the* central question of the philosophy of history, and of a practical historical theology. It constitutes both the problem and the resource of history.

Meaning in history, then, is neither merely constructed nor simply discovered; rather, history presents us with a variety of possibilities, a

8. See Don S. Browning, "Social Theory," in *The Blackwell Companion to Modern Theology*, ed. Gareth Jones (Malden, MA: Blackwell), 76-77.

9. Also discussed in Browning, *Marriage and Modernization*, 13, 181-82

movement in history itself (Hegel called it the Dialectic) which presents us with choices in the present (Kierkegaard called it the Moment). History never achieves complete objectivity and synthesis; it always requires interaction with intentional beings to realize the choices it offers, some of which are better than others, and some of which are disastrous.

Choice requires a leap (again to recall Kierkegaard), but not one done in total ignorance. To borrow from John Polkinghorne, it is a leap into the light and not into the dark. Yet choices must be made before all the evidence is in. Choices about human sexuality and families must be made now, in the historical moment, before we can have all the data we need. Indeed, there is never enough data. In this respect, it is like global warming; if we wait until all the data are in, it will be too late.

Don Browning's Insights and Oversights in History

There is much to celebrate in their work of Don Browning and his colleagues. His rejection of the rival icons of "lifestyle choice" and "family values," which both embody the now-globalizing American religion of freedom; his analysis of the colonization of the life-world by both the bureaucratic state and the global economy; and his refusal to restrict his metaphors or symbols for God to love — all these represent important achievements in the conversation. "Critical familism" is an attractive and constructive program. Even my criticisms cluster chiefly on something I admire, the integration of theory and application.

In Browning's wide-ranging discussions of family history and theory, I see four problems, all of which relate to the circular character of historical interpretation and the dynamic character of history itself. It is not that he does not recognize the historicity of history and interpretation; it is rather that its implications are insufficiently realized.

First, the hermeneutical circle itself needs to be historicized. The four moments of descriptive theology, historical theology, systematic theology, and strategic practical theology[10] seem to confine history to one part of the circle. Historical theology, however, is itself a circle within the circle (creating epicycles and other patterns). Interpretation goes from the present to the past to the future and returns to the present, changed. But the present is *already* changed by the past and the future before interpret-

10. Don S. Browning, *A Fundamental Practical Theology* (Minneapolis: Fortress, 1991), 58-59.

ers "leave" the present; that is one of the things, paradoxically, they learn on their trips. Moreover, they learn that the past and future are shaped by the present as well. This means that the *entire* hermeneutical circle is changed by history, and that historical theology cannot be confined to one moment. Browning is superior to most interpreters in understanding that the present reaches out to both the past and future.[11] Nevertheless, his travels to the past seem to arrive at a stable, formed past no longer subject to change, and no longer actively changing the present.

In this sense, the dialectical character of what Browning describes as the "brute aspects"[12] of human experience applies also to history. As the alcoholic painfully learns that drinking does not "work," history itself forces upon us the recognition that our interpretation of it is not working and must change.

A second issue is that the concept of a "classic" needs to be reconsidered. Browning rightly understands that our interrogation of history starts with some questions, and I fully agree (though others will debate) that questions of marriage and family should begin with the present crisis.[13] Yet once that move begins, he turns to the monuments, "texts and events," that shape present practices.[14] But present practices are shaped by far more than these texts and events; why is the historical research limited to these? The concept of a "classic" is clearly different in today's social infrastructure; many of my students do not recognize "lilies of the fields," as a common metaphor, simply because the are not familiar enough with the Bible. Of course they are wrong if they think the Bible does not shape culture, but the book is not a "classic" for them in the same sense as for earlier epochs. Aquinas, Luther, and Calvin are probably not canonical at your neighborhood megachurch, though they are surely present there. This ought not lead us to entertain such conceits as the elimination of authorship, intention, and canon; but classics are still not what they used to be.

A third observation is that Browning treats historical epochs, particularly modernity, too much as discrete entities. Periodization is a necessary and useful task, and indeed corresponds to real events in history. Nevertheless, periods are not discrete, and too rigid an adherence to periodization can obscure important phenomena. The boundary between modernity and pre-modernity, of particular concern in the family debate,

11. Browning, *Fundamental Practical Theology,* 181-82.

12. Browning, *Fundamental Practical Theology,* 184-86.

13. This never eliminates or replaces the need for more or less "pure" historical research, the painstaking work of archives, data, and shovels; it rather is presupposed.

14. Browning, *Fundamental Practical Theology,* 184.

is fluid. Modernity took different forms in different areas. Moreover, the date for the beginning of the modern era is disputable. It probably begins with the formation of the massive capital that made the colonization and exploration of the fifteenth and sixteenth centuries possible. Or, if the term "modern" is made to coincide with "industrializing," then another word must be found for the era which commences with that capital formation and colonization.[15] A clearer sense of when and where modernity begins will help clarify this project, even as it calls into question whether the term "modernization" is too broad.

This leads to my fourth point. Browning needs to give more attention to the role of post-Reformation developments, particularly the development of sectarian and Pietist movements in Germany, the Netherlands, and England. Sectarianism (Anabaptists, Mennonites, Hutterites, and others) promoted voluntarism, developed in communal directions, and played important roles in the development of democracy; some, notably Quakers, were influential in abolition and more public status for women. Pietism arose in response, sociologically, to the deeply weakened structures of urbanizing families in Protestant Europe, particularly with respect to prostitution and alcohol (Jakob Spener in Halle and John Wesley in England). Pietism's heir, nineteenth-century American Methodism and revivalism, receives its due,[16] but the links to seventeenth- and eighteenth-century economic and social upheaval are missing. This is ironic given that one of Browning's best case studies focuses on a black Pentecostal church, which has much Pietism in its family tree.[17] The omission of these movements is, in part, related to questions of periodization and "classics." It reflects, perhaps, a view that the Reformation is the last important event before industrialization, and therefore neglects the important events in between. It also reflects the limitations of focusing on "classics": neither of these movements produced theological classics.[18]

All this historicizes the circle, and underscores the task of hitting a

15. Ernst Troeltsch dates modernity from the fifteenth century, with the beginnings of colonialism, imperialism, and the modern unified state, but acknowledges another major change with the revolutions of the eighteenth century. See Ernst Troeltsch, *Der Historismus und seine Probleme* (Tübingen: Mohr Siebeck, 1922), 751-53, 765.

16. Browning, *Marriage and Modernization*, 34-35; Browning et al., *From Culture Wars to Common Ground*, 84-86.

17. Browning, *Fundamental Practical Theology*, 26-33, 243-91.

18. In no way do I mean to suggest that Pietism and Methodism had no theology; yet they produced no theological systems on the order of the scholasticism that the Lutheran Pietists so vigorously disputed.

moving target from a moving target. What meaning can we extract from history, what responses should we make to the possibilities it provides us in the moment, given the hermeneutical circle no one can break and the research no one can ever finish? In this I have proceeded far enough along the path of raising questions and should start risking some answers of my own, continuing to engage Browning's work along the way.

The Current Contradiction in Carnal Knowledge

Thus far I have presented history both as a challenge and a resource for a practical theology of marriage, family, and sexuality; in turn, the present situation of families poses a challenge for historiography and history. The task now is to discern the circumstances of the present, to use them to help discern the directions and possibilities history provides us, and to decide how we will respond. In the remainder of this chapter, I undertake the perilous challenge of trying to illustrate, in broad yet fragmentary strokes, how this process may work. Here I will develop my second thesis, that the historical contradiction in marriage and family is part of a broader contradiction in intimacy. In this I take many of the insights of Browning and his team and try to put them into a more dynamic historical perspective.

A broader view of history makes clear that we are dealing with a contradiction not merely in family, marriage, and sexuality, but much larger. Put brusquely, this is a contradiction between the human needs for interpersonal, intergenerational, and intersexual intimacy and a world infrastructure that systematically frustrates and denies those needs. These needs are an "order of creation" in terms of Lutheran doctrine, or adaptive for survival in evolutionary terminology,[19] a "brute fact" ignored only with dire consequences. This process of a contradiction in human intimacy is itself a continuation and perhaps nearing the culmination of the process of rationalization described at the beginning of the past century by Max Weber. The needs for intimacy have their source in the kin altruism and parental investment referenced by Browning; they increase, and are increasingly frustrated, as the "colonization of the life-world" by technical rationality continues.[20]

19. This does not mean that "orders of creation" and "adaptation" are equivalent terms. That is a question for another time.

20. Browning, *Marriage and Modernization,* 106-13, 19; Browning et al., *From Culture Wars to Common Ground,* 60.

I use the specifically Hegelian (or Marxist) language of contradiction to underscore the conflict, urgency, and necessity for an "overcoming" *(Aufhebung)* or upheaval in the situation. "Resolution" is too weak to describe what must happen. The contradiction in which the human need for intimacy is caught will soon reach a point beyond which it cannot continue.

Intimacy can be defined in terms of its absence, seen in the reduction of human relationships exclusively to cash transactions, to manipulation instead of response, to abuse rather than appreciation. The opposite of intimacy is apparent when — for understandable and sometimes good reasons — the sufferer from abuse refuses to let others cross the boundaries marked by the scars of that abuse. Yet the isolation itself compounds the suffering, and often plays a role in the cycle of future abuse. Intimacy is the opposite of another classic Marxist term, "alienation," whether from self or others. It may be circular to characterize intimacy as a non-abusive, nurturing and regenerating connection, but it is a fitting circle.

In any case, the word is not limited to family, marriage, and sexuality. It is important see it in its broader sense: It applies to intergenerational relations and to intersexual relations generally, for both are particularly troubled in our time. These relations are alienated by the same contradiction that weakens families. Large numbers of children have no significant relationships with adult men in their lives, and large numbers of adult men have no significant relationships with any women (including friends) or children in their lives.[21] The same holds true for the separation of the elderly and the young.

Let us look at some of the historical dynamics and infrastructure of this upheaval. First, present changes in family structure, moving from broader and broader to smaller and smaller family units, or simply to disconnected individuals, are of extraordinarily long duration, and will not easily be stopped. Rationalizing economic forces, particularly those that require workers to be as fluid and mobile as cash, do not make for stable relationships. Economic forces pull parents apart. Ironically, the ability to have sexual relations with virtually no risk of pregnancy seems to have increased distrust and decreased intimacy between men and women in general. Social differentiation increasingly separates the very young from the adolescent, young adults from the mature, adults from the frail elderly. Intimacy across any of the above boundaries becomes difficult. At the same time, it appears that this cannot continue much longer without massive psychological trauma to the species.

21. Browning et al., *From Culture Wars to Common Ground,* 79.

Manifestations of this isolation and lack of intimacy are widespread. One sees it in the massive increase in work hours for the middle classes and the almost graveyard-like stillness of residential neighborhoods during the day. It appears in violent behavior by children, including those who are well-educated and have ample material opportunities. Among the signs of this isolation and lack of intimacy is the evidence amassed by Browning that correlates lessened expectations for children of single parent households.[22] None of this, of course, suggests that overworked middle-class parents or overwhelmed single parents are morally inferior to parents who have more time for their children. This is a question of an historically emerging infrastructure. The call for a combined sixty-hour work week for parents proposed by Browning and his coauthors in *From Culture Wars to Common Ground* is an audacious first step toward changing that structure. The structural changes it would require from boardroom to playground to port of entry are massive.

Of course, historical comparisons are difficult because precious little past data, and no future data, are available. Were there really more opportunities for intimacy in the twelfth or seventeenth centuries, or even in the 1950s? Yet the frequency of contemporary complaints about the absence of intimacy stand in contrast to past complaints (certainly legitimate) about stifling relationships. This contradiction has grown with great strides in equality, freedom, and reproductive health for women, mostly in Euro-North American-Pacific Rim society, achievements that will not be reversed. But once again it will not do simply to mutter "who's to say?" nor to declare "*we* will say!" Nor will mere compromise suffice. Something new must be said, and something will.

Another aspect (among many) of this contradiction is the increasingly close encounters between radically different cultural and religious interpretations of marriage and family. The most visible of these is the contradiction between Islamic Shari'a and Western family law. It should be no secret that much of the conflict between some Muslims (particularly in Europe) and the "West" has to do with differing views of the family. Denunciations of Western immorality are not rare among Muslims, nor limited to so-called "radicals" or "fundamentalists."[23]

Those who believed that these contradictions will simply disappear

22. Browning et al., *From Culture Wars to Common Ground,* 55-58.

23. For an example of how French Muslims debate how to raise children in a "land of unbelief," see Gilles Kepel, *The War for Muslim Minds: Islam and the West* (Cambridge, MA: Harvard University Press, 2004), 250-53.

through "assimilation" have, thus far, proved wrong. One quite irenic American imam has proposed that not only Muslims but all religious groups in America should be allowed to live under their own family law, enforced by their own jurists or advisors to the courts.[24] This is, of course, unthinkable under American and European jurisprudence (at least for the foreseeable future). More significant for the immediate future are the conflicts that will happen in India, particularly West Bengal, and parts of sub-Saharan Africa, as Muslim populations become the majority.

Browning's recent work has helped to open a dialogue with Islam (along with Judaism and Confucianism) on this issue, and is an important first step in that direction.[25] Juxtaposing this with analysis of how contemporary Western theorists, such as Susan Moller Okin, regard Islam's potential for gender equality brings together streams of thought usually kept separate. The convergence noted by Browning between the medieval Muslim jurist al-Ghazalli and Thomas Aquinas on kin altruism and inclusive fitness is significant and worth further exploration. It does not, however, begin to explain the discontent many Muslims living in the West feel with Western sexual mores and practices. A fuller interpretation of the dialectic between Islam and the West will require a thick description of the present infrastructure of Muslim-Western relations, including the social and economic dislocation of Muslims in Europe and North America. This is another case where expansion beyond the focus on classic texts, attention to infrastructure and superstructure, and a sense of the dynamics of history can render the inquiry more fruitful.[26]

Overcoming Family History with Family History: Opportunities for Response

My role is chiefly one of response to change, both present and future, to contradictions that are unstable and unable to continue in their present

24. Feisal Abdul Rauf, *What's Right with Islam: A New Vision for Muslims and the West* (San Francisco: HarperSanFrancisco, 2004), 109-11.

25. Browning, *Marriage and Modernization*, 122-25, 145-51.

26. Similar issues apply to Browning's engagement with Judaism and East Asian/Confucian family patterns and teachings. See Don S. Browning et al., *Sex, Marriage and Family in the World Religions* (New York: Columbia University Press, 2005). In each case, the unique histories of these cultures' and religions' interactions with the now-globalizing West will need analysis, as will a close attention to infrastructure and non-textual sources.

form. This is not a counsel of passivity but rather of looking for the *kairos*, the right moment to act with history rather than against it or in an attempt to force it.[27]

Here I focus on theological responses of two kinds: (1) a public theology, in which the church can add its voice to the public discourse, using publicly accessible criteria to advocate for the common good of families; and (2) a semi-public theology, focused on what the church can and must do in its own life to advance the good of human intimacy, including marriage, family, and sexuality. To develop the public practical theology, I seek those insights which can speak to a historicized public good in an age of privatization; for the semi-public practical theology I propose goals and practices which need *not* appeal to publicly accessible criteria, although the criteria are neither strictly private nor inaccessible (hence "*semi*-public"). This distinction is very similar to that drawn by Browning between a "more public language" and a "confessional language,"[28] as well as to the programmatic division between how the Church should address public policy and address its own life.[29] The chief distinction here is that semi-public theology is more "countercultural."[30] Using both types of theology, I argue for the relevance of forgiveness and sanctification in a practical theology of families and sexuality, going beyond the symbols of creation and providence to reclaim a Trinitarian character for the project.[31]

It is well to recall once more that history teaches us that the past is never what it used to be. But history also reminds us that past changes themselves can also be changed, and that past directions of change are not fixed. Even though the past should not be restored, we can retrieve some of its wisdom. And though we should not repeat the mistakes of the future, we can learn from them.

27. There are, no doubt, many other kinds of response to which the church ought to pay close attention. One in particular is the formation of new relationships and communities of (new and genuine? ersatz?) intimacy on the Internet through regular conversations, blogging, chatgroups, and the like.

28. Browning, *Marriage and Modernization*, 130.

29. Browning et al., *From Culture Wars to Common Ground*, 306-34.

30. Browning, "Empirical Considerations in a Practical Theology of Families," uses the term. My combination of public and semi-public theology is very close to his approach to both "critically resist and selectively support" the changes modernity has brought about in families.

31. Browning, *Fundamental Practical Theology*, 194-99 draws three metaphors from Reinhold Niebuhr, though "Redeemer" is not as fully developed.

Public Practical Historical Theology: The Church's Word and Action in Public

It is a truism that the church should call all participants in society to a recollection of the importance of the public good, and particularly the public good of thriving families — both as an intrinsic good and as an instrumental good in the building of a healthy and functional society. Yet the nature of the "public" and of the "good" are changing dramatically. The church itself does not have a clear public standing, nor is it clear who does. The "public" has broadened to include both sexes, more economic classes, and more cultures; yet it is more elusive, fragmented, and difficult to address. It is a challenge to articulate thriving families as a "public good" when many audiences have no conception of how something "public" can be "good." Instead, the good is increasingly privatized. The political right privatizes the good economically and spatially, compressing it into privately controlled wealth and sometimes even gated communities, with a publicly funded national security state to protect it from terrorism and immigration. The political left, though still in relative disarray, seeks to privatize the good in terms of personal lifestyle choice and public economic support for those choices. In a tragic irony, with both wings claiming to support families ("family values" or "working families"), neither is able to provide much real assistance.[32]

The church must oppose patriarchy and all forms of domestic violence, abuse, and neglect while endorsing strong two-parent families on the basis of publicly testable empirical evidence. At the same time, it must support all families and demand strong social and political protection for children and working parents. Eliminating patriarchy is not enough. New contradictions have emerged, especially a lack of protection for vulnerable populations and isolated individuals not connected to any strong social network. This leads directly to the principle of subsidiarity as developed in Roman Catholic social teaching — that families and all familial relationships ought to be supported first of all by the relationships and structures closest to them (friends, relatives, voluntary associations, local support networks), and only by the

32. For more of this analysis of the failings of the political, and religious, left and right, see Kyle Pasewark and Garrett Paul, *The Emphatic Christian Center* (Nashville: Abingdon, 1999), 109-26, 230-40. Much of this discussion is dated by events since 2001, but much has simply been exacerbated by the development of the national security state to combat terrorism.

broader services of society and state when all the closer supports have failed.[33]

Yet both the broader structures as well as the nearby supports are under great stress and have been weakened in the emerging privatization of almost everything. Even the "good" is being privatized. And when the public is ironically unable to grasp the very idea of a "public good," it is difficult for marriage to be seen as anything other than a contract for personal fulfillment. There is an urgent need to make the social value of stable families and of reducing domestic violence and neglect more visible. The equal-regarding marriage and opportunities for both genders should be consistent with the public good, and the public good seen as valuable. How can a public theology contribute to this debate?

The costs of physical and sexual abuse, especially of children, are staggering. A promising area for contributions by a public theology is in building a worldwide struggle against physical and sexual abuse, and for thriving, especially of children, and in families. Definitions of abuse will continue to be contested — genital mutilation is a vivid example — but the globalization of the sex trade is bringing all cultures into the contradictory web of intimacy and abuse, and illustrates how some kinds of agreement across boundaries will become both possible and necessary. This can be and is already a global issue in which religious communities have a particular interest. It is also a case in which meaning cannot be infinitely deferred; decisions must be made now.

My reference to "costs" suggests another area where history can be made to work for us instead of against us. There is no doubt that one of the long-term forces of modern history has been the power of measurement, particularly the measurement of costs. Until now, however, that has worked almost exclusively against families, for children have never counted on the balance sheet nor has domestic work been counted as an expense (except for the wealthy who pay others to do it). This could be changed — dramatically — if the economic costs of abuse and dysfunctional families to society made their way into cost accounting. Economic systems have benefited all too much from cheap labor, but they also require healthy societies, educated and functional workforces and markets, and controlled health care and law enforcement costs. If the connection between these costs and the costs of the destruction of families and human intimacy were closely correlated, it could make a major difference in

33. As articulated by Leo XIII in *Rerum Novarum;* see Browning et al., *From Culture Wars to Common Ground,* 238-41; Browning, *Marriage and Modernization,* 137-39.

the social and political will to do something about them as a means of controlling social expenses.

I am *not* proposing that human intimacy is good because it can cut business costs. I am proposing that it cuts *some* costs because it is good (even if it is costly in other ways)[34] and that this could be an honest and worthwhile strategic move. Indeed, an appeal to a "common" good defined by costs and benefits may still work where other appeals to the "public" good might fall on deaf ears. Social and economic reforms may be quickly accepted, even by capital, if they are seen to be in its own interest.

Theologically, the previous considerations come under the doctrines of creation and providence, and therefore the First Person of the Trinity. But there is more to be done here than simply to create and sustain families. There is a desperate need to undo the damage done by patriarchy, neglect, abuse, and the reduction of human relationship to cash values. Trust, particularly trust between women and men, between one generation of children and the generations of parents who preceded them, cannot be restored by fiat. Here, too, the church has another gift to offer to the public discussion — the value of forgiveness and reconciliation in restoring trust. This brings the Second Person of the Trinity into the equation.[35]

God knows that we have had enough of cheap forgiveness and cover-ups (nearly the same thing) both within and without the church, particularly with respect to sexual abuse. Stopping abuse comes first, and there is much work yet to do for government, families, and the church. But reconciliation of some kind cannot be infinitely deferred, and is necessary to prevent repeat offenses, unless all offenders are locked up permanently. Shaming an offender usually simultaneously shames a victim (which the offender likely is), which, in turn, fuels the cycle of abuse. Without some reconciliation — while continuing to provide protection — the cycle of guilt and repetition will continue. Here the church can help society see the common good of *costly* forgiveness and reconciliation, which take place only where it is frankly acknowledged that forgiveness costs both the one who forgives and the one who is forgiven. Where both parties accept that a wrong has been done that neither can make unhappen, a first step is taken.

34. Social capital is, after all, a form of *capital,* which by definition represents deferred benefits for the short term. Wisely invested capital, however, is less expensive in the long run than short-term profits.

35. I do not, of course, mean to suggest that social forgiveness and reconciliation must be done in the name of Christ; rather, the Church can offer the gift and example of the social value of forgiveness and reconciliation.

Sexual abuse and violence receive most attention in this area, and they need yet more. However, the damage done by economic havoc and the divorce and family instability that ensue from it both receive much less scrutiny. Here the need for forgiveness and reconciliation is not yet even on the horizon, and awareness of the damage will probably need to increase before public reconciliation can even be discussed. The link between economic stress and marital instability in particular is beneath the radar of both the religious and the political left and right. History will press these contradictions, however — particularly the close tie between lack of true intimacy and abuse — until recognition is forced.

Semi-Public Practical Historical Theology: The Church's Inner Word and Action

A *semi-public* historical theology concerns the Word spoken to the church itself, still on behalf of the world and the human race. In part, this concerns how the church can take up its share of the work that subsidiarity implies.

One of the chief characteristics of this historical moment in American society is, as I have argued, an increased desire for renewed intimacy in all forms. That absence is felt at exponentially higher and more painful level in the more vital relationships of parent and child, lover and spouse; it is one of the factors that brings people into congregations, and its absence there is a chief complaint. How can the church respond to the moment at hand by promoting communities of intimacy and subsidiarity within itself? Nor need one look far for signs of the broader contradiction of intimacy within the present history of the church. Current ambivalences regarding same-sex relationships and ordination, required celibacy and women's ordination, the tone of discussion over sexual abuse, and the absence of discussion regarding divorce and adultery (except when it involves the pastor!) are all indicative of it. But what meaning can be extracted from this contradiction, from the resources of the past and the future?

Some can come through the preaching, liturgical, and teaching ministry of the church, the Word the church proclaims to itself. Drawing on the doctrines of creation, providence, and sin, the church must teach that sexuality and marriage are a divine gift, no matter how bitterly frustrating and painful they can become. But these affirmations, alongside candid acknowledgments of pain and brokenness, should not be reserved for marriage liturgies and marital counseling; they should be in ordinary homilies on the wedding in Cana, or Judah and Tamar (whose irregular liaison is part of Christ's family tree, and thus ironically part of the world's reconciliation).

The existence of sexual abuse, exploitation, and violence in the church must be denounced in no uncertain terms, and the work of authorities who prosecute these be supported (a little Romans 13 is in order here). But if Jesus befriended prostitutes, he befriended sex offenders as well. They are both objects of Christ's redeeming love, and no offender begins recovery without overcoming shame and believing that she or he is a worthwhile person. If sex offenders have no welcome within the church, who does? Signs of that redeeming Word are almost nowhere to be seen in today's "mainline" churches. Yes, our children and ourselves are to be protected, but where is the prophetic word about the release of *these* prisoners? The Gospel's history of costly forgiveness must be reclaimed, not least within the church.

There are resources in the historical theology of the church for this. Reconciliation, forgiveness, and friendship that overcame (or tried to overcome) sexual and class and ethnic boundaries are evident in Paul's writings and the Jesus movement, as Browning and the New Testament scholars upon whom he and his colleagues have relied have rightly shown.[36] But where else? This sense of a *costly* forgiveness and reconciliation need to be recovered and expanded beyond current concerns for boundaries to the classical sense of restoring damaged relationships.

One other place in which these events were enacted in history of Christianity is in the Protestant sectarian and Pietist movements of the sixteenth through eighteenth centuries.[37] Repudiating or demanding reform of existing social structures, they formed small, close-knit communities, sometimes comprised of near-strangers, committed to resisting what they perceived as — and often were — unjust and dehumanizing social structures. German Pietism may be understood in part as a movement to help displaced rural people struggling to adapt to pre-industrial urbanization, while Methodism performed a similar task for massive

36. Frequently cited references for Paul include Galatians 3:28; 1 Corinthians 11:17-22, 12:12-20ff., and 16:19; Romans 16:1-15; evidence for the Jesus movement, whether traceable to Jesus or not, include Matthew 9:10-13 and Luke 7:31-35. See Browning, *Marriage and Modernization*, 60-66.

37. I absolutely do not mean to suggest that this never happened anywhere else since New Testament times. Specifically, I omit monasticism solely because of the obvious difference of celibacy. Nevertheless, it is likely that the monastic movement offers much in this respect as well.

numbers of workers in industrializing England. So, too, did aspects of antislavery movements, which were more at home in these than in the established churches, though betrayed in both. The fervent Pietist rejections of alcohol and makeup, which struck later generations as hypocritical moralism, served to counter alcoholism and to distinguish working-class women from prostitutes.

Some of these movements manifested a family-like sense of group intimacy and support that were important in the growth of the early church. Some of this appears to be replicated in aspects of the Pentecostal movement, and also in the growing twelve-step movements, of which Alcoholics Anonymous is only the best-known. Strong personal connection, support, and intimacy among members plays an essential role in twelve-step movements, which initially drew in part on Christian practice and theology but are now detached and more "spiritual" in orientation. Sadly (for the church), many members of these movements find a healing and redemptive intimacy in them that they cannot find in congregations.

Pietism and sectarianism exemplify, in part, what I mean by a "semi-public" theology: they speak a language that looks for neither public verification nor approval, but seeks rather to change the inner community and self first, and thereby to change the "outer" world (sometimes intentionally, sometimes not). It is not a private or secret language, inaccessible to the "outside" world; but neither is it universal nor able to secure universal agreement.

The languages of pietism, sectarianism, and twelve-step movements all share broadly in a commitment to personal transformation, change, and responsibility. In theological terms, this reflects the doctrine of personal sanctification and the work of the Holy Spirit. We have thus already introduced the work of the Third Person of the Trinity, and brought historical practical theology to a point where it can fully engage Trinitarian theology. Marriage, family, and sexuality can be, and usually have been, part of this language of transformation and personal sanctification.

In just this sense of transformation and sanctification, marriage, family, and sexuality can be seen as *sacramental* in character. That is, they can be seen as commitments to greater personal and community responsibility and transformation than the "outer" world requires. In public language such transformation is frequently subsumed under the category of "growth," but it is just as easy for individuals to grow apart as to grow together. Reclaiming a sacramental view of marriage recaptures the sense that marriage is not an only act of two people witnessed by others, but an act of the Word, an act of the church community, a divine blessing, effectual apart from the worthiness of the recipients, and can be profaned and violated but not undone — though often necessary to dissolve.[38]

Both the sacramental and the sanctified views of marriage and family conflict with the minimalist view of marriage dominant in Western society and powerful in many Protestant bodies as well. Such a view logically points in the direction of stronger requirements for marriage within the church, and for more sect-like structures to support these obligations. Such requirements will certainly include more pre-marital counseling and perhaps longer waiting periods, and may or may not include baptism, membership, confirmation, church involvement, as well as covenantal obligations for both partners.

It may be objected that making these *requirements* rather than recommendations undermines the Gospel of grace or makes the church less inclusive. Perhaps, instead, they will help those who seek a church wedding discern their true reasons for doing so, and strengthen both their and the church's commitment to marriage and family. Having certain requirements for marriage does not constitute a limitation on redemptive grace.

Sects and sect-like movements have, historically, been the movements most successful, at least initially, in transforming society. If the world of marriage and family is bound up in a historical contradiction which requires an overcoming or transformation, the history on which the church can draw is precisely those movements which have been most effective in transformation. Such movements have called people to aspire to higher standards; while these requirements have repelled some, they have attracted and been liberating for others. They also share dangerous tendencies which must be combated, including self-righteousness, authoritarianism, patriarchy, and eventual smugness and exclusiveness. The *critical* part of critical familism must be vigilant with respect to these tendencies within sect-like groups.

Conclusion

I have sketched a picture of an historical contradiction between human intimacy and social infrastructure as the broader framework in which we

38. Protestants are not likely to give marriage the status of a sacrament that it has in Roman Catholicism, nor should they. One reason is that it often can and must be dissolved. Others are that marriage is not limited to Christians, nor necessary for grace. But it can be viewed as sacramental *within* the Church.

find the current contradiction of family, marriage, and sexuality. This contradiction will not resolve itself simply, but will be overcome through a transformation or upheaval of some kind. I have suggested ways in which the church can discern signs of the new transformation with some possible responses, both in a public theology and practice and in a semi-public, sect-like theology and practice. I have also attempted to retrieve the Trinitarian dimension of this theology. In the end, this more Hegelian view of history has reached much the same conclusions as Browning and his colleagues, with calls for more research and more historicizing of the project.

A public theology in support of the common goods of marriage and family based on publicly verifiable criteria, and a semi-public theology supporting a sacramental and sanctified view of marriage, family and sexuality based on criteria that are semi-public: these are the outcomes. But it is never apart from semi-public discourse and action that history is transformed.

11 Response

Don S. Browning

The essays in this volume are designed to test and improve an approach to theology called "practical theology," or more specifically, "fundamental practical theology." Furthermore, they intend to examine this approach as it applies to a major issue facing American society and the churches, the issue of the future of families.

Over the last 20 years, I have been elaborating this particular approach to theology, and for well over a decade I have been addressing the situation of families using this practical theological method. The Religion, Culture, and Family Project (RCF) was a large research project using the approach of fundamental practical theology to guide its orientation to what eventually became two multivolume series on family, marriage, and children.

The Influence of Erik Erikson

Before my turn to practical theology and the specific concern with the family, I spent many years addressing issues dealing with the relation of theology to the social sciences, particularly the relation of theology to psychology. Some of the authors in this volume, such as Steven Tipton and Bonnie Miller-McLemore, address this early work, especially my writings on Erik Erikson in *Generative Man* (1973, 1975) and later articles designed to clarify what I said in that book.[1] The essay by Richard Osmer,

1. Don Browning, *Generative Man: Society and the Good Man in Philip Rieff, Nor-*

more than others, addresses my practical theological method and then helpfully applies it to teaching a practical theological course on family with first-year seminarians. Mary Stewart Van Leeuwen, without discussing my practical-theological method as such, also tests some of the central ideas of the RCF Project, and my written and co-written books on family, in the context of teaching evangelical college students about family issues. I will address the important essays of Osmer and Van Leeuwen later in my response. Addressing their essays will enable me to return to the link between practical theology and the family research.

Christian Love as Equal Regard

I first will turn to a central theme that runs through a number of essays in this book. This has to do with the meaning of Christian love as equal regard and what it implies as an ideal governing the lives of families, especially Christian families. The essays by M. Christian Green, Bonnie Miller-McLemore, Timothy Jackson, and Rebekah Miles directly address, and sometimes challenge, various aspects of this ethical concept. I have argued that all families and marriages, not just Christian families and marriages, should be ordered and inspired by love as equal regard. Christian families should live by equal regard but should also do more. The equal regard of Christian families, in addition, should be enriched by forgiveness and stimulated by self-sacrifice to renew and sustain love as equal regard and mutuality when it is under stress and imbalance.

But the concept of love as equal regard is complex. This is why so many of the essays in this volume address it. It is easily misunderstood. Even these careful essays often do not always get it quite right, at least from my perspective. So let me briefly define love as equal regard and then clarify it more fully in the paragraphs that follow.

As I use the concept, love as equal regard has two dimensions to it. First, it has what moral philosophers call a deontological dimension, and second and subordinate to the first dimension it has what moral philosophers call a teleological dimension. The deontological dimension has to do with respecting the other — all others — as ends in themselves and

man Brown, Erich Fromm, and Erik Erikson (Philadelphia, PA: Westminster Press, 1973; Dell, 1975); "Generativity, Ethics, and Hermeneutics: Revisiting Erik Erikson," in *Christian Ethics and the Moral Psychologies* (Grand Rapids, MI: Wm. B. Eerdmans, 2006), 146-65.

never only tools, instruments, or means serving just one person's interests, aims, and satisfactions. Christians anchor this respect for the other in their belief that all humans — including but not restricted to one's spouse, children, and close relations — are made in the image of God and reflect in their personhood the sacredness of the divine. But the concept of love as equal regard has as well a teleological element having to do with willing and actively aiming for the good of the loved one. In the equal-regard love ethic, doing good for the other is essential, although subordinate, to treating the other as an end. This may seem strange, but here is what it means. Doing good must be subordinate to respecting the other in order to protect against manipulating or coercing another person for, as we often say, his or her "own good." But how do we gain tested knowledge of the goods that equal regard tries to actualize?

Stephen Pope: Using Evolutionary Psychology

Stephen Pope's perceptive essay is useful for clarifying how I employ evolutionary psychology to illuminate the goods of life that love as equal regard should bring into existence. We know the good of life, first of all, through our inherited normative practices. As Alasdair McIntyre and Paul Ricoeur have forcefully argued, these practices, especially in their more classic forms, contain the tested goods that meet the basic needs of human life.[2] For instance, we do not invent the good of literacy or even the good of a healthy diet. Literacy and good eating are practices that have been discovered, refined, and passed along as traditions from the past. These practices and the goods they deliver can be refined, improved, or even altered somewhat by science and other disciplines, but these fields of knowledge do not create these goods from thin air; they come first from inherited customs and habits. Even then, however, these goods should be considered mainly as premoral goods that can only become fully moral goods if they are organized justly and fairly within the full context of love as equal regard. For example, a person enjoying the good of a healthy diet is not necessarily a moral person nor is the diet itself a moral good. Whether that person is morally good depends on how he or she justly and fairly organizes the good of

2. Alasdair MacIntyre, *After Virtue* (Notre Dame, IN: University of Notre Dame, 1981), 57; Paul Ricoeur, *Oneself as Another* (Chicago: University of Chicago Press, 1992), 152-53.

healthy food with other goods, including the good of nutrition needed by other people.

But sometimes our traditions, especially in changing circumstances, are interpreted as sending contradictory messages about the premoral goods and goals of life. As Stephen Pope has so perceptively pointed out, when a religio-cultural tradition such as Christianity is in internal conflict over its judgments about premoral goods, the practical Christian ethicist might turn to the social sciences, including evolutionary psychology, for clarification. The ethicist would do this in order to gain "distanciated" insights into the premoral goods of life that might help mediate the conflict of goods in a tradition's interpretation of inherited normative practices.

An example will help. Modernity has put a tremendous amount of pressure on families. This has led to high rates of divorce, nonmarital births, the detachment of fathers from their offspring, and increased rates of child poverty and neglect. Because of these trends, the question has arisen as to whether children really need both of their biological parents in order to grow and flourish. Furthermore, the question has arisen as to whether parents need to marry or stay married in order to raise their children successfully.

Pope has pointed out correctly that I use insights derived from evolutionary psychology to show both the reality and importance of kin-altruism as a bio-psychological account of the naturalistic conditions of parental investment, especially the investment and care of fathers for their offspring. Evolutionary psychology helps explain why natural parents, on average, are likely to be more invested in their offspring than other parental arrangements. Marriage reinforces invested parenting and may be crucial for the overall care and well-being of children. However, kin altruism does not itself demand or create the justice and mutuality implied by the idea of love as equal regard. But when equal regard is applied to families, both tradition and the distanciated scientific evidence of evolutionary psychology bear witness to the importance of both mothers and fathers for the care of children. These two sources — tradition first and science second — reinforce each other in testifying to the good for children of the committed, intact mother-father team. It is especially important for clarifying the naturalistic conditions contributing to paternal care and investment — a norm that the Christian tradition has upheld on the grounds of both revelation plus the supplements of naturalistic observation.

Love as Equal Regard: Green, Miller-McLemore, Jackson, and Miles

I will amplify this brief summary of my understanding of love as equal regard in responding to the insightful comments of several of the essays in this volume. I will not follow the order of the chapters as they appear in the table of contents. It will help us focus our dialogue if I concentrate on the many comments dealing with the meaning and ramifications of the marital and family love ethic of equal regard.

I begin with the essay by M. Christian Green. Green joins Miller-McLemore in identifying herself as a theological feminist. Her scholarship has been motivated by a central question: are there resources within the Christian tradition for an ethic articulating the equal obligations and importance of fathers as well as mothers in both the family's domestic care *and* its economic productivity? Green, who has an academic background in law and theological ethics, is concerned with the neglect in recent American family law of the obligations and contributions of fathers to their children. She is concerned about how psychologist Carol Gilligan's feminist ethics of care has been used to overemphasize in the law the role of maternal care, at the neglect of paternal care, for child well-being. Green agrees with me in finding resources for a more balanced ethic in the theories of marital friendship and parental investment, both paternal and maternal, in the Aristotelian-Thomistic tradition of Western philosophy and theology. She even finds evidence for the continuing influence of these thinkers in the liberal family theories of John Locke and the feminist theories of Lisa Cahill and Martha Nussbaum.

Green introduces a very important revision to the Aristotelian-Thomistic tradition in her concept of equity. For her, there must be a balancing or compensatory feature in love if it is to be truly equal. She does not use this illustration, but I take it that she means that for equal regard to exist between rich and poor, the poor must receive compensatory supports in order to overcome obstacles to their progress. She also suggests that for long-term equality to exist between husband and wife or parent and child, one party must extend extra giving, and maybe even sacrifice, to help the weaker party recover or eventually achieve the capacity for equality and mutuality. By giving the concept of equity this dynamic meaning, she in effect is amending the meaning of both equity and friendship in Aristotle. Equity for Aristotle meant giving the more honorable person the greater portion and the less honorable party the smaller portion. In contrast, equity means for Green that equal regard must be flexible and shift with the dynamics of life. I agree and have tried to make similar points without laboring, as has Green, to redefine the concept of equity, at least as Aristotle used it. I learned to appreciate how love must shift with dynamics of life during my early studies of the life-cycle theories of Erik Erikson. Green, Tipton, and McLemore appropriately point out the early importance of Erikson for my theological ethics, including my later work on marriage and family.

My remarks on Green's dynamic theory of equity set the stage for addressing the perceptive comments of Miller-McLemore. As I indicated above, she is quite aware of the influence of Erikson on both my early and later thinking. It is indeed true, as Tipton's essay demonstrated in detail, that Erikson influenced my concern to maintain the generative relation of fathers with children — a role that the forces of modernization and globalization increasingly put at risk.

McLemore makes another point that bears more directly on the love ethic of equal regard as she believes that I interpret it. She complains, somewhat differently than Timothy Jackson does, that I underemphasize the role of sacrificial love in equal regard. She points out that love as equal regard contrasts with those versions of Christian love that define it predominantly as sacrificial giving to the other. She is, however, aware that in many of my writings I fully acknowledge the necessity in Christian love of sacrificial love to actualize and restore equal regard under the conditions of finitude and sin. McLemore believes, however, that I only emphasize the conditions of sin whereas, in fact, I emphasize both.[3] Because both finitude and sinfulness touch even marriage and family life, a love ethic of equal regard requires acts of self-sacrifice to address them even though it is not itself the goal of Christian love. Martyrdom is not the end or telos of Christian love.

McLemore is right at least in one respect; I often write about the self-sacrificial moment of the equal-regard ethic as "transitional." In this sense, sacrificial love is the effort needed to promote or restore love as equal regard and mutuality when these are absent or have broken down due to either finitude or sin or, as is usually the case, both. McLemore thinks the word "transitional" suggests speedy or temporary and for this reason does not capture the fullness of Christian love. However, I would remind her that in chapter 10 and elsewhere in our co-authored *From Culture Wars to Common Ground* (1997; 2000), we developed a life-cycle the-

3. See, for example, the discussion in *Religious Thought and the Modern Psychologies* (Minneapolis, MN: Fortress Press, 2004), 77-78.

ory of love as equal regard.[4] There we argued that love as equal regard should not be interpreted to mean moment-by-moment equality of the kind that demands keeping score or adding up credits and debits in a short-term frame of reference. In that book, we used Erikson's life-cycle theory to develop a view of love as equal regard that acknowledges the rhythms of the entire cycle of the generations from infancy to old age as well as the relation of husband and wife facing the challenges of birth and child care. This cycle contains shifting patterns of dependency, vulnerability, and strength that love as equal regard must address and balance. Clearly, as McLemore herself argues, parents will and shall make long-term sacrifices for their children. But, even then, equal regard should constitute the horizon of parental care. Good parental care should warmly and constantly expect children to grow up and treat both others and parents with equal regard — as ends in themselves deserving respect and the recognition of their human needs. If we remember that equal regard is a life-cycle ethic that takes into account the inevitable imbalances of finitude and sin over the entire cycle of the generations, then McLemore's concern for the transitional character of self-sacrifice as too fleeting can be answered.

Timothy Jackson also questions the faithfulness of love as equal regard to Christianity. In addition, he questions its adequacy for an ethics of marriage and family. Jackson does me the honor of comparing me with Søren Kierkegaard. When put up against a giant such as Kierkegaard, it is not surprising that, in the mind of Jackson, I lose. Jackson, however, mistakenly equates the love ethic of equal regard with an ethic of reciprocity. For this reason, he thinks it is a "conditional" ethic, one that would abandon the other if he or she were not to reciprocate one's respect and efforts to do good. But, as Jackson must know, the justice component of equal regard is inspired both by the Christian principle of neighbor love that says "you shall love your neighbor as yourself" (Matt. 19:19) and philosophical reflections on it by Kant, Paul Ricoeur, Louis Janssens, Eugene Outka, and others. Love as equal regard is not, in any of these perspectives, a conditional principle. Loving the other with equal regard is unconditional; it is not conditioned as such by reciprocal return. The Christian must respect the other as an end in him or herself and as a child of God (made in the image of God) regardless of obstacles, resistances, rejections,

4. Don Browning, Bonnie Miller-McLemore, Pamela Couture, Brynolf Lyon, and Robert Franklin, *From Culture Wars to Common Ground* (Louisville, KY: Westminster John Knox, 1997, 2000), 24, 180-81, 287-301.

or failures to reciprocate. Nonetheless, loving the neighbor as oneself (which perfectly exhibits the logic of love as equal regard) demands that the person exhibiting equal regard has the right to expect to be treated with equal regard as well. This is true even though in the Christian love ethic being treated with equal regard is not a prior condition for treating others with equal regard.

Jackson has, however, another concern. Like McLemore, but for different reasons, he believes Christian love is primarily self-sacrificial action for the good of the other. He too is uncomfortable with my formulation, following the thought of Louis Janssens, that sees the self-sacrificial demand of the cross as a transitional ethic required to promote or restore the equal regard and mutuality of genuine community. Careful analysis, however, of Jackson's own view of Christian love reveals only a small difference with my position. Jackson also acknowledges that Christian love does not require self-sacrifice and martyrdom as ends in themselves. He believes Christian love only requires an "openness" to self-sacrifice. I submit, however, that the difference between "openness" to sacrificial love and sacrificial love as a "transition" is indeed slight. This is especially true in light of the unconditional nature of equal regard as I define it and the life-cycle rhythms that require parents and spouses to endure long periods of sacrificial giving with only the faintest hope of realizing or restoring actual equal regard.

Jackson overlooks the truth that the nonviolent love ethic of both Gandhi and Martin Luther King, Jr., exemplifies the authenticity of love as equal regard. The entire purpose of nonviolent self-sacrificial protest is to demand equal regard from the oppressor even as the oppressed sustain affirmation for the personhood of the individual or group oppressing them. Jackson's discontent with the place of self-regard in Christian love undercuts the logic of nonviolent love as well as the role of self-regard in love as equal regard between spouses and between parents and their children. One of the goals of parental love is to enable children to develop the capacity for genuine equal regard, mutuality, and community with others, including their own parents.

In the essay by Rebekah Miles, other aspects of love as equal regard came to light, i.e., the proposal for society to provide a 60-hour workweek in the paid economy for married couples with children. Miles and her husband serve as fair warning to all authors: be careful what you write because someone might take you seriously and actually put into practice what you advocate. This happened in the Miles family.

Rebekah and her husband read *From Culture Wars to Common*

Ground and actually experimented with the 60-hour workweek that we propose there. In this book, we argued that equal regard was a social ethic as well as an ethic for individual couples and families. For couples with children who want, or are financially required, to carry responsibilities of both paid employment and domestic life, society must accommodate and support this need. Miles is correct when she observes that the 60-hour workweek proposal functions as both a critique and reform of the social structures of modern societies. It is designed to save families with children from the ravages of the market. It is fashioned to shape modern industrial societies so that couples have time for their children, their intimate lives, and their vocations. We joined the 60-hour workweek proposal with other recommendations such as the 30-hourwork week for single parents on welfare and more flex time job opportunities. We even proposed a Parental Bill of Rights that would allow a parent to leave the workforce for several years to care for a child with the guarantee of a monthly income and job training for re-absorption into the market at approximately the same level when he or she wants to return to paid employment.

Miles took the 60-hour proposal a bit more rigidly than we intended. Rather than pursuing the 60-hour workweek, Miles' husband left paid employment and dedicated himself to child care and volunteer service while Miles became the sole breadwinner. Miles believes we failed to investigate and support that option, which she holds is closer to the Christian calling. It was not our purpose to privilege paid employment over volunteering, as Miles believes we did. Clearly, from a Christian perspective, volunteer service as a vocation should be applauded. Our message was aimed more to the institutions of government and market than to individual couples as such. It was a demand for social reform. We developed the idea in the early 1990s when newspapers were full of articles about the explosion of dual-income families and 90- to 100-hour workweeks for couples, even after children were born. This new regime of work was exacting great stress on spouses and parental relationships and a great toll on child and adult well-being. Salaries were declining in relation to inflation, and more and more married couples felt compelled to seek paid employment to make ends meet.

In conclusion, I agree with Miles. If couples can afford it, volunteer work in contrast to paid employment might contribute both stimulation and domestic balance of the kind the equal-regard love ethic would require. But in acknowledging this, I add a word of caution. I urge Miles to agitate for the social reforms needed to provide more part-time jobs, flex jobs, home-based employment, inexpensive and high-quality child care, and the many other reforms that are required for the great majority of couples who both need and want paid employment. The 60-hour week for couples with children may be good social policy even though some couples may elect to organize their lives around volunteering. Without taking such positive action, Miles' laudable support for volunteer service may return us to the divided spheres of the 1950s, the family ideals of the nineteenth century, and the contemporary social vision of Focus on the Family and other such conservative groups.

John Wall and Critical Hermeneutics

I now turn to the slightly different concerns of John Wall. He addresses and extends the critical hermeneutic philosophy that undergirds so much of my later work in fundamental practical theology and theological ethics. I sometimes combine these two terms — practical theology and theological ethics — and refer to what I do as a "practical-theological ethics." My response to Wall will prepare us to address the practical interests of Osmer and Van Leeuwen. Wall acknowledges the importance of hermeneutics to my work on both family issues and the disciplines of practical theology and theological ethics. Most of my family research and writings of the last two decades have been ordered by a critical hermeneutical methodology.

What does this mean? Briefly, hermeneutics is a perspective on philosophy and interpretation theory that says all human understanding is like a dialogue or conversation entailing an exchange of questions, listening, and answering. Hermeneutics is especially well illustrated when we try to understand what Hans-Georg Gadamer called our "effective history" — the great cultural and religious classics that have shaped our own social experience even in ways we do not consciously acknowledge.[5] Hermeneutics becomes critical when insights into the meaning and purpose of life are tested either by enduring principles within the tradition such as the Golden Rule and neighbor-love (or its philosophical elaboration in Kant's categorical imperative) or by "distantiated" (to be distinguished from "objective") insights of the empirical sciences, especially when tradi-

5. Hans-Georg Gadamer, *Truth and Method* (New York: Crossroad, 1982), 267-68.

6. Paul Ricoeur, *Hermeneutics and the Human Sciences* (Cambridge: Cambridge University Press, 1981), 59-62.

tion makes statements about empirical realities, which it often does.[6] The point is, when it comes to understanding something, hermeneutics puts the priority on practical dialogue and locates empirical testing as secondary, i.e., a kind of useful distance to the historical conversation aimed at understanding and testing that which has formed us.

Wall wants to extend my use of critical hermeneutics by bringing it into the emerging new field of childhood studies. He aspires to contextualize empirical studies of children by seeing them as distantiated elements within a wider historical-interpretive dialogical and critical reappropriation of certain classic images of childhood in the cultural and religious history that shape the experience of Americans. Since Christianity has had massive influence on the cultural sensibilities of the U.S., Wall has special interest in the Christian tradition.

Wall wants a new emphasis on an ethics and theology called "childism." As feminism brought the interpretive voices of women into theology and ethics, Wall wants to bring the interpretive voices of children into these disciplines. Children, he insists, should be part of the interpretive dialogue and bring with them their own cultural and religious experience and histories. Of course, children do not have the capabilities to be their own interpreters. Hence, Wall argues that adults must listen to the voice — the experience and questions — of children and seek to enrich understanding of children by collaborating with them in interpreting the cultural and religious classics that have formed them. He proposes pursuing these collaborative acts of understanding with the secondary help of the distanciating critiques of the empirical sciences as well as the critical potential of the abiding principle of equal regard.

In a different language, my co-authors and I recommended in chapter 10 of *From Culture Wars to Common Ground* something close to what Wall is proposing. There we envisioned family life as a complex dialogue between husband and wife and their respective religio-cultural heritages. We suggested that parents should treat their children as having emerging interpretive capacities of their own. Wall's view of childism envisions this interpretive process as a dialectic between "top down" (the messages of our normative traditions) and "bottom up" (the voice and experiences of children). Wall states well what we were starting to express in that chapter.

We painted a normative picture of family as a critical hermeneutical dialogue between parents, children, and their religio-cultural classics — preferably in concert with a wider community of interpretation such as church, synagogue, or mosque. This idea points to a compelling model for how parents can be authoritative without being authoritarian, i.e., how they can open a religious and moral tradition to their children without extinguishing their children's developing powers of interpretation. Family as an emerging community of critical hermeneutical dialogue expresses an ideal of family as living a life-cycle ethic of love as equal regard. Parents, in a mutual interpretive dialogue with each other, *invite children to join them* with the goal of becoming mutually authoritative interpreters and dialogue partners with their parents, church, or synagogue of a classical moral and religious tradition.

Osmer, Van Leeuwen, and Paul: Practical Theology in History, the Present, and the Future

The concluding three essays address more directly my practical theological work. Osmer and Van Leeuwen do this in the context of teaching classes. Paul to some extent does this as well. But Paul is interested in the relation of practical theology to historical theology, especially as it pertains to understanding the contemporary state of intimacy. As an historian, however, he is concerned as much about the future as he is the past. Hence, his essay provides provocative suggestions about how a practical theology of marriage and family should relate to history, the present, and the future — a fitting concern for the concluding chapter of this volume.

My earlier response to Wall provides a transition into engagement with the helpful essay by Richard Osmer. Osmer has been a close associate of mine in developing and re-evaluating the fields of practical theology. Practical theology is often thought to refer to the theological disciplines that order the internal life of churches — religious education, pastoral care, liturgics, homiletics, missions, etc. The new practical theology that Osmer and I have worked to develop in the American Association of Practical Theology and the International Academy of Practical Theology introduces a critical hermeneutical perspective to those disciplines and brings them into closer association with theological ethics and moral philosophy. Osmer nicely summarizes my use of Hans-Georg Gadamer and shows that hermeneutical dialogue for the purpose of understanding is actually a practical enterprise designed to inform our various everyday practices. I am fully sympathetic with his desire to institutionalize the hermeneutic approach to practical theology in the classroom teaching process. I also have tried to institutionalize hermeneutical practical theology in the classroom through a teaching method that invited students to identify issues of great concern to them, describe those issues, research the religious and cultural classics of the past to determine how they inform the issue, and then return to propose concrete strategies to address the issue. Osmer does something like this in his excellent course syllabi that he shares with us. I applaud this approach to teaching and believe it has much to offer family studies and a myriad of other practical issues facing church and society.

I agree with Osmer on seeing my four movements of fundamental practical theology — descriptive, historical, systematic, and strategic — as each entailing Gadamer's hermeneutical circle. I take seriously his desire to replace my "historical theological" step with what he calls "interpretive theology." But finally I resist it. It is precisely because I think he is right to see each of these steps as involving Gadamer's interpretive circle that I resist his proposal to rename the historical movement and call it the "interpretive" step. From my perspective, all four movements entail the interpretive circle, as Osmer himself suggests. Therefore, I believe there are strong reasons to retain the unique importance of the crucial task of historical theology, i.e., the interpretation *specifically* of the religious and cultural classics that have formed us.

Although Mary Stewart Van Leeuwen has not been, as Osmer has, a colleague in the practical-theology movement, she was an important contributor to the Religion, Culture, and Family Project and watched it unfold as a multi-dimensional practical-theology research project. By this I mean that the RCF Project, as I indicated above, exhibited the four movements of practical theology — description of the family issue, historical retrieval, systematic and ethical theological critique, and strategic interventions designed to strengthen family policy in both church and society. From this perspective, Van Leeuwen herself is a kind of practical theologian. In her writings, she critically retrieves the Christian tradition for the renewal of marriage and family but with a strong, although subordinate, use of the social sciences for clarifying issues pertinent to gender and child well-being.

Van Leeuwen joins Osmer in wanting to institutionalize a practical approach to teaching family studies. Her students are primarily Evangelicals. Like a good practical theologian, she describes these students. She depicts them as theologically conservative but pummeled by market values on sex and marriage and about as widely experienced in oral, anal, and genital sex as the average secular youth of our society. They also have been socialized into a view of marriage and family built around the divided gender spheres of the nineteenth and first half of the twentieth centuries. Yet these Evangelical students, like most Americans, will experience a world in which both husbands and wives are employed in the wage economy. Van Leeuwen works hard to retrieve for her students a view of Christian families in which the ethic of equal regard can help achieve intact families where husbands and wives have, in principle, equal opportunities and obligations in paid work, politics, and domestic life.

Van Leeuwen wants to open the equal-regard marriage and family to her students whereas Miles wants to remind students that the dual income equal-regard family is not the only way to go. Both messages are important, depending on the specific contexts of the teaching situation. Van Leeuwen would probably agree with Miles; both parents should not be forced to participate in the wage economy. But in our society, there is enormous pressure, and sometimes necessity, for this to happen. Christian critical familism tries to find a middle way by making the world of paid employment more flexible and less all-consuming so that families in modern societies can sustain themselves financially, contribute to a productive society, and still have time to love each other, care for their children, and volunteer their time to the needy and vulnerable.

Garrett Paul's rich chapter raises a host of important questions. Space allows room to address only two of the most central. First, Paul and I agree that the human motivation for doing history is basically practical and motivated by our present situation, concerns, practices, and questions. We search history to learn how we were shaped by the past and to determine which of our inherited norms and narratives can serve us in the present and future. Paul and I are both informed by European hermeneutics — especially the thought of Gadamer and Ricoeur. In short, we agree that practical thinking has an unavoidable historical dimension and that historical thinking is inevitably practical as well. Paul raises the question, however, as to whether I use Gadamer and Ricoeur's concept of "the classics" in a rigid and historically undynamic way. He wonders if I understand how the great classics of the Christian past — in my case the marriage and family classics that have shaped Christianity and much of Western law and culture — also have been affected by multiple social-systemic factors of an economic and political kind in both their creation and reception.

My answer is that I try to understand this interaction. I would remind him that we both, as his essay attests, actually bring together hermeneutic perspectives on the relation of practical and historical reflection with the multidimensional theory of action found in Max Weber. Weber believed that history was mainly moved by meanings (hence, his appreciation for the role of religion) but always in interaction with material and social-systemic forces as well.[7] Therefore, in my family and marriage writings, I have been interested in how normative ideas (the classics of Genesis, Aristotle, the New Testament, Augustine, Aquinas, etc.) on marriage and family have interacted with material and social-systemic processes such as farming, herding, ancient Mediterranean urban life, capitalism, socialism, and modernity's headlong plunge into the use of technical rationality (à la Weber). As a constructive practical theologian, covering at times huge swaths of history, I doubtless missed many nuances. But I have tried to resist interpreting the marriage and family classics of the past as if they took place in no identifiable or important social, material, and cultural contexts. Even as Paul himself acknowledges, I give a large amount of attention to how Christian claims about marriage play out in the context of the technical rationality of modern societies. This is an insight that gets to the heart of Paul's own important observations about how our intensified search for intimacy is being frustrated by the great global infrastructures of our increasing rationalized societies, undercutting close relationships of all kinds — parent-child, kinship, friendship, and yes, husband-wife. I agree and appreciate Paul's extension of this insight.

Paul has a second concern that I wish to address. He believes that I have failed to take seriously the resources of Protestant Pietism for addressing the contemporary family situation of the church. He is right. I have neglected it. I acknowledge my guilt. But why is this omission interesting? Paul wants both a *public practical theology* and a *semi-public practical theology* to address the contradictions of intimacy in a globalizing world. He acknowledges that his distinction is similar to mine between *public practical theology* and *confessional practical theology.* He used his distinction to drive home the point that the church's inner renewal on matters of sex, marriage, and family actually may be more important in the future than its discourse in a public practical theology. Furthermore, he believes that a sound inner-ecclesial practical theology on these matters will have an impact on the wider society — hence, be a kind of semi-public theology.

I agree. The churches cannot have an impact on society if they do not have a strong confessional or semi-public practical theology of marriage, family, and intimacy. As my colleagues and I argued in the last

7. Max Weber, *The Protestant Ethic and the Spirit of Capitalism* (New York: Charles Scribner's Sons, 1958), xiv, 90-91.

chapter of *From Culture Wars to Common Ground,* the inner-ecclesial tasks of the church, both theological and strategic, must precede its public witness.[8] Here the Pietist tradition may have much to teach, as Paul believes.

However, Paul is wise not to make too great a distinction between the inner-ecclesial and outer-public task of practical theology, thus the usefulness of his phrase "semi-public" practical theology. In our kind of modern and dynamic society, the walls between church and other social systems are porous. If our inner-ecclesial theological language does not analyze and address the wider problems that face sexuality and intimacy in society as a whole, our churches, I fear, will fail in speaking to both the lives of the faithful as well as the wider public.

My Gratitude

I want to conclude by expressing my sincere appreciation to all my friendly critics. I have learned much and have a clearer understanding of what I have been trying to say over the years in my practical-theological and family writings. I also want to express my profound gratitude to M. Christian Green, John Witte, and Amy Wheeler for having the idea of organizing this exchange. And finally, thanks must go to Craig Dykstra of the Division of Religion of the Lilly Endowment, Inc. for supporting the Religion, Culture, and Family Project and this volume of critique and imaginative probes into the future. The Religion, Culture, and Family Project would have been impossible without the vision and resources of the Lilly Endowment.

8. Don Browning, Bonnie Miller-McLemore, Pamela Couture, Brynolf Lyon, and Robert Franklin, *From Culture Wars to Common Ground* (Louisville, KY: Westminster John Knox, 1997, 2000), 306-22.

Contributors

Herbert Anderson, Ph.D., is Professor Emeritus of Pastoral Theology at the Catholic Theological Union in Chicago

Carol Browning is an organist, pianist, mother of Elizabeth and Christopher Robert, and equal-regard spouse.

Don S. Browning, Ph.D., is Alexander Campbell Professor Emeritus of Ethics and the Social Sciences, the University of Chicago Divinity School

Lisa Sowle Cahill, Ph.D., is J. Donald Monan Professor of Theology, Boston College

M. Christian Green, J.D., M.T.S., Ph.D., is Visiting Lecturer on Ethics at Harvard Divinity School

Timothy P. Jackson, Ph.D., is Associate Professor of Christian Ethics, Candler School of Theology at Emory University

Martin E. Marty, Ph.D., is Fairfax M. Cone Distinguished Service Professor at The University of Chicago

Rebekah Miles, M.Div., Ph.D., is Associate Professor of Ethics, Perkins School of Theology at Southern Methodist University

Bonnie J. Miller-McLemore, Ph.D., is E. Rhodes and Leona B. Carpenter Professor of Pastoral Theology and Counseling at Vanderbilt University Divinity School

Richard Robert Osmer, M.Div., Ph.D., is Thomas W. Synnott Professor of Christian Education at Princeton Theological Seminary

Garrett E. Paul, Ph.D., is Professor of Religion at Gustavus Adolphus College

Stephen J. Pope, Ph.D., is Professor of Theology at Boston College

David Popenoe, Ph.D., is Professor of Sociology Emeritus and Co-Director of the National Marriage Project at Rutgers University

Mary Stewart Van Leeuwen, Ph.D., is Professor of Psychology and Philosophy at Eastern University

Steven M. Tipton, Ph.D., is Professor of Sociology of Religion at Emory University and its Candler School of Theology

Linda Waite, Ph.D., is Lucy Flower Professor in Urban Sociology at the University of Chicago

John Wall, Ph.D., is Professor of Religion and Ethics and Associate at the Center for Children and Childhood Studies at Rutgers University

Amy Wheeler, B.A., is Associate Editor and Director's Associate of the Center for the Study of Law and Religion at Emory University

Barbara Dafoe Whitehead, Ph.D., is Co-Director of the National Marriage Project at Rutgers University

John Witte, Jr., J.D., is Jonas Robitscher Professor of Law and Director of the Center for the Study of Law and Religion at Emory University

Bibliography of Don Browning's Writings

Books, Articles, Chapters in Books, Journal Articles, Editor of Special Issues

1963

"A Doctrine of the Atonement Informed by the Psychotherapeutic Process." *The Journal of Pastoral Care* 17 (Fall 1963): 136-147.

1964

"Theology and Psychotherapeutic Psychology." *Frontiers* 25 (February 1964): 20-24.

1965

"Psychological and Ontological Perspectives on Faith and Reason." *The Journal of Religion* 45:4 (October 1965): 296-308.

1966

Atonement and Psychotherapy. Philadelphia: Westminster Press.

"Pastoral Care and Public Ministry." *The Christian Century* 83:39 (September 1966): 1176-1178.

1967

"A Theological Perspective on Homosexuality." *Christian Medical Society Journal* 19:3 (May-June 1967): 12-18.

1968

Pastoral Care and the Poor, a special issue of *Pastoral Psychology* 19:182 (March 1968).

"Faith and the Dynamics of Knowing." In Peter Homans (ed.). *Essays in Divinity.* Chicago: University of Chicago Press.

"Analogy, Symbol, and Pastoral Theology in Tillich's Thought." *Pastoral Psychology* 19:181 (February 1968): 41-54. Memorial Issue on Paul Tillich.

"The Challenge of the Poor." *Pastoral Psychology* 19:182 (March 1968): 5-6. Editorial.

"Religion, Revelation, and the Strengths of the Poor." *Pastoral Psychology* 29:182 (March 1968): 32-40.

"The Relation of Psychology to History." *Criterion* (Winter 1968): 17-20.

1969

Pastoral Care and the Poor, a second special issue of *Pastoral Psychology* 20:198 (November 1969).

"The Influence of Psychology on Theology." In William Oglesby (ed.). *Essays in Honor of Seward Hiltner.* Nashville: Abingdon Press: 121-135.

"Pastoral Care and Social Ethics." *Pastoral Psychology* 20:198 (November 1969): 5-6. Editorial.

1971

"Psychological and Ontological Perspectives on Faith and Reason." In Ralph James (ed.). *Process Theology Reader.* Indianapolis: Bobbs Merrill.

"Pastoral Care and the Poor." In Howard Clinebell (ed.). *Community Mental Health.* Nashville: Abingdon Press.

"Generative Man and the Future of Sexuality." *Criterion* (Spring 1971): 17-22.

1972

"Reason and Ecstasy: Psychological and Philosophical Notes on the Counterculture." *Zygon* 7:2 (June 1972): 80-97.

1973

Generative Man: Society and the Good Man in Philip Rieff, Norman Brown, Erich Fromm, and Erik Erikson. Philadelphia: Westminster Press. Finalist for National Book Award in Philosophy and Religion, 1974. Issued as a Delta paperback, 1975.

"Psychiatry and Pastoral Counseling: Moral Context or Moral Vacuum?" *The Christian Century* (February 6, 1973): 158-161.

"New Trends in Pastoral Care." *The Christian Century* (September 5, 1973): 849-51.

"Thinking Small about Larger Things." *Criterion* (Winter 1973): 9-11.

1974

"Theological Reflections on Rogers, Perls and Schultz." *Dialogue* 13 (April 1974): 104-109.

1975

Philosophies of the Person, a special issue of *Zygon* 10:2 (June 1975).

Social Science Interpretations of Religion, a special issue of *Zygon* (June 1975).

"William James's Philosophy of the Person: The Concept of the Strenuous Life." *Zygon* 10:2 (June 1975): 162-174.

"Method in Religious Living and Clinical Education." *Journal of Pastoral Care* 29:3 (September 1975): 157-167.

"Preface to a Practical Theology of Aging." *Pastoral Psychology* 23:229 (Winter 1975): 151-167.

1976

The Moral Context of Pastoral Care. Philadelphia: Westminster Press. Translated as *Norman ed waarden in het pastoraat,* Uitgeurij De Toorts: Nederlandse vertaling, 1978. Issued as paperback, 1983.

1977

"Monistic Dimensions in Humanistic Psychology: A Process Theology Perspective." In Widick Schroeder (ed.). *Belief and Ethics.* Chicago: Quest Press.

"Pastoral Care and Models of Training in Counseling." *Contact: The Interdisciplinary Journal of Pastoral Studies* (1977): 12-19. Reprinted in *Journal of Supervision and Training in Ministry* (Winter 1979): 98-105.

1978

"Erik Erikson and the Search for a Normative Image of Man." In Peter Homans (ed.). *Childhood and Selfhood: Essays on Erikson, Religion and Modernity.* Lewisburg, PA: Bucknell University Press.

1979

"Images of Man in Contemporary Models of Pastoral Care." *Interpretation: A Journal of Bible and Theology* 33:2 (1979): 144-156. Translated as "Menschbilder in zeitgenössischen Modellen der Seelsorge." *Wege zum Menschen* 33 (October 1981): 406-418.

"William James's Philosophy of Mysticism." *The Journal of Religion* 59:1 (January 1979): 56-70.

"Homosexuality, Theology, the Social Sciences and the Church." *Encounter* 40:3 (Summer 1979): 223-244.

With Bernie Lyon. "Sociobiology and Ethical Reflection." *Theology Today* 36:2 (July 1979): 229-239.

"Hypocrisy: Modern and Christian Solutions." *Criterion* 18:3 (Autumn 1979): 28-30.

1980

Pluralism and Personality: William James and Some Contemporary Cultures of Psychology. Lewisburg, PA: Bucknell University Press.

"Pastoral Theology in a Pluralistic Age." *Pastoral Psychology* 29:1 (Fall 1980): 32-42.

1981

"Toward a Practical Theology of Care." *Union Seminary Quarterly Review* 36:2-3 (Winter/Spring 1981): 159-172.

1982

Religion and the Economic Order. Edited with David Krueger. Chicago: The Disciples Divinity House.

Untitled review articles of *Human Nature and History: A Response to Sociobiology* by Kenneth Bock and *The Expanding Circle: Ethics and Sociobiology* by Peter Singer. *Theology Today* 38:4 (January 1982): 539-541.

"The Estrangement of Pastoral Care from Ethics." In Steve Kepnes and David Tracy (eds.). *The Challenge of Psychology to Faith.* New York: Concilium–The Seabury Press, 1982. Also published in foreign-language editions.

"On Religious Education in a Pluralistic World." *The Journal of Religion* 6:4 (October 1982): 418-424. Article review of Thomas H. Groome's *Christian Religious Education: Sharing Our Story and Vision.*

1983

Religious Ethics and Pastoral Care. Philadelphia: Fortress Press.

Practical Theology: The Emerging Field in Religion, Church and World. Edited and introduced. San Francisco: Harper & Row.

"Integrating the Approaches: A Practical Theology." In Carl Dudley (ed.). *Building Effective Ministry.* San Francisco: Harper & Row.

Untitled review article of *Faith, Authenticity, and Morality,* by Donald Evans. *Religious Studies Review* 9:1 (January 1983): 37-41.

"Practical Thinking in Ministry and in Religion and Psychological Studies." *Criterion* (Winter 1983).

"Response to Ruth Tiffany Barnhouse." *Anglican Theological Review* 65:4 (October 1983): 412-417.

"Toward a Practical Theology of Care." *The Drew Gateway* 53:2 (Winter 1983): 1-22.

1984

Untitled review of *Freud and Man's Soul* by Bruno Bettleheim. *Theology Today* 41:1 (April 1984): 127-129.

"Psychology as Religio-ethical Thinking." *Journal of Religion* 64 (April 1984): 139-157.

"The Revival of Practical Theology." *The Christian Century* 101:4 (February 1-8, 1984): 134-144.

1985

"Introduction to Pastoral Counseling." In Robert Wicks, Richard Parsons, and Donald Capps (eds.). *Clinical Handbook of Pastoral Counseling.* Mahwah, NJ: Paulist Press.

"Practical Theology and Political Theology." *Theology Today* 42:1 (April 1985): 15-33.

1986

"Counseling," "Ethical Problems in Psychoanalysis," and "Psychology and Ethics." In James Childress and John Macquarrie (eds.). *The Westminster Dictionary of Christian Ethics.* Philadelphia: Westminster Press.

With Brynolf Lyon. "Faith Development and the Requirements of Care." In Craig Dykstra, and Sharon Parks (eds.). *Faith Development and Fowler.* Birmingham, AL: Religious Education Press.

"Fulfillment and Obligation in the Modern Psychologies." *Anglican Theological Review* 68:4 (October 1986): 287-301.

"Hospital Chaplaincy as Public Ministry." *Second Opinion* 1 (1986): 66-76.

"Globalization and the Task of Theological Education." *Theological Education* 23:1 (Autumn 1986): 43-59.

1987

Religious Thought and the Modern Psychologies. Minneapolis, MN: Fortress Press. Second edition, 2004.

"Practical Theology and Religious Education." In Lewis Mudge and James Poling (eds.). *Formation and Reflection: The Promise of Practical Theology.* Philadelphia: Fortress Press.

"The Challenge of the Future to the Science-Religion Dialogue." *Zygon* 22 (1987): 35-39.

"Medicine, Modernization, and Religion in the People's Republic of China." *Second Opinion* 4 (1987): 10-29.

"Metaphor and Obligation in Some Modern Psychologies." *Anglican Theological Review* 69:1 (January 1987): 54-68.

"Mapping the Terrain of Pastoral Theology: Toward a Practical Theology of Care." *Pastoral Psychology* 36:1 (Fall 1987): 10-28.

"The Protestant Church in the People's Republic of China." *The Christian Century* 104:7 (March 4, 1987): 218-221.

1988

"Pastoral Care and the Study of the Congregation." In Barbara Wheeler and Joseph Hough (eds.). *Beyond Clericalism and Theological Education.* Atlanta: Scholars Press.

"Hospital Chaplaincy as Public Ministry." *Journal of Health Care Chaplaincy* 2:1 (1988): 3-16.

"Pastoral Counselor as Ethicist: What Difference Do We Make?" *The Journal of Pastoral Care* 42:4 (Winter 1988): 283-296. Reprinted in *Criterion* 29:3 (Autumn 1990): 6-11.

1989

The Education of the Practical Theologian: Responses to Joseph Hough and John Cobb's "Christian Identity and Theological Education." Edited with David Polk and Ian S. Evison. Atlanta, GA: Scholars Press.

"Religious Education as Growth." In Mary Boys (ed.). *Practical Theological Reflection and Action.* New York: The Pilgrim Press.

"Religious Education for Practical Theological Thinking and Action." In Nelle G. Slater (ed.). *Tensions between Citizenship and Discipleship.* New York: The Pilgrim Press.

"Rethinking Homosexuality." *Christian Century* 106 (October 11, 1989): 911-916. Article review of *The Construction of Homosexuality* by David Greenberg.

1990

"The Psychoanalytic Interpretation of St. Augustine's *Confessions:* An Assessment and New Probe." In Joseph H. Smith and Susan A. Handelman (eds.). *Psychoanalysis and Religion.* Baltimore: Johns Hopkins University Press.

"Methods and Foundations for Pastoral Studies in the University." In Adrian Visscher (ed.). *Les Études Pastorales a L'Université.* Ottawa: University of Ottawa Press.

"Citizenship, Saintliness and Health: Relations between Religion and the Clinical Psychological Disciplines." *Contact: The Inter-disciplinary Journal of Pastoral Studies* 102:2 (1990): 2-11.

1991

A Fundamental Practical Theology. Minneapolis, MN: Fortress Press. Issued as a paperback, 1995. Now being translated into Chinese.

Religious and Ethical Factors in Psychiatric Practice. Edited with Thomas Jobe and Ian S. Evison. "Introduction" by D. S. Browning and Ian S. Evison, 1-19, and D. S. Browning, "The Protestant Responses to Psychiatry: Contributions to a Public Philosophy for Psychiatry," 20-41. Chicago: Nelson-Hall.

Does Psychiatry Need a Public Philosophy? Edited with Ian S. Evison. "Introduction," and "A Public Philosophy for Psychiatry: A View from Theology," by Don Browning. Chicago: Nelson-Hall.

With Carol Browning. "The Shape of the Family: A New Love Ethic." *The Christian Century* 108:33 (November 13, 1991): 1060-1062. Republished as "The Church and the Family Crisis." In Paul Jerrold et al. (eds.). *Moral Issues and Christian Response.* Fort Worth, TX: Harcourt Brace, 1998.

"Family Ethics and the Ethics of Ministerial Leadership." In James Wind et al. (eds.). *Clergy Ethics in a Changing Society.* Louisville: Westminster John Knox Press.

"Toward a Fundamental and Strategic Practical Theology." In Barbara Wheeler and Edward Farley (eds.). *Shifting Boundaries: Contextual Approaches to the Structure of Theological Education.* Louisville, KY: Westminster Press.

"Auf dem Uege zu einer Fundamentalen und Strategischen Practichen Theologie." In Karl Ernst Nipkow, Dietrich Rössler, Friedrich Schweitzer (eds.). *Practische Theologie und Kultur der Gegenwart: Ein Internationaler Dialog.* Gütersloh: Gütersloher Verlagshaus Gerd Mohn.

1992

Habermas, Modernity, and Public Theology. Edited with Francis Fiorenza. New York: Crossroad.

With Carol Browning and Ian Evison. "Family Values and the New Paternalism." *The Christian Century* 109:19 (June 3, 1992): 572-573.

"Altruism and Christian Love." *Zygon: A Journal on Religion and Science* 27[4] (December 1992): 421-436. Also published in *Altruismus: Aus der Sicht von Evolutionsbiologie, Philosophie, und Theologie.* Evangelischen Academie Locuum, 1996.

"Psychology in Service of the Church." *Journal of Psychology and Theology* 20:2 (1992): 127-136.

1993

With Ian Evison. "The Family Debate: A Middle Way." *Christian Century* 110:21 (July 14-21, 1993): 712-716.

"The Religion Culture and Family Project: An Interim Report." *Criterion* 32:2 (Spring 1993): 5-11.

1994

"A Conversation with Don S. Browning." *Initiatives in Religion: A Newsletter of Lilly Endowment Inc.* 3:1 (Winter 1994): 3-4.

"Egos without Selves: A Practical Theological Critique of the Family Theory of the Chicago School of Economics." *Annual of the Society of Christian Ethics* (Autumn 1994): 127-145.

"Is the Family a Conservative Issue?" Rerum Novarum Lecture, Catholic Archdiocese of Melbourne, Australia. June 6, 1994. *Concilium.* Brescia: Queriniana, 1995. Also printed as "Re-Building the Nest: Families and the Need for a

New Social Agenda." *Just Reading* 3. Melbourne, Australia: Catholic Archdiocese of Melbourne, 1994.

"Congregational Studies as Practical Theology." In James Lewis and James Wind (eds.). *The Study of Congregations.* Chicago: University of Chicago Press.

1995

With Carol Browning. "Better Family Values: A New Paradigm for Family Policy Can Bridge the Partisan Gap." *Christianity Today* 39:2 (February 9, 1995): 29-32.

"Chastening Liberalism." *Christian Century* 112[4] (February 1-8, 1995): 121-124.

"Children, Mothers, and Fathers in the Post-Modern Family." In Pam Couture and Rodney Hunter (eds.). *Pastoral Care and Social Conflict*, 71-85. Nashville: Abingdon Press.

"The Family and the Male Problematic." *Dialog* 34[2] (Spring 1995): 123-130.

"Contractual Problems." *The Christian Century* (June 7-14, 1995).

"Religion and Family Ethics: A New Strategy for the Church." In Clark Wade Roof and Nancy Ammerman (eds.). *Work, Family, and Religion in Contemporary Society.* New York: Routledge.

"Christian Ethics and the Family Debate: An Overview." In *The Annual of the Society of Christian Ethics.* Washington, DC: Georgetown University Press, 1995: 251-262.

"Altruism, Civic Virtue, and Religion." In Mary Ann Glendon and David Blankenhorn (eds.). *Seedbeds of Virtue.* New York: Madison Books.

"The Nature and Criterion of Theological Scholarship." *Theological Education* 32: 1 (1995).

1996

With David Balch, Lisa Sowle Cahill, Pamela Couture, and Mary Stewart Van Leeuwen. "Family Values, Christian Values: A Roundtable Discussion." *The Christian Century* (January 31, 1996).

"Biology, Ethics, and Narrative in Christian Family Theory." In Jean Bethke Elshtain and David Popenoe (eds.). *Promises to Keep.* Lanham, MD: Rowman & Littlefield.

"Diagnosis Maybe; Solution, No." *Society,* 33:5 (July-August 1996).

"Immanence and Transcendence in Pastoral Care and Preaching." *Journal for Preachers* 20:1 (Advent 1996): 22-32.

1997

With Bonnie Miller-McLemore, Pam Couture, Bernie Lyon, and Robert Franklin. *From Culture Wars to Common Ground: Religion and the American Family Debate.* Louisville, KY: Westminster John Knox. Second edition, 2000.

"Practical Theology and the American Family Debate." *International Journal of Practical Theology* 1 (1997): 136-160.

"Fatherhood and Religion: The University of Chicago Project." *Newsletter of the National Fatherhood Initiative*, 1997.

"Can Psychology Escape Religion?" *International Journal of Psychology of Religion* 7:1 (1997): 1-12. An adapted version published by the Gregorian Pontifical Institute in a book collection celebrating twenty-five years of its department of psychology. Edited by Father Franco Imoda (1997).

1998

With Herbert Anderson, Ian Evison, and Mary Stewart Van Leeuwen (eds.). *The Family Handbook.* Louisville, KY: Westminster John Knox Press.

"The Task of Religious Institutions in Strengthening Families." Jointly issued by the Religion, Culture and Family Project and the Communitarian Network.

"Marriage and the American Family Debate." *Circuit Rider* (July-August 1998): 6-8.

"Self-Sacrifice, Self-Fulfillment, and Mutuality: The Evolution of Marriage." *The Responsive Community* (Winter 1997-98): 58-62. Reprinted as "Mutual Respect Between Spouses Will Improve Marriage" in *What Will Improve Male/Female Relationships: Chapter Four of Male/Female Roles: Opposing Viewpoints.* San Diego: Greenhaven Press, Inc., 2000.

1999

"When Theory Meets Practice: Communitarian Ethics and the Family." *The Responsive Community* (Winter 1998-99): 52-61. This article was later published in *Marriage in America.* Rowman & Littlefield, 2000.

With Carol Browning and John Wall. "Marriage as Public Policy," *The Christian Century* (January 20, 1999): 44-45.

"Fatherhood as a Point of Convergence: Beyond Old Categories." In Don Eberly (ed.). *The Faith Factor in Fatherhood.* New York: Lexington Books.

With Bonnie Miller-McLemore. In "Globalisation and the Family — A Practical Theological Analysis." Pam Couture and Paul Ballard (eds.). *Globalisation and Difference: Practical Theology in a World Context.* Fairweather, Cardiff, UK: Cardiff Academic Press.

With Carol Browning. "Black Fatherhood/Whole Fatherhood," *The Christian Century* (Summer 1999). Republished as "Confronting Fatherhood in Black America," *The Chicago Tribune* (September 26).

"Ehe: Praktisch-theologisch." In *Religion in Geschichte und Gegenwart.* Tübingen: J. C. B. Mohr–Paul Siebeck. Band 2, C-E: 1085-1088.

"Eheberatung." In *Religion in Geschichte und Gegenwart.* Tübingen: J. C. B. Mohr–Paul Siebeck. Band 2, C-E: 1090-1091.

"Ehescheidung: Praktisch-theologisch," In *Religion in Geschichte und Gegenwart.* Tübingen: J. C. B. Mohr–Paul Siebeck. Band 2, C-E: 1101-1102.

With John Wall and Thomas Needham. "The Ethics of Relationality: The Moral

Views of Therapists Engaged in Marital and Family Therapy." *Family Relations* (April 1999) 48 2: 139-151.

Toward a Fundamental and Strategic Practical Theology." In Friedrich Schweitzer and Johannes A. Van der Ven (eds.). *Practical Theology — International Perspectives.* Frankfurt am Main; New York: Peter Lang.

"Apologetik: Praktisch-theologisch." In Hans Betz et al. (eds.). *Religion in Geschichte und Gegenwart.* Tübingen: J. C. B. Mohr–Paul Siebeck. Band 1, A-B: 626-629.

"The Challenge and Limits of Psychology to Theological Ethics." *Annual of the Society of Christian Ethics* 19 (1999): 133-143.

2000

"Familie: Socializations-theoretisch." In *Religion in Geschichte und Gegenwart.* Tübingen: J. C. B. Mohr–Paul Siebeck. Band 3, F-H: 21-22.

"The Task of Religious Institutions in Strengthening Families," and "When Theory Meets Practice: Communitarian Ethics and the Family." In Martin King Whyte (ed.). *Marriage in America: A Communitarian Perspective.* New York: Rowman & Littlefield.

With Gloria Rodriguez. "Toward a Public Philosophy of Faith-Based and Community-Based Organizations in Their Service to Families." Prepared for a leadership roundtable sponsored by the Annie E. Casey Foundation and Morehouse College, December 2000.

"Christian Equal Regard and the Male Problematic." In Wallace Alston (ed.). *Theology in Service of the Church: Essays in Honor of Thomas Gillespie.* Grand Rapids, MI: Wm. B. Eerdmans.

"Hermeneutik als Grundlage und Aufgabe praktische-theologischer Ethik." In Wilhelm Gräb et al. (eds.). *Christentum und Spätmoderne.* Stuttgart, Germany: Verlag W. Kohlhammer.

2001

The Human Image of God. Edited with Hans-Georg Ziebertz, Friedrich Schweitzer, and Hermann Häring. Leiden: Brill; Boston: Köln.

"World Family Trends." In Robin Gill (ed.). *The Cambridge Companion in Christian Ethics.* Cambridge; New York: Cambridge University Press.

With Max L. Stackhouse (eds.). *God and Globalization: The Spirit and the Modern Authorities* Harrisburg, PA: Trinity Press International.

"What Kind of Love? The Equal Regard Marriage and Children," *American Experiment Quarterly* (Summer 2001): 47-53.

"The World Situation of Families: Marriage Reformation as a Cultural Work." In Adrian Thatcher (ed.). *Celebrating Christian Marriage.* Edinburgh, Scotland: Continuum.

"The Dialectic of Archaeology and Teleology in Christian Family Theory" in "Essays in Honor of Philip Hefner." *Currents in Theology and Mission* 28: 3-4 (June-August, 2001): 298-306.

"What Is Marriage: An Exploration." In Dana Mack and David Blankenhorn (eds.). *The Book of Marriage.* Grand Rapids, MI: Wm. B. Eerdmans.

2002

With Gloria Rodriguez. *Reweaving the Social Tapestry: Toward a Public Philosophy and Policy of Families.* New York: W. W. Norton, Inc.

With Katherine Anderson and Brian Boyer (eds). *Marriage — Just a Piece of Paper.* Grand Rapids, MI: Wm. B. Eerdmans.

With John Wall, William Doherty, Stephen Post, and Mary Stewart Van Leeuwen (eds.). *Marriage, Health, and the Professions: Implications of the Health Values of Marriage for the Practice of Law, Medicine, Ministry, Therapy, and Business.* Grand Rapids, MI: Wm. B. Eerdmans.

"The Language of Health Versus the Language of Religion: Competing Models of Marriage for the 21st Century." In Alan Hawkins et al. (eds.). *Revitalizing the Institution of Marriage for the 21st Century: An Agenda for Strengthening Marriage.* Westport, CT: Praeger Press.

"Should Churches Know About the Communitarians?" *Family Ministry* 16:1 (Spring 2002): 75-78.

"The Relation of Practical Theology to Theological Ethics." In Michael Welker and Friedrich Schweitzer (eds.). *Reconsidering the Boundaries Between Theological Disciplines.* Münster, Germany: LIT Verlag, 2002.

"Science and Religion on the Nature of Love." In Stephen Post et al. (eds.). *Altruism and Altruistic Love: Science, Philosophy and Religion in Dialogue.* Oxford: Oxford University Press.

"Violence, Authority, and Communities of Reconstruction." In J. S. Dreyer and J. A. Van der Ven, (eds.). *Divine Justice — Human Justice.* Pretoria, South Africa: Research Institute for Theology and Religion.

"Ricoeur and Practical Theology." In John Wall, William Schweiker and David Hall (eds.). *Paul Ricoeur and Contemporary Moral Thought.* New York; Hampshire, UK: Routledge.

2003

Marriage and Modernization: How Globalization Threatens Marriage and What to Do about It. (The 1998 Cadbury Lectures). Grand Rapids, MI: Wm. B. Eerdmans Publishing Co.

With David Blankenhorn and Mary Stewart Van Leeuwen (eds.). *Does Christianity Teach Male Headship? The Equal-Regard Marriage and Its Critics.* Grand Rapids, MI: Wm. B. Eerdmans Publishing Co.

"Feminism, Family, and Women's Rights: A Hermeneutic Realist Perspective." *Zygon* 38:2 (June 2003): 317-54.

"Critical Familism, Civil Society, and the Law." *Hofstra Law Review* 32:1 (Fall 2003): 313-329.

2004

"Mutuality, Reason, and Family Policy." In Herbert Anderson Foley et al. (eds.). *Mutuality Matters: Family, Faith, and Just Love.* Lanham, MD: Rowman & Littlefield.

"The Meaning of Family in the Universal Declaration of Human Rights." *Evidence* 12 (Summer 2004): 25-34.

"Theology and Social Theory." In Gareth Jones (ed.). *Blackwell's Companion to Modern Theology.* Oxford: Blackwell Publishing.

"An Ethical Analysis of Erikson's Concept of Generativity." In Ed de St. Aubin, Dan McAdams, Tae Chang Kim (eds.). *The Generative Society.* Washington, DC: American Psychological Association.

2005

"Good Christian Men: How Faith Shapes Fathers." *The Christian Century* 122:1 (January 11, 2005): 18-22.

Foreword, xx-xxvi. In John Witte and Robert M. Kingdon. *Sex, Marriage, and Family in John Calvin's Geneva: Courtship, Engagement and Marriage.* Grand Rapids, MI: Wm. B. Eerdmans Press.

"Moral Development." In William Schweiker (ed.). *Religious Ethics: The Blackwell Companion.* Oxford: Blackwell Publishing.

"Zygon at 40: Its Past and Possible Future." *Zygon* 40:3 (September 2005): 529-534.

2006

Christian Ethics and the Moral Psychologies. Grand Rapids, MI: Wm. B. Eerdmans Publishing Co.

Universalism vs. Relativism: Making Moral Judgments in a Changing, Pluralistic, and Threatening World. Lanham, MD: Rowman & Littlefield.

Sex, Marriage, and Family in the World Religions. Edited with Christian Green and John Witte. New York: Columbia University Press.

American Religions and the Family. Edited with David Clairmont. New York: Columbia University Press.

"After the Loving: The Collapse of Marriage." *The Christian Century* 123:3 (February 7, 2006): 24-29.

"The United Nations Convention on the Rights of the Child: Should It Be Ratified and Why?" *Emory International Law Review* 20:1 (Spring 2006): 167-184.

With Elizabeth Marquardt. "What about the Children? Liberal Cautions on Same-Sex Marriage." In Robert George and Jean Bethke Elshtain (eds.). *The Meaning of Marriage: Family, State, Market, and Morals.* Dallas, TX: Spence Publishing Company.

"Christian Marriage and Public Policy." In *Christian Reflection: A Series in Faith and Ethics.* Waco, TX: Baylor University Center for Christian Ethics: 19-28.

"Human Dignity, Human Complexity, and Human Goods." In R. Kendall Soulen and Linda Woodhead (eds.). *God and Human Dignity.* Grand Rapids, MI: Wm. B. Eerdmans.

2007

Equality and the Family: A Fundamental Practical Theology of Children, Mothers, and Fathers in Modern Societies. Grand Rapids: Wm. B. Eerdmans Publishing Co.

General Editor of Book Series

Theology and Pastoral Care Series (1982-1986).

Published by Fortress Press, Philadelphia, PA.

Don S. Browning, *Religious Ethics and Pastoral Care.*

Don Capps, *Life Cycle Theory and Pastoral Care.*

Regis Duffy, *A Roman Catholic Theology of Pastoral Care.*

Nelson Thayer, *Spirituality and Pastoral Care.*

Alistair V. Campbell, *Professionalism and Pastoral Care.*

K. Brynolf Lyon, *Toward a Practical Theology of Aging.*

Elaine Ramshaw, *Ritual and Pastoral Care.*

Don Capps, *Pastoral Care and Hermeneutics.*

Thomas C. Oden, *Care of Souls in the Classic Tradition.*

Herbert Anderson, *The Family and Pastoral Care.*

Ralph Underwood, *Empathy and Confrontation.*

James Fowler, *Pastoral Care and Faith Development.*

Robert Katz, *Judaism and Pastoral Care.*

Studies in Practical Theology Series (1998-2005).

Edited with Hans Van der Ven, James Fowler, and Friedrich Schweitzer. Wm. B. Eerdmans Publishing Co., Grand Rapids, MI.

Hans Van der Ven, *The Moral Foundation of the Self.*

Gerben Heitink, *Practical Theology.*

Richard Osmer and Friedrich Schweitzer, *Religious Education between Modernization and Globalization.*

Robert L. Browning and Roy A. Reed, *Forgiveness, Reconciliation, and Moral Courage: Motives and Designs for Ministry in a Troubled World.*

F. Gerrit Inmink, *Faith: A Practical Theological Reconstruction.*

Theology for the Twenty-First Century: A Series (1997-2003).
Edited with Wallace Alston and Robert Jenson. Trinity Press International, Harrisburg, PA.

Gerhard Sauter, *What Dare We Hope? New Perspectives on Eschatology.*

John Polkinghorne and Michael Welker (eds.), *The End of the World and the Ends of God.*

Max L. Stackhouse and Peter Paris (eds.), *God and Globalization,* Vol. 1.

Max L. Stackhouse and Don Browning (eds.), *God and Globalization,* Vol. 2.

Max L. Stackhouse and Diane B. Obenchain (eds.), *God and Globalization,* Vol. 3.

Family, Religion, and Culture Series (1997-2000).
Edited with Ian Evison.

A ten-book series supported by a grant from The Lilly Endowment, Inc. and published by Westminster John Knox, Louisville, KY.

Don Browning, Bonnie Miller-McLemore, Pamela Couture, Robert Franklin, and Bernie Lyon, *From Culture Wars to Common Ground: Religion and the American Family Debate.*

Anne Carr and Mary Stewart Van Leeuwen (eds.), *Religion, Feminism, and the Family.*

Max Stackhouse, *Covenant and Commitments.*

Ted Peters, *For the Love of Children: Genetic Technology and the Future of the Family.*

Phyllis Airhart and Margaret Bendroth (eds.), *Faith Traditions and the Family.*

John Witte, *From Sacrament to Contract: Marriage, Religion, and Law in the Western Tradition.*

Leo Perdue, John Collins, Carol Meyers, and Joseph Blenkinsopp, *Families in Ancient Israel.*

David Balch and Carolyn Osiek, *Families in the New Testament World.*

Bernie Lyon and Archie Smith (eds.), *Tending the Flock.*

Herbert Anderson, Don Browning, Ian Evison, and Mary Stewart Van Leeuwen (eds.), *The Family Handbook.*

Religion, Marriage, and Family Series (1998-).
Edited with John Wall, David Clairmont, and from 2003 with John Witte. Wm. B. Eerdmans Publishing Co., Grand Rapids, MI.

Stephen Post, *More Lasting Unions.*

Marcia Bunge (ed.), *Childhood in Christian Theology.*

Dana Mack (ed.), *The Book of Marriage.*

John Wall, Don Browning, William Doherty, Stephen Post, and Mary Stewart van Leeuwen (eds.), *Marriage, Health, and the Professions: Implications of the Health Values of Marriage for the Practice of Law, Medicine, Ministry, Therapy, and Business.*

Katherine Anderson, Don Browning, and Brian Boyer (eds.), *Marriage — Just a Piece of Paper?*

David Balch and Carolyn Osiek (eds.), *Early Christian Families in Context.*

Don Browning, *Marriage and Modernization: How Globalization Threatens Marriage and What to Do about It.*

John Witte, Jr., and Eliza Ellison (eds.), *Covenant Marriage in Comparative Perspective.*

Timothy P. Jackson (ed.), *The Morality of Adoption: Social-Psychological, Theological, and Legal Perspectives.*

John Witte Jr., and Robert M. Kingdon, *Sex, Marriage, and Family in John Calvin's Geneva,* Vol. 1: *Courtship, Engagement, and Marriage.*

David Blankenhorn, Don Browning, and Mary Stewart Van Leeuwen (eds.), *Does Christianity Teach Male Headship? The Equal-Regard Marriage and Its Critics.*

Don Browning, *Christian Ethics and the Moral Psychologies.*

Don Browning, *Equality and the Family: A Fundamental, Practical Theology of Children, Mothers, and Fathers in Modern Societies.*

Index